# Glory of Jaina

## Religion, Philosophy and Science

# Contents

# Preface

This book is based upon many scripts and texts on the subject and is published with the intention that it may serve to people who want to know about Jainism. It is hoped that this book will be useful to all who are interested in the Indian solutions of familiar philosophical problems. Its foremost aim has been to give a connected and so far as possible within the limits of a single volume, a comprehensive account of the subject. I have made use of the standard works on the subject published in the past.

Jainism is one of the most ancient religion of India. Although Jainism has fewer followers than Hinduism and Sikhism it has had an influence of Indian culture for over 2500 years, making significant contributions in philosophy, logic, art and architecture, grammar, mathematics, astronomy, astrology and literature.

The word Jainism goes back to *jina*, which, derived from the Sanskrit root ji 'to conquer' means 'victor' i.e. one that successfully subdued his passions and obtained mastery over himself. The creed to which the name is applied is not an off-shoot or a sub-sect of Buddhism as it was once taken to be, but is quite independent of it. Lord Mahavira was born in India in 599 BC and regarded as the last of a line of 24 holy and spiritually enlightened beings, the Tirthankaras.

Jainism is a religion of love and compassion above all else. Jains believe that the universe is eternal. They believe in the eternity of the soul. There are thought to be multitudes of souls or life-modas, which are all independent and eternal.

Of all religions of the world, Jainism is the only religion which has the principle of Ahimsa as its central doctrine. The other religions also speak of Ahimsa whenever convenient but they never offer such loyalty to the principle of ahimsa as is found in Jainism. It has only given maximum attention to the important practical aspects of the theory of Ahimsa so that Ahimsa, in its minutest details, can be actually observed both by the law followers and ascetics in their everyday life.

It is true that some quite good books on Jainism have appeared in the past in English, but none of them, so far as I know, satisfactorily caters for the needs of a beginner in the subject, or is as handy, intelligible and yet comprehensive as the average reader would desire it to be. Most of the sections and informations contained in this treatise have been collected from various articles on the subject and the idea of expanding them, with the necessary additions and alterations in to a book first occured to me when I came across some of the volumes on Hinduism. Later on, some of my colleagues and friends suggested me the need of a similar work, and now, when it is ready, I believe it will serve the purpose for which it has been designed. Consistently with the aim of this publication the various chapters are calculated to provide a clear and brief exposition of the subject with which they deal, and an effort has been made to keep the matter and the form as close to the original sources as possible.

I am indebted to a number of writers, both olden times and my times, for some of the valuable material contained in this book.

Finally, I thank to Smt. Poonam Goel of M/S Raj Publications for taking keen interest in the publication of the book.

# 1

# Jain Religion

The religion which enjoins adoration and worship of Jinas or the religion which is propounded by Jinas is knows as the Jain religion.

Jina means one who has conquered the internal enemies and impurities of the soul like attachment (raga) and hatred (dwesha). He is known as Parmatma (the great soul), Sarvajna (omniscient), and Savadarshee (omnipotent). Such Jinas have been in existence from times immemorial. No beginning can be traced for them, and the Jain Religion has also no beginning. It is a very ancient religion. It teaches us to become Jina and those who follow it are called Jains.

According to Jain conception the period of time consists of two cycles, ascending (utsarpinee) and descending (avasarpini). In each of these two cycles, twenty-four Tirthankaras (Jinas) came into existence. They are called Tirthankaras because they are to become the propounders of the sacred order of religion. The last Tirthankar was Lord Mahavir. Some say that Lord Mahavir was the founder of

Jainism, but this is incorrect. Twenty-three Tirthankaras existed before Lord Mahavir flourished. In their times Jainism also flourished and before that also Jainism existed. By their extraordinary perception and knowledge, Tirthankaras who come from time to time, bring the fundamental principles into light again. They preach them, propound them, and also spread them.

The souls of Tirṭhankaras, from the very moment of their births, are gifted with superb knowledge and are very highly meritorious. They renounce their kingly status, cast aside their riches and worldly pleasures, and adopt asceticism. By the performance of extremely severe penances, they destroy all sins accumulated during their past births, burn all karmas, inculcate a spirit of equanimity towards friends and foes both, attain the status of Vitaraga i.e, where there is no attachment or hatred towards anyone, and gain omniscient knowledge. Those souls (atmas) who have thus become Parmatmas are of two kinds, Jeevan-mukta and Videhmukta. Those who have destroyed the four Ghati Karmas are called Jeevan-mukta.

*Jnana-varaniya,*
*Darsana-varniya,*
*Mohaniya, and*
*Antaraya*

Those who have destroyed the four further Karmas, known as Aghati Karmas are called Videhmukta or Siddha.

Nama, Gotra, Ayushya, and Vedniya

Jeevanmukta Parmatmas, Arhats, or Arihants impart their rare and unprecedented teachings to all to realize true happiness and ultimately attain the eternal bliss of the final beatitude (Moksha). The principles of Jain religion having been propounded by Veetraga (souls with no attachment or hatred) and Sarvajna (Omniscient) are universally wide and based on truth and for that very reason their universal beneficence can be said to be established and proved.

Ahimsa Parmo Dharma (nonviolence is the paramount religion) epitomize the true essence of Jainism. This suggests that one should bear love towards all living beings, as they are considered potentially divine in whatever form they exist. All of them have the capacity to be liberated from the endless cycle of birth and rebirth and attain eternal bliss. Attainment of the purity and liberation of the soul are achieved by the means of Right Faith, the Right Knowledge and the Right Conduct.

Jainism allows full freedom to all human beings to observe the vows and practice self-discipline. The vows to be observed by monks and nuns are stricter than those for lay people. The Jain religion preaches that even the smallest of the small living beings (jivas) should be given protection and should not be hurt. It is the teaching of Jainism that all living beings in the world desire to live. Death is not desired by anyone. All beings desire happiness, and dislike misery.

There is life (Jiva) even in earth, water, fire, air, and vegetables. The soul in all worldly living beings is potentially like the soul in us. There is no difference in the soul of an ant and that of an elephant, though the very same soul (Atma) takes the form of an ant as well as that of an elephant.

Contraction and expansion are its characteristic attributes and due to the bondage of karmas a soul finds itself born in any one of the eighty-four lack of forms of existence.

If any living being is ill disposed towards us, even so we must love and give protection to it, whether it is an animal or man. This is the magnanimity of Jain Religion. What a height of eminence! What a noble sentiment for universal welfare!

The Jain Religion preaches the Doctrines of Ahimsa (nonviolence), Satya (truth), Asteya (nonstealing), Brahmacharya (celibacy) and Aparigraha (nonattachment).

Anger, pride, deceit, greed, attachment, aversion all these are our terrible foes. One should be away from them.

Avoid nocturnal meals, look the ground you tread upon lest any injury may be done to any living being, filter water and other liquids and then use them.

Do not speak ill of anybody, nor feel jealous. Avoid strives and quarrels. Maintain mutual good-will and do not do evil to anybody. Be delighted at the, sight of virtuous. Be desirous of allaying the sufferings of the unhappy. Be friendly towards all living beings. By giving pain to others, one will have to experience bitter fruits. Therefore, one desiring happiness should make others happy. Inculcate the spirit of equanimity towards others. Be charitable, try to uplift the poor and the afflicted, observe the best moral standards in your conduct i.e. make your character an ideal one, practice austerities to the best of your abilities and lead a life of the pure and noble thinking. This is the principal message of the Jain Religion. The details will be found in the following pages.

It is extremely difficult to get this human existence. One should therefore shake off idleness and indolence, instill and practice religion and, thereby, enjoy the endless and unobstructed happiness of the final beatitude.

**Anekantvada**

It is the doctrine of Jain Philosophy that the ultimate principle is always logical and there can be no principle devoid of logic. The Jain mode of explaining everything logically is very charming. One finds deliberative exhortations on any subject in all its facts, may they be constructive or obstructive, enlightening or destructive, consumptive, or nutritive. The main reason for this is the exquisitely beautiful system of logic and reasoning known as "Syadvad". The principles of Jain Philosophy are based on the theory of Syadvad. It is the best means of arriving at the truth or of ascertaining fundamental principles and it is because of this that the Jain Philosophy is at the helm of all philosophies and the Jain Religion is the perfect religion. The word Syadvad is composed of two words 'Syat' and 'Vada'. Syat means in a sense or from a certain standpoint (Apeksha) and Vada points at Principle or School. One thing from one standpoint or point of view appears to be of a certain type while from another point of view the same thing appears to be of a different type. Therefore, to comprehend the full aspect of a thing one must take into account several points of view. This being the belief of Syadvad, it is sometimes also known as "Anekantvada" as well (i.e. that school of thought which takes into account more than one point of view).

To understand the true nature of Syadvad, Apeksha-vada or Anekantvada one must properly follow the two parables viz, (1) The other side of the shield, and (2) The story of Blind Men and the Elephant.

## Parable-1 Other side of the Shield

On the outskirts of a village a statue was erected in honor of one of its hero. It had a sword in one hand and a shield in the other. One side of the shield was covered with gold while the other one was covered with silver. Two unknown persons came there each from the opposite direction and began expressing their views. One said that the statue was beautiful and more so because its shield was covered with gold. The other said that the shield was not covered with gold but was with silver. A quarrel ensued between them. A wise man came from the village by that time and said that the shield was covered with gold as well as silver. Let both of you just exchange your places and see the other side of the shield. Both realized their error and apologized to each other for fighting falsely.

### Parable-2 Blind Men and Elephant

Once a royal retinue was stopping at a village to spend their afternoon. The village folks came there and amongst them there were six blind men. All had heard a lot about elephants but none had ever been able to see one. They requested the care-taker to allow them to touch the elephant so that they may be able to make out what the elephant could be like. They were permitted to do so. The first who came across the ears stated that the elephant was like a tusk weeding tool (Supada). The other caught hold of the trunk and stated that the elephant was like a big wooden pestle. The third touched the tusks and said it was like a big windpipe. The fourth touched the legs and said it was like a big pillar. The fifth felt the stomach and said it looked like a water-bag. The sixth had a tail in his hand and said it appeared to him like a broom. Each thought that his version was right and others were wrong. The care-taker said that none of them had ever seen the elephant fully. Each one had merely seen one limb and from that data each one had given his surmises about the whole elephant. This was, therefore, the cause of their quarrel. He explained the whole position, and all the blind men became silent and departed.

By these parables, one thing certainly becomes clear that the same thing can be explained from different stand points and any description of a thing would be true from one stand point but from this it cannot mean that the other points of view cannot be right. From the above it follows that to comprehend the real nature of any thing one must pay due regard to all points of view. Viewing things in this light, one will have to admit that everything in this world involves endless points of view and has endless characteristics.

Any one of the standpoints to which one has to resort for expounding a thing is called Naya (standpoint). In Naya, there is only partial truth, but in denying other characteristics that statement could result in falsehood. Suppose there is an elderly person of 75 years and he has a son aged 45 and the latter has a son aged 15. Now if the son who is aged 45 is only addressed as "father," this form of address will result in falsehood because from the standpoint of his 75 years old father he is also a son. If the 45-year-old man is only styled a "son," that too would be wrong because from the standpoint of his 15-year-old son, he is also a father. Similarly, one person is known as "Arya" from standpoint of territory; or as "Vaishya" from standpoint of Verna; or as "Oshwal" from standpoint of his sub-caste or say "Nagori" from standpoint of the village or as a son, father, husband or brother from the standpoints respectively of his father, son, wife or sister. In this way, from various standpoints, it is possible to have different characteristics in one and the same thing.

Syadvada if properly understood reveals the true nature of a thing. What is the nature of this world? How many things have existed therein? What are their attributes? etc. Perfect solution of all such quarries is obtained by Syadvada. It is an unprecedented gift of the Jain Religion to the world. If its secret is properly understood, all false schools of philosophy would end and the earnest desires for universal brotherhood will shine to the fullest extent.

# 2

# Theory of Karma (Law of Causation)

Everyone in this world desires happiness and dislikes misery, but we find that one is a millionaire while another is a pauper; one is healthy while another is diseased; one is white while another is black; one is handsome while another is ugly; one is stout while another is lean; one is intelligent while another is an idiot; one is a master while another is a slave. Similarly, we find the high and the low, the mutilated and the lame, the blind and the deaf, and many such oddities. What is the reason for all these conditions? People would say that it is due to individual luck. What is that luck? Who made it? Who governs it? How can you be free from all the above oddities and truly be happy? The Jain religion shows us the correct path to follow and we shall see in the following pages how to do it.

As said above there are many oddities in this world. It will have to be admitted that behind all of this some powerful force is at work. This force is called "karma". We are unable to perceive karma by our naked eyes, yet we are able to know it from its actions.

The thrones of mighty monarchs are gone, the proud

and the haughty have been humiliated in a moment and reduced to ashes. What is the principal cause of all this? It is karma. Even amongst the twins born of the same mother we find one an idiot and another intelligent, one rich and another poor, one black and another white. What is all of this due to? They could not have done any deeds while they were in their mother's womb. Why then should such oddities exist? We have then to infer that these disparities must be the result of their deeds in their past births though they are born together at one time.

In Jain philosophy the word karma has quite a different and unique significance. The starting principle of Jainism is that there is an eternal union between soul and matter. This union though without a beginning is not without an end. Once the union is entirely broken, when the soul is free from the slightest vestige of contact with matter, nothing can bind it again. It is liberated.

The activity of soul which invites and enables matter of an exceptionally subtle form to flow into it, as also the matter which actually does flow into the soul, is technically called Karma. The thought activity is called Bhava-Karma, and the actual matter flowing into the soul and binding it is called Dravya Karma. It is a substance. It is in itself inert matter, lifeless like a pebble, but in combination with jiva (life) its potency is immense, beyond calculation and measure. It then keeps the jiva itself bound and fettered. A prisoner, dancing constantly at karma's every beck and gesture. At each step, the momentum for a new movement is gained. At each embrace of matter, the delighted deluded soul throbs and vibrates for a fresh embrace. Matter is ever ready to attack the soul and to flow into it with its billion insinuations, to keep alive the vigorous bondage of the living by the nonliving. It is so very fine and subtle, that it cannot be perceived, recognized, discerned by any the most highly developed sensory organ, or by the most perfected microscope. It eludes all efforts of the chemist and the physicist to calculate, measure, graph, photograph, use, harness, or control it. It is millions of times finer and subtler than the waves of sound, light, or electricity, or the electrons and protons conceived by man. Yet this matter is ever and anon surrounding us on all sides, and permeating through and through every particle of our body and soul. There is no space where it is not. It is perceivable, appreciable, and knowable by the omniscients. Its workings, metamorphoses, make-ups, and changes are explained by Acharyas, who have heard the voice of the omniscient, and who have transmitted the knowledge thus directly acquired from the omniscient to others through the past millenniums, by mouth and in writings.

Karma is the original cause, the first the ultimate, which keeps the universe going. All phenomena, all changes, all manifestations are due to karmic effects. Jain saints, the masters of wisdom, have analyzed the workings of karma in the most minutest details in the Jain Shastras.

Karmic matter never remains in an isolated condition. As soon as it takes form, it combines with the physical or fluid body, which stimulates it into activity. The stimulation into activity is called asrava or inflow, and when it combines is called bandha or bondage.

The karmic molecules produce their effect after a certain period. This duration is called abadhakala or quiescence.

The action or effect is called udaya or operation.

The period for which it continues to operate is called sthiti, and this varies with the mildness or intensity of passions.

The natural siddance, falling or shedding off, of karmic molecules in due course during the period of duration is called nirjara or shedding. This can also be effected earlier, and the operation and duration period can be shortened, by austerities. The duration and effect or fruition of karmas can be increased or decreased. A person is the maker and master of his destiny. He can make himself happy or miserable, he can rise above circumstances, and can make a hell of heaven and a heaven of hell. A karma bound in one life may produce its effect in the same life, in the next, or in a life thereafter.

Just as gold is mixed with mud in the mines, the soul is covered with karmas from the infinite past. Just as gold is purified by means of acids and other processes, the soul is purified and freed from karmas by the process of mercy, charity, penance, self control, etc. The soul then attains salvation.

The living souls (jivatmas) are infinitely infinite. Each has a distinct entity. If these were parts and parcels of one soul we would have found every one happy or miserable at the happiness or misery of any one of them. However, what we see is entirely different. If one eats sweets he alone enjoys sweetness. At the death of one, all do not die. From this we have to conclude that though similar in nature the soul of each individual has a distinct existence. The soul which gets absolved from karma becomes a Parmatma. Such a soul is not affected by karmas again and is not born again. There are no births and deaths for such a soul. It becomes Siddhatma.

The soul gets covered with karmas mainly due to attachment (raag) and hatred (dwesha). The fruits of karmas i.e, actions would be good or bad according to the nature of actions (good or bad) done. One who has self control and can resist from acquiring karmas i.e. One who has no attachment or hatred is called Jina and the religion which teaches us to become a Jina is known as Jainism. Those who follow this religion are Jains. To follow the Path of Liberation it is not necessary to be born a Jain. However one should lead a life which is in accord with Jainism and conforms to the type and measure of faith, knowledge, and conduct leading to the goal. If that be so the soul may be sure that he or she is a liberal being and on a path to truth and freedom from the miseries and limitations of embodied existence.

One would ask how many types of karmas exist? How do they bind the soul? How are their fruits are realized, and how they wear away or get destroyed? All of this is shown in detailed in the Jain Shastras. Karma can be divided into eight main classes. They have 148 sub-classes.

The main classes are:

(1) **Jnanavarniya**: Knowledge obscuring karma; it is matter which obscures the soul's attribute of knowledge (5 subclasses).

(2) **Darshanavarniya**: Conation obscuring karma; it is matter which obscures the soul's attribute of conation, perception (9 sub-classes).

(3) **Vedniya**: Feeling karma; it is karma which mundane souls (embodied souls) come in contact with agreeable or disagreeable objects, which in their turn cause the feelings of pleasure or pain in the soul, according to their various degrees of attachment and aversion therein (2 sub-classes).

(4) **Mohaniya**: Deluding karma; it is karma which obscures the attributes of right belief, and right conduct of the soul (28 sub-classes).

(5) **Ayushya**: Age karma; this keeps one in bondage of four forms of existence i.e. hellish, sub-human, human, and celestial. It causes and determines the sojourn of a soul into a particular body (4 sub-classes).

(6) **Nama**: Body making karma; this gives the soul a distinguishing form of existence, determines its classes. It causes condition of existence, formation of different kinds of bodies, and the change from one to another condition of existence (93 sub-classes).

(7) **Gotra**: Family determining karma; this imparts a high or low status in life i.e. by which a soul is to take birth in a high or a low family (2 sub-classes).

(8) **Antaraya**: Obstructive karma; this creates hindrance in the ways of the soul's giving of gifts or achieving of things, in its abilities and in its use and enjoyment. It obscures the infinite power of the soul (5 sub-classes).

Numbers 1, 2, 4 and 8 are called Ghatiya Karmas.

Numbers 3, 5, 6 and 7 are called Aghatiya Karmas.

Ghatiya karmas are called so because they destroy the manifestation of the real and essential attributes of the soul. The manifestation of these attributes in mundane souls varies inversely of the proportionate decrease of the forces of these four destructive karmas.

The Aghatiya karmas are called so because they do not obscure the real attributes of the soul, but affect only the external environments of the soul and pertains to body.

As said above there are mainly eight kinds of classes (Prakrites) of karmic matter and these eight classes have 148 sub-classes. The subclasses are:

(1) Jnanavarniya - knowledge obscuring karma (5).

1. Mati jnan - obscures sensory knowledge
2. Shruta jnan - obscures scriptural knowledge
3. Avadhi jnan - obscures visual knowledge
4. Manahparyaya jnan - obscures mental knowledge
5. Keval jnan - obscures perfect knowledge

(2) Darshnavarniya - conation obscuring karma (9).

6. Chakshu darshan - obscures ocular conation
7. Achakshu darshan - obscures nonocular conation

8. Avadhi darshan - obscures visual conation

9. Keval darshan - obscures perfect conation

10. Nidra darshan - obscures sleep conation

11. Nidra-Nidra darshan - obscures deep sleep conation

12. Prachala darshan - obscures drowsiness conation

13. Prachala-Prachala darshan - obscures heavy drowsiness conation

14. Styasagriddhi darshan - obscures somnambulism conation

(3) Vedaniya - feeling karma (2).

15. Sata - Pleasure

16. Asata - Pain

(4) Mohaniya - deluding karma

(A) Darshana Mohaniya - deludes right belief (3)

17. Mithyatva - wrong belief

18. Samyag mithyatva - right-wrong belief

19. Samyaktva Prakriti - right belief clouded by slight wrong belief

(B) Charitra Mohaniya - deludes right conduct (25)

Kashaya - Passions (16)

Anantanubandhi - right beleif preventing passions (4)

20. Krodha - anger

21. Mana - pride

22. Maya - deceit

23. Lobha - greed

Apratyakhyana varaniya - partial vow preventing passions (4)

24. Anger

25. Pride

26. Deceit
27. Greed

Pratyakhyana varaniya - total vow preventing passions (4)

28. Anger
29. Pride
30. Deceit
31. Greed

Samjvalana - prevents perfect conduct

This is the slightest degree of passion and coexists with self restraint of a higher order. It relates to the four passions (4).

32. Anger
33. Pride
34. Deceit
35. Greed

Akashaya - quasi passions, slight or minor passions (9).

36. Hasya - laughter
37. Rati - indulgence
38. Arati - ennui; dissatisfaction
39. Shoka - sorrow
40. Bhaya - fear
41. Jugupsa - disgust; aversion; hiding one's own, and publishing other people's shortcomings
42. Striveda - feminine inclination
43. Purusveda - masculine inclination
44. Napumsakaveda - common Sex

(5) Ayu - age karma (4)

45. Narakayu - hellish age

46. Tiryanchayu - sub-human age
47. Manushyayu - human age
48. Devayu - celestial age

(6) Nama - body making karma (93)

Gati - condition of existence (4)

49. Narak - hellish
50. Tiryanch - sub-human
51. Manushya - human
52. Deva - celestial

Jati - genus of beings (5)

53. Ekendriya - one-sensed
54. Dvindriya - two-sensed
55. Tendriya - three-sensed
56. Chaundriya - four-sensed
57. Panchendriya - five-sensed

Sharira - bodies (5)

58. Audarika - The physical body of all men and animals.
59. Vaikrjyika - The fluid body of hellish and celestial beings which they can change at will.
60. Aharaka - Assimilative, the spiritual man like emanation from the head of a saint in doubt, in the sixth spiritual stage.
61. Taijasa - Electric body of mundane souls which always accompanies the Karmana.
62. Karmana - Karmic body found in all mundane souls.

Angopanga - major and minor limbs (3)

63. Audarika - physical
64. Vaikriyika - fluid
65. Aharaka - assimilative

66. Nirman - proper formation of limbs in relation to their situation (sthana) and dimensions (pramana)

Bandhana - molecular bondage (5)

67. Audarika - physical
68. Vaikriyika - fluid
69. Aharaka - assimilative
70. Taijasa - electric
71. Karmana - karmic

Samghat - molecular interfusion (5)

72. Audarika - physical
73. Vaikriyika - fluid
74. Aharaka - assimilative
75. Taijasa - electric
76. Karmana - karmic

Samsthan - figure of the body (6)

77. Samachaturasra - Symmetrical; perfect symmetry all around.
78. Nyagrodha - Banyan like; short in lower but large parimandala in upper extremities like a banyan tree
79. Svati - Tapering; like a snake-hole, broad in lower but narrow in the upper extremities, reverse of the last.
80. Kubjaka - Hunchback
81. Vamana - Dwarf
82. Hundaka - Unsymmetrical; disproportionate, deformed

Samhanana - bones, muscle etc. (6)

83. Vajra rishabha aracha - adamantine, nerves, joints samhanana and bones
84. Vajra narcha samhanana - adamantine joints and bones
85. Naracha samhanana - unbreakable joints and bones

86. Ardha naracha samhanana - semi-unbreakable joints and bones

87. Kilita samhanana - riveted bones

88. Asamprapta sripatika - loosely jointed bones samhanana

Sparsha - touch (8)

89. Kathora - hard

90. Komala - soft

91. Guru - heavy

92. Laghu - light

93. Ruksha - rough

94. Snigdha - smooth

95. Shita - cold

96. Ushna - hot

Rasa - tastes (5)

97. Tikta - pungent

98. Katuka - bitter

99. Kashaya - astringent (saline)

100. Amla - acid

101. Madhura - sweet

Gandha - smell (2)

102. Sugandha - sweet-smelling; fragrant

103. Durgandha - evil-smelling; malodorous

Varna - color (5)

104. Krishna - black

105. Nila - blue

106. Rakta - red

107. Pita - yellow

108. Shukla - white

Anupurvi - Migratory form; the power of retaining the form of the last incarnation during transmigration, i.e. in the passage from one to another condition of existence.

109. Naraka Anupurvi - hellish migratory form

110. Tiryanch Anupurvi - sub-human migratory form

111. Manushya Anupurvi - human migratory form

112. Deva Anupurvi - celestial migratory form

113. Agurulaghu - neither too heavy to move, nor too light to have stability

114. Upaghata - having a self destructive limb or organ, as a stag's horns

115. Paraghata - destructive; possessing a limb or organ fatal to others, such as a lion's claws

116. Atapa - hot light; radiant heat; possesses a brilliant body, which is hot to others but not to the possessor, as the gross radiant earth bodied beings in the sun

117. Udyota - cold light, phosphorescence

118. Uchchhvasa - respiration

Vihayogati - movement; capacity of moving in space (2)

119. Shubha - graceful

120. Ashubha - awkward

121. Pratyeka - individual body; a body enjoyable by one Sharira soul only

122. Sadharana - common body; possessed and enjoyable by many souls, e.g. a potato

123. Trasa - mobile, with bodies having 2, 3, 4, and 5 senses

124. Sthavara - immobile, with bodies having one sense only, i.e. the sense of touch

125. Subhaga - amiable personality even though not beautiful
126. Durbhaga - unrepossessing even though beautiful
127. Susvara - sweet voiced; musical
128. Duhsvara - harsh voiced; noisy
129. Shubha - beautiful (body)
130. Ashubha - ugly (body)
131. Sukshma - fine (body) uncuttable and all pervasive
132. Badara - gross (body)
133. Paryapti - capable of developing the body fully
134. Aparyapti - incapable of developing the body fully
135. Sthira - steady (circulation of blood, bile, etc.)
136. Asthira - unsteady (circulation of blood, etc.)
137. Adeva - impressive appearance such as may affect others
138. Anadeya - nonimpressive, dull appearance
139. Yashah Kirti - bringing good name even if one does not do good actions
140. Ayashah Kirti - notoriety; bringing bad name, even if one does good actions
141. Tirthankara - a Tirthankara's career with all its grandeur when he preaches and completes his ministry

(7) Gotra - family determining karma (2)

142. Uchcha Gotra - high family
143. Nicha Gotra - low family

(8) Antaraya - obstructive karma (5)

144. Dana Antaraya - charity obstructive
145. Labha Antaraya - gain obstructive

146. Bhoga Antaraya - obstruction of enjoyment, of consumable things

147. Upabhoga Antaraya - obstruction of re-enjoyment of nonconsumable things

148. Virya Antaraya - obstruction of power of exercise of one's capacities.

Some Acharyas treat the 93 subclasses of the body, making karma differently and the total of subclasses of all karmas is taken as 97, 107, 148, 158, or 168. Mainly in all Jain books the total of 148 is considered for all purposes.

# 3

# Six Dravyas (Substances)

We now look at the Six Dravyas, or fundamental substances, their attributes and modifications.

The universe consists mainly of two substances, living (jiva) and nonliving (ajiva).

The living alone has consciousness, and the power to attend and to know.

The nonliving has neither consciousness, attention, nor knowledge.

This nonliving is of five kinds:

(1) Matter (Pudgala) i.e. table, chair, brick, stone, etc. Matter is of many kinds, but the most mighty kind is karmic matter, which the mundane soul wears and which is the self wound matter to keep the soul moving in "Samsara."

(2) Principle of Motion (Dharma) is an essential auxiliary of the motion of souls and matter.

(3) Principle of Rest (Adharma) is a similar auxiliary of the cessation of the movements of souls and matter.

(4) Time (Kala) in virtue of which things become old, new, or continue in their existence.

(5) Space (Akasha) which gives their place or location to all substances.

Space consists of the universe (Loka) and the non-universe (Aloka). Space and time are both extensive and infinite.

These six, Jiva, Pudgala, Dharma, Adharma, Kala, and Akasha, are called the six substances or Dravyas.

Dravya literally means flowing, or continuing. It is called so because it flows or continues the same through all its modifications. It is called "sat" or existence also.

Existence or substance is a collective name for a trinity unity of birth (utpada), decay (vyaya), and continuance (dhrauvya).

Further, a substance is a group of attributes (guna) and modifications (paryaya).

Some attributes are general or common for all six substances, others are special. Common attributes are necessary for the existence of the group as a group or substance. These are infinite but six are principal:

(1) Astitva - Indestructibility; permanence; the capacity by which a substance cannot be destroyed.

(2) Vastutva - Functionality; capacity by which a substance has function.

(3) Dravyatva - Changeability; capacity by which it is always changing in modifications.

(4) Prameyatva - Knowability; capacity by which it is known by someone, or of being the subject matter of knowledge.

(5) Agurulaghutva - Individuality; capacity by which one attribute or substance does not become another and the substance does not lose the attributes whose grouping forms the substance itself.

(6) Pradeshatva - Spatiality; capacity of having some kind of location in space.

Chetanatva, consciousness, amurtavta, and immateriality

- are common attributes of the class of substance, or group of attributes, called soul.

Achetanatva, unconsciousness, murtatva, and materiality - are common to motion, rest, time and space.

Achetanatva, unconsciousness, amurtatva, and immaterially - are common to matter.

Vishesha Gunas are special attributes of a particular substance. These distinguish one group from the others, and are:

### 1. Jiva - Soul

(1) Knowledge. In its full form it arises only in the absence of knowledge obscuring karma.

(2) Conation. In its full form it arises only in the absence of conation obscuring karma.

(3) Bliss. In its full form it arises only in the absence of all the four destructive karmas, etc.

(4) Power. In its full form it arises only in the absence of obstructive karmas, etc.

(5) Right Belief. In its full form it arises only in the absence of deluding karma.

(6) Right Conduct. In its full form it arises only in the absence of deluding karma.

(7) Avyavadha. Undisturbable, due to the absence of Vedaniya or feeling karma, neither pleasure nor pain.

(8) Avagaha. Penetrability, due to the absence of age karma.

(9) Agurulaghutva. Due to the absence of family determining karma.

(10) Sukshmatva. Fineness due to the absence of body making karma.

The first six are Anujivi attributes, which coexist in

and constitute the substance. They arise fully only on the destruction (kshya) of the four destructive (ghatiya) karmas, i.e. Conation and knowledge-obscuring, deluding and obstructive karmas.

The last four are pratijivi attributes, which merely indicate the absence of their opposites. They arise fully on the destruction (kshya) of the four nondestructive (aghatiya) karmas, i.e. feeling, age, family determining, and body making karmas,

II. Pudgala matter has special attributes:

(1) touch (2) taste (3) smell (4) color

III. Dharma has for its special attribute the quality of being the medium of motion.

IV. Adharma is the medium of rest.

V. Akasha or space's special attribute is to give place to all substances.

VI. Kala or time's special attribute is to bring about modifications (paryaya).

Modifications occur only with reference to attributes. This alone is what is meant by birth and decay. Modifications or conditions change, i.e. a new condition is born, i.e, comes into existence (utpada) and the old one decays, i.e. goes out of existence (vyaya).

The essential attributes of the substance always persist through all these modifications. It must be clearly understood and constantly remembered that substance is one; the birth and decay in its modifications, and the continuance of the substance (dhrauvya) itself are only three aspects of viewing one and the same thing.

Also substance (dravya), attribute (guna), and modification (paryaya) are three mutually interpervasive aspects of the trinity. Attribute is nothing different from substance and modification. So for all the three. When we talk or think of one, we necessarily talk or think of the remaining two. The soul with omniscience sees the whole trinity in its entirety at one and the same time.

In the universe, the jiva dravya or soul, is found mixed with nonliving matter. Death is a most universal and eternal phenomenon. The body is living; when death intervenes, the body becomes lifeless, or dies. Life has left the body. This, life is the soul; the body represents the grossest and most visible form of matter, with which the life was clothed, and which was "living" only so long as life or soul was united with it. The soul is a self existing entity and its existence is well proved. Since it is formless, it is not perceptible to our eyes. We do not see wind, but its effect is felt. Because of the effect the cause exists. The effect (actions) of atma i.e. soul is perceptible in a living man because a living man moves, walks, plays, does work, and even thinks in various ways. All this is not perceptible in a dead man.

A moment before death movements are perceptible in a living man but the moment after death nothing is perceived in the dead body. Death does not mean annihilation of anything, soul or matter. It is only a separation of the outer body from the soul, which is still combined with two material but fine bodies, i.e. electric and karmic. It is only when the soul obtains liberation, that it becomes permanently pure and completely rid of all combination with matter. By careful comparison we can find a trace to the characteristic features of life and its differences from lifelessness.

The first thing we notice in one, who was living but is dead now, is that his senses do not act. He cannot touch, taste, smell, see, or hear. He has no vitality of the senses. Also he is powerless. He cannot act, speak, or think. He has no force, no vitality of body, speech, or mind. Many of these things may be absent also in a living man who is asleep, in a trance, or otherwise unconscious. Therefore, all over the world we examine the man's respiration. If it is there, we say, he still lives. If not, we say, "He has breathed his last." This respiration is a sure sign of life.

To sum up the distinction between the living and nonliving substances we may say that a nonliving substance does not have

(1) the vitality of the five senses,

(2) the power of body, speech, and mind,

(3) respiration, and

(4) age.

These four may be called the four (or with their subdivisions ten) vitalities of living beings. It is noticeable that all these four or ten are also a manifestation of one underlying real fact, that of consciousness.

In a dead body the sensory organs are there and the eye may be impressed with color and form as before, but there is no consciousness behind it which in life received, recorded, and responded to the ocular stimulus. The four or ten vitalities are sure signs to distinguish the living from the nonliving, but in reality it is consciousness which distinguishes life from lifelessness. All this goes to prove that body and soul are two different things. Body is the abode of the soul.

When the duration of time of the existence of soul in the body comes to an end, the body is left and the soul according to the Ayu Karma (its deeds in this birth by which he earns the life span of the next birth) goes away to another place, takes a new birth, and there lives in a new body. When the duration in that birth comes to an end, it goes away to a third birth. There he puts on a third body. In this way from the eternal past, the line of births and deaths continues according to karma (deeds of each soul).

The matter (pudgala) referred to above is of six kinds:

(1) Gross-gross matter (solid) e.g. a mountain, pillar of iron etc.

(2) Gross (liquid), e.g. water, oil etc.

(3) Gross-fine, e,g. shade, sunshine.

(4) Fine-gross, e.g. fragrance, sound, sweetness etc.

(5) Fine, matter capable of becoming karmic matter. It cannot be perceived by the senses.

(6) Fine-fine, matter which has for its atoms the combinations of two or more ultimate atoms (parmanu). According to some saints it is the ultimate atom itself.

The inflow of the above said karmic matter towards the soul is caused by the vibratory activity of mind, speech, and body. Colored by passions (kashaya) of anger, pride, deceit, and greed mainly. The inflow leads to bondage of soul by karmic matter. The vibrations determine the kind (prakriti) and the quantity (pradesha) of the karmic matter to be drawn towards and bound to the soul. The passions determine the duration (sthiti) of the bondage, and the mild or intense fruition (anubhaga) of the karma at its maturity.

# 4

# Seven Tatvas (Principles)

The Tatvas or the Principles are seven:

(1) Jiva, soul,

(2) Ajiva, non-soul,

(3) Asrava, inflow,

(4) Bandh, bondage,

(5) Samvara, the check of inflow,

(6) Nirjara, the shedding of previously bound up karmas,

(7) Moksha, liberation from all karmic contact.

## I & II. Jiva & Ajiva

All that exists is included in one or other of the two principles, soul and non-soul. While a man is alive, it is the soul in his body which perceives and knows all objects. A body without soul is incapable of perceiving or knowing anything. Material objects such as a pen, table or chair cannot feel or know anything. They are unconscious or inanimate substances. The soul is the only conscious substance. Looked at from the real point of view even a mundane i.e. embodied soul is pure, peaceful, all knowing and all blissful. It is potentially so. From the practical point of view such a soul experiences various kinds of pain and pleasure in different conditions of life. The universe teems with infinite living forms. How to observe, analyse, and classify them? This may be done in three different ways:

(1) Soul-classes (Jiva Samasa). There are obvious differences of body, sense and mind in different classes of souls. The body is primarily the basis of this classification. This in Jainism is technically called soul classes (Jiva Samasa).

(2) Soul-quest (Margana). It comprises other inner differences in species, sex, passion, knowledge, conation, etc. In soul quest, the embodied condition of the soul, i.e. the mixed living and non-living condition, is primarily the basis.

(3) Spiritual Stages (Gunasthan). They concern the purely-inner progress of the soul. In these spiritual stages, the progress of the soul from iguorance and delusion to perfect self-absorption is traced.

Soul-classes (Jiva Samasa). From the protoplasm of the germ-cell to a full blown human-being, there is an infinite number of mundane souls or living beings in the universe. The protoplasm so far as is known at present has no ears to hear, no eyes to see, no nose; to smell, no tongue to taste, it has only the sense of touch. The human being has all the five senses fully developed and distinct, and a mind also which is also a sort of additional and higher sense (a quasi-sense), the organ of which sense is invisibie to us. In Jainism, it is an organ which is made up of subtle matter called Manovargana or mental matter and its form is like a lotus with eight petals near the heart. We can divide mundane souls into six classes.

(1) With the sense of touch only

(2) With touch and taste

(3) With touch, taste and smell

(4) With touch, taste, smell, and sight

(5) With touch, taste, smell, sight, and hearing

(6) With touch, taste, smell, sight, hearing, and mind

One-sensed souls cannot be known by our senses. They can penetrate all matter. They are everywhere in the universe. They are not obstructed by, and they do not obstruct others. They die their own death.

Some of the above seven kinds are born with the capacity to develop, others die before acquiring the capacjty to develop. Each one of the seven may, therefore, be developable or non-developable. Thus, there may be said to be fourteen soul-classes in all. A further distinction can be considered. Some mundane souls can voluntarily change their place in space; others cannot. Observation will show that all one-sensed souls are immobile and that all the other souls are 406 soul classes of mundane souls as under:

(1) Sub-human, one to four-sensed - 81

One-sensed in earth, water, fire, air, vegetable, trunk, creeper, plant, tree, root.

(2) Sub-human, five-sensed - 42

In work region, highest, middle, lowest enjoyment regions.

(3) Human, five-sensed - 13

In work region Arva Khanda and Mlichha Khanda. In highest, middle, lowest and distorted enjoyment regions.

(4) Celestial, five-sensed - 172

In 1st to 16th Heaven, 9 Graiveyaka, 9 Anudisha, 6 Anuttara.

(5) Hellish, five-sensed - 98

In 1st to 7th Hell

Total Soul classes 406

**Soul quests (Marganas).** There are 14 soul quests as under

(1) **Gati.** Conditions of existence are 4: human, sub-human, hellish and celestial. Margana is a condition in which a mundane soul is necessarily found. There are four such sets, of existence.

(2) **Indriya.** Senses are 5: touch, taste, smell, sight and hearing.

(3) **Kaya**. Body is of 6 kinds: earth, water, fire, air, vegetable (all immobile) and mobile bodies.

(4) **Yoga.** Soul's vibrations are of 15 kinds:

1 - 8are mind and speech vibrations, each being true, false, mixed true and false, and neutral i.e, neither true nor false;

9 - 15 are body vibratious.

9 - Body vibration physical.

10 - Body vibration physical mixed with karmic.

11 - Body vibration fluid.

12 - Body vibration fluid mixed with karmic.

13 - Body vibration assimilative.

14 - Body vibration assimilative mixed with physical.

15 - Body vibration karmic.

(5) **Veda.** Sex is of 3 kinds:

masculine, feminine, common.

(6) **Kashaya**. Passions are of 4 kinds:

anger, pride, deceit, greed.

(7) **Jnana**. Knowledge is of 8 kinds:

sensitive, scriptural, visual, mental, perfect and wrong sensitive, wrong scriptural, wrong visual.

(8) **Samyam.** Restraint is of 7 kinds:

equanimity, recovery of equaninity after downfall, pure and absolute non-injury, slightest delusion, passionless, partial control, non-control.

(9) **Darshana**. Conation is of 4 kinds:

occular, non-occular, visual, perfect.

(10) **Leshya.** Thought paint is of 6 kinds:

black, blue, dove-gray, yellow, pink, white.

(11) **Bhavya**. It is of 2 kinds:

capacity or incapacity of being liberated.

(12) **Samyaktva.** Right Belief is of 6 kinds:

subsidential, destructive, destructive-subsidential, wrong-belief, downfall, mixed right and wrong belief.

(13) **Sanjna.** It is of 2 kinds:

rational and irrational.

(14) **Akaraka**. It is of 2 kinds:

Taking or not taking, no karmas or assimilative matter.

All these divisions of soul quests are marked out with reference to the results of the operation of different karmas. The pure soul has perfect knowledge, perfect conation, right belief, and pure right conduct. These have no reference to any operation of karmas. The pure soul is free from all these distinctions of soul quests.

Spiritual Stages (Gunasthana). These are dealt with in a separate chapter.

The non-soul comprises the other five real and independent substances mentioned below, which, taken together with the soul, make up the six substances (Dravyas) described previously.

(1) Pudgala, matter is the most prominent, and plays a very important part in the amphitheatre of the universe. The special attribute of matter-substance (Pudgala) are touch, taste, smell, and colour. It exists either in the form of atoms or of molecules. Only gross molecules are cognizable by the senses; fine, electric and karmic molecules which compose the electric and the karmic

bodies of all mundane souls are not cognizable by the senses.

(2) Dharma Dravya, medium of motion is a single, immaterial substance, pervading throughout the whole of the universe. It is essentially an auxiliary cause of motion for soul and matter.

(3) Adharma Dravya, medium of rest is also a single, immaterial substance, pervading throughout the whole universe. It is also an essentially auxiliary cause of rest for soul and matter.

(4) Akasha Dravya, space is a single infinite immaterial substance. Its function is to give place to all substances.

(5) Kala Dravya, time is an immaterial substance. It is an auxiliary camse of bringing about modifications in all substances.

**III & IV. Asrava and Bandha**

The most important combination of soul and matter is our body. It is also manifest that this body is constantly changing, in virtue of our activity of mind, speech and body.

A feeling of modesty in the mind of the maiden paints her cheeks with blush. A sad thought gives one a long face. Criminal broodings breed a criminal look in a man or woman. The pious chanting of a hymn or prayer gilds one with the calm detachment and glory of the halo of a priest or devotee. Our food, dress, play and work, all bring about constant changes in the body. Matter attracts matter. Generally the law of nature is "like to like". The matter of bad thoughts attracts matter of bad thought, and ultimately becomes the father of a bad habit. This attraction of good or bad matter by the soul in virtue of its mental, vocal, or bodily activity, is called infow (Asrava).

Every mundane soul has a karmic body, formed of karmic molecules. The universe is full of karmic molecules.

Inflow of these molecules towards the soul, caused by its ows vibratory activities, through mind, speech, and body, is the third principle Asrava.

The mundane inflow is of 39 kinds, according to its causes:

5 caused by the activity of the 5 senses,

4 caused by the activity of the 4 passions,

5 caused by the activity of the 5 sins:

injury, lies, theft, unchastity, and worldly attachment,

25 caused by 25 kinds of activities which are the effects of the 14 causes, viz., 5 senses, 4 passions, and 5 sins of vowlessness.

When these molecules are so attracted towards the soul, they are assimilated in the existing karmic body. The causes of assimilation or bondage are the soul's vibratory activities and passions. This process is known as Bandha (bondage) the fourth principle.

The process of inflow and bondage of karmic matter go on simultaneously.

The main auxiliary causes of both of them are:

(a) wrong belief (Mithyatva),

(b) vowlessness (Avirati),

(c) passions (Kashaya), and

(d) soul's vibratory activities of mind, speech and body (Yoga).

If the vibratory activity is with passion, the inflow leads to bondage of soul by karmic matter. It is called Samparayika or mundane inflow.

If it is without passion, i.e. purely vibratory in the llth, 12th and 13th spiritual stages and does not lead to bondage it is called Iryapatha or transient or fleeting inflow.

The causes of inflow of the eight karmas are as under:

1 & 2. Knowledge and conation-obscuring karmas.

The inflow of knowledge and conation obscuring karmic matter is caused by the following:

(1) Depreciation of those who are learned in the scriptures.

(2) Concealment of knowledge.

(3) Envy, jealousy, refusal to impart knowledge out of envy.

(4) Obstruction. Hindering the progress of knowledge.

(5) Denying the truth, proclaimed by another, by body and speech.

(6) Refuting the truth, although it is known, to be such.

### 3. Feeling Karma, Vedaniya Karma

The inflow of pain bringing feeling (Asata Vedaniya) karmic matter is due, to the following feelings and acts:

(1) Dukha, pain

(2) Shoka, sorrow,

(3) Tapa, repentence, remorse

(4) Akrandana, weeping

(5) Badha, depriving of vitality

(6) Paridevana, piteous or pathetic moaning to attract conpassion.

These 6 can be produced in one's own self, in another, or both in one's self and another. Thus, there are 18 forms of this inflow.

The following are the causes of inflow of pleasure bearing feeling (Sata Vedaniya) karmic matter:

(1) Bhuta anukampa, compassion for all living beings

(2) Vraty anukampa, compassion for the vowers

(3) Dana, charity

(4) Saraga samyam, self-control with slight attachment

(5) Samyam asamyam, restraint by vows of some, but not of others

(6) Akama nirjara, equanimous submission to the fruition of karma

(7) Bala tapa, austerities not based upon right knowledge

(8) Yoga, contemplation

(9) Kshanti, forgiveness

(10) Shauch, contentment

**4. Deluding Karma, Mohaniya Karma**

The inflow of Darshana Mohaniya, right belief deluding karmic matter is caused by

Avarnavada,

defaming the Omsiscient Lord, Arhat Kevali;

the Scriptures Shruta;

the Saint's brotherhood,

Sangha;

the true relegion,

Dharma; and

the celestial beings, Deva,

e.g. saying that the celestial beings take meat or wine, etc. and to offer these as sacrifices to them.

The inflow of Charitra Mohaniya, right conduct deluding karmic matter is caused by the intense thought activity produced by the rise of the passions and of the quasi passions, no-kashaya, e.g. joking about truth, etc., disinclination to take vows, etc., including in evil society, etc.

**5. Age, Ayu Karma**

The inflow of Narakayu, Hellish Age Karma is caused by too much worldly activity and by attachment to too many wordly objects or by too much attachment e.g. committing breaches of the first five vows of non-killing, truth, non-stealing, chastity, non-attachment to worldly possessions. The point to be noted is that it is not the possession or ownership of worldly wealth which is sinful but it is the attachment to it which is a sin. A man may be in the world; but he must not be of it.

The infow of Tiryancha-ayu, Sub-human Age Karma is caused by Maya, deceit, e.g, cheating others, preaching the false doctrines, etc.

The infow of Manushya-ayu, Human Age Karma is caused by slight worldly activity and by attachment to a few wordly objects or by slight attachment. Natural humble dis-position is also the cause of Human Age Karma.

Vowlessness and sub-vowlessness with slight worldly activity and slight attachment are causes of the inflow of all kinds of Age Karmas. Not taking the vows of laymen and not adopting the restrictions (Shila) but having slight attachment to the world and activity in it, can be the cause of the infow of Age-karmic matter of all four kinds.

The inflow of Deva Ayu, Celestial Age Karma is caused by the following:

(1) Saraga Samyam, self-coutrol with slight attachment found in monks only.

(2) Samyam Asamyam, restraint of some vows, but not of others, found in laymen only.

(3) Akama Nirjara, equanimous submission to the fruition of karma.

(4) Bala Tapa, austerities not based upon right-knowledge.

Right belief is also the cause of Celestial Age Karma, but only of the heavenly order. It applies to human and sub-human beings only. A celestial or hellish right believer binds the human age karma. Note also that if a human or sub-human being has bound a particular Age Karma before gaining right belief, he must enjoy that.

**6. Body Making, Nama Karma**

The inflow of Ashubha Nama, a bad body making karma is caused by a non-straightforward or deceitful working of the mind, body or speech or by Visamvada, wrangling, etc., wrong belief, envy, back-biting, self-praise, censuring others, etc.

The inflow of Shubha-Nama, a good body making karma is caused by the causes which are opposite of the above viz. by straightforward dealings with body, mind and speech; by avoiding disputes, etc., right belief, humility, admiring praiseworthy people, etc.

The inflow of Tirthankara body making karma is caused by meditation (Bhavana) of the following 16 matters:

(1) Darshana Vishuddhi, purity of right belief. Pure right belief is with 8 Angas or the following 8 qualities:

(a) Nisshankita. Free from all doubt.

(b) Nishkankshita. Free from worldly desire.

(c) Nirvichikitsita. Free from repulsion from anything.

(d) Amudbadrishtitva. Free from superstitious belief.

(e) Upa-brimhana or more popularly, Upa-guhana. Advancement in one's own attributes. Free from a tendency to proclaim the faiths of others.

(f) Sthiti-karana. To help oneself or others to remain steady in the path of truth.

(g) Vatsalya. Tender affection for one's brother on the path of liberation.

(h) Prabhavana. Propagation of the path of liberation.

(2) Vinaya sampannata. Reverence for means of liberation and for those who follow them.

(3) Shila vrateshnanatichara. Faultless observance of the 5 vows, and faultless subdual of the passions.

(4) Abhikshna jnanopayoga. Ceaseless pursuit of right-knowledge.

(5) Samvega. Perpetual apprehension of mundane miseries.

(6) Shaktitas tyaga. Giving to others, gift of knowledge, food, medicine etc., according to one's capacity.

(7) Shaktitas-tapa. The practice of austerities, according to one's capacity.

(8) Sadhu samadhi. Protecting and reassuring to saints or removing their troubles.

(9) Vaiyavrittya karana. Serving the meritorious.

(10) Arhat bhakti. Devotion to Arhats or Omniscient Lords.

(11) Acharya bhakti. Devotion to Acharyas or heads of the orders of saints.

(12) Bahu shruta bhakti. Devotion to Upadhyayas or teaching saints.

(13) Pravachana bhakti. Devotion to Scriptures.

(14) Avashyaka parihari. Not neglecting one's six important daily duties.

(15) Marga prabhavana. Propagation of the Path of Liberation.

(16) Pravachana vatsalatva. Tender affection for one's brothers on the Path of Liberation.

Even one of these, if properly contemplated and with right belief, brings about the inflow of Tirthankara body making karma.

**7. Family determining, Gotra Karma**

The inflow of low family determining karma is caused by the following:

(1) Paraninda, speaking ill of others.

(2) Atma prashansa, praising oneself.

(3) Sadgunochchhadana, concealing the good qualities of others.

(4) Asad guna udbhavana, proclaiming in oneself the good qualities which one does not possess.

The inflow of high family determining karma is caused by the opposites of the above i.e.:

(1) Para prashansa, praising others.

(2) Atma ninda, denouncing oneself.

(3) Parsad gunandbhanana, proclaiming the good qualities of others.

(4) Atmasad guna uchchhadana, not proclaiming one's own good qualities.

(5) Nichaih Vritti, an attitude of humility towards one's betters.

(6) Anutseka, not being proud of one's own achievements or attainments.

**8. Obstructive, Antraya Karma**

The inflow of Antaraya Karma is caused: by disturbing others in charity, gain, enjoyment of consumable things, enjoyment of non-consumable things, and making use of their powers.

Note that the inflow of 7 Karmas, i.e. of all except the age karma, is going on always in souls influenced by the passions, and of the age karma also on special occasions; but the predominance of the above causes will determine the intensity of fruition (anubhaga) of their particular inflow.

The special occasions of Age Karma are eight in one man's life, as follows:

Suppose a man's life is to be 81 years long. The first

occasion for binding the age karma will be on his passing 2/3 of it, i.e. when he is 54. The second on his passing 2/3 of the remainder i.e. when he is 72. The third on his passing 2/3 of the remainder, i.e. when he is 78. The fourth on his passing 2/3 of the remainder, i.e. when he is 80. Similarly the fifth when he is 80 years, 8 months. The sixth is at 80 years, 10 months and 20 days. The seventh at 80 years, 11 months, 16 days and 16 hours. The eighth at 80 years, 11 months, 25 days, 13 hours, and 20 minutes. If no age karma is bound yet, the ninth is the last antar muhurta of his life. The point is that the man is born with his particular age karma already bound. Therefore, he must bind the age karma of his next incarnation at the latest at the last moment.

(1) Wrong Belief. It is of 5 kinds:

(a) Ekanta. Taking only one aspect of a many sided thing.

(b) Viparita. Perverse belief, e.g. animal sacrifices lead to heaven. Injury to auyone cannot be a cause of merit.

(c) Samshaya. Doubt, scepticism, hesitation, e.g. as to Path of Liberation.

(d) Vinaya. Veneration. Taking all religions and Gods, even the so-called religions which enjoin cruel or immoral practices, to be equally worthy of pursuit.

(e) Ajnana. Wrong belief caused by ignorance. Indiscrimination of good and bad. Wrong belief is caused by Nisarga, inborn error; or by Adhigama, preaching of another.

(2) Avirata. Vowlessness, Non-renunciation is of 12 kinds:

Lack of compassion for 6 classes of embodied souls; and lack of restraint of 5 senses and 1 mind.

(3) Pramada. Carelessness is of 15 kinds:

(1) Food (bhojana katha)

(2) Women (stri katha)

(3) Politics (rajya katha)

(4) Scandal (desha katha)

(5-9) Senses

(10-13) Passions

(14) Affection

(15) Sleep

(4) Kashaya. Passions are four: anger, pride, deceit and greed.

(5) Yoga. Vibrations in the soul, through mind, speech and body, are of 15 kinds:

Mind: (1) Satya mana, true mind.

(2) Asatya mana, false mind.

(3) Ubhaya mana, mixed true and false mind.

(4) Anubhaya mana, neither true nor false.

Speech: (1) Satya Vachana, true.

(2) Asatya Vachana, false.

(3) Ubhaya Vachana, both.

(4) Anubhaya Vachana, none.

Body: (1) Audarika, physical.

(2) Audarika mishra, i,e. physical with karmic.

(3) Vakriyika, fluid.

(4) Vakriyika mishra, Fluid with karmic.

(5) Aharaka, Assimilative.

(6) Aharaka mishra, i.e. Assimilative with physical.

(7) Karmana, Karmic.

Note that the Taijasa, Electric Body, is always found with the Karmic Body. It never has an independent yoga. The electric molecules are drawn like the karmic molecules by the vibrations set in the soul by yoga of any kind.

Karmic matter is bound to the soul by the vibrations (yoga) of mind, speech and body, coloured by passions

(Kashaya) of anger, pride, deceit, and greed mainly. The vibrations determine the kind (Prakriti) and the quantity (Pradesha) of the Karmic matter to be drawn towards and bound to the soul. The passions determine the duration (Sthiti) of the bondage and the mind or intense fruition (Anubhaga) of the karma at its maturity.

**Kinds of Bondage**

There are eight kinds of Prakritis of Karmic matter and 148 sub-classes as already mentioned in Chapter II.

**The Quantity of Bondage**

As to Pradesha, accoiding to the nature caused by their names from all around, due to the differences is the vibrations (yoga) in the soul-activty, not perceptible by the senses, the karmic molecules enter and become one and stay with every Pradesha of the soul. They come in infinite numbers, every moment, to each soul. The particular number of the molecules actually absorbed is called Pradesha-bandha.

**Duration of Bondage**

The maximum durations are as under:

Knowledge and Conation obscuring karmas, Feeling Karmas and Obstructive karmas 30 crore x crore Sagaras.

This is possible in a rational five sensed, fully developable (Paryapta) soul, who has wrong belief (Mithyatva).

**Deluding Karma**

70 crore x crore Sagaras.

Nama and Gotra Karmas:

33 crore x crore Sagaras for each.

This is also possible as above.

Ayu, Age Karma: 33 Sagaras.

The minimum durations are as under:

Feeling Karma: 12 Muhurtas

= 12 x 48 minutes

= 12 x 48/60 = 48/5 = 9hours, 36 minutes.

Gotra Karma: 8 Muhurtas.

Nama Karma: 8 Muhurtas.

Knowledge obscuring Karma

Conation obscuring Karma

Obstructive obscuring Karma

Deluding obscuring Karma

One Antar-muhurta which ranges from 1 Samaya and 1 Avali at the lowest to 48 minutes minus one Samaya.

Fruition of Karma.

It is according to the name of the karma, e.g. knowledge obscuring karma prevents the acquisition of knowledge and so on.

V. Samvara.

Checking of inflow and bondage of karmic molecules is called Samvara (stoppage). The main auxiliary causes of stopping the inflow and bondage of karmic molecules are:

(a) right belief,

(b) observance of vows,

(c) passionlessness, and

(d) restraint of soul's vibratory activities.

The causes of inflow and bondage are given above.

Wrong belief (Mithya Darshan) is stopped (Samvara) in the 4th Spiritual Stage (guuasthana), vowlessness (Avirata) in the 5th and 6th, carelessness (Pramada) in the 7th, passion (Kashaya) in the 8th, 9th and 10th, vibration (Yoga) in the 14th Stage.

Samvara or Stoppage of Inflow is produced by the following:

(A) 3 kinds of Gupti, preservation.

(B) 5 kinds of Samiti, carefulness.

(C) 10 kinds of Dharma, observances.

(D) 12 kinds of Anupreksha, meditation.

(E) 22 kinds of Parishaha Jaya, subdual of sufferings.

(F) 5 kinds of Charitra, conduct.

By austerities is caused the shedding of karmic matter, and also stoppage of inflow.

(A) 3 preservations, Gupti, proper control (Nigraha) over (1) mind, (2) speech, and (3) body.

(B) 5 carefulness.

(1) Samyak Irya Samiti, Proper care in walking.

(2) Samyak Bhasha Samiti, Proper care in speaking.

(3) Samyak Eshna Samiti, Proper care in eating.

(4) Samyak Adana Nikshepa Samiti, Proper care in lifting and laying.

(5) Samyak Utsarga Samiti, Proper care in excreting.

(C) 10 observances:

(1) Uttama kshama, supreme forgiveness.

(2) Uttama mardava, supreme humility.

(3) Uttama arjava, supreme straight forwardness (Honesty).

(4) Uttama shaucha, supreme contentment.

(5) Uttama satya, supreme truth.

(6) Uttama samyama, supreme restraint.

(7) Uttama tapa, supreme austerities.

(8) Uttama tyaga, supreme renunciation.

(9) Uttama akinchanya, supreme non-attachment, not taking the non-self for one's own self.

(10) Uttama brahmacharya, supreme chastity.

(D) 12 Meditations:

(1) Anitya Anupreksha, Everything is subject; to change or transitory but note that as substance everything is permanent. Only condition is transitory.

(2) Asharana Auupreksha. Unprotectiveness, helplessness.

The soul is unprotected from the fruition of karmas, death, pain, pleasure success, failure are the necessary, results of our acts in this or past lives.

(3) Samsara Anupreksha, Mundaneness, soul, moves in the cycle of existences and cannot attain true happiness till he is out of it.

(4) Ekatva Anupreksha. Loneliness, I am alone the doer of my actions and the enjoyer of the fruits of them.

(5) Anyatva Anupreksha. Separateness, otherness. The world, my relatives and friends, my body and mind, they are all distinct and separate from my real self.

(6) Ashuchi Anupreksha. Impurity, the body is impure and dirty. Purity is of 2 kinds: of the Soul itself; and of the body and other things. This last is of 8 kinds.

(7) Ashrava Anupreksha, Inflow. The inflow of Karma is the cause of my mundane existence and it is the product of passions, etc.

(8) Samvara Anupreksha, Stoppage. The inflow must be stopped.

(9) Nirjara Anupreksha, Shedding. Karmic matter must be shed from or shaken out of the soul.

(10) Loka Anupreksha, Universe. The nature of the Universe and its constituent elements in all their vast variety proving the insignificance and miserable nothingness of man in time and space.

(11) Bodhi Durlabha Asupreksha. Rarity of Right Path. It is diffcult to attain right belief, knowledge and conduct.

(12) Dharma svakhya tattva Anupreksha. Nature of Right Path as said by the Conquerors. The true nature of Truth, i.e., the three fold path to real Liberation. These must be meditated again and again.

(E) 22 Sufferings.

For the sake of non-falling-off from the Path of Liberation, and for the shedding of karmic matter, whatever sufferings are undergone calmly and with religious renunciation are called the Sufferings (Parishaha). They are:

(1) Hunger

(2) Thirst

(3) Cold

(4) Heat

(5) Troubles from insect-bites, mosquitoes, etc.

(6) Nakedness, To bear calmly the troubles of climate, unpopularity, etc., due to the vow of absolute possessionlessness, i.e. nakedness

(7) Ennui, dissatisfaction, languor

(8) Women. Resisting temptations from and desire for women

(9) Walking too much, not to feel the fatigue, but to bear it calmly

(10) Continuous sitting in one posture, not to disturb the posture of meditation, even if there is danger from lion, snakes, etc.

(11) Sleeping, resting on the hard earth

(12) Abuse

(13) Beating

(14) Begging. To resist the temptation of begging even when there is great need of protection of body, mind, etc.

(15) Failure to get alms

(16) Disease

(17) Contact with thorny shrubs, etc.

(18) Dirt. Discomfort from dust, etc.

(19) Respect or disrespect by admirers or enemies

(20) To resist conceit of knowledge and to be full of humility

(21) Lack of knowledge. Not to be pained, even though it is felt that one does not know much

(22) Slack belief, e.g., on failure to attain supernatural powers, even after great piety and austerities to begin to doubt the truth of Jainism and its teachings.

(F) 5 Charitras. They are:

(1) Eqnanimity

(2) Recovery of equalimity after a fall from it

(3) Pure and absolute non-injury

(4) All but entire freedom from passion

(5) Ideal and passionless conduct (Parihar Vishuddhi)

VI. Nirjara.

The shedding of karmas already bound with a soul, at maturity, or prematurely, is called Nirjara. The premature shedding of karmas is caused by pure thought activities, brought about by the practice of right kind of austerities.

The shedding on maturity is a natural and automatic process. But it is a long process.

Therefore a shorter method is adopted; deliberate activity may hasten the ripening of a karma and the shedding of its matter.

To illustrate, we wish evil to our neighbour A : the thought activity invites the karmic matter into the soul (ashrava), the matter comes and binds the soul (bandha). This karma may take two months to bear its full fruits; in the meantime it is an evil load for the soul. To get lightness and to get rid of the karma, the soul may deliberately feel an opposite kind of feeling towards other neighbours B, C, and D, or towards A himself. A still surer way is to practise austerity. By removing the mind from the demands and impulses of the body, and by mortifying the physical man through not listening to its greed and temptations, matter may be overcome and the soul freed from the bondage.

The natural maturing of a Karma and its separation from the soul is called Savipaka Nirjara. Inducing a karma to leave the soul by means of a contrary karma, or by means of ascetic practices, is called Avipaka Nirjara (Riddance without fruition).

The causes of stopping of inflow of karmic matter given previously are also causes of the shedding of the karmas already bound to the soul. In addition to these, austerities (tapa) also cause the shedding before its time. Tapa, austerities are external and internal.

External austerities are six:

(1) Anashana, Fasting.

(2) Avamodarya, Eating less than one's fill, or less than one has appetite for.

(3) Vritti parisankhyana, Taking a mental vow to accept food from a house-holder, only if a certain condition is fulfilled, without letting anyone know about the vow.

(4) Rasa parityaga, Daily renunciation of one or more of 6 kinds of delicacies: ghee (butter, clarified butter), milk, curd, sugar, salt, oil.

(5) Vivikta shayyasana, sitting and sleeping in a lonely place, devoid of animate beings.

(6) Kaya-Klesha, Mortification of the body, so long as the mind is not disturbed.

Internal austerities are also six:

(1) Prayashchitta, Expiation.

(2) Vinava, Reverence.

(3) Vaiyavritya, Service of the saints or worthy people.

(4) Swadhyaya, Study.

(5) Vyutsarga, Giving up attachment to the body, etc.

(6) Dhyana, Concentration.

VII. Moksha,

Liberation is freedom from all karmic matter as a result of the non-existence of the cause of bondage and the shedding off of all karmas previously bound. The total separation of soul from the bondage of all karmic matter is liberation (Moksha). It is the state of a Siddha, the condition of perfection. Continuous devotion to Apta (own soul), study of the scriptures, and meditation of the seven principles, cause the subsidence of wrong belief (Mithyatva) and of the four error feeding passions (Anantanubandhi Kashaya) and as a cousequence the real Right Belief, which is an attribute of the soul, shines forth in its true splendour. At this stage the Right Believer is fully convinced of the true amd pure nature of his own soul, and this is Real Right Belief.

**Punya (merit) and Papa (demerit)**

Two more are added to the above said seven principles. These are Punya (merit) and Papa (demerit).

Know good karmas as merit and bad karmas as demerit. Non-self, whether merit or demerit, is not conducive to the freedom of the soul. People generally love merit and hate demerit, because the latter brings pain and the former pleasure. Really pleasure also is not beneficial, because a mundane soul indulging in sense pleasures remains aloof from the path of spiritual purity. Every gratification of sense pleasure reates desire for further gratification. For obtaining such gratifications one has to employ means, which may be fair or foul, and, he inevitably binds bad karmas. He goes on sinking deeper and deeper in the mire and his chances of extricating himself become lesser and lesser. A wise man should wean himself away from both merit and demerit, and concentrate all attention to contemplation of pure soul. From the practical point of view, people prefer merit to demerit, and therefore, engage themselves in such acts and thoughts as bring in merit for the following reasons:

(1) Cause of bondage of each is different; good thoughts bring merit (Punya), and bad thoughts demerit (Papa).

(2) Nature of each is different. Good karmas are pleasure bearing feeling karma, high family, good body-making, good age karma classes; while bad karma are pain bearing feeling karma, low family, bad body-making, bad age karma, and the four destructive karmas, knowledge obscuring, conation obscuring, delusion and obstructive karmas.

(3) Fruition of each is different. Merit (Punya) result in pleasure and demerit (Papa) in pain.

(4) The result in each is different. Merit (Punya) leads on to the Path of Liberation ultimately and demerit (Papa) to the path of bondage.

From the real point of view, however, both merit and demerit lead the soul further into the vortex of transmigration because:

(1) Both are caused by impure thought activity of the soul

(2) Both have got material karmic nature

(3) Fruition of both is harmful to real happiness of soul

(4) Both lead towards the path of bondage.

Passionate thought activity and soul vibration cause inflow and bondage of karma, good or bad. Both are bondages, hindering the purity and freedom of soul. Merit bondage is like fetters made of gold and the demerit bondage is like iron fetters, causing the soul to wander in the cycle of existences because fruits of good or bad karmas have to be enjoyed. A wise Right Believer should, therefore, see that merit and demerit both are derogatory to the Path of Liberation, and true peace and happiness. Thus he should have regard and liking only for self-absorption, based on Right Belief, Right Knowledge and Right conduct of Soul in its own true nature, as the true Path of Liberation. Although in the lower Spiritual Stages, when long-continued self-absorption is not possible, one is obliged to take resort to good deeds, such as, worship of Arhats and Saints, devotion to and services of the Acharyas, charity, and study of scriptures in order to keep away Pramada or lines of thoughts and deeds not beneficial for soul advancement. Such good deeds are performed with the object of self improvement and not for the gratification of sense desire. There is, however, a constant effort for attaining the high status of self-absorption.

# 5

# Fourteen Gunasthanas
## (Spiritual Stages)

According to Jain Philosophy there are 14 Spiritual Stages (Gunasthanas) of thought activities, which a soul, desirous of being liberated and of attaining perfection has to pass through.

The 14 Spiritual Stages which trace the progress of the soul from delusion to a condition of perfection are useful as a practical preliminary. In its highest essence the soul neither needs nor is capable of any divisions or stages; it is always itself infinite. The 14 Spiritual Stages are:

### (1) Mithyatva, Wrong Belief, Delusion

The thoght activity of the soul due to the operation of the Right Belief Deluding Karmas. In this, the soul does not believe in the right path to liberation. All 28 sub-classes of Mohaniya i.e. deluding karma may be present in this first and lowest stage. From here the soul always goes to the 4th Gunasthana.

### (2) Sasadana, Downfall

The second and third stages are the intervening

progressive stages of thought activities between wrong belief and right belief of the 4th stage. In the 2nd stage the three kinds of right belief deluding karmas are existent, but in an inoperative condition. The remaining 25 are operative. The duration of this stage is the shortest, viz. at the most 6 Avalis, or winks or twinklings of an eye. This is a stage, which is not touched by the soul in its progress. It is only one of the possible 3 stages, which the soul occupies if it suffers a downfall from the 4th stage. These 3 downward stages are the 1st, 2nd and 3rd. When there is operation in the 4th stage of one of the four Anantanubandhi Kashayas, error feeding passions, the soul falls down to the 1st stage through the 2nd and the thought activity in the passage through, is called Sasadana.

**(3) Mishra, mixed right and wrong belief**

Operation of Samyak mithyatva mohaniya karmas or Mishra Mohaniya. Belief in right and wrong at one and the same time. This is reached on falling down from the 4th stage. From the 3rd, the soul may come down straight to the 1st or rise to the 4th stage. But the operation of the error feeding passions without operation of wrong belief brings about the downfall of the soul from the 4th to the 2nd stage. In the 3rd stage, only 22 causes delusion are operative, namely, 21, i.e., all except the 4 error feeding passions of right conduct deluding karma, and only 1, i.e. mixed right and wrong belief of the right belief deluding karma.

**(4) Avirata Samyaktva, Vowless Right-Belief**

A soul which enters the 4th stage is said to have reached the threshold of Liberation. At this stage the soul has got only right belief. The soul here has belief in the Path of Liberation, but cannot observe the rules of conduct for attaining Liberation. Here only 21 causes of delusion are operative. There is no right belief deluding karma except of the 3rd kind i.e. when the right belief is clouded by wrong belief.

**(5) Desha Virata, partial vows, i.e. taking the partial vows**

All the 11 Pratimas or stages of a layman's life come in this stage. As soon as the soul begins to follow the practical vows of a layman, it is said to enter the 5th stage. Here only 17 causes of delusion are operative. The four partial vow preventing passions become quiescent here.

**(6) Pramata Virata, imperfect vows**

After renunciation of all worldly objects, still occasionally to turn the mind to the service or needs of the body. This is Pramattabhava, careless slackness in concentration. Henceforth, the stages are all in the life of a muni, saint. Here only 13 causes of delusion operate. The 4 total vow preventing passions become quiescent. The 6th stage is also a retrogressive one. It is reached by a soul which is going down from the 7th stage. But such a downfallen soul may regain the 7th stage from the 6th. Indeed this can go on for a long, long time.

**(7) Apramata Virata, Perfect vows**

Renouncing the careless slackness of the 6th Gunasthana, and being absorbed in spiritual contemplation (righteous contemplation of tbe highest type). From here there are 2 Shrenis, or ways of ascent,

(1) Upashama Shreni in which the right conduct deluding karma subsides,

(2) Kshapaka Shreni in which it is being destroyed. This last is the necessary way to Moksha, liberation.

**(8) Apurva Karana, New thought activity**

Karana or thought activity which the sain't soul had never yet acquired. This is the beginning of the first Shukladhyana, pure concentration on the pure Atma or

Self. In the 7th and 8th stages 13 causes of delusion operate but their operation is mild.

**(9) Anivritta Karana, Advanced thought activity**

Special thought activity of a still greater purity. A stage of Pratham Shukladhyan. Here 7 causes of delusion operate, 6 slight passions no-kashyas subside or are destroyed.

**(10) Suksma Samparaya, Slightest delusion**

All passions are destroyed or have subsided, except very slight nominal greed. This is also, first Shukladhyana.

**(11) Upashanta moha or Upashanta kashaya subsided delusion**

A thought activity which is produced by the subsidence of the entire right conduct deluding karmas. This is also first Shukladhyana. A saint must fall down from here, but if strong enough, he can resume his ascent from the Kshapaka mode of ascent in the 8th stage. Here all 28 causes of delusion subside. Here the soul can stay at the most for one antar muhurt. After falling down to any of the lower stages up to 7th, the soul can go up the destructive ladder to the 8th and higher stages, skipping the 11th or the highest point of the subsidential ladder on its way from the 10th to the 12th stage, the highest point of the destructive ladder, where delusion does not subside but is entirely destroyed.

**(12) Kshina moha, delusionless**

The entire right conduct deluding karmas are destroyed, in this stage, and the thought activity produced belongs to the 2nd Shukladhyana. The saint attaining this, does so directly from the 10th stage without passing through the 11th stage.

**(13) Sayoga Kevali, Vibrating Perfect Soul**

Before commencing this, the soul must have destroyed the three remaining destructive karmas knowledge obscuring, conation obscuring, and obstructive karmas. The soul is subject to mundane vibratory activity due to body making karma. A saint after destroying all the four Ghati karmas by dint of meditation and self-realisation enters the 13th stage of Vibratory Omniscient (Sayoga-Jina), when he is known as Arhat or the Worshipful Lord. The Soul becomes Arhat or Perfect Soul in human body with vibrations in it. Preaching and peregritnations belong to this stage. The Worshipful Lord proclaims Truth to the world.

**(14) Ayoga Kevali, Vibrationless Perfect soul**

When the same soul or the Worshipful Lord is about to be entirely freed from karmas and his vibratory activity has ceased, the soul is said to have entered the 14th stage of Non-vibrating Omniscient Lord (Ayoga Jina). During the very short period of this stage the soul destroys the remaining four Aghati karmas i.e. Vedniya, Nama, Gotra and Ayu karmas. Then the soul leaving the body goes to Siddhalaya at the top of the universe, is finally free from all the karmas and has accomplished all that was to be accomplished, liberation Moksha. Such a soul is known as a Perfect Soul (Siddha). The soul is a pure soul substance full of the infinite attributes of omniscience, omnipotence, etc. In one word the soul is itself God.

Thus, it will be seen that all these 14 Spiritual Stages are due to wrong belief, vowlessness, carelessness, passions and vibratory activity. Carelessness (Pramada) in intensity or mildness lasts from the 1st to the 6th stage of imperfect vow. Therefore, the first six stages are referred to by the word "Pramatta". All the other eight stages are meditation and free from carelessness in pursuing the Path of Self-realisation, and are described as "Apramatta". The stages are indices of degrees of progressing thought activities. They are mere steps of ladder to reach the abode of Liberation. When the top is reached, the ladder is left behind. Thus the soul in its essence is devoid of any distinction of stages.

While a saint remains in the 6th and the 7th stages and improves his qualifications, so that he has the capacity of controlling the whole order of saints and supervises their general conduct, he is said to be head of the order of saints or an Acharya, and as such he follows and practises the five kinds of conduct. They are as follows:

(a) Darshanachara, Conduct of right belief. Performance of all those duties which keep right belief firm.

(b) Jnanachara, Conduct of knowledge. Minute and detailed study of the scriptures, with the view of increasing right knowledge.

(c) Charitrachara, Conduct of observing saintly character. Thirteen kinds of rules of conduct are to be observed as under:

Five vows:

(1) non-injury
(2) truth
(3) non-stealing
(4) chastity
(5) possessionlessness

The saints have to observe these rules fully, without any blemish or transgression

Carefulness in:

(6) walking
(7) speaking
(8) eating
(9) lifting up and laying down
(10) excreting

Control of:

(11) Mind

(12) Speech

(13) Body

Observing these rules regularly and flawlessly with the idea of realising the self is called Charitrachara.

(d) Tapachara,

Conduct of austerities is the proper and regular observance of 12 kinds of austerities (tapas) as fasting, etc.

(e) Viryachara,

Conduct of soul force means the development of soul force and repulsion of the karmic forces with the view of attaining liberation.

An Acharya, as defined above, himself practises and observes all the above mentioned five kinds of conduct, and instructs the saints of his order to do the same.

Any saint of the order who is in the 6th and the 7th stages, is well versed in Jain scriptures and is capable of teaching and instructing other saints of the order, is called the preceptor (Upadhaya),

All other saints who are neither Acharyas nor Upadhyas are known as Sadhus. They may be in any spiritual stage from the 6th to the 12th stages, when delusion is absolutely destroyed. From the 8th to the 12th, all are the progressive stages of meditation. In these stages a saint is deeply absorbed in meditation and self realisation.

From the above, we note that a soul when it observes and follows the 13 rules of conduct, remains either in the condition of an Acharya, Upadhyaya or a Sadhu and the attainment of the condition of being an Arhat or a Siddha is an outcome of the observance of the rules of right conduct. The Arhat or Arihant and the Acharya, Upadhyaya and

Sadhu are said to be Mahan Atmas (great souls). All the above five i.e. the Arihants, Siddhas, Acharyas, Upadhyayas, and Sadhus are called five Supreme Dignitaries (Pancha Parmeshthi). It is only these five Dignitaries, who are worshipped by the Jainas in general. The most miraculous benedictory hymn (Navakar Mantra) which every Jain usually recites everyday consists of Namaskar to this Panch Parmeshthi. This Mantra comprises an adoration of qualities. In it, we have the praise of the highest souls (Siddhas) who have completely realised all the natural and inherent qualities of the soul and of those qualified persons who are on their way to realization.

6

# Three Jewels of Jainism

The Path of Liberation is the combination of right belief Samyak Darshan), right knowledge (Samyak Jnana), and right conduct (Samyak Charitra) the Three Jewels of Jainism. Following this path the soul reaches its ultimate goal, Nirvana. Nirvana is the condition of the soul when it is free from all karmic dirt and regains its own pure inherent nature. Then it is all blissful, all knowing, all powerful, ever lasting, having accomplished all that was to be accomplished.

The Jain Philosophy explains all points in a two-fold manner. The Nishchaya, Mukhya, Shuddha, Satyartha, Bhutartha, or Dravyartha Naya, is that aspect which views things from an absolute standpoint, unaffected by the influence of surrounding circumstances.

Vyavahara, Upachara, Ashuddha, Asatyartha, Abhutartha, or Paryarthika Naya contemplates the same objects in their varying conditions under outside influences.

This study of the two-fold aspect of substances, is essentially necessary for a full and perfect comprehension of an object. From the Nishchaya Naya i.e. Real point of view man viewed as the Jiva is pure consciousuess, and is immaterial.

Again, as encased in the body, it is from Vyavahara Naya i.e. Practical point of view, said to possess weight, colour and other attributes of matter. It has varying degrees of consciousness according as it is in one sensed, two sensed, three sensed, four sensed and five sensed form of life. The vast majority of people in the world are so very much engrossed in mundane pursuits, that they pay no attention, and bestow no thought to find out the reality of their own selves; and therefore they go deeper into the more of mundane meanderings.

"Know thyself," has been the precept and practice of all serious searchers after the truth about soul. The high saints point out Vyavahara for the guidance of the ignorat. They first describe things as they ordinarily and seemingly appear and gradually they lead to the real aspect. If attention is confined to vyavahara only and no effort is made to grasp the real aspect, there would be no real progress and one would be unable to evolve the spiritual side and would ever remain involved in mazes temporal. It is therefore essentially necessary that one should know both the real and practical aspects of things.

If one adopts the Nishchaya view only, one would altogether neglect the rules of conduct which serve as stepping stones to spiritual progress. If the Vyavahara view alone is adhered to, realisation of the true self, Moksha, would become impossible of attainment.

In the universe, Jivas exist in two conditions. There are the pure, uncontaminated Jivas, exhibiting all the attributes of perfection. They are omniscient. Omniscience is just the seeing of the whole Truth. It is a full and direct manifestation of the soul, knowledge is the essence of soul. There is no soul without knowledge, Non-omniscience is merely a result of the soul being obscured by the conation obscuring and knowledge obscuring karmas. These being destroyed, Omniscience the real natural characteristic of the Soul manifests itself. Such omniscient jivas want nothing, they are above desire, and they are ever happy. They are Mukta Jivas.

The Samsari Jivas or embodied souls are contaminated by combination with fine molecules of fine karmic matter, which obscure their inherent attributes such as omniscience, peace and beatitude. It is this Karmic combination, which is the inducing cause for attracting fresh Karmic matter to the soul, and keeping up the state of contamination. There is a limit to the period for which karmic matter can remain combined and bound up with a soul, but before the expiry of that period, the activities of body, mind and speech, and the passions and emotions, generated by the karmic molecules already in contact, create a condition which attracts other karmic molecules for bondage with the soul, and thus the process of falling off of old, and the bondage of fresh karmas goes on and on.

The karmas are ever changing in their intensity, duration, kind and quantity. The stoppage of this process of bondage and the elimination of all karmas can be attained by effort, of which the ultimate result is nirvana, emancipation, liberation from the karmas. The ultimate object of human existence is to attain perfect purity of soul, its condition of inherent perfection. The obstacle to such attainment is ignorance, illusion, or Moha, and when that is removed, the inherent attribuies appear and the latent becomes patent. The latent potentialities become fully, manifested, and the imperfect soul becomes perfect soul, Parmatma.

Jiva and matter both have the capacity of modification. The modification, however, would not go beyond the scope of their respective attributes. A Jiva would in spite of all modifications remain a Jiva, and would never get modified into matter; and so would matter never get modified into

and greatness. He is enamoured of spiritual happiness, which is far beyond the gratification of senses. He should not exhibit a feeling of disgust at the various conditions caused by hunger, thirst, cold, heat, etc. or at the sight of excrement, etc. He should realise the true nature of things as they, are and should look at everything with a dispassionate attitude. Physical conditions due to the operation of karmas should induce in him a feeling of pity and not disgust. A true believer who has faith in seven Tattvas should never have a superstitious belief in a fallacious scripture, an unreal doctrine, or a false deity. Similarly he should not search for and proclaim the faults, defects and discrepances of others.

06. Sthitikarana Anga is the 6th pillar of Right Belief

It means steadiness. The right believer should be firm, and should strengthen others who are vacillating. One should always drive away the inroads of scepticism on himself or others by constant reassuring and argument, and should never yield to sceptical thoughts.

07. Vatsalya Anga means that the right believer should have affection for co-religionists. He should ever cherish feelings of deep affection for religion, which brings about the treasure of spiritual happiness, and also for co-religionists.

08. Prabhavana Anga is the 8th pillar of Right Belief. It is a desire to enhance the glory of the Faith.

The learned saints have said six Padas regarding soul as the basis of Right Belief:

1. There is soul. Just as there are other substances in the universe, similarly there is a soul substance also. On account of certain attributes, just as the existence of other substances has been proved, similarly on account of its attribute chetan, consciousness the existence of soul has been proved.

2. The soul is ever-lasting. Soul is of permanent duration. Other substances owe their existence to circumstances. Soul is a self entity because no circumstances are experienced for its origin or birth. Chetan attribute is not likely to be produced due to combination of any other substance. Therefore, that which has its existence without any circumstances cannot have its destruction due to any circumstances. As such soul is ever-lasting.

3. The soul is the doer. All substances are full with some actions and results thereof are seen. The soul is also full with actions and is therefore the doer thereof. In the real sense self-absorption is its action but in the practical sense it is the doer of karmas due to thought activities.

4. The soul is the enjoyer. There is always the fruit of whatever action is done. Such is the experience. There is fruit of poison if it is consumed, there is fruit of sugar if it is taken, there is fruit of fire touch if that is done, there is fruit of snow touch if that is done. Similarly, there is fruit of whatever way the soul acts, viz., with passions or without passions. The soul is therefore the enjoyer of those actions which he does.

5. There is Moksha (Liberation). The soul is the doer of karmas and the enjoyer of the fruits of its karmas. However, there is destruction of these karmas also, because as intensity of passions gets lessened by practice the karmas get destroyed that way. Pure self (without karma) is Moksha or liberation from karmas.

6. There is remedy for Moksha. If there is always bondage only of karmas, then these can be no release from same. But there are remedies swch as Right Belief, Right Knowledge, Right Conduct, which are contrary for the bondage of karmas and by the practice of which intensity of karmas gets lessened and gradually the karmas get destroyed. There are, therefore, the remedies for attainment of Moksha.

These six truths are said by the learned Saints as the basis of Right Belief.

**Right Knowledge (Samyak Jnana)**

Those who have attained Right Belief as above, should devote themselves to the acquisition of Right Knowledge, which though simultaneous with Right Belief is yet distinguishable from it and has to be striven for, as an effect following Right Belief.

Right Belief and Right Knowledge both are two distinct attributes of Jiva. They respectively are obscured by two destructive karmas, Darshanavaraniya and Jnanavaraniya. On the attainment of Right Belief, the knowledge then becomes Right Knowledge; but because of the existence of knowledge obscuring karma in operation, it not perfect. Therefore, it is necessary to make constant endeavours for advancement of knowledge as long as omniscience is not evolved. The conquerors (Jinas) have called Right Knowledge the effect and Right Belief the cause. Lamp and light go together; still the lamp precedes the light, and light cannot be said to precede the lamp. In the same way there is relation of cause and effect between Right Belief and Right Knowledge, though both are almost simultaneous.

It should be free from three main defects:

(a) Doubt (Samashaya)

(b) Perversity (Viparyaya), and

(c) Indefiniteness or Vagueness (Anadhyavasaya).

Practical Right Knowledge is the acquisition of the detailed knowledge of all the seven principles, explained previously, with the help of the Jain Scriptures and should be free from the above said three main defects. Real Right Knowledge is to know the true and real nature of the soul as quite distinct from all other non-soul substances.

Constant contemplation of, and unflinching devotion to, the subject matter of practical Right Knowledge is an auxiliary cause to the attainment of real Right Knowledge. Further, it comprises correct reading, writing and pronouncing of letters and words, correct understanding, both combined, at proper time, with reverence, propriety of behaviour, zeal, and desire for its propagation. Just like eight pillars of Right Belief there are eight pillars also of Right Knowledge as set out below:

(1) Grantha - Reading, writing and pronouncing every letter and word correctly.

(2) Artha - Understanding the meaning and full significance of words, phrases and the text.

(3) Ubhya - Reading, writing and speaking with full and proper understanding of the import of what is read, written and spoken.

(4) Kala - Observance of regularity, punctuality and propriety of time. Improper and unsuitable occasions should be avoided.

(5) Vinaya - Reverent attitude.

(6) Sopadhana - Propriety of behaviour.

(7) Bahumam - Zeal.

(8) Aninhana - No concealment of knowledge or of its sources,

If knowledge is pursuied in the manner stated above, it will be properly and progressively acquired and promulgated.

## Right Conduct (Samyak Charitra)

After Right Belief and Right Knowledge, the third but the most important path to the goal of Moksha is Right Conduct, the three together forming what is collectively known as Ratna Traya, the "Jewels Three" of Jainism.

Right Belief and Right Knowledge would not lead to Moksha, which is attainable only after the destruction of all karmic contact, and this can only be accomplished through Right Conduct.

A Right Believer, who has fully realised the true and real nature of his own soul, and is bent upon getting rid of the karmic filth which is in bondage with his soul, tries to follow Right Conduct.

It is Right Knowledge which makes conduct right. Conduct following ignorance can never be designated as right. Therefore, Right Conduct follows Right Knowledge. The main object in following Right Conduct is to be free from attachment and aversion, and from all impure thought activities and to attain the condition of equanimity.

It is of two kinds. The complete conduct of a saint, and the partial discipline of a disciple or a layman, Shravak.

From the real point of view, Right couduct is an inherent attribute of Jiva, in its pure condition.

Practical Right Conduct consists in observing the following five vows:

1. Ahimsa - refraining from doing injury to any of the mundane souls.
2. Satya - refraining from falsehood.
3. Asteya - refraining from theft.
4. Brahmacharya - chastity.
5. Aparigraha - Non-attachment.

Laymen observe these partially (Anuvrata) while saints observe them fully (Mahavrata).

We now look into the details of these vows.

1. Ahimsa: Refraining from doing injury to any mundane soul.

Any injury whatsoever to the material or conscious

vitalities caused through passionate activity of mind, body or speech is Himsa. Under the influence of passion, a person injures the natural purity of Jiva; and, as a result of the working of passions, he loses his life forces, or life itself, and similarly, causes pain to others, or even the deprivation of vitalities or of life itself. Passion is thus the moving cause which leads to himsa.

The word Prana means vitality. It is of two kinds. Bhava Prana, conscious vitalities are the attributes of Jiva such as consciousness, peacefulness, happiness, power. The conscious vitalities are possessed by all Jivas alike.

Dravya Prana are material vitalities. They are ten, the five senses of touch, taste, smell, sight, and hearing, the three forces of body, speech, and mind, and breathing and age.

With reference to the possession of material vitalities Jivas differ and are divided into the following six classes:

(1) Ekendriya, one sensed, such as earth bodied, fire bodied, air bodied, vegetable bodied. They have four vitalities: age, breathing, body force, and sense of touch.

(2) Dvendriya, two sensed, such as worms, conch, shell. These have six vitalities: the previous four, and speech force and sense of taste.

(3) Treendriya, three sensed, e.g. bug, ant, scorpion, lice. They have seven vitalities: sense of smell is added to the above six.

(4) Chaturendriya, four sensed, e.g. wasp, moth, fly, bee. They possess the sense of sight also and have eight vitalities.

(5) Panchendriya Asaini, Irrational, five sensed, such as a kind of serpent found in water. They have nine vitalities, the sense of hearing being added to the preceding eight. They are rarely found.

(6) Panchendriya Saini. Rational, five-sensed. They include

hellish, celestial and human beings, beasts, birds, fowl, fishes, serpents, etc. They have ten vitalities, mind force being added to the above nine.

The degree of Himsa varies with the motive which causes it, and the vitalities injured. The higher the number of vitalities possessed by a Jiva, the greater is the himsa in killing it.

Himsa has been said of two kinds:

Anarambhi or Samkalpi and Arambhi.

The first one may be translated as "Intentional Injury". It can be avoided by every thinking person without any difficulty or harm to himself.

The second one Arambhi Himsa may be sub-divided as Udyami, Graharambhi, and Virodhi.

Udyami Himsa is unavoidably committed in the performance of necessary domestic purposes such as preparation of food, keeping the house, body, clothes clean, construction of buildings, wells, gardens, and keeping cattle.

Virodhi is that which is unavoidably committed in defence of person and property, against thieves, robbers, etc. One who has adopted the discipline of a saint practises complete Ahimsa. A true believer in the householder's stage abstains from Samkalpi Himsa, but is unable to abstain from Arambhi, although he tries his best to avoid it as far as possible, and is ever making progress in such endeavour.

Further, those who desire avoiding himsa should, first of all take care to renounce wine, flesh, honey, and the five Udumbar fruits, viz., gular, anjeera, banyan, peepal and pakar, all belonging to the fig class. Honey, wine, butter, flesh are all the result of extrerne fermentation and the birth place of lives of the same genus. The five fruits referred to are birth places of mobile lives. A Jain disciple would renounce all the above non-eatables.

Also Himsa is inevitable in eating at night. It should, therefore, be renounced. One, who has perfectly renounced Himsa, will not utter a word which is likely to give pain to auother; will not do any act which may cause injury to another; will not harbour any thoughts prejudicial to another; will not make anybody else utter words likely to cause pain to another, nor commit acts likely to injure another, nor entertain feelings of ill will towards another; and will not approbate or encourage others who by words, deeds or thought cause pain to another. This nine fold renunciation is perfect renunciation.

### 2. Satya: Refraining from Falsehood

Wrong statement throught carelessness is falsehood. It may be:

(1) denial of the actual existence of a substance with reference to its position, time or nature

(2) affirmation of what does not exist, with reference to position, time awd nature

(3) where it is wrongly described

(4) speech condemnable, sinful, or disagreeable.

Himsa is inevitable in such cases, because of careless indulgence.

### 3. Asteya: Refraining from Theft

This is the appropriation of what is not given. It causes injury and is himsa, for property is as dear as life and there is thoughtless indulgence.

### 4. Brahmacharya: Sexual Purity, Chastity

In sexual intercourse there is obvious himsa, due to the killing of mobile germs in the act. Sexual indulgence otherwise has root in desire, and hence is himsa. If unable to live without a wife, let other females be abjured. Many a householder is not sufficiently advanced to give up sex desire altogether. It is only the ascetics who do so. The house holder also should, however, observe the vow of Brahmacharya to a limited extent by total abstinence from all sexual desires with reference to females other than his own wife.

### 5. Aparigraha, Non-attachment: Attachment of temporalities

Affectionate regard for external objects is due to illusion and is attachment clinging to externals. Even if one has renounced all tangible property, the feeling of attachment itself is a clinging to externals. Possession (Parigraha) is external and internal (Bahiranga and Antaranga Parigraha).

Internal possessions are fourteen:

(1) Wrong belief

(2) Desire for sexual enjoyment with woman

(3) Desire for sexual enjoyment with man

(4) Desire for sexual enjoyment with both

(5) laughter

(6) indulgence

(7) enui

(8) sorrow

(9) fear

(10) disgust

(11) anger

(12) pride

(13) deceit

(14) greed

External possession is of living or non-living objects. Abjuring all possession is Ahimsa; and all appropriation internal as well as external is himsa. Himsa, the central sin, is included in every other of the remaining four: falsehood, theft, sexual impurity, and possession of goods. Internal attachment, the desire for worldly objects prejudically affects the purity of the soul, and this injury to the pure nature of the soul constitutes himsa. External possession or the actual possession of temporalities creates attraction and love for them, which defiles soul purity and, therefore, amounts to himsa. Both internal and external attachment should, therefore, be given up by one who practises the principle of Ahimsa.

## Supplementary Vows

A layman is required to follow the seven supplementary vows (Sheelas) also, as they are helpful in the proper observance of the first five main vows. Just as the encircling walls guard town, so do Sheelas (supplementary vows) protect the Anu-Vratas. Out of these seven, the following are called Gunavratas (Multiplicative vows) because they raise the value of the first five vows multifold.

## Gunavratas

(1) Dig Vrata, a vow to limit worldly activities to fixed points in all the 10 directions, north, south, east, west, north-east, north-west, south-east, south-west, above and below. This brings the merit of Ahimsa with regard to what is beyond such limits.

(2) Desha Vrata, a vow to limit worldly activities for a fixed period only. This means that one shall not, during a certain period of time, proceed beyond a certain village, market, street, or house or have anything to do with objects beyond that limit. This secures Ahimsa in regard to what is beyond such confines.

(3) Anartha Danda Vrata. Taking a vow not to commit purposeless sin. It is of five kinds:

(a) Apa Dhyan, thinking ill of others.

(b) Papodesha, preaching ill of others.

(c) Pramada Charya. Inconsiderate conduct, such as uselessly breaking the boughs of trees.

(d) Himsa dan, preparing or supplying instruments of attack.

(e) Dushruti, reading or listening to improper literature.

The remaining four supplementary vows are the following Shiksha-vratas or disciplinary vows; so called because they are preparatory to the discipline of an ascetic's life.

**Shiksha Vratas**

(1) Samayika. Taking a vow to devote a fixed period everyday, once, teice or thrice, at sunrise, sunset and noon to the contemplation of the self for spiritual advancement. By giving up Rag-Dwesha," affection and aversion and observing equauimity, in all objects, one should practise samayika, equanimity, continuously, as per set procedure, which brings about a realisation of the true nature of self.

(2) Proshadhopvasa. Taking a vow to fast on four days of the month, i.e. the two Ashtamis and the two Chaturdashis. To strength the daily practice of Samayika a discipline, one must observe fasting, twice each fortnight. Free from all work, and having given up affection for the body etc., one should commence fasting at middle of the day previous to Proshadha day (which is the 8th and the 14th day of each lunar fortnight). One should then retire to a secluded spot, renounce all sinful activities, abstain from indulgence in all objects of the senses, and observe due restraint of body, speech and mind, and pass time in spiritual contemplation, perform

Samayika, engage himself in self study and worship of Jina. The Proshadha day, the second night, and the half of the third day should carefully be passed in the above manner. He who having set himself free from all sinful activities, passes 16 Yamas (48 hours) in the above manner certainly observes the vow of Ahimsa in its thoroughness, for that period.

(3) Bhogopabhoga Pariman. Taking a vow everyday to limit one's enjoyment of consumable and nom-consumable things. Bhoga means enjoyment of an object which can only be used once, such as food and drink, fruits and flowers. Upabhoga means enjoyment of an object which can be used several times, such as furniture, dresses, ornaments, buildings. Himsa is incurred from the use of articles of Bhoga and Upabhoga. One should, therefore, ascertain the reality of things, and renounce these two also, in accordance with his own capacity. The use of all Anant Kaya vegetatables such as potato, ginger, radish must be given up, Anant Kaya or Sadharana vegetable is that which infinite Jivas adopt as their one and common body. In Pratyeka vegetable only one jiva pervades throughout the body. Butter is the birth place of numerous Jivas. Fresh butter if not at once melted on fire and strained away, becomes the place of generation of innumerable Jivas. This is visibly apparent in what is called fermentation. Fermentation in the case of butter, actually commences at once, though it is not visible early. Just like honey, wine and flesh, butter should also be renounced or enjoyment should be limited.

(4) Atithi Samvibhag. Taking a vow to take one's food only after feeding ascetics or others, with a part of it. The food offered should be pure and with reverence.

The house-holder is also the observer in the last moments of his life, of the process of Sallekhana, peaceful death, which is characterised by non-attachment to the world and by a suppression of the passions. The last thought should be of a calm renunciation of the body, and this thought should ever be present long before death, supervenes. This is, Ahimsa, because all passions have been duly subdued. Thus, the house-holder's vows are twelve with the last or peaceful death as their supplement.

The following 11 stages of spiritual progress (Pratimas) have been laid down for a layman.

(1) Darshan (Faith) Pratima.

A layman who entertains Right Belief, and follows the five main vows to a limited extent is classed in this stage. He must have a perfect and intelligent, well-reasoned faith in Jainism, i.e., he must have a sound knowledge of its doctrines and their applications in life.

(2) Vrata (Vow) Pratima.

In this stage he observes the five main vows to a limited extent (Anuvratas), without transgression and follows the seven supplementary vows i.e. three Gunavratas and four Shiksha Vratas. In short, he must not destroy any kind of life, must not tell a lie, must not make use of another person's property without the owner's consent, must be chaste, must limit his necessities of life, and avoid the use of food which involves unnecessary killing of living beings. The three Guna-Vratas are special vows relating to the limitation and determination of his daily work, food, and enjoyment. The remaining four vows relate to his meaitation in the morning, noon and evening, to his keeping fast on certain days, limiting enjoyment everyday of consumable and non-consumable things, and to his duty of daily giving charity in the form of knowledge, medicine, comfort or protection, and food.

(3) Samayika (worship) Pratima.

In this state he practises faultless contemplation

regularly, three times, in the morning, at midday and in the evening, at least for 48 minutes everytime. Worship means self contemplation and purifying one's ideas and emotions.

(4) Proshadhopavasa (Fortnightly must fast) Pratima.

In this stage, he observes regularly a fast faultlessly twice a fortnight i.e. on the 8th and 14th days of each lunar fortnight.

(5) Sachitta Tyaga Pratima.

In this stage he does not take animate water and vegetable, etc. Sachitta Tyaga means abstinence from the flesh of conscious creatures. He refrains from taking fresh vegetable because they are living.

(6) Ratri Bhukta Tyaga Pratima. (Abstinence from eating at night).

He does not take or give food or drink at night. There are minute living beings which no amount of light can reveal or disperse, and which must be consumed with meals after sunset.

(7) Brahmacharya Celebacy Pratima.

He gives up sexual intercourse even with his wife.

(8) Arambha Tyaga Pratima.

He gives up all professions and all means of earning money and all worldly occupations. Abandonment of merely all worldly engagements and occupations.

(9) Parigraha Tyaga Pratima.

He gives up all desire for objects of the world and abandons all property; except a very few limited number of clothes and utensils.

(10) Anumati Tyaga Pratima.

He would not even offer advice on any worldly matter.

(11) Uddishta Tyaga Pratima.

> In this stage he would not accept food which is prepared particularly for him. He will only accept food which is respectfully offered by a house-holder at the time when he goes out for food.

The last three stages 9 to 11 are preparatory to the monk's life. They enjoin a gradual giving up of the world and retiring into some very quiet place to acquire the knowledge of Truth and ultimately to become fit to be a teacher of the Path to Liberation.

Six Daily Duties. Every Jain house-holder is ordinarily required to perform the following six daily duties:

(1) **Deva-Puja.** Worship of the Arhats, the adorables.

(2) **Guru Bhakti.** Devotion to the Gurus or Preceptor saints.

(3) **Svadhyaya.** Study of the scriptures.

(4) **Samyama.** Control of the five senses and the mind. In practising Samyam, it is necessary to renounce certain objects of enjoyments with the idea of self-control.

(5) **Tapa.** Austerities such as meditating upon, the nature of soul, every morning and evening, for a fixed time.

(6) **Dana or Charity.** Giving of food, knowledge, medicine, and protection.

The causes and processes of mundane ailments are adumbrated in the Jaina karma philosophy. Their remedies are the 11 Stages (Pratimas) of the house-holder's life; and the vows, common to the house-holder and the monk, but followed in a more extended and intensive way by the latter.

A saint while observing the five main vows fully and without any transmigration, has to observe the following eight rules of conduct also:

I. Five kinds of caution (Samiti).

(a) Irya Samiti, proper care is walking.

(b) Bhasha Samiti, proper care in speaking.

(c) Eshna Samiti, proper care in eating.

(d) Adana Nikshepa Samiti, proper care in lifting and placing the bowl, etc.

(e) Utsarga Samiti, proper care while attending calls of nature.

II. Three kinds of Restraint (Gupti)

(a) of mind

(b) of word

(c) of body

These eight rules of conduct taken together with the five vows make the thirteen rules of practical Right Conduct laid down for a saint.

**Six Essential Daily Duties of a Saint (Avashyaka)**

From the real point of view this means that a really true and independent saint must refrain from all good and bad thought activities. At the same time it is necessary for him not to engage himself in the flickering thought activities concerning various attributes and modifications of all the six substances (Dravyas). He should devote his whole attention to the realisation of the pure nature of his own self. It is only in this condition of self absorption that a saint is said to perform Avashyaka Karma (Independent Action)

From the practical point of view they may be briefly described as follows:

(1) Pratikramana -

Repentence means the statement of the sins and

transgressions committed by a saint, during the performance of his daily routine; and making penance for them.

(2) Pratyakhyana -

Renpnciation means resolving to avoid particular thought activities and actions in future, which tend to disturb the performance of essential duties.

(3) Stuti - praising

(4) Vandana -

Prostration to the worshipful saints. They are both aspects of devotion which are practised with the object of getting rid of impure thought activities.

(5) Samayika - Equanimity.

In practising Samayika a saint resorts to some undisturbed solitude, and calmly and cheerfully withdraws all his thought activities, and meditates upon his own soul and its various attributes and modifications.

(6) Kayotsarga -

This is the relinquishment of attachment to the body and all other objects associated with it.

If a saint or a layman merely observes his respective duties and vows, without having self absorption as his real aim, he falls far short of the standard and cannot be called the real follower of the Path of the Conquerors. He is known as a Bahir Atma or external soul, while a saint or a layman who believes in Avashyaka Karma of self absorption and tries to work up to that, and does not restrict himself merely to the observance of external formalities, is called an Antar Atma, internal soul. Nirvana is the result brought about by the practice of self absorption, which is the combination of real Right Belief, real Right Knowledge and real Right Conduct.

Among the Jains there are two main sects:

Swetambaras and Digambaras.

The Svetambaras are subdivided into Murtipujak, Sthanakvasi and Terapanthi. The latter two do not believe in idol-worship.

The three main groups of Digambaras are Bisapanthi, Tarahapanthi and Taranapanthi. They believe in idol-worship.

The observance of the great vows are uniform for all the Jains except that the vow of Aparigraha (non-possession) is followed in its full sense by Digambar monks only, who remain unclad. A peacock feather broom and a water pot (tumbdu) are the possessions of Digambar Monks. They keep standing while they eat from the cavity of their palms.

Sthanakvasi and Terapanthi monks and nuns carry a piece of cloth tied on their mouth (Muhapatti) which distinguishes them from other monks and nuns.

Murtipujak monks and nuns carry a Muhapatti in their hand and they hold it at a distance from the mouth while delivering religious discourses. Some critics call the Jainas Idolatrous, The answer to them is that the Jainas do not worship the stone, silver, gold or diamond of which the images of Jinas are made. They worship the qualities of Total Renunciation of the World, the Acquisition of undisturbable harmony with the infinite, and the identity of the Liberated Soul with peace everlasting, which these images represent.

The itinerary of any Jain Pilgrim includes places where the Jinas (Tirthankaras) attained Moksha and became Siddhas. There are five such places associated with twenty-four Tirthankaras.

Mt. Kailas (Astapada) is associated with Rishabha the first Tirthankara.

Sammeta Shikharji (Mt. Parasnath), is associated with twenty other Jinas;

Champapuri is associated with Vasupujya the twelfth Tirthankara,

Mt. Girnar is associated with Neminath the twenty-second Tirthankara, and

Pawapuri is associated with Mahavira the last of the twenty-four Jinas or Tirthankaras. Lord Mahavira attained Nirvana at Pawapuri in 527 B C.

Pilgrims also visit places considered holy because of their association with various events in the lives of the Jinas.

Rajagriha the Tirth of five Hills, is famous because Lord Mahavir's Samavasarana (the assemblage of celestials, men and beasts that heard the Preachings of Mahavira) was held there.

Similarly, the Shatrunjaya Mountain in Saurashtra is holy because Rishabha the first Tirthankara had visited it. It was also here that Bharat, the son of Rishabha, built a magnificent temple. On the slopes of Shatrunjaya millions of Jain monks have come to meditate and seek Moksha. The place is considered very sacred. It has more than 800 shrines and 5000 images of the Tirthankaras.

Like Shatrunjaya, the twin mountains of Mangi Tungi with their cave temples are revered because from there countless monks of the Digambara Sect have attained Moksha.

In this category the Hill of Muktagiri can also be included. On full moon day of Kartik, there is a big festival at this Tirtha.

Near Muktagiri there is the Tirtha of Antariksha Parshvanatha. It is claimed that here the image of Parshvanatha defies the law of gravitation. It is suspended and does not touch its pedestal.

At Sravanbelagola, Mysore on Doddabetta or Vindhyagiri there is a collossal image of Bahubali, the son of the first Jina Rishabha. Known as Gomateswara the image (57 feet high) is carved out of single rock aud was erected in the 10th, century.

The Dilwara Jain Temples on Mt. Abu are a great attraction for Jains. The architecture is exquisite.

Some Jain Tirthas are known as "Atishaya Kshetras," as, each of them has a certain miraculous event associated with it. Among such places is the famous Kshetra of Shri Mahavirji in Rajasthan. The temple of Rikhabdevji in the Aravallis, near Udaipur also known as the temple of Shri Kesariaji is also a great attraction for Jain Pilgrims. To this deity everyday is offered Kesar (Saffron) and Chandan (Sandalwood), the exquisite fragrance of which engulfs the temple and forever lingers in the air.

The temple of Ranakpur (Rajasthan) on the western fringe of the Aravallis breathes an atmosphere of sublime peace. This Adinatha Temple was built in the 15th century. It covers an area of over 40,000 Sq. ft. and the richly carved (1444) pillars are arranged in such a way that the image of Lord Adinath can be seen from any point. There are no miracles associated with this shrine. But the pious chanting, echoing within its spacious interior, awakens the pilgrim's deepest yearnings for contact with the Divine.

The above are some prominent Jain Pilgrim centres. Pilgrimage is good from the practical point of view but the real aim of a seeker to the Path of Liberation should be self absorption, which is the combination real Right Belief, Knowledge and Conduct.

# Conclusion

We have seen that the oddities which are found in this world are all due to the effects of different kinds of karmas. We have seen the causes of inflow and bondage of eights kinds of karmas and their sub-classes. We have seen how this inflow can be checked and how the shedding of karmas already bound can be done.

The pure soul is free from all karmic matter and is full of the infinite attributes of omniscience, omnipotence, etc. It is only when the soul forgets its own true self (Swabhava) and gets attracted towards material things due to Rag, Dwesha etc. (Vibhava) there is inflow and bondage of karmic matter with the soul and the cycle of mundane existence continues.

It is the duty or Dharma of every mundane soul to get itself liberated from such existences (i.e. from its condition of Vibhava) and bring to its pure true self (i.e. condition of Swabhava) with its natural and inherent attributes and thus achieve true happiness.

The Fourteen Gunasthanas show us how the soul

reaches higher and higher ladder of Spiritual Advancement from Wrong Belief to Right Belief, then to Vows, then to perfectly careful Vows, then to passionless, and then to a cessation of the Vibratory Activity of body, speech, and mind.

A mundane Soul is beset with five kinds of innate evils or imperfections.

The Wrong Belief is shed at the end of the 1st,

Vowlessness at the end of the 4th,

Carelessness at the end of the 6th,

Passions at the end of the 10th, and

Vibratory Activity at the end of the 13th Spiritual Stage.

The Three Jewels of Jainism, Samyak Darshan, Samyak Jnan, and Samyak Charitra, teach us how to tread the Path of Liberation and ultimately to achieve the desired goal—Moksha.

The whole Drama of life is played or danced together by the living soul being in close grasp of lifeless matter. Lifeless space is the stage, lifeless time is the duration and lifeless Dharma and Adharma the indispensable assistants for the dancers to move or to rest. The exercise of dancing is their eternal movement in the cycle of mundane existences.

Every pilgrim on the Path of Liberation (Moksha) must be constantly careful to avoid all passionate thought activities. Every action of his will be performed with due care and caution and the commission of himsa would be avoided altogether.

The acquisition of internal purification follows the practice of self control or conquest over the cravings of the body, and the ravings of the mind, a supreme subjection of sense desires, mastering of passions and governance of emotions. The joys of yoga, of communion with the highest, are only known to those who have experienced them. They are above all earthly pleasures, they lead to heavenly happiness, and ultimately to the realization, the attainment to Godhood, Siddhasthan, Parmatma Pada, the true happiness where the soul is identified with limitless, perfect, direct, completed knowledge, of all that is, that was, that shall be, simultaneous, in all their varying forms and conditions, is supremely self satisfied, is omniscient, and omnipotent, forever and ever, in the unending eternity of time and space.

To achieve this condition requires supreme effort. It is difficult for a layman at once to do so. He has therefore to proceed gradually on the Path of Liberation. He should at least aim that his next birth should be better circumstanced than the present one, not with regard to sense pleasures, but with regard to his spiritual advancement, and he should try to concentrate his efforts in that direction. If such efforts are made and continued his soul is likely to rise higher and higher in spiritual advancement in subsequent births and ultimately after several births may reach the desired goal, the condition of Siddha.

# 7

# Jain Ethics

## Ten Virtues of Monks

Along with the five great vows, monks strive after the ten-fold virtues of a self controlled ascetic. The layperson follows these virtues partially.

| | |
|---|---|
| Kshamaa | Forbearance, Forgiveness |
| Maardava | Modesty, Humility |
| Aarjava | Straightforwardness, Candor |
| Saucha | Contentment |
| Satya | Truthfullness |
| Samyam | Self-restraint, Control of Senses |
| Tapa | Austerity, Penance |
| Tyaga | Renunciation |
| Akinchanya | Non-attachment |
| Brahmacharya | Celibacy, Chastity |

Monks are required to bear equanimity towards all living beings, friends and foes alike.

In addition to the ten fold virtues Monks live on alms, do not eat food at night, do not use any kind of conveyance, and do not possess any property.

Jain Dashlakshni parva which begins from Bhaadaravo Sud 5, and ends, Bhaadravo Sud 14, Ananta-chaturdashi, is the celebration of ten virtues, Each day is dedicated to one virtue.

Bhaadaravo Vad 1, is called Kshamaavaanee day. This is the day of forgiving and asking forgiveness.

## **Twelve Bhavnas** (Reflections or Thoughts)

Jain religion puts a significant emphasis on the thought process of a human being. A person's behavior and his actions are the reflection of his internal thoughts, day in and day out. It is not the action but intention behind the action results in the accumulation of Karma.

One should be very careful about his thoughts, how he thinks, and the subject matter of his thought.

To make room for pure thoughts, and to drive out the evil ones, Jainism recommends to meditate the following twelve thoughts or Bhavnas.

The twelve Bhavnas described here are the subject matters of one's meditation, and how to occupy one's mind with useful, religious, beneficial, peaceful, harmless, spiritually advancing, Karma preventing thoughts. They cover a wide field of teachings of Jainism. They are designed to serve as aids to spiritual progress, produce detachment, and lead the aspirants from the realm of desire to the path of renunciation. They are reflections upon the fundamental facts of life, intended to develop purity of thought and sincerity in the practice of religion.

The reflections are also called Anupreksha*s*, longings, thoughts, aspirations, or Bhavnas.

1. Anitya Bhavna -Impermanence of the world
2. Asarana Bhavna - No one provides protection
3. Samsara Bhavna - No permanent relationship in universe
4. Ekatva Bhavna - Solitude of the soul
5. Anyatva Bhavna - Separateness
6. Asuci Bhavna - Impureness of the body
7. Asrava Bhavna - Influx of karma
8. Samvara Bhavna - Stoppage of influx of karma
9. Nirjara Bhavna - Shedding of karma
10. Loka Bhavna - Transitory of universe
11. Bodhi-durlabha - Unattainability of right faith, Bhavna knowledge, and conduct
12. Dharma Bhavna - Unattainability of true preceptor, scriptures, and religion

**1. Anitya Bhavna - Impermanence of the world**

Under this reflection, one thinks that in this world every thing such as life, youth, wealth, property, etc. are transient or subject to alteration. Nothing in the universe is permanent, even though the whole universe is constant. Spiritual values are therefore worth striving for as soul's ultimate freedom and stability. This will help to break all earthly attachments.

**2. Asarana Bhavna - No one provides protection**

Under this reflection, one thinks that he is helpless against death, old age, and disease. The only way he can conquer death and disease is by destroying all his karma. The soul is his own savior, and to achieve total freedom and enlightenment, one takes refuge to the true path and to the five best personalities. They are Arihanta, Siddha, Acharya, Upadhyay and Sadhus. The refuge to others are due to delusion, and must be avoided.

**3. Samsara Bhavna - No permanent relationship in universe**

Under this reflection, one thinks that the soul transmigrates from one life to the other in any of the four forms, human, animal, hellish, and heavenly.

The continual cycle of birth, life, and death is full of pain and miseries, and has not yet ended. There are no permanent worldly relations like father, mother, friend, foe, etc. It is we who establish these relations and live accordingly.

This kind of thought will help minimize or stop any attachments to anybody, other living beings, or objects. The soul must achieve ultimate freedom from it, which is liberation or Moksha.

**4. Ekatva Bhavna - Solitude of the soul**

Under this reflection, one thinks that the soul is solitaire, and lonely in existence. The soul assumes birth alone, and departs alone from the life form. The soul is responsible for its own actions and karmas. The soul will enjoy the fruits, and suffer bad consequences of its own action alone. Such thoughts will stimulate his efforts to get rid of karmas by his own initiative and will lead religious life.

**5. Anyatva Bhavna - Separateness**

Under this reflection, one thinks that soul is separate from any other objects or living beings of the world. Even his body is not his. At the time of death, soul leaves the body behind. The body is matter, while the soul is all consciousness.

The soul therefore should not develop attachment for worldly objects, and other living beings. He should not allow himself to be controlled by desires, greed, and urges of the body.

**6. Asuci Bhavna - Impureness of the body**

Under this reflection, one thinks about the constituent element of one's body. It is made of impure things like blood, bones, flesh, etc. It also generates impure things like perspiration, urine, stool, etc.

The soul, which resides within the body, is unattached to the body. It is alone and pure. The body ultimately becomes nonexistent, but the soul is eternal. Therefore emotional attachments to the body is useless.

**7. Asrava Bhavna - Influx of karma**

Under this reflection, one thinks about karma streaming into the soul. Every time he enjoys or suffers through the senses (touch, taste, smell, sight, and hearing) he makes his karma increase. This thought will make him more careful, and will try to stop the influx of karmas.

**8. Samvara Bhavna - Stoppage of influx of karma**

Under this reflection, one thinks about stopping evil thoughts, and becomes absorbed in achieving spiritual knowledge, meditation, etc. This prevents the influx of karma.

**9. Nirjara Bhavna - Shedding of karma**

Under this reflection, one thinks about the evil consequences of karma, and striving to destroy the previously acquired karma by austerity and meditation.

**10. Loka Bhavna - Transitory of universe**

Under this reflection, one thinks about the real nature of this universe. Judging from the standpoint of substance, it is eternal but from the standpoint of modification it is transitory.

Thus all objects of the world come into existence and perish. This thought makes him understand the true nature of reality, which is necessary for right knowledge.

**11. Bodhi- durlabha Bhavna - Unattainability of right faith, knowledge, and conduct**

Under this reflection, one thinks that it is very difficult for the transmigrating soul to acquire right faith, right knowledge, and right conduct in this world. Therefore, when one's has the opportunity to be a religious person, take the advantage of it to develop right religious talent. This thought will strengthen one's effort to attain them, and live accordingly.

**12. Dharma Bhavna - Unattainability of true preceptor, scriptures, and religion**

Under this reflection, one thinks that the true preceptor, scriptures, and religion are excellent shelters in this world full of agony. All other things lead to misery and suffering.

### Four Bhavnas or Virtues

Besides the twelve Bhavnas described above Jainism has laid great importance on the following four Bhavnas or virtues.They are mentioned here for clarification.

| | | |
|---|---|---|
| Amity, love, and friendship | - | Maitri |
| Appreciation, respect and joy | - | Pramoda |
| Compassion | - | Karuna |
| Equanimity and tolerance | - | Madhyastha |

### Twelve Vows Of Layperson

The five great vows (Maha-vratas) can be adopted by monks who are very keen about the uplift of their souls and ready to sacrifice all worldly enjoyments and family ties.

For those who want to remain in family life and for whom complete avoidance of five principle sins are difficult, Jain ethics specifies the following twelve vows to be carried out by the householder.

Of this twelve vows, the first five are main vows of limited nature (Anuvratas). They are somewhat easier in comparison with great vows (Maha-vratas). The great vows are for the monks.

The next three vows are known as merit vows (Guna-vratas), so called because they enhance and purify the effect of the five main vows and raise their value manifold. It also governs the external conduct of an individual.

The last four are called disciplinary vows (Shikhsa-vratas). They are intended to encourage the person in the performance of their religious duties. They reflect the purity of one's heart. They govern one's internal life and are expressed in a life that is marked by charity. They are preparatory to the discipline of an ascetic's life.

Three merit vows (Gunavrats) and four disciplinary vows (Shikhsa-vratas) together are known as Seven vows of virtuous conduct (Shilas).

A person may adopt these vows, according to his individual capacity and circumstances with the intent to adopt ultimately as a great vows.

The layperson should be very careful while observing and following these limited vows. These vows being limited or restricted vows may still leave great scope for the commitment of sins and possession of property.

The twelve vows are described as follows:

Five Main Vows of Limited Nature (Anuvratas):

1. Non-violence Anuvrat - Ahimsa Anuvrat (Sthula Pranatipat Viraman)

2. Truthfulness Anuvrat - Satya Anuvrat (Sthula Mrisavada Viraman)

3. Non-stealing Anuvrat - Achaurya Anuvrat (Sthula Adattadana Viraman)

4. Chastity Anuvrat - Bhramacharya Anuvrat (Sthula Maithuna Viraman)

5. Non-attachment Anuvrat- Aparigraha Anuvrat (Sthula Parigraha Viraman)

Three Merit Vows (Guna-vrats):

6. Dik Vrata - Limited area of activity vow

7. Bhoga-Upbhoga Vrata - Limited use of consumable & non-consumable items vow

8. Anartha-danda Vrata - Avoidance of purposeless sins vow

Four Disciplinary Vows (Siksha-vratas):

9. Samayik Vrata - Meditation vow of limited duration

10. Desavakasika Vrata - Activity vow of limiting space

11. Pausadha Vrata - Ascetic's life Vow of limited duration

12. Atithi Samvibhaga Vrata - Limited charity vow

**1. Non-violence Anuvrat (Ahimsa Anuvrat)**

In this vow, a person must not intentionally hurt any living being (plants, animals, humans etc.) or their feeling either by thought, word or deed, himself, or through others, or by approving such an act committed by somebody else.

Intention in this case applies selfish motive, sheer pleasure and even avoidable negligence. He may use force, if necessary, in the defense of his country, society, family, life, property, religious institute.

His agricultural, industrial, occupational living activities do also involve injury to life, but it should be as minimum as possible, through carefulness and due precaution.

**Four stages of violence are described**

Premeditated Violence: to attack someone knowingly

Defensive Violence: to commit intentional violence in defense of one's own life

Vocational Violence: to incur violence in the execution of one's means of livelihood

Common Violence: to commit violence in the performance of daily activities

Premeditated violence is prohibited for all. A householder is permitted to incur violence defensively and vocationally provided he maintains complete detachment. Common violence is accepted for survival, but even here, one should be careful in preparing food, cleaning house, etc. This explains the Jain's practices of filtering drinking water, vegetarianism, not eating meals at night, and abstinence from alcohol.

Nonviolence is the foundation of Jain ethics.

Lord Mahavir says:

> 'one should not injure, subjugate, enslave, torture or kill any living being including animals, insects, plants, and vegetables.'

This is the essence of religion. It embraces the welfare of all animals. It is the basis of all stages of knowledge and the source of all rules of conduct. The scriptures analyze the spiritual and practical aspects of nonviolence and discuss the subject negatively and positively.

**2. Truthfulness Anuvrat (Satya Anuvrat)**

The second of the five limited vows is Truth. It is more than abstaining from falsehood. It is seeing the world in its real form and adapting to that reality. The vow of truth puts a person in touch with his inner strength and inner capacities.

In this vow, a person avoids lies, such as giving false evidence, denying the property of others entrusted to him, avoid cheating others etc. The vow is to be followed in thought, action, and speech, and by doing it himself or by getting it done through others.

He should not speak the truth, if it harms others or hurts their feelings. He should, under these circumstances, keep silence.

**3. Non-stealing (Achaurya / Asteya) Anuvrat**

In this vow, a person must not steal, rob, or mis-appropriate others goods and property. He also must not cheat and use illegal means in acquiring worldly things, nor through others or by approving such an act committed by others.

**4. Chastity (Bhramacharya) Anuvrat**

The basic intent of this vow is to conquer passion and to prevent the waste of energy. Positively stated, the vow is meant to impart the sense of serenity to the soul.

In this vow, the house holder must not have a sensual relationship with anybody but one's own lawfully wedded spouse. Even with one's own spouse, excessive indulgence of all kinds of sensual pleasure need be avoided.

**5. Non-possession/ Non-attachment (Aparigraha) Anuvrat**

Non-possession is the fifth limited vow. As long as

a person does not know the richness of joy and peace that comes from within, he tries to fill his empty and insecure existence with the clutter of material acquisitions.

Lord Mahavir said, security born of material things is a delusion. To remove this delusion, one takes the vow of non-possession and realizes the perfection of the soul.

One must impose a limit on one's needs, acquisitions, and possessions such as land, real estate, goods, other valuables, animals, money, etc. The surplus should be used for the common good. One must also limit the every day usage of number of food items, or articles and their quantity.

This Jain principle of limited possession for householders helps in equitable distribution of wealth, comforts, etc., in the society.

Thus Jainism helps in establishing socialism, economic stability, and welfare in the world.

Non-possession, like non-violence, affirms the oneness of all life and is beneficial to an individual in his spiritual growth and to the society for the redistribution of wealth.

**6. Dik Vrata - Limited Area of Activity Vow**

This vow limits one's worldly activities to certain area in all the ten directions; north, south, east, west, north-east, north-west, south-east, south-west, above and below. He gives up committing sins in any place outside the limited areas. This vow provides a space limit to the commitments of sins not restricted by the limited vows of non-violence. Thus outside the limited area, the limited vows assumes the status of full vow (Maha-vratas).

**7. Bhoga-Upbhoga Vrata - Limited use of Consumable/ Non-consumable items vow**

Generally one commits the sin by one's use or

enjoyment of consumable (Bhoga) and non-consumable (Upbhoga) things.

Consumable (Bhoga) means enjoyment of an object which can only be used once, such as food, drink, fruits and flowers.

Non-consumable (Upabhoga) means enjoyment of an object which can be used several times, such as furniture, cloths, ornaments, buildings etc.

One should, therefore, limit the use of these two items in accordance with his own need and capacity by taking this vows.

This vow provides the time limit to the commitments of sins not restricted by Aparigraha Anuvrata.

**8. Anartha-danda Vrata - Avoidance of Purposeless Sins Vow**

One must not commit unnecessary or purposeless sin or moral offense as defined below. Thinking, talking, or preaching evil or ill of others.

Doing inconsiderate or useless acts such as walking on the grass unnecessarily. Manufacturing or supplying arms for attack.

Reading or listening, improper literature, or carelessness in ordinary behavior.

Thus this vow is of great practical importance. It makes life more vigilant and sin-proof.

**9. Samayik Vrata - Limited Meditation Vow**

Meditation of the soul and its relationship with nature is known as Samayik.

By giving up affection and aversion (Rag and Dvesha), observing equanimity in all objects, thinking evil of no one, and being at peace with the world, one should practice this vow of meditation (Samayik).

This vow consists in sitting down at one place for at least 48 minutes concentrating one's mind on religious activities like reading religious books, praying, or meditating. This vow may be repeated many times in a day. It is to be observed by mind, body, and speech.

The meditation of 48 minutes makes a person realize the importance of a life long vow to avoid all sinful activities and is a stepping stone to a life of full renunciation.

**10. Desavakasika Vrata - Limited Duration of Activity Vow**

This vow sets the new limit within the limitations already set by Dik Vrata and Bhoga-Upbhoga Vrata. The general life long limitation of doing business in certain areas and the use of articles are further restricted for a particular days time of the week.

This means that one shall not, during a certain period of time, do any activity, business, or travel beyond a certain city, street, house or have anything to do with the enjoyment of objects beyond that limit.

**11. Pausadha Vrata - Limited Ascetic's Life Vow**

This vow requires to live the life of a monk for a day. During this time one should retire to a secluded place, renounce all sinful activities, abstain in seeking pleasure from all objects of the senses, observe due restraint of body, speech and mind. A person follows five great vows (Mahavratas) completely during this time. He passes his time in spiritual contemplation, perform meditation (Samayik), engage in self study, and worship Gods (Arihants and Siddhas).

This vow promotes and nourishes one's religious life and provides training for ascetic life.

**12. Atithi Samvibhaga Vrata - Limited Charity Vow**

One should give food, clothes, medicine, and other

articles of its own possession to monks, nuns, and a pious person. The food offered should be pure and with reverence.

One should not prepare any foods specially for monks because monks are not allowed to have such foods. Donating of one's own food and articles to monks and others, provides an inner satisfaction and raises one's consciousness to higher level. It also saves him from acquiring of more sins if he would have used the same for his nourishment, comfort and pleasure.

## Peaceful Death

In the final days of life, a householder observes peaceful death. The house-holder can attain a peaceful death (Sallekhana) if he truly follows the above twelve vows. The peaceful death is characterized by non-attachment to the worldly objects and by a suppression of the passions at the time of death. The last thought should be of a calm renunciation of the body, and this thought should ever be present long before death supervenes.

## Conclusion

By performing these twelve vows, a lay follower may live a righteous life and advance towards a fuller and more perfect life, and conquer desire.

While earning wealth, supporting family, and taking up arms to protect himself, his family, his country, etc. against intruder, he is taught self restraint, love and enmity.

On one hand, he is debarred from doing any harm to himself, to his family, to his country, or to humanity by his reckless conduct. On the other hand, by giving up attachments he gradually prepares himself for the life of ascetics.

If one goes deeper into the rules laid down, he will find that practice of limiting the number of things to be

**8**

# Jain Mysticism

## Fourteen Auspicious Dreams of Mother Trishala

Queen Trishala, mother of Lord Mahavir at midnight saw fourteen beautiful and auspicious dreams after conception. They were:

1. Elephant
2. Bull
3. Lion
4. Goddess Laxmi
5. Garland of Flowers
6. Full Moon
7. Sun
8. Large Flag
9. Silver Urn
10. Lotus-Lake
11. Milky-Sea
12. Celestial Air-plane
13. Heap of Gems
14. Smokeless Fire

### 1. Elephant

The first dream Queen Trishala saw was of an elephant. She saw a big, tall, and impetuous elephant. It had two pairs of tusks. The color of the elephant was white and its whiteness was superior to the color of marble. It was an auspicious elephant, and was endowed with all the desirable marks of excellence.

This dream indicates that her son will guide the spiritual chariot, and save human beings from misery, greed, and attraction of life.

### 2. Bull

The second dream Queen Trishala saw was of a bull. The color of the bull was also white, but it was brighter than white lotuses. It glowed with beauty and radiated a light all around. It was noble, grand, and had a majestic hump. It had fine, bright, and soft hair on his body. Its horns were superb and sharply-pointed.

This dream indicates that her son will be a spiritual teacher of great ascetics, kings, and other great personalities.

### 3. Lion

The third dream Queen Trishala saw was of a magnificent lion. Its claws were beautiful and well-poised. The lion had a large well-rounded head and extremely sharp teeth. Its lips were perfect, its color was red, and its eyes were sharp and glowing. Its tail was impressively long and well-shaped. Queen Trishala saw this lion descending towards her and entering her mouth.

This dream indicates that her son will be as powerful and strong as a lion. He will be fearless, almighty, and capable of ruling over the world.

### 4. Goddess Laxmi

The fourth dream Queen Trishala saw was of the

Goddess Laxmi, the Goddess of wealth, prosperity and power. She was seated at the top of mountain Himalaya. Her feet had a sheen of golden turtle. She had a delicate and soft fingers. Her black hair was tiny, soft, and delicate. She wore rows of pearls interlaced with emeralds and a garland of gold. A pair of earring hung over her shoulders with dazzling beauty. She held a pair of bright lotuses.

This dream indicates that her son will attain great wealth, power, prosperity.

**5. Garland of Flowers**

The fifth dream Queen Trishala saw was of a celestial garland of flowers descending from the sky. It smelled of mixed fragrances of different flowers. The whole universe was filled with fragrance. The flowers were white and woven into the garland. They bloomed during all different seasons. A swarm of bees flocked to it and they made a humming sound around the region.

This dream indicates that the fragrance of her son's preaching will spread over the entire universe.

**6. Full Moon**

The sixth dream queen Trishala saw was of a full moon. It presented an auspicious sight. The moon was at its full glory. It awoke the lilies to bloom fully. It was bright like a well polished mirror. The moon radiated whiteness like a swan. It inspired the oceans to surge skyward. The beautiful moon looked like a radiant beauty-mark in the sky.

This dream indicates that her son will have a great physical structure, and be pleasing to all living beings of the universe.

**7. Sun**

The seventh dream Queen Trishala saw was of a huge

disc of sun. The sun was shining, and destroying darkness. It was red like the flame of the forest. Lotuses bloomed at its touch. The sun is the lamp of the sky and the lord of planets. The sun rose and an put to end the evil activities of the creatures who thrive at night.

This dream indicates that the teaching of her son will destroy anger, greed, ego, lust, pride, etc. from the life of the people.

**8. Large Flag**

The eighth dream Queen Trishala saw was of a very large flag flying on a golden stick. The flag fluttered softly and auspiciously in the gentle breeze. It attracted the eyes of all. Peacock feathers decorated its crown. A radiant white lion was on it.

This dream indicates that her son will be great, noble, and a well respected leader of the family.

**9. Silver Urn**

The ninth dream Queen Trishala saw was of a silver urn (kalash) full of crystal-clear water. It was a magnificent, beautiful, and bright pot. It shone like gold and was a joy to behold. It was garlanded with strings of lotuses and other flowers. The pot was holy and untouched by anything sinful.

This dream indicates that her son will be perfect in all virtues.

**10. Lotus-Lake**

The tenth dream Queen Trishala saw was of a lotus lake (padma-sagar). Thousands of lotuses were floating on the lake which opened at the touch of the sun's rays. The lotuses imparted a sweet fragrance. There were swarms of fish in the lake. Its water glowed like flames of fire. The lily-leaves were floating on the water.

This dream indicates that her son will help to liberate the human beings who are tangled in the cycle of birth, death, and misery.

**11. Milky-sea**

The eleventh dream Queen Trishala saw was of a milky sea. Its water swelled out in all directions, rising to great heights with turbulent motions. Winds blew and created waves. A great commotion was created in the sea by huge sea animals. Great rivers fell into the sea, producing huge whirlpools.

This dream indicates that her son will navigate through life on an ocean of birth, death, and misery leading to Moksha or liberation.

**12. Celestial air-plane**

The twelfth dream Queen Trishala saw was of a celestial airplane. The airplane had eight thousands magnificent gold pillars studded with gems. The plane was framed with sheets of gold and garlands of pearls. It was decorated with rows of murals depicting bulls, horses, men, crocodiles, birds, children, deers, elephants, wild animals, and lotus flowers. The plane resounded with celestial music. It was saturated with an intoxicating aroma of incense fumes. It was illuminated with a bright silvery light.

This dream indicates that all Gods and Goddesses in heaven will respect and salute to his spiritual teaching and will obey him.

**13. Heap of Gems**

The thirteenth dream Queen Trishala saw was of a great heap of gems, as high as Mount Meru. There were gems and precious stones of all types and kinds. These gems were heaped over the earth and they illuminated the entire sky.

This dream indicates that her son will have infinite virtues and wisdom.

**14. Smokeless Fire**

The fourteenth dream queen Trishala saw was of a smokeless fire. The fire burned with great intensity and emitted a radiant glow. Great quantities of pure ghee and honey were being poured on the fire. It burned with numerous flames.

This dream indicates that the wisdom of her son will excel the wisdom of all other great people.

After having such fourteen wonderful dreams, Queen Trishala woke up. Her dreams filled her with wonder. She never had such dreams before. She narrated her dreams to King Siddharth.

The king called the soothsayers for the interpretation of dreams and they unanimously said, "Sir, her Highness will be blessed with a noble son. The dream augur the vast spiritual realm, the child shall command. Her Highness will become the Universal Mother."

After nine months and fourteen days, Queen Trishala delivered a baby boy. The boy was named Vardhaman meaning ever increasing.

Immediately after the birth of prince Vardhaman, Indra, the King of Heaven, arrived with other gods and goddesses. He hypnotized the whole city including mother Trishala and King Siddharth.

He took baby Vardhaman to Mount Meru and bathed him. He proclaimed peace and harmony by reciting Bruhat Shanti during the first bathing ceremony of the new born Tirthankara.

After renunciation and realization of Absolute Self Knowledge, Prince Vardhaman became Lord Mahavir, the twenty fourth and the last Tirthankara of Jain religion.

**Five Bodies and Eight Vargnas**

A liberated soul does not have a material body, mind, speech, and does not breathe. The soul is totally free from all karmas. It merely exists in Moksha in the permanent blissful state.

As far as a worldly soul is concerned it possesses a material body along with some other types of bodies. These bodies are made up from different types of varganas (matters). Jainism explains that eight types of vargana exist in the universe. Every space in the universe is filled with these vargana. When five of the eight vargana when attach to the worldly soul they create five different bodies. The remaining three vargana provide three different functions to the material body.

**The eight Vargnas (matters) are**

| | | |
|---|---|---|
| **Audaric vargana** | - | creates the physical body of the living being |
| **Tejas vargana** | - | creates the Tejas body to the living being which provides heat and digestion power to the audaric body. |
| **Karman vargana** | - | creates Karmic or Causal body |
| **Aharac vargana** | - | creates Aharac body, which is very small in size and is possessed by some unique soul |
| **Vaikriya vargana** | - | creates Vaikriya body, which can be converted into very small or large in size |
| **Breathing vargana** | - | provides breathing |
| **Mind vargana** | - | provides mind for thinking |
| **Speech vargana** | - | provides speech |

9

# Jain View of the Universe

**Six Universal Entities** (Substances or Dravyas)

## Structural View Of The Universe

Jain Philosophy does not give credence to the theory that the God is a creator, survivor, or destroyer of the universe. On the contrary, it asserts that the universe has always existed and will always exist in exact adherence to the laws of the cosmos. There is nothing but infinity both in the past and in the future.

The world of reality or universe consists of two classes of objects:

Living beings (conscious, chetan, jiva) and

Non-living objects (unconscious, achetan, ajiva)

Non-living objects are further classified into five categories

| | |
|---|---|
| matter | (Pudgal) |
| space | (Akas) |
| medium of motion | (Dharmastikay) |
| medium of rest | (Adharmastikay) |
| time | (Kaal or Samay) |

The five nonliving entities together with the living beings, totaling six are aspects of reality in Jainism. They are also known as six universal entities, substances or dravyas.

These six entities of the universe however do undergo countless changes, but nothing is lost or destroyed. Everything is recycled in another form.

**The Concept of Reality or Entity or Substance (Dravya)**

A reality is defined to have an existence (Sat).

Each reality or entity continuously undergoes countless changes known as origination and destruction. This is known as Paryaya of a substance.

In the midst of changes its qualities remain unchanged which is called permanence. This is also known as Gunas of the substance.

Hence every entity (substance or object) in the universe has three aspects:

Origination - Utpada (continuous changes)

Destruction - Vyaya (continuous changes)

Permanence - Dhrauvya (permanent)

Both attributes (Gunas) and modes (Paryayas) are inseparable from an entity.

The same principle can be explained differently as follows:

An entity is permanent (nitya) from the stand point of its attributes or qualities (Guna). This is known as substancial stand point (dravyarthik naya).

An entity is transient (anitya) from the stand point of its forms or modifications (Paryaya). This is known as modal stand point (Paryayarthik Naya).

A natural description of reality takes into consideration these three aspects:

- permanence in the midst of change
- identity in the midst of diversity
- unity in the midst of multiplicity

The modifications that an entity undergoes refer to the various shapes and forms into which a substance is transformed, either naturally or artificially.

*Examples:*

A living being through the process of growth, undergoes various changes, such as childhood, youth, and old age. These changes are the natural modifications of the living being.

Childhood, youth, and old age are transient forms (Paryaya) of a living being. The soul of a living being is permanent (Dravya).

Clay is molded by a potter into various shapes. Gold is crafted by a goldsmith into various ornaments. These changes are artificial modifications of the nonliving being.

- ornaments and clay shapes are transient (paryaya)
- gold and clay are permanent (dravya)

While undergoing various modifications, either natural or artificial, the basic substance remains unchanged and is permanent, while the forms change and are transient.

**The six universal substances**

As explained above Jainism believes that the universe is made from the combination of the six universal substances. All of the six substances are indestructible, imperishable, immortal, eternal and continuously go through countless changes.

| | | |
|---|---|---|
| Soul/Consciousness | - Jiva | (Living being) |
| Matter | - Pudgala | (Nonliving being) |
| Medium of motion | - Dharma | (Nonliving being) |

| | | |
|---|---|---|
| Medium of rest | - Adharma | (Nonliving being) |
| Space | - Akasa | (Nonliving being) |
| Time | - Kaal | (Nonliving being) |

**Soul (Jiva)**

Its essential characteristic is consciousness. This is the only knowing substance. It possesses perfect knowledge, perfect vision, perfect power, and perfect bliss. It also possesses the property of contraction and expansion like that of light. They are of innumerable numbers. Living being can not be created or can not be destroyed. The total number of living beings remain same in the entire universe at all the time.

There are two types of Souls (Living beings):

**Free (Mukta) Soul**

Free soul is defined as a pure consciousness, a soul that has completely exhausted all of its karma. It is a liberated soul. It is also known as Siddha. All siddhas are defined as Gods in Jainism.

Liberated souls or Gods do not possess a body.

They possess perfect knowledge, vision, power, and bliss.

They live in Moksha, which is located on the top of Lokakas.

They never return again into the cycle of life, death, pain, and pleasure.

There are an innumerable number of liberated souls.

All Tirthankaras and other Keval-jnanis become siddhas at the end of their life (death).

**Worldly (Samsari) Soul**

It possesses a body (plants, naraki, tiryanch, human, or

angel) and wanders into the cycle of life and death.

It is covered with karma particles.

It possesses limited knowledge, vision, power, and bliss.

It suffers from birth, death, pain, and pleasure.

There are a innumerable number of worldly souls.

It is the doer of all kinds of karmas (actions), and enjoyer of the fruit of the karmas.

It is capable of becoming free from worldly life.

Worldly souls are divided according to the number of senses they possess.

There are total five senses a living being may possess. touch, taste, smell, sight, and hearing.

One sense (Ekendria)

- possesses one sense - touch only
- it cannot move own its own accord
- they are subdivided into five categories

Soul possesses earth as its body - Prithvikaya

Soul possesses water as its body - Apakaya

Soul possesses fire as its body - Agnikaya

Soul possesses air as its body - Vayukaya

Soul possesses vegetable as its body - Vanaspatikaya

Two senses (Be-indriya)

A living being possesses two senses - touch and taste ex. worms, leeches.

Three senses (Tre-indriya)

A living being possesses three senses - touch, taste, and smell ex. ants, lice.

Four senses (Chau-indriya)

A living being possesses four senses - touch, taste, smell, and sight ex. flies, bees.

**Five senses** (Panch-indriya)

A living being possesses five senses - touch, taste, smell, sight, and hearing ex. animals, birds, human, heavenly, and hellish beings, etc.

A soul with one to four senses does not a possess mind.

A soul with five senses may possess a mind.

## Matter (Pudgala)

It is matter or body.

It has senses (touch, taste, smell, sight, and hearing).

They are of infinite number

It possesses color

It does not have consciousness or knowledge.

The smallest particle of matter is known as Parmanu (atom).

A paramanu occupies only one pradesa (unit of space)

There are four divisions of matter:

Skandha (whole-matter):

Any object which has a mass of matter can be called skandha.

ex. stick, stone, knife, a particle of sand

Skandha-desa (portion of matter):

Desa means a part, portion, or division. An undetached portion of skandha is called skandha-desa When a part of the skandha (skandha-desa) is separated from the whole, it also becomes another skandha. A hand of a statue when undetached is known as a skandha-desa but when separated from the statue is known as Skandha.

Skandha-pradesa (smallest particle of matter):

The smallest undetached portion of skandha, which cannot be further divided is called skandha-pradesa.

Paramanu or Anu (atom):

When the smallest portion of the matter is separated from its skandha, it is called paramanu or anu. Parmanu matter can not be further sub-divided, cut, or pierced.

**Karmic Matter (Karma Pudgala):**

Karma is one of the categories of matter. It is known as karmic matter (karma pudgala). Karma particles are of very fine matter not perceptible to the senses. The entire universe is filled with such karmic matter.

Every living being is covered by karmic matter from the beginning of time. It is the karmic matter that keeps the soul away from realization of its true nature or liberation.

**Medium of Motion (Dharma)**

Medium of motion helps in the movement of soul and matter.

ex. water provides medium for fish to move

It does not possess senses, color, or body.

It does not have a consciousness or knowledge.

It exists in Lokakas.

**Medium of Rest (Adharma)**

Medium of rest helps to rest soul and matter.

ex. People rest in the shade of a tree

It does not possess senses, color, or body.

It does not have consciousness or knowledge.

It exists in Lokakas.

**Space (Akasa)**

Space provides room to soul, matter, dharma, adharma, and time.

It pervades everywhere (infinite).

It is the support of everything and thus it is self supported.

It has no form, color, taste, smell, and touch.

It does not perform any action (inactive), however it does give accommodation to soul and matter of their actions.

It is one and whole.

Where medium of motion and rest substances exist, it is called Lokakas.

The remaining space is empty and is called Alokakas.

**Time (Kaal)**

There are two views exist in Jainism with regards to time.

One view: Time is an imaginary thing, it has no real existence.

Another view: Time has a real existence consisting of innumerable time atoms.

The changes in living being and non-living being substances are measured in the units of time. However time is not the cause of the changes to living being and non-living substances.

The smallest indivisible portion of time is called Samaya.

Combination of samayas are: moment, second, minute, hour, day, month, year, etc.

| | | |
|---|---|---|
| innumerable samayas | = | one avali (time required to blink a eye) |
| 16,777,216 avalis | = | one muhurt (48 minutes) |
| 30 muhurts | = | one day |
| 15 days | = | one fortnight |
| 2 fortnights | = | one month |
| 12 months | = | one year |
| innumerable years | = | one palyopama |
| 1,000,000,000,000,000 palyopamas | = | one sagaropama |

# 10

# Jain Puja

## Meaning Of Ashta Prakari Puja

Generally Jains use the following eight items to perform *puja of a Tirthankara in the temple.* Symbolically each item represents a specific religious virtue and one should reflect on it while performing puja.

1. Jala Puja: Water
2. Chandan Puja: Sandal-wood
3. Pushpa Puja: Flower
4. Dhup Puja: Incense
5. Dipak Puja: Candle
6. Akshat Puja: Rice
7. Naivedya Puja: Sweet food
8. Fal Puja: Fruit

### 1. Jala Puja: (Water)

Water symbolizes the ocean. Every living being continuously travels through life's ocean of birth, death, and misery. This puja reminds that one should live his life with honesty, truthfulness, love, and compassion towards all living beings. This way one will be able to cross life's ocean and attain liberation (Moksha). This is known as samyak-darshana, samyak-jnana, and samyak-charitrya in the Jain religion.

**2. Chandan Puja: (Sandal-wood)**

Chandan symbolizes knowledge (jnana). By doing this puja, one should thrive for right knowledge. Jainism believes that the path of knowledge is the main path to attain Moksha or liberation. Bhakti or devotion helps in the early stages of one's effort for liberation.

**3. Pushpa Puja: (Flower)**

The flower symbolizes conduct. Our conduct should be like a flower, which provides fragrance and beauty to all living beings without discrimination. We should live our life like flowers full of love and compassion towards all living beings.

**4. Dhup Puja: (Incense)**

Dhup symbolizes monkhood life. While burning itself, incense provides fragrance to others. Similarly, true monks and nuns spend their entire life selflessly for the benefit of all living beings. This puja reminds that one should thrive for a ascetic life.

**5. Dipak Puja: (Candle)**

The flame of dipak represents a pure consciousness, i.e. a soul without any bondage of a karma or a liberated soul. In Jainism, such a soul is called a Siddha or God. The ultimate goal of every living being is to become liberated. By doing this puja one should thrive to follow five great vows; non-violence, truthfulness, non-stealing, chastity, and non-possession. Ultimately these vows will lead to liberation.

**6. Akshat Puja: (Rice)**

Rice is a kind of grain which is nonfertile. One cannot grow rice plants by seeding rice. Symbolically, it means that rice is the last birth. By doing this puja one should thrive to put all the efforts in life in such a way that this life becomes one's last life, and after the end of this life one will not be reborn again.

**7. Naivedya Puja: (Sweet food)**

Naivedya symbolizes tasty food. By doing this puja, one should thrive to reduce or eliminate attachment to tasty food. Healthy food is essential for survival, however one should not live for tasty food. Ultimate aim in one's life is to attain a life where no food is essential for survival. That is the life of a liberated soul who lives in Moksha for ever in ultimate blissful state.

**8. Fal Puja: (Fruit)**

Fruit is a symbol of Moksha or liberation. If we live our life without any attachment to worldly affairs, continue to perform our duty without any expectation and reward, be a witness to all the incidents that occur surrounding us, truly follow monkhood life, and have a love and compassion to all living beings, we will attain the fruit of liberation. This is the last puja symbolizing the ultimate achievement of our life.

# 11

# Jain Principles

### Nine Tattvas (Principles)

The nine tattvas, or principles, are the single most important subject of Jain philosophy. It deals with the karma theory of Jainism, which provides the basis for the path of liberation. Without the proper knowledge of this subject, a person can not progress spiritually. The true faith and understanding of this subject brings about right faith (samyak-darshana), right knowledge (samyak-jnana), and right conduct in an individual.

### Nine Tattvas (Principles)

1. Jiva - soul or living being (Consciousness)
2. Ajiva - non-living substances
3. Asrava - cause of the influx of karma
4. Bandh - bondage of karma
5.*Punya - virtue
6.*Papa - sin

* Punya and Papa are the diverse results of Asrava and Bandh. Some exponents of Jains do not treat them as separate tattvas. According to them, there are only seven principles instead of nine.

7. Samvara - arrest of the influx of karma

8. Nirjara - exhaustion of the accumulated karma

9. Moksha - total liberation from karma

1. Jiva (soul) Substance:

Explained in The Six Universal Substances chapter.

2. Ajiva (Non-living) Substances:

Explained in The Six Universal Substances chapter.

### 3. Asrava (Cause of the influx of karma) -

Asrava is the cause which leads to the influx of good and evil karma which lead to the bondage of the soul.

Asrava may be described as attraction in the soul toward sense objects.

The following are causes of influx of good and evil karma:

Mithyatva - ignorance

Avirati - lack of self restraint

Kasaya - passions like anger, conceit, deceit, and lust

Pramada - unawareness or unmindfulness

Yoga - activities of mind, speech, and body

In addition to the above causes, the five great sins; violence, untruth, stealing, sensual indulgence, and attachment to worldly objects are also the cause of the influx of karmas.

### 4. Bandha (Bondage of karma)-

Bandha is the attachment of karmic matter (karma pudgala) to the soul. The soul has had this karmic matter bondage from eternity.

This karmic body is known as the karmana body or causal body.

Karmic matter is a particular type of matter which is attracted to the soul because of its ignorance, lack of self restraint, passions, unmindfulness, activities of body, mind, and speech.

The soul, which is covered by karmic matter, continues acquiring new karma from the universe and exhausting old karma into the universe through the above mentioned actions at every moment.

Because of this continual process of acquiring and exhausting karma particles, the soul has to pass through the cycles of births and deaths, and experiencing pleasure and pain. So under normal circumstances the soul can not attain freedom from karma, and hence liberation.

Karmic matter attaching to the soul assumes four forms:

| | |
|---|---|
| Prakriti bandha | - Type of karma |
| Sthiti bandha | - Duration of karma |
| Anubhava bandha | - Intensity of attachment of karma |
| Pradesa bandha | - Quantity of karma |

## Prakriti Bandha

When karmic matter attaches to the soul, karma will obscure its essential nature of:

> perfect knowledge, vision, bliss, power, eternal existence, non-corporeal, and equanimity.

Prakriti bandha is classified into eight categories, according to the particular attribute of the soul that it obscures.

Jnana-varaniya

It covers the soul's power of perfect knowledge.

Darasna-varaniya

It covers the soul's power of perfect visions.

Vedniya

It obscures the blissful nature of the soul, and thereby produces pleasure and pain.

Mohniya

It generates delusion in the soul in regard to its own true nature, and makes it identify itself with other substances.

Ayu

It determines the span of life in one birth, thus obscuring its nature of eternal existence.

Nama

It obscures the non-corporeal existence of the soul, and produces the body with its limitations, qualities, faculties, etc.

Gotra

It obscures the souls characteristics of equanimity, and determines the caste, family, social standing, etc.

Antaraya

It obstructs the natural energy of the soul and prevents it from attaining liberation. It also prevents a living being from doing something good and enjoyable.

**Ghati and Aghati karmas**

The above eight karmas are also categorized into two groups, known as ghati and aghati karmas.

**Ghati Karmas**

Jnana-varaniya, Darasna-varaniya, Mohaniya, and Antaraya karmas are called Ghati karmas (dangerous karmas) because they obscure the true nature of the soul.

**Aghati Karmas**

> Ayu, Nama, Gotra, and Vedniya karmas are called Aghati karmas. They do not obscure the original nature of the soul. However, they associate with the body of the soul. Hence they can not destroyed by the soul so long as it possesses a body.

When a person destroys all of his ghati karmas, at that time he attains keval-jnana. However, he continues to live as a human being because none of his aghati karmas are destroyed. He can only attain liberation after all of his aghati karmas are destroyed. Hence he attains liberation after his death.

When a person attains keval-jnana, he is known as an Arihant. If an Arihant establishes the four fold order of Monks, Nuns, Sravaka, (male layperson), and Sravika (female layperson) then the Arihant is called a Tirthankara. Other Arihantas are known as ordinary Kevali. After Nirvana (death) both Tirthankaras and ordinary Kevalis are called Siddhas.

All Siddhas are unique individuals, but they all possess perfect knowledge, vision, power, and bliss. Hence from the qualities and attributes point of view all Siddhas are same.

**Sthiti Bandha**

When karmic matter attaches to the soul the duration of the attachment is determined at that time according to the intensity or dullness of the soul's passions.

**Anubhava Bandha or Rasa Bandha**

What fruits the karmic matter will produce is determined at the time of attachment by varying degrees of passions.

**Pradesa Bandha**

The quantum of karmic matter that is drawn towards

the soul for attachment is determined by the intensity or dullness of the soul's action.

**5. Punya (Virtue)**

The influx of karmic matter due to good activities of the mind, body, and speech with the potential of producing pleasant sensations is called punya or virtue.

Activities such as offering food, drink, shelter, purifying thought, physical and mental happiness, etc. result in producing punya karmic matter.

**6. Papa (Sin)**

The influx of karmic matter due to evil activities of the mind, body, and speech with the potential of producing unpleasant sensations is called papa or sin.

Activities such as violence, untruth, theft, unchastity, attachment to objects, anger, conceit, deceit, lust, etc. result in producing papa karmic matter.

**7. Samvara (Arrest of Karma)**

The method which arrests fresh karma from coming into the soul is samvara. This process is a reverse of asrava.

It can be accomplished by constant practice of:

- restraint of mind, body, and speech
- religious meditation
- conquest of desire
- forgiveness, tenderness, purity, truth, austerity, renunciation, unattachment, and chastity

**8. Nirjara**

Nirjara is the exhaustion of karmic matter already acquired.

- The karmas exhaust themselves by producing their results when it is time for them to do so.

- Unless they are exhausted before they are mature and start producing results, it becomes difficult to be free. By that time, new karmic matter begins to pour in.
- Therefore, it becomes necessary for one who desires final liberation to exhaust all karmas before maturity. This is called nirjara.

Nirjara is to be done by rigorous austerities.

## External Nirjara

| | |
|---|---|
| Anasan | - complete abstinence of eating and drinking |
| Alpahara | - reduction in the quantity of food one normally eats |
| Ichhanirodha | - control of desire for food and material things |
| Rasatyaga | - complete abstinence of eating or drinking juicy and tasty foods such as honey, alcohol, butter, milk, tea, sweets, juice etc. (no attachments to the taste of the foods) |
| Kayaklesa | - control of passions by discipline |
| Samlinata | - sitting in a lonely place in due posture with senses withdrawn |

## Internal Nirjara

| | |
|---|---|
| Prayaschita | - repentance for the breach of vows |
| Vinaya | - appropriate behavior towards a teacher |
| Vaiyavrata | - selfless service to the suffering and deserving |
| Svadhyaya | - studying/listening of religious scriptures |
| Bhutsarga | - non-attachment to the body |
| Subha-dhyana | - religious meditation |

## 9. Moksha

Moksha is the liberation of the living being (soul) after complete exhaustion or elimination of all karmas.

A liberated soul regains totally its original attributes of perfect knowledge, vision, power, and bliss. It climbs to the top of Lokakas and remains there forever in its blissful and unconditional existence.

It never returns again into the cycles of birth, life, and death.

This state of the soul is the liberated or perfect state, and this is called "Nirvana."

# 12

# Jain Texts

Jaina Sutras, Translated from the Prakrit by Hermann Jacobi, 1884(from: Sacred Books of the East vol. 22) *Akaranga Sutra Kalpa Sutra*

## About Jainism

## Akaranga Sutra

## First Book

## First Lecture,

## Called

## Knowledge of The Weapon

## First Lesson

O long-lived (Gambusvamin)! I (Sudharman) have heard the following discourse from the venerable (Mahivira): (1) Here many do not remember whether they have descended in an eastern direction (when they were born in this world), or in a southern, or in a western, or in a northern direction, or in the direction from above, or in the direction from below, or in a direction intermediate (between the cardinal points), or in a direction intermediate between these (and the cardinal points). (2) Similarly, some do not know whether their soul is born again and again or not; nor what they were formerly, nor what they will become after having died and left this world. (3) Now this is what one should know, either by one's own knowledge or through the instruction of the highest (i.e. a Tirthakara), or having heard it from others: that he descended in an eastern direction, or in any other direction (particularised above). Similarly,some know that their soul is born again and again, that it arrives in this or that direction, whatever direction that may be. (4) He believes in soul, believes in the World believes in rewards, believes in action (acknowledged to be our own doing in such judgments as these): 'I did it;' 'I shall cause another to do it;' 'I shall allow another to do it.' In the world, these are all the causes of sin, which must be comprehended and renounced. (5) A man that does not comprehend and renounce the causes of sin, descends in a cardinal or intermediate direction, wanders to all cardinal or intermediate directions, is born again and again in manifold births, experiences all painful feelings. (6) About this the Revered One has taught the truth (comprehension and renunciation). For the sake of the splendour, honour, and glory of this life, for the sake of birth, death, and final liberation, for the removal of pain, all these causes of sin are at work, which are to be comprehended and renounced in this world. He who, in the world, comprehends and renounces these causes of sin, is called a reward-knowing sage (muṇi). Thus I say'. (7)

**Second Lesson**

The (living) world is afflicted, miserable, difficult to instruct, and without discrimination. In this world full of pain, suffering by their different acts, see the benighted ones cause great pain. (1) See! there are beings individually embodied (in earth; not one all-soul). See! there are men who control themselves, (whilst others only) pretend to be houseless (i.e. monks, such as the Bauddhas, whose conduct differs not from that of householders), because one destroys this (earth-body) by bad and injurious doings, and many other beings, besides, which he hurts by means of earth, through his doing acts relating to earth. (2) About this the Revered One has taught the truth: for the sake of the splendour, honour, and glory of this life, for the sake of birth, death, and final liberation, for the removal of pain, man acts sinfully towards earth, or causes others to act so, or allows others to act so. This deprives him of happiness and perfect wisdom. About this he is informed when he has understood or heard, either from the Revered One or from the monks, the faith to be coveted. (3) There are some who, of a truth, know this (i. e. injuring) to be the bondage, the delusion, the death, the hell. For this' a man is longing when he destroys this (earth-body) by bad, injurious doings, and many other beings, besides, which he hurts by means of earth, through his doing acts relating to earth. Thus I say. (4)

As somebody may cut or strike a blind man (who cannot see the wound), as somebody may cut or strike the foot, the ankle, the knee, the thigh, the hip, the navel, the belly, the flank, the back, the bosom, the heart, the breast, the neck, the arm, the finger, the nail, the eye, the brow, the forehead, the head, as some kill (openly), as some extirpate (secretly), (thus the earth-bodies are cut, struck, and killed though their feeling is not manifest). (5)

He who injures these (earth-bodies) does not comprehend and renounce the sinful acts; he who does not injure these, comprehends and renounces the sinful acts. Knowing them, a wise man should not act sinfully towards earth, nor cause others to act so, nor allow others to act so. He who knows these causes of sin relating to earth, is called a reward-knowing sage. Thus I say. (6)

**Third Lesson**

(Thus I say): He who acts rightly, who does .pious work, who practises no deceit, is called houseless. (1) One should, conquering the world, persevere in that (vigour of) faith which one had. on the entrance in the order; the heroes (of faith), humbly bent, (should retaintheir belief in) the illustrious road (to final liberation) and in the world (of water-bodies); having rightly comprehended them through the instruction (of Mah1vira), (they should retain) that which causes no danger (i.e. self-control). Thus I say. (2) A man should not (himself) deny the world of (water-bodies), nor should he deny the self. He who denies the world (of water-bodies), denies the self; and he who denies the self, denies the world of (water-bodies). (3)

See! there are men who control themselves; others pretend only to be houseless; for one destroys this (water-body) by bad, injurious doings, and many other beings, besides, which he hurts by means of water, through his doing acts relating to water. (4) About this the Revered One has taught the truth: for the sake of the splendour, honour, and glory of this life, for the sake of birth, death, and final liberation, for the removal of pain, man acts sinfully towards water, or causes others to act so, or allows others to act so. (5) This deprives him of happiness and perfect wisdom. About this he is informed when he has understood and heard from the Revered One, or from the monks, the faith to be coveted. There are some who, of a truth, know this (i.e. injuring) to be the bondage, the delusion, the death, the hell. For this a man is longing when he destroys this (water-body) by bad and injurious doings, and many other beings, besides, which he hurts by means of water, through his doing acts relating to water. Thus I say. (6)

There are beings living in water, many lives; of a truth, to the monks water has been declared to be living matter. See! considering the injuries (done to water-bodies), those acts (which are injuries, but must be done before the use of water, e.g. straining) have been distinctly declared. Moreover he (who uses water which is not strained) takes away what has not been given (i.e. the bodies of water-lives). (A Bauddha will object): 'We have permission, we have permission to drink it, or (to take it) for toilet purposes.' Thus they destroy by various injuries (the water-bodies). But in this their doctrine is of no authority.

He who injures these (water-bodies) does not comprehend and renounce the sinful acts; he who does not injure these, comprehends and renounces the sinful acts. (7) Knowing them, a wise man should not act sinfully towards water, nor cause others to act so, nor allow others to act so. He who knows these causes of sin relating to water, is called a reward-knowing sage. Thus I say. (8)

**Fourth Lesson**

(Thus I say): A man should not, of his own accord, deny the world (of fire-bodies), nor should he deny the self. He who denies the world (of fire-bodies), denies the self; and he who denies the self, denies the world (of fire-bodies). (1) He who knows that (viz. fire) through which injury is done to the long-living bodies (i.e. plants), knows also that which does no injury (i.e. control); and he who knows that which does no injury, knows also that through which no injury is done to the long-living bodies. (2) This has been seen by the heroes (of faith) who conquered ignorance; for they control themselves, always exert themselves, always mind their duty. He who is unmindful of duty, and desiring of the qualities (i.e. of the pleasure and profit which may be derived from the elements) is called the torment (of living beings). Knowing this, a wise man (resolves): 'Now (I shall do) no more what I used to do want only before.' (3) See! there are men who control themselves; others pretend only to be houseless; for one destroys this (fire-body) by bad and injurious doings, and many other beings, besides, which he hurts by means of fire, through his doing acts relating to fire. About this the Revered One has taught the truth: for the sake of the splendour, honour, and glory of this life, for the sake of birth, death, and final liberation, for the removal of pain, man acts sinfully towards fire, or causes others to act so, or allows others to act so. (4) This deprives him of happiness and perfect wisdom. About this he is informed when he has understood, or heard from the Revered One or from the monks, the faith to be coveted. There are some who, of a truth, know this (i.e. injuring) to be the bondage, the delusion, the death, the hell. For this a man is longing, when he destroys this (fire-body) by bad and injurious doings, and many other beings, besides, which he hurts by means of fire, through his doing acts relating to fire. Thus I say. (5)

There are beings living in the earth, living in grass, living on leaves, living in wood, living in cowdung, living in dust-heaps, jumping beings which coming near (fire) fall into it. Some, certainly, touched by fire, shrivel up; those which shrivel up there, lose their sense there; those which lose their sense there, die there. (6)

He who injures these (fire-bodies) does not comprehend and renounce the sinful acts; he who does not injure these, comprehends and renounces the sinful acts. Knowing them, a wise man should not act sinfully towards fire, nor cause others to act so, nor allow others to act so. He who knows the causes of sin relating to fire, is called a reward knowing sage. Thus I say. (7)

**Fifth Lesson**

I shall not do (acts relating to plants) after having entered the order, having recognised (the truth about these acts), and having conceived that which is free from danger (i.e. control).'

He who does no acts (relating to plants), has ceased from works; he who has ceased from them is called 'houseless.' (1) Quality is the whirlpool (avatta=samsara), and the whirlpool is quality. Looking up, down, aside, eastward, be sees colours, hearing he hears sounds; (2) longing upwards, down, aside, eastward, he becomes attached to colours and sounds. That is called the world; not guarded against it, not obeying the law (of the Tirthakaras), relishing the qualities, conducting him-self wrongly, he will wantonly live in a house (i.e. belong to the world).(3)

See! there are men who control themselves; others pretend only to be houseless,for one destroys this(body of a plant) by bad and injurious doings, and many other beings, besides, which he hurts by means of plants, through his doing acts relating to plants. (4) About this the Revered One has taught the truth: for the sake of the splendour, honour, and glory of this life, for the sake of birth, death, and final liberation, for the removal of pain, man acts sinfully towards plants, or causes others to act so, or allows others to act so. This deprives him of happiness and perfect wisdom. About this he is informed when he has understood, or heard from the Revered One. or from the monks, the faith to be coveted. There are some who, of a truth, know this (i.e. injuring) to be the bondage, the delusion, the death, the hell. For this a man is longing when he destroys this (body of a plant) by bad and injurious doings, and many other beings, besides, which he hurts by means of plants, through his doing acts relating to plants. Thus I say. (5)

As the nature of this (i.e. men) is to be born and to grow old, so is the nature of that (i.e. plants) to be born and to grow old; as this has relson, so that has reason'; as this falls sick when cut, so that falls sick when cut; as this needs food, so that needs food; as this will decay, so that will decay; as this is not eternal, so that is not eternal; as this takes increment, so that takes increment; as this is changing, so that is changing. (6) He who injures these (plants) does not comprehend and renounce the sinful acts; he who does not injure these, comprehends and renounces the sinful acts. Knowing them, a wise man should not act sinfully towards plants, nor cause others to act so, nor allow others to act so. He who knows these causes of sin relating to plants, is called a reward-knowing sage. Thus I say (7).

**Sixth Lesson**

Thus I say. There are beings called the animate, viz. those who are produced 1. from eggs (birds, &c.), 2. from a fetus (as elephants, &c.), 3. from a fetus with an enveloping membrane (as cows, buffaloes, &c.), 4. from fluids (as worms, &c.) 5, from sweat (as bugs, lice, &c.), 6. by coagulation (as locusts, ants, &c.), 7. from sprouts (as butterflies, wagtails, &c.), 8. by regeneration (men, gods, hell-beings). This is called the Samsara (1) for the slow, for the ignorant. Having well considered it, having well looked at it, I say thus: all beings, those with two, three, four senses, plants, those with five senses, and the rest of creation, (experience) individually pleasure or displeasure, pain, great terror, and unhappiness. Beings are filled with alarm from all directions and in all directions- See! there the benighted ones cause great pain. See! there are beings individually embodied. (2)

See! there are men who control themselves; others pretend only to be houseless, for one destroy this (body of an animal) by bad and injurious doings, and many other beings, besides, which he hurts by means of animals, through his doing acts relating to animals. (3) About this the Revered One has taught the truth: for the sake of the splendour, honour, and glory of this life, for the sake of birth, death, and final liberation, for the removal of pain, man acts sinfully towards animals, or causes others to act so, or allows others to act so. This deprives him of happiness and perfect wisdom. About this he is informed, when he has understood, or heard from the Revered One or from the monks, the faith to be coveted. There are some who, of a truth, know this (i.e. injuring) to be the bondage, the illusion, the death, the hell. For this a man is longing, when he injures this (body of an animal) by bad and injurious doings, and many other beings, besides, which he hurts by means of animals, through acts relating to animals. Thus I say. (4)

Some slay (animals) for sacrificial purposes, some kill (animals) for the sake of their skin, some kill (them) for the sake of their flesh, some kill them for the sake of their blood; thus for the sake of their heart, their bile, the feathers of their tail, their tail, their big or small horns, their teeth, their tusks, their nails, their sinews, their bones; with a purpose or without a purpose. Some kill animals because they have been wounded by them, or are wounded, or will be wounded. (5)

He who injures these (animals) does not comprehend and renounce the sinful acts; he-who does not injure these, comprehends and renounces the sinful acts. Knowing them, a wise man should not act sinfully towards animals, nor cause others to act so, nor allow others to act so. He who knows these causes of sin relating to animals, is called a reward-knowing sage. Thus I say. (6)

**Seventh Lesson**

He who is averse from (all actions relating to) wind, knows affliction. Knowing what is bad, he who knows it with regard to himself, knows it with regard to (the world) outside; and he who knows it with regard to (the world) outside, knows it with regard to himself: this reciprocity (between himself and) others (one should mind). Those who are appeased, who are free from passion, do not desire to live. (i)

See! there are men who control themselves; others pretend only to be houseless, for one destroys this (wind-body) by bad and injurious doings, and many other beings, besides, which he hurts by means of wind, through his doing acts relating to wind. (2) About this the Revered

One has taught the truth: for the sake of the splendour, honour, and glory of this life, for the sake of birth, death, and final liberation, for. the removal of pain, man acts sinfully towards wind, or causes others to act so, or allows others to act so. This deprives him of happiness and perrfect wisdom. About this he is informed when he has understood, or heard from the Revered One or from the monks, the faith to be coveted. There are some who, of a truth, know this to be the bondage, the delusion, the death, the hell. For this a man is longing when he destroys this (wind-body) by bad and injurious acts, and many other -beings, besides, which he hurts by means of wind, through his doing acts relating to wind. Thus I say. (3)

There are jumping beings which, coming near wind, fall into it. Some, certainly, touched by wind, shrivel tip; those which shrivel up there, lose their sense there; those which lose their sense there, die there. (4)

He who injures these (wind-bodies) does not comprehend and renounce the sinful acts; he who does not injure these, comprehends and renounces the sinful acts. Knowing them, a wise man should not act sinfully towards wind, nor cause others to act so, nor allow others to act so. He who knows these causes of sin relating to wind, is called a rewardknowing sage. Thus I say. (5)

Be aware that about this (wind-body) too those are involved in sin who delight not in the right conduct, and, though doing acts, talk about religious discipline, who conducting themselves according to their own will, pursuing sensual pleasures, and engaging in acts, are addicted to worldliness. He who has the true knowledge about all things, will commit no sinful act, nor cause others to do so, &c. (6) Knowing them, a wise man should not act sinfully towards the aggregate of six (kinds of) lives, nor cause others to act so, nor allow others to act so. He who knows these causes of sin relating to the aggregate of the six (kinds of) lives, is'called a reward-knowing sage. Thus I say. (7)

## Second Lecture

## Conquest of The World

### First Lesson

Quality is the seat of the root, and the seat of the root is quality. He who longs for the qualities, is overcome by great pain, and he is careless. (For he thinks) I have to provide for a mother, for a father, for a- sister, for a wife, for sons, for daughters, for a daughter-in-law, for my friends, for near and remote relations, for my acquaintances, for different kinds of property, profit, meals, and clothes. Longing for these objects, people are careless, suffer day and night, work in the right and the wrong time, desire wealth and treasures, commit injuries and violent acts, direct the mind, again and again, upon these injurious doings (described in the preceding lecture). (1) (Doing so), the life of some mortals (which by destiny would have been long) is shortened. For when with the deterioration of the perceptions of the ear, eye, organs of smelling, tasting, touching, a man becomes aware of the decline of life, they after a time produce dotage. Or his kinsmen with whom he lives together will, after a time, first grumble at him, and he will afterwards grumble at them. They cannot help thee or protect thee, nor canst thou help them or protect them. (2) He is not fit for hilarity, playing, pleasure, show. Therefore, ah! proceeding to pilgrimage, and thinking that the present moment is favourable (for such intentions), he should be steadfast and not, even for an hour, carelessly conduct himself. His youth, his age, his life fade away.

A man who carelessly conducts himself, who killing, cutting, striking, destroying, chasing away, frightening (living beings) resolves to do what has not been done (by any one)-him his relations with whom he lived together, will first cherish, and he will afterwards cherish them. But they cannot help thee or protect thee, nor canst thou help them or protect them. (3)

Or he heaps up treasures for the benefit of some spendthrifts, by pinching himself. Then, after a time, he falls in sickness; those with whom he lives together will first leave him, and he will afterwards leave them. They cannot help thee or protect thee, nor canst thou help them or protect them. (4)

Knowing pain and pleasure in all their variety, and seeing his life not yet decline, a wise man should know that to be the proper moment (for entering a religious life); while the perceptions of his ear, eye, organs of smelling, tasting, touching are not yet deteriorated, while all these perceptions are not yet deteriorated, man should prosecute the real end of his Soul. Thus I say. (5)

**Second Lesson**

A wise man should remove any aversion (to control); he will be liberated in the proper time. Some, following wrong instruction, turn away (from control). They are dull, wrapped in delusion. While they imitate the life of monks, (saying), 'We shall be free from attachment,' they enjoy the pleasures that offer themselves. Through wrong instruction the (would-be) sages trouble themselves (for pleasures); thus they sink deeper and deeper in delusion, (and cannot get) to this, nor to the opposite shore. Those who are freed (from attachment to the world and its pleasures), reach the opposite shore. Subduing desire by desirelessness, he does not enjoy the pleasures that offer themselves. Desireless, giving tip the world, and ceasing to act, he knows, and sees, and has no wishes because of his discernment'; he is called houseless. (1)

(But on the contrary) he suffers day and night, works in the right and the wrong time, desires wealth and treasures, commits injuries and violent acts, again and again directs his mind upon these injurious doings; for his own sake, to support or to be supported by his relations, friends, the ancestors, gods, the king, thieves, guests, paupers, Sramanas. (2 )

Thus violence is done by these various acts, deliberately, out of fear, because they think 'it is for the expiation of sins,' or for some other hope. Knowing this, a wise man should neither himself commit violence by such acts, nor order others to commit violence by such acts, nor consent to the violence done by somebody else.

This road (to happiness) has been declared by the noble ones, that a clever man should not be defiled (by sin). Thus I say. (3)

**Third Lesson**

'Frequently (I have been born) in a high family, frequently in a low one; I am not mean, nor noble, nor do I desire (social preferment).' Thus reflecting, who would brag about his family or about his glory, or for what should he long? (1)

Therefore a wise man should neither be glad nor angry (about his lot): thou shouldst know and consider the happiness of living creatures. Carefully conducting himself, he should inind this: blindness, deafness, dumbness, one-evedness, hunchbackedness, blackness, variety of colour (he will always experience); because of his carelessness he is born in man), births, he experiences various feelings. (2)

Not enlightened (about the cause of these ills) he is afflicted (by them), always turns round (in the whirl of) birth and death. Life is dear to many who own fields and houses. Having acquired dyed and coloured (clothes), jewels, earrings, gold, and women, they become attached to these things. And a fool who longs for life, and worldly-minded, laments that (for these worldly goods) penance, self-restraint, and control do not avail, will ignorandy come to grief. (3)

Those who are of a steady conduct do not desire this (wealth). Knowing birth and death, one should firmly walk the path (i.e. right conduct), (and not wait for old age to commence a religious life),

For there is nothing inaccessible for death. All beings are fond of life, like pleasure, hate pain, shun destruction, like life, long to live. To all life is dear. (4)

Having acquired it (i.e. wealth), employing bipeds and quadrupeds, gathering riches in the three ways [by action, order or consent, that is, mind, body or speech] whatever his portion will be, small or great, he will desire to enjoy it. Then at one time, his manifold savings are a large treasure. Then at another time, his heirs divide it, or those who are without a living steal it, or the king takes it away, or it is ruined in some way or other, or it is consumed by the conflagration of the house. Thus a fool doing cruel deeds which benefit another, will ignorantly come thereby to grief. (5)

This certainly has been declared by the sage. The), do not cross the flood, nor can they cross it; they do not go to the next shore, nor can they go to it; they do not go to the opposite shore, nor can they go to it.

And though hearing the doctrine, he does not stand in the right place; but the clever one who adopts the true (faith); stands in the right place (i.e. control).

He who sees by himself, needs no instruction, But the miserable, afflicted fool who delights in pleasures, and whose miseries do not cease, is turned round in the whirl of pains. Thus I say. (6)

**Fourth Lesson**

Then, after a time, he falls in sickness: those with

whom he lives together, first grumble at him, and he afterwards grumbles at them. But they cannot help thee or protect thee, nor canst thou help them or protect them. (1)

Knowing pleasure and pain separately, they trouble themselves about the enjoyment (of the external objects). For some men in this world have (such a character that) they will desire to enjoy their portion, whether it be large or small, in the three ways. Then, at one time, it will be sufficiently large, with many resources. Then, -at another time, his heirs divide it, or those who have no living steal it, or the king takes it away, or it is ruined in some way or other, or it is consumed by the conflagration of the house. Thus a fool, doing cruel acts, comes ignorantly to grief. (2)Wisely reject hope and desire, and extracting that thorn (i.e.pleasure) thou (shouldst act rightly). People who are enveloped by delusion do not understand this: he who (gathers wealth) will, perhaps, nbt have the benefit of it.

The world is greatly troubled by women. They (viz. men) forsooth say, 'These are- the vessels (of happiness).' But this leads them to pain, to delusion, to death, to hell, to birth as hell-beings or brute beasts. The fool never knows the law. (3)

Thus spake the hero: 'Be careful against this great delusion; the clever one should have done with carelessness by considering death in tranquillity, and that, the nature of which is decay (viz. the body); these (pleasures), look ! will not satisfy (thee). Therefore have done with them! Sage, look! this is the great danger, it should overcome none whomsoever. He is called a hero who is not vexed by (the hardships caused) by control. He should not be angry because the (householder) gives him little. If turned off, he should go. Thou shouldst conform to the conduct of the sages.' Thus I say. (4)

**Fifth Lesson**

That for this (viz. pleasure) the wants of the world

should be supplied by bad injurious doings: for one's own sons, daughters, daughters-in-law, kinsmen, nurses, kings, male and female slaves, male and female servants, for the sake of hospitality, of supper and breakfast, the accumulation of wealth is effected. (1)

(This is) here for the enjoyment of some men. (But a wise man) exerting himself, houseless, noble, of noble intellect, of noble perception recognises the proper moment (for all actions). He should not accept, nor cause others to accept, or permit them to accept anything unclean. Free from uncleanlinesshe should wander about. (2) Being not seen in buying and selling, he should not buy, nor cause others to buy, nor consent to the buying of others. This mendicant who knows the time, the strength (of himself), the measure (of all things), the practice, the occasion (for begging, &c.), the conduct, the religious precepts, the true condition (of the donor or hearer), who disowns all things not requisite for religious purposes, who is under no obligations, he proceeds securely (on the road to final liberation) after having cut off both (love and hate). Clothes, alms-bowls, blankets, brooms, property, straw mats, with regard to these things he should know (what is unclean). When he receives food he should know the quantity required. This has been declared by the Revered One: he should not rejoice in the receipt of a gift, nor be sorry when he gets nothing. Having got much, one should not store it away; one should abstain from things not requisite for religious purposes. With a mind different (from that of common people) a seer abandons (these things). This is the road taught by the noble ones, well acquainted with which one should not be defiled (by sin). Thus I say. (3)

Pleasures are difficult to reject, life is difficult to prolong. That man, certainly, who loves pleasures, is afflicted (by their loss), is sorry in his heart, leaves his usual ways, is troubled, suffers pain. The farsighted one who knows the world, knows its inferior part (hell), its upper part (heaven), its side-long part (the state of brute beasts). He who knows the relation (of human affairs, viz.) that he who desires for the world is always turned round (in the samsAra), is called among mortals a hero, who liberates those who are fettered. (4)

As the interior (of the body is loathsome), so is the exterior; as the exterior, so is the interior. In the interior of the body he perceives the foul interior bumours, he observes their several courses (or eruptions). A well-informed man knowing (and renouncing the body and pleasures), should not eat (his saliva); he should not oppose himself to the (current of knowledge). Certainly, that man who engages in worldly affairs, who practises many tricks, who is bewildered by his own doings, acts again and. again on that desire which increases his unrighteousness Hence the above has been said for the increase of this (life). (A man addicted to pleasures) acts as if immortal, and puts great faith (in pleasure); but when he perceives that this body sustains pains, he cries in his ignorance. Therefore keep in your mind what I say. (5)

A heretic professes to cure (the love of pleasure), while he kills, cuts, strikes, destroys, chases away, resolves to do what has not been done before. To whom he applies the cure-enough of that fool's affection; or he who has (the cure) applied, is a fool. This does not apply to the houseless. Thus I say. (6)

**Sixth Lesson**

He who perfectly understands (what has been said in the preceding lesson) and follows the (faitb~ to be coveted, should therefore do no sinful act, nor cause others to do one. Perchance he meditates a sin (by an act against only) one (of the six aggregates of lives); but he will be guilty (of sin against) every one of the six. Desiring happiness and bewailing much, he comes ignorantly to grief through his own misfortune. (i) Through his own carelessness every one produces that phase of life in which the vital spirits are pained. Observing (the pain of mundane existence, one should) not (act) with violence. This is called the true knowledge (and renunciation). He who ceasing from acts relinquishes the idea of property, relinquishes property itself. That sage has seen the path,(to final liberation) for ' whom there exists no property. Knowing this, a wise man, who knows the world and has cast off the idea of the world, should prudently conquer the obstructions to righteousness. Thus I say. (2)

The hero does not tolerate discontent,

The hero does not tolerate lust.

Because the hero is not careless,

The hero is not attached (to the objects of the senses).

Being indifferent against sounds (and the other) perceptions, detest the comfort of this life.

A sage adopting a life of wisdom, should treat his gross body roughly.

The heroes who have right intuition, use mean and rough food.

Such a man is said to have crossed the flood (of life), to be a sage, to have passed over (the samsara), to be liberated, to have ceased (from all activity). Thus I say. (3)

A sage is called unfit who does not follow the law and fails in his office. (But on the contrary) he is praised as a hero, he overcomes the connection with the world, he is called the guide (or the right way). What has been declared to be here the unhappiness of mortals, of that unhappiness the clever ones propound the knowledge. (4)

Thus understanding (and renouncing) acts, a man who recognises the truth, delights in nothing else; and he who delights only in the truth, recognises nothing else. As (the law) has been revealed for the full one, so for the empty one; as for the empty one, so for the full one. But he (to whom the faith is preached) will perhaps disrespectfully beat (the preacher). Yet know, there is no good in this (indiscriminate preaching). (But ascertain before) what sort of man he is, and whom he worships. He is called a hero who liberates the bound, above, below, and in the sideward directions. He always conforms to all knowledge (and renunciation); the hero is not polluted by the sin of killing. he is a wise man who perfectly knows the non-killing, who searches after the liberation of the bound. The clever one is neither bound nor liberated; he should do or leave undone (what the hero does or does not do); he should not do what (the hero) leaves undone:

> Knowing (and renouncing) murder of any kind and worldly ideas in ' all respects.

He who sees himself, needs no instruction. But the miserable and afflicted fool who delights in pleasures and whose miseries do not cease, is turned round in the whirl of pains . Thus I say. (5)

End of the Second Lecture, called Conquest of the World.

**Third Lecture**

**Called**

**Hot and Cold**

**First Lesson**

The unwise sleep, the sages always wake. Know, that in this world the (cause of) misery brings forth evil consequences! Knowing the course of the world, one should cease from violent acts. He who correctly possesses these (sensual perceptions), viz. sounds, and colours, and smells, and tastes, and touches (1), who self-possessed, wise, just, chaste, With right comprehension understands the world, he is to be called a sage, one who knows the law, and righteous. He knows the connection of the whirl (of births) and the Current (of sensation with love and hate). Not minding heat and cold, eqvanimous against pleasure and pain, the Nirgrantha does not feel the austerity of penance. Waking and free from hostility, a wise man, thou liberatest (thyself and others) from the miseries. (2)

But a man always benighted, subject to old age and death, does not know the law. Seeing living beings suffering, earnestly enter a religious life. Considering this, O prudent one, look!

Knowing the misery that results from action,

The deluded and careless one returns to life;

Disregarding sounds and colours, upright,

Avoiding Mara one is liberated from death.

Carefully abstaining from pleasures and ceasing from bad works he is a hero, guarding himself, who is grounded in knowledge. (3) He who knows the violence done for the sake of special objects, knows what is free from violence; he who knows what is free from violence, knows the violence done for special objects. For him who is without karman, there is no appellation. The condition of living beings arises from karman.

Examining karman and the root of karman, viz. killing, examining (it) and adopting its contrary, he is not seen by both ends. Knowing this, a wise man who knows the world and has cast off the idea of the world, should prudently conquer the obstructions to righteousness Thus I say. (4)

**Second Lesson**

Look, Sir, at birth and old age here,

Examine and know the happiness of the living,

Thence the most learned, I knowing (what is called) the highest good,

He who has right intuition, commits no sin. (1).

Undo the bond with mortals here;

He who lives by sins, is subject to both

Desirous of pleasures they heap up karman,

Influenced by it they are born again. (2)

Killing (animals) he thinks good sport, and derives mirth from it:

Away with that fool's company, he increases his own unrighteousness. (3)

Thence the most learned, knowing (what is called) the highest good,

Aware of the punishment, commits no sin;

Wisely avoid the top and the root!

Cutting them off, he knows himself free from karman.(4)

That man will be liberated from death; he is a sage who sees the danger, knowing the highest good in this world, leading a circumspect life, calm, guarded, endowed (with knowledge, &c.), always restrained, longing for death, he should lead a religious life. Manifold, indeed, appear sinful actions; therefore prove constant to truth ! Delighting in it, a wise nian destroys all karman. (1)

Many, indeed, are the plans Of this man (of the world); he will satisfy his desires; he (thereby causes) the slaughter of others, the pain of others, the punishment of others, the slaughter, the blame, the punishment of a whole province. Doing such things, some have exerted themselves. (2)

Therefore the second (i.e. the wrong creed) is not adhered to. The knowing one seeing the vanity (of the world) [knowing the rise and fall of the souls], the Brahman follows the unrivalled (control of the Gainas). He should not kill, nor cause others to kill, nor consent to the killing of others. 'Avoid gaiety, not delighting in creatures (i.e. women), having the highest intuition,' keeping off from sinful acts. (3)

And the hero should conquer wrath and pride,
Look at the great hell (as the place) for greed.
Therefore the hero abstaining from killing,
Should destroy sorrow, going the road of easiness
Here now the hero, knowing the bondage,
Knowing sorrow, should restrain himself.
Having risen to birth among men,
He should not take the life of living beings.

**Third Lesson**

Knowing the connection of the world, (carelessness is not for his benefit).' 'Look at the exterior (world from analogy with thy own) self; [then] thou wilt neither kill nor destroy (living beings);' viz. out of reciprocal regard [well examining] he does no sinful act. What is the characteristic of a sage?' Recognising the equality (of all living beings), he appeases himself.' (1)

Knowing the highest good, onc should never be careless;
Guarding one's self, always prudent, one should pass life on the right road.

'One should acquire disregard of sensual enjoyment, being with a great one (i.e. a god) or the small ones (men).' When one knows whence men come and where they go, and when both ends are out of sight, one is not cut, nor slit, nor burnt, nor struck (2) by any one in the whole world.

Some do not remember what preceded the present: 'what has been his past? what will be his future?' Some men here say: 'what has been his past, that will be his future.'

There is no past thing, nor is there a future one

So opine the Tathagatas.

He whose karman has ceased and conduct is right, who recognises the truth (stated above) and destroys sinfulness (thinks):

What is discontent and what is pleasure? not subject to either, one should live;

Giving up all gaiety, circumspect and restrained, one should lead a religious life. (3)

Man! Thou art thy own friend; why wishest thou for a friend beyond thyself? Whom he knows as a dweller on high, him he should know as a dweller far (from sin); and whom he knows as a dweller far (from sin), him he should know as a dweller on high. Man! restraining thyself (from the outward world) 'thou wilt get free from pain.' Man, understand well the truth! exerting himself in the rule of truth a wise man overcomes Mara. (4)

'The gifted man, following the law, sees well his true interest.' In a twofold ways, for the sake of life's splendour, honour and glory (some men exert themselves), wherein they go astray. The gifted, touched by calamity, are not confounded. 'Mind this! the worthy one, in this world, gets out of thr creation' Thus I say. (5)

**Fourth Lesson**

That man (i.e. the liberated) conquers wrath, pride, deceit, and greed. This is the doctrine of the Seer who does not injure living beings and has put an end (to acts and to samsara). Preventing propensity to sin destroys former actions. He who knows one thing, knows all things; and he who knows all things, knows one thing. He who is careless in all respects, is in danger; he who is not careless in all respects, is free from danger. (1)

He who conquers one (passion), conquers many; and he who conquers many, conquers one. 'Knowing the misery of the world' rejecting the connection with the world, 'the heroes go on the great journey,' they rise gradually; 'they do not desire life.' (2)

He who avoids one (passion), avoids (them all) severally; and he who avoids them severally, avoids one. Faithful according to the commandment (of the Tirthakaras), wise, and understanding the world according to the commandment - such a man is without danger from anywhere. There are degrees in injurious acts, but there are no degrees in control. (3)

He who knows wrath, knows pride; he who knows pride, knows deceit; he who knows deceit, knows greed; he who knows greed, knows love; he who knows love, knows hate; he who knows hate, knows delusion; he who knows delusion, knows conception; he who knows 'conception, knows birth; he who knows birth, knows death; he who knows death, knows hell; he who knows hell, knows animal existence; he who knows animal existence, knows pain.

Therefore, a wise man should avoid wrath, pride, deceit, greed, love, hate, delusion, conception, birth, death, hell, animal existence, and pain.

This is the doctrine of the Seer, who does not injure living beings and has put an end (to acts and to samsara). Preventing the propensity to sin destroys former actions. Is there any worldly weakness in the Seer? There exists none, there is none. Thus I say. (4)

End of the Third Lecture, called Hot and Cold.

**Fourth Lecture**

**Called**

**Righteousness**

**First Lesson**

The Arhats and Bhagavats of the past, present, and future, all say thus, speak thus, declare thus, explain thus:

answer, reply: For all sorts of living beings pain is unpleasant, disagreeable, and greatly feared. Thus I say. (6)

**Third Lesson**

Reflect and observe that whether you go to this world or to that beyond, in the whole world those who are discerning beings', who abstain from cruelty relinquish karman. They are flesh-subduing, called duty-knowing, upright men, aware that pain results from actions.' Thus say those who have right intuition. (1)

All the professors, conversant with pain, preach renunciation. Thus thoroughly knowing karman, observing the commandment, wise, unattached (to the world), recognising thy Self as one, subdue the body, chastise thyself, weaken thyself: 'just as fire consumes old wood!' Thus with a composed mind, unattached, 'unhesitatingly avoid wrath!' Considering the shortness of life 'know pain, or what will come;' one shall feel the several feelings; and perceive the world suffering under them. (2)

Those who are free from sinful acts are called anidina. Hence a very wise man should not be inflamed (by wrath). Thus I say. (3)

**Fourth Lesson**

One should mortify (one's flesh) in a low, high, and highest degree, quitting one's former connections, and entering tranquillity. Therefore a hero is careful, a person of pith, guarded, endowed (with knowledge, &c.), and always restrained. Difficult to go is the road of the heroes, who go whence there is no return (final liberation). Subdue blood and flesh. (1)

That man is called a worthy one, a hero, one to be followed, who living in chastity [guarding his eyes] shakes off the aggregate.

He who desires the current of karman, is a fool who

has-not cut off the fetters of, nor conquered the connection with, (the world.) For such as dwell in darkness, and are without knowledge, there is no success in faith. Thus I say.(2)

'Whence should he have it, who does not get it early, late, or in the middle of life?' But the discerning one is awakened, and ceases to act. See that it is good to be so! Cutting off that 'whence bondage, cruel death, and dreadful pain,' 'and the (desire for) external (objects) flow, he who among mortals knows freedom from acts,' 'seeing that acts will bear fruit, the knower of the sacred lore, parts from (karman).' (3)

There are those who have established theniselves in the truth, who (were, are, or will be) heroes, endowed (with knowledge), always exerting themselves, full of equanimity, valuing the world (as it deserves) in the east, west, south, north. We shall tell the knowledge of them who (were, &c.) heroes, endowed (with knowledge), always exerting themselves, full of equanimity, valuing the world (as it deserves).

Is there any worldly weakness in the Seer? There exists none, there is none. Thus I say. (4)

End of the Fourth Lecture, called Righteousness.

**Fifth Lecture,**

**Called**

**Essence of The World**

**First Lesson**

Many entertain cruel thoughts against the world with a motive or without one; they entertain cruel thoughts against these (six classes of living beings). To him, pleasures are clear. Therefore he is near death. Because he is near death, he is far (from liberation). But he who is neither near (death) nor far (from liberation), considers the life of a slow and ignorant fool as similar to a dewdrop trembling on the sharp point of the blade of Kusa grass which falls down when shaken by the wind. A fool, doing cruel acts, comes thereby ignorantly to grief. Through delusion he is born, dies, &c.' Being conversant with the deliberation about this delusion, one is conversant with the samsara; being not conversant with that deliberation, one is not conversant with the samsara. He who is clever, should not seek after sexual intercourse. But having done so, (it would be) a second folly of the weak-minded not to own it. Repenting and excluding (from the mind) the begotten pleasures, one should instruct others to follow the commandment. Thus I say. (1)

See! many who desire colours, are led around (in the samsara), they (experience) here again and again feelings (i.e. punishment). Many live by injurious deeds against the world, they live by injurious deeds against these (living beings). Also the fool, suffering (for his passions), delights in bad acts here, mistaking that for salvation which is none. Many (heretics) lead the life of a hermit (in order to avoid worldly sorrows and pains). (2)

Such a man has much wrath, much pride, much conceit, much greed; he delights in many (works), acts frequently like a stage-player or a rogue, forms many plans, gives way to his impulses, is influenced by his acts though he pretends to be awakened: (thinking) that nobody will see him. Through the influence of ignorance and carelessness the fool never knows the law. Men! unhappy creatures, world-wise are those who, not freeing themselves from ignorance, talk about final liberation: they turn round and round in the whirlpool (of births). Thus I say. (3)

**Second Lesson**

Many do not live by injurious deeds against the world, they do not live by injurious deeds against these (living beings). Ceasing from them, making an end of them, he perceives: this is a favourable opportunity; he who searches for the right moment for this body (should never be careless). This is the road taught by the noble ones. (1)

When he has become zealous for the law, he should never be careless, knowing pain and pleasure in their various forms. Men act here on their own motives; it has been declared that they suffer for their own sins. Neither killing nor lying, he should (patiently) bear (all unpleasant) feelings when affected by them. That man is called a true monk. (2)

Those who are not given to sinful acts are (nevertheless) attacked by calamities; but then the steadfast will bear them. (he has to bear) them afterwards as (he has done) before (his conversion). (The body) is of a fragile, decaying nature, (it is) unstable, transient, tineternal, increasing and decreasing of a changeable nature. Perceive this as its true character. For him who well understands this, who delights in the unique refuge, for the liberated and inactive there is no passage (from birth to birth). Thus I Say. (3)

Many are attached to something in the world - be it little or much, small or great, sentient or nonsentient - they are attached to it (here) amongst these (householders). Thus some incur great danger. For him who contemplates the course of the world and does not acknowledge these attachments (there is no such danger). Knowing that that which is well understood is well practised, man! with thy eyes on the highest good, be victorious (in control). Among such men only is real Brahmanhood. Thus I say. (4)

1 have heard this, and it is in my innermost heart; and the freedom from bonds is in your innermost heart. He who has ceased (to have worldly attachments), the houseless, suffers with patience a long time.

The careless stand outside, the careful lead a religious life. Maintain rightly this state of a sage. Thus I say. (5)

**Third Lesson**

Many are not attached to something in this world, they are not attached to it among these (householders). He is a wise man who has heard and understood the word of the learned ones. Without partiality the law has been declared by the noble ones. As I have destroyed here the connection with the world, so is the connection elsewhere difficult to destroy. Therefore I say: One should not abandon firmness. (1) Some who early exert themselves,do not afterwards slide back; some who early exert themselves, afterwards slide back; those who do not early exert themselves, (can of course) not' slide back. That man also is of this description, who knowing the world (as worthless nevertheless) follows its ways. 'Knowing this, it has been declared by the sage.' Here the follower of the commandment, the wise, the passionless, he who exerts himself before morning and after evening, always contemplating virtue and hearing (the merit of it) will become free from love and delusion. 'Fight with this (your body)! why should you fight with anything else?' Difficult to attain is this (human body) which is worth the fight. For the clever ones have praised the discernment of wisdom; the fool who falls from it, is liable to birth, &c. (2) In this (religion of the Gainas the cause of the fool's fall) has been declared (to depend) on colour and killing. But a sage who walks the beaten track (to liberation), regards the world in a different way. 'Knowing thus (the nature of) acts in all regards, he does not kill,' he controls himself, he is not overbearing. (3)

Comprehending that pleasure (and pain) are individual, advising kindness, he will not engage in any work in the whole world: keeping before him the one (great aim, liberation), and not turning aside, 'living humbly, unattached to any creature! The rich (in control) who with a mind endowed with all penetration (recognises) that a bad deed should not be done, will not go after it. What you acknowledge as righteousness, that you acknowledge as sagedom (mauna); what you acknowledge as sagedom, that you acknowledge as righteousness. It is inconsistent with weak, sinning, sensual, ill-conducted house-inhabiting men. (4) 'A sage, acquring sagedom, should subdue his body.' 'The heroes who look at everything with indifference, use mean and rough (food, &c.)' Such a man is said to have crossed the flood (of life), to be a sage, to have passed over (the samsara), to be liberated, to have ceased (from acts). This I say. (5)

**Fourth Lesson**

For a monk who has not yet reached discrimination, it is bad going and difficult proceeding when he wanders (alone) from village to village. Some men (when going wrong) will become angry when exhorted with speech. And a man with wary pride is embarrassed with great delusion (1) There are many obstacles which are very difficult to overcome for the ignorant and the blinded. Let that not be your case! That is the doctrine of the clever one (Mahavira). Adopting the (Akarya's) views, imitating his indifference (for the outer world), making him the guide and adviser (in all one's matters), sharing his abode, living carefully, acting according to his mind, examining one's way, not coming too near (the akarya), minding living beings, one should go (on one's business). (2)

(A monk should according to the akarya's order) go and return, contract or stretch (his limbs), thoroughly clean (what ought to be cleaned). Sometimes, though a monk be endowed with virtue and walks in righteousness, living beings, coming in contact with his body, will be killed. (If this happens through mere carelessness) then he will get his punishment in this life; but if it was done contrary to the rules, he should repent of it and do penance for it. Thus he who knows the sacred lore, recommends penance combined with carefulness. (3) (When a monk) with fully developed intuition and knowledge, calm, guarded, endowed (with knowledge), always restrained, perceives (a woman tempting him), he should consider within himself: what will this person do? The greatest temptation in this world are women. This has been declared by the sage. (4)

When strongly vexed by the influence of the senses, he should eat bad food, mortify himself, stand upright, wander from village to village, take no food at all, withdraw his mind from women. First troubles, then pleasures; first pleasures, then troubles: thus they are the cause of quarrels. Considering this and well understanding it, one should teach oneself not to cultivate (sensuality). Thus I say. He should not speak of women, nor look at them, nor converse with them, nor claim them as his own, nor do their work. Careful in his speech and guirding his mind, he should always avoid sin. He should maintain this sagedom. Thus I say. (5)

**Fifth Lesson**

Thus I say: a lake is full of water, it is in an even plain, it is free from dust, it harbours (many fish). Look! he (the teacher) stands in the stream (of knowledge) and is guarded in all directions. Look! there are great Seers in the world,wise, awakened, free from acts. Perceive the truth: from a desire of (a pious) end they chose a religious life. Thus I say. (I)

He whose mind is always wavering, does not reach abstract contemplation. Some, bound (by worldly ties), are followers (i. e. understand the truth); some who are not bound, are followers. How should he not despond who amongst followers is a non-follower? 'But that is truth beyond doubt, what has been declared by the Ginas.' (2)

Whatever a faithful, well-disposed man, on entering the order, thought to be true, that may afterwards appear to him true; what he thought to be true, that may afterwards appear to him untrue; what he thought to be untrue, that may afterwards appear to him true; what he thought to be untrue, that may afterwards appear to him true. What he thinks to be true, that may, on consideration, appear to him true, whether it be true or untrue. What he thinks to be untrue, that may, on consideration, appear to him untrue, whether it be true or untrue. But hewho reflects should say unto him who does not reflect: Consider it to be true. Thus the connection (i. e. the continuity of sins) is broken. (3)

Regard this as the course of,the zealous one, who stands (in obedience to the spiritual guide). In this point do not show yourself a fool!

As it would be unto thee, so it is with him whom thou intendest to kill. As it would be unto thee, so it is with him whom thou intendest to tyrannise over. As it would be unto thee, so it is with him whom thou intendest to torment. In the same way (it is with him) whom thou intendest to punish, and to drive away. The righteous man who lives up to these sentiments, does therefore neither kill nor cause others to kill (living beings). He should not intentionally cause the same punishment for himself. (4)

The Self is the knower (or experiencer), and the knower is the Self. That through which one knows, is the Self. With regard to this (to know) it (the Self) is established. Such is he who maintains the right doctrine of Self. This subject has truly been explained. Thus I say. (5)

**Sixth Lesson**

Some not instructed (in the true law) make (only a show) of good conduct; some, though instructed, have no good conduct. Let that not be your case! That is the doctrine of the clever one. Adopting the (akarya's) views, imitating his indifference (for the outer world), making him the guide and adviser (in all one's matters), sharing his abode, conquering (sinfulness), one sees the truth; unconquered one should be one's own master, having no reliance on anything (in the world). He who is great and withdraws his mind from the outer world, should learn the teaching (of the Tirthakaras) through the teaching (of the akarya); by his own innate knowledge, or through the instruction of the highest, or having heard it from others. A wise man should not break the commandment. Examining all (wrong) doctrines from all sides and in all respects, one should clearly understand, (and reject) them. 'Knowing the delight of this world, circumspect and restrained, one should lead the life of an ascetic.' Desiring liberation, a hero should, through the sacred lore, ever be victorious. Thus I say. (1)

The current (of Sin) is said to come from above, from below, and from the sides; these have been declared to be the currents through which, look, there is sinfulness.

'Examining the whirlpool, a man, versed in the sacred lore, should keep off from it.' Leaving the world to avert the current (of sin), such a great man, free from acts, knows and sees the truth; examining (pleasures) he does not desire them. (2) Knowing whence we come and whither we go, he leaves the road to birth and death, rejoicing in the glorious (liberation). 'All sounds recoil thence, where speculation has no room,' nor does the mind penetrate there. The saint knows well that which is without support. (3)

(The liberated) is not long nor small nor round nor triangular nor quadrangular nor circular; he is not black nor blue nor red nor green nor white; neither of good nor bad smell; not bitter nor pungent nor astringent nor sweet; neither rough nor soft; neither heavy nor light; neither cold nor hot; neither harsh nor smooth; he is without body, without resurrection, without contact (of matter), he is not feminine nor masculine nor neuter; he perceives, he knows, but there is no analogy (whereby to know the nature of, the liberated. soul); its essence is without form; there is no condition of the unconditioned. There is no sound, no colour, no smell, no taste, no touch-nothing of that kind. Thus I say. (4)

End of the Fifth Lecture, called Essence of the World.

**Sixth Lecture,**

**CALLED**

**THE CLEANING.**

**FIRST LESSON.**

He who is awakened amongst men, preaches; the man to whom all these classes of lives are well known, preaches the unparalleled wisdom. He praises the road to liberation for those who well exert themselves, who have forsworn cruelty, are zealous and endowed with knowledge. Thus some great heroes are victorious; but, look, some others who are wanting in control do not understand (the welfare of) their souls. Thus I say. (1)

As in a lake a greedy leaf-covered tortoise cannot rise tip; as the trees do not leave their-place (though shaken by storms, &c.): thus men, born in various families, cry bitterly because they are attached to the objects of the senses; on account of their sinfulness they do not reach liberation. (2)

Now look at those who are born in these families to reap the fruit of their own acts:

Bolls and leprosy, consumption, falling sickness, blindness and stiffness, lameness and hump-backedness,

Dropsy and dumbness, look! apoplexy(?) and eye-disease, trembling and crippledness, elephantiasis and diabetes,

These are the sixteen diseases enumerated in due order; besides them many illnesses and wounds occur.

Contemplating their (i.e. the creatures') death, knowing their births in higher and lower regions, contemplating the fruit (of their acts), hear about this according to truth.

There are said to be blind beings dwelling in darkness; once or frequently meeting this lot, they experience pleasant and unpleasant feelings. This has been declared by the awakened ones. (3) There are beings endowed with voice, with taste, waterbeings dwelling in water, beings living in the air: 'beings torment beings. See the great danger in this world;' many pains (are the lot) of the creatures. Men who are given to their lusts, come to destruction through their weak, frail body. 'The fool works hard, thinking' that the unhappy one suffers many pains. 'Knowing that these diseases are many, should the afflicted search after (remedies)?' See! they are of no avail, have done with them! Sage! see this great danger! Do not hurt anybodyl Contemplate. Be attentive! I shall proclaim the doctrine of renunciation. (4)

To reap the fruit of their acts they are born in these various families, they increase, are born, grow up, become awakened, and leave the world in due order as great sages. The lamenting parents say to them who proceed on the glorious road: 'Do not leave us!' (5) Consulting their own pleasure, indulging their passions, 'making a noise, the parents cry:' No man who leaves his parents is (fit to become) a flood-crossing sage! (The ascetic) does not take refuge there (in his family); for what could attract him there?

He should always maintain this knowledge! Thus I say.(6)

**Second Lesson**

Though some know the misery of the world, have relinquished their former connections, have given up case, live in chastity, and, whether monk or layman, thoroughly understand the law, they are not able (to persevere in a religious life). The ill-disposed, giving up the robe, alms-bowl, blanket, and broom, do not bear the continuous hardships that are difficult to bear. He who prefers pleasures will, now or after an hour, be deprived (of the body, not to recover it) for an infinite space of time. And thus they do not cross (the samsara), for the sake of these pleasures which entail evil consequences and are associated with others of their kind. (1)

But some who embrace the law, will practise it, being careful about its outward signs; not giving way to worldliness, but bein- firin. Knowing (and renouncing) all lust, a devout man becomes a great sage when he breaks all bonds, thinking: Nothing belongs to me. A man who, thinking, I am I, exerts himself for this (creed), ceases (to act), is houseless, walks about bald-headed. The naked, fasting (monk), who combats the flesh, will be abused, or struck, or hurt; he will be upbraided with his former trade, or reviled with untrue reproaches. Accounting (for this treatment) by his former sins, knowing pleasant and unpleasant occurrences, he should patiently wander about. Quitting all worldliness one should bear all (disagreeable) feelings, being possessed of the right view. (2)

Those are called naked, who in this world, never returning (to a worldly state), (follow) my religion according to the commandinent. This highest doctrine has here been declared for men. Delighted with this, destroying that (i.e. the effect of works), he will successively give up sinfulness, after having come to a knowledge of it. Here (in our religion) some live as single mendicants. Therefore a wise man should lead the life of an ascetic by collecting pure alms or any alms in all sorts of families. 'If (the food) be of good or bad smell, or if dreadful beasts inflict pain on (other) beings'- all that happens to you, you will firmly bear it. Thus I say. (3)

**Third Lesson**

A sage who is well instructed in the law and leads

a life of abstinence, is always a destroyer of the effects of works. To a mendicant who is little clothed and firm in control, it will not occur (to think): My clothes are torn, I shall beg for (new) clothes; I shall beg for thread; I shall beg for a needle; I shall mend (my clothes); I shall darn them; I shall repair them; I shall put them on; I shall wrap myself in them. (1)

The unclothed one, who excels in this (abstinence), will often be molested by (sharp blades of) grass, by cold, heat, gnats, and mosquitoes. The unclothed one, who effects scarcity (of his wants or of his karman), bears these and various other hardships. He is fit for penance, as has been declared by the Revered One. Understanding this in all respects and with his whole mind, he should perfectly know righteousness. The great heroes (i.e. the Tirthakaras) who for a long time walked in the former years, the worthy ones bore the troubles (mentioned above); endowed with perfect knowledge they had lean arms and very little flesh and blood. He who discontinues (to sin) and is enlightened, is said to have crossed (the samsara), to be liberated, and to have ceased (to act). Thus I say. (2)

But can discontent lay hold of a mendicant, who has ceased to act and leads a religious life, for a long time controlling himself? He advances in his spiritual career and exerts himself. As an island which is never covered with water, so is the law taught by the noble ones (a safe refuge for those in danger). They are free from desires, free from murder, beloved, wise, learned. For their benefit has been the exertion of the Revered One; as birds (feed) their young ones, so are the disciples regularly to be instructed day and night. Thus I say. (3)

**Fourth Lesson**

The disciples are thus regularly instructed, day and

night, by the knowledge-endowed great heroes, receiving knowledge from them. Some, being seduced from the calmness of the mind, adopt rough manners. Some, living in chastity, dispute the authority (of the teacher), others hear and understand his words; they intend to lead a godly life, but having left the world, they are not qualified (for a religious life). Others, being incensed by lusts, greedy, sensual, 'do not care for abstract meditation and religious instruction: these men speak harshly unto the teacher.' It is a second folly of the slow-minded to call virtuous, calm, religiously living men worthless.

Some, turning from (control), assign its difficulty as their reason (for doing so); others, falling from the pure knowledge and defiling the creed, though not without devotion, for the love of life. change (their vows). 'When they feel the hardships (of a religious life) they slide back, for their love of life.' Their leaving the world is a bad leaving. (1)

Those who deserve to be called fools, are born again and again. Standing low (in learning or control) they will exalt themselves (and say) in their pride: I am learned. They speak harshly unto the passionless; they upbraid them with their former trades, or revile them with untrue reproaches. The wise, therefore, should know the law. Thou lovest unrighteousness, because thou art young, and lovest acts, and sayest: 'Kill beings;' thou killest them or consentest to their being killed by others. (Such a man) thinks contemp-tuously: A very severe religion has been proclaimed. Sinking in opposition to the law, he is called murderer. Thus I say.(2)

Some think: What have I to do with this or that man? Thus they leave father and mother, kith and kin, like heroes exerting themselves, free from murder. Look! the pious and calm become desponding; the rising, cast down. Those troubled with sensuality, the cowardly men become perverters of the faith. Therefore the reputation of some becomes bad. He is an apostate ascetic! He is an apostate ascetic I

Look! Some, though living with religious, pious, calm, and worthy (monks), are not religious, nor pious, nor calm, nor worthy. Knowing them, the learned, the wise, the steadfast hero will always be victorious through the right faith. Thus I say. (4)

**Fifth Lesson**

Staying in or between houses, in or between villages, in or between towns, in or between counties, a monk is attacked by murderers, or is subject to the hardships (of a mendicant's life). A hero should bear these hardships. (1)

A Saint, with right intuition, who cherishes compassion for the world, in the east, west, south, and north, should preach, spread, and praise (the faith), knowing the sacred lore. He should proclaim it among those who exert themselves, and those who do not, among those who are willing to hear (the word). (2)

Not neglecting tranquillity, indifference, patience, liberation, purity, uprightness, gentleness, and freedom from worldly cares, one should, with due consideration, preach the law of the mendicants to all sorts of creatures. (3)

With due consideration preaching the law of the mendicants, one should do no injury to one's self, nor to anybody else, nor to any of the four kinds of living beings. But a great sage, neither injuring nor injured, becomes a shelter for all sorts of afflicted creatures, even as an island, which is never covered with water. (4)

Thus a man who exerts himself, and is of a steady mind, without attachment, unmoved (by passion) but restless (in wandering about), having no worldly desires, should lead the life of an ascetic.

Having contemplated the beautiful law, the discerning one is liberated.

Therefore look at worldliness, ye men, fettered in fetters!

Those whom lust conquers, sink; therefore do not shrink from the hard (control)! He who knows (and renounces) perfectly and thoroughly these injurious acts, from whom the injurers do not shrink, 'who has shaken off wrath, pride,' delusion, and greed, 'he is called a removed one.' Thus I say. (5)

On the decay of the body (he does not despond, but deserves) his appellation, 'the leader of the battle.' The sage who has reached the other side, unafflicted and unmoved like a beam, being in the power of death, desires death as the dissolution of the body. Thus I say. (6)

End of the Sixth Lecture, called the Cleaning.

**Seventh Lecture,**

**Called**

**Liberation**

**First Lesson**

I say: To friendly or hostile (heretics) one should not give food, drink, dainties and spices, clothes, alms-bowls, and brooms; nor exhort these persons to give (such things), nor do them service, always showing the highest respect. Thus I say. (1)

(A heretic may say): Know this for certain having or not having received food, &c. (down to) brooms, having or not having eaten (come to our house), even turning from your way or passing (other houses; we shall supply your wants). Confessing an individual creed, coming and going, he may give, or exhort to give, or do service (but one should not accept anything from him), showing not the

one gown, or with no clothes-aspiring to freedom from bonds. Penance suits him. Knowing what the Revered One has declared, one should thoroughly and in all respects conform to it. (1)

When it occurs to a blessed mendicant that he suffers pain, and cannot bear the influence of cold, he should not try to obviate these trials, but stand fast in his own self which is endowed with all knowledge. 'For it is better for an ascetic that he should take poison.' Even thus he will in due time put an end to existence. This (way to escape trials) has been adopted by many who were free from delusion; it is good, wholesome, proper, beatifying, meritorious. Thus I say. (2)

**Fifth Lesson**

A mendicant who is fitted out with two robes, and a bowl as third (article), will not think: I shall beg for a third robe. He should beg for robes which are allowed to be begged for; he should wear the clothes, &c. &c. This is the whole outfit of one who wears clothes. But know further, that after the winter is gone and the hot season has come, one should leave off the used-up garments; having left off the used-up garments, (one should) be clad with the undermost garment, with a gown, or with no clothes at all-aspiring to freedom from bonds. Penance suits him. Knowing what the Revered One has declared, one should thoroughly and in all respects conform to it. (1) ,

When the thought occurs to a mendicant that through illness he is too weak, and.not able to beg from house to house-and on-his thus complaining a householder brings food, &c., obtained (without injuring life), and gives it him-then he should, after deliberation, say: O long-lived householder! it does not become me to eat or drink this food, &c., or (accept) anything else of the same kind. (2)

A mendicant who has resolved, that he will, when

sick, accept the assistance of fellow-ascetics in good health, when they offer (assistance) without being asked, and that vice versa he, when in health, will give assistance to sick fellow-ascetics, offering it without being asked-(he should not deviate from his resolution though he die for want of help). (3)

Taking the vow to beg (food, &c.) for another (who is sick), and to eat (when sick) what is brought by another; taking the vow to beg, &c., and not to eat what is brought; taking the vow not to beg, &c., but to eat what is brought; taking the vow neither to beg, &c., nor to eat what is brought (one should adhere to that vow). Practising thus the law as it has been declared, one becomes tranquil, averted from sin, guarded against the allurements of the senses. Even thus (though sick) he will in due time put an end to existence. This (method) has been adopted by many who were free from delusion; it is good, wholesome, proper, beatifying, meritorious. Thus I say. (4)

**Sixth Lesson**

A mendicant who is fitted out with one robe, and a bowl as second (article), will not think: I shall beg for a second robe. He should beg for such a robe only as is allowed to be begged for, and he should wear it in the same state as he receives it. This is, &c. (see lesson 4, § 1).

But when the hot season has come, one should leave off the used-up clothes; one should be clad with one or no garment-aspiring to freedom from bonds. Knowing what the Revered One, &c. (see lesson 5, §1)

When the thought occurs to a mendicant: 'I am myself, alone; I have nobody belonging to me, nor do I belong to anybody,' then he should thoroughly know himself as standing alone-aspiring to freedom from bonds. Penance suits him. Knowing what the Revered One has declared, one should thoroughly and in all respects conform to it. (1)

A male or female mendicant eating food &c. should not shift (the morsel) from the left jaw to the right jaw, nor from the right jaw to the left jaw, to get a fuller taste of it, not caring for the taste (of it)-aspiring to freedom from bonds. Penance suits him. Knowing what the Revered One has declared, one should thoroughly and in all respects conform to it. (2)

If this thought occurs to a monk: 'I am sick and not able, at this time, to regularly mortify the flesh,' that monk should regularly reduce his food; regularly reducing his food, and diminishing his sins, 'he should take proper care of his body, being immovable like a beam; exerting himself he dissolves his body.' (3)

Entering a village, or a scot-free town, or a town with an earth-wall, or a town with a small wall, or an isolated town, or a large town, or a sea-town, or a mine, or a hermitage, or the halting-places of processions, or caravans, or a capital-a monk should beg for straw; having begged for straw he should retire with it to a secluded spot. After having repeatedly examined and cleaned the ground, where there are no eggs, nor living beings, nor seeds, nor sprouts, nor dew, nor water, nor ants, nor mildew, nor waterdrops, nor mud, nor cobwebs he should spread the straw on it. Then he should there and then effect (the religious death called) itvara [fasting to death while keeping within a limited space]. (4)

> This is the truth: speaking truth, free from passion, crossing (the samsara), abating irresoluteness,

Knowing all truth and not being known, leaving this frail body, overcoming all sorts of pains and troubles through trust in this (religion), he accomplishes this fearful (religious death). Even thus he will in due time put an end to existence. This has been adopted by many who were free from delusion; it is good, wholesome, proper, beatifying, meritorious. Thus I say. (5)

**Seventh Lesson**

To a naked monk the thought occurs: I can bear the pricking of grass, the influence of cold and heat, the stinging of flies and mosquitos; these and other various painful feelings I can sustain, but I cannot leave off the covering of the privities. Then he may cover his privities with a piece of cloth.

A naked monk who perseveres in this conduct, sustains repeatedly these and other various painful feelings: the grass pricks him, heat and cold attack him, flies and mosquitos sting him. A naked monk (should be) aspiring to freedom from bonds. Penance suits him. Knowing what the Revered One has declared, one should thoroughly and in all respects conform to it. (1)

A monk who has come to any of the following resolutions,-having collected food, &c., I shall give of it to other monks, and I shall eat (what they have) brought; (or) having collected food, &c., I shall give of it to other monks, but I shall. not eat (what they have) brought; (or) having collected food, &c., I shall not give of it to other monks, but I shall eat (what they have) brought; (or) having collected food, &c., I shall not give of it to other monks, nor eat (what they have) brought; (2) (or) I shall assist a fellow-ascetic with the remnants of my dinner, which is acceptable and remained in the same state in which it was received, and I shall accept the assistance of fellow-ascetics as regards the remnants of their dinner, which is acceptable and remained in the same state in which it was received;, (that monk should keep these vows even if he should run the risk of his life) - aspiring to freedom from bonds. Penance suits him. Knowing what the Revered One has declared, one should thoroughly conform to it. (4)

(The last two paragraphs of the last lesson are to be reproduced here.) Thus I say. (5)

**Eighth Lesson**

The wise ones who attain in due order to one of the unerring states (in which suicide is prescribed), those who are rich in control and endowed with knowledge, knowing the incomparable (religious death, should continue their contemplation). (1)

Knowing the twofold (obstacleso i.e. bodily and mental), the wise ones, having thoroughly learned the law, perceiving in due order (ihat the time for their death has come), get rid of karman. (2)

Subduing the passions and living on little food, he should endure (hardships). If a mendicant falls sick, let him again take food. (3)

Be should not long for life, nor wish for death; he should yearn after neither, life or death. (4)

He who is indifferent and wishes for the destruction of karman, should continue his contemplation.

Becoming unattached internally and externally, he should strive after absolute purity. (5)

Whatever means one knows for calming one's own life, that a wise man should learn (i. e. practise) in order to gain time (for continuing penance). (6)

In a village or in a forest, examining the ground and recognising it as free from living beings, the sage should spread the straw. (7)

Without food he should he down and bear the pains which attack him. He should not for too long time give way to worldly feelings which overcome him. (8)

When crawling animals or such as live on high or below, feed on his flesh and blood, he should neither kill them nor rub (the wound). (9)

Though these animals destroy the body, he should

not stir from his position. After the Asravas have ceased, he should bear (pains) as if he rejoiced in them. (10)

When the bonds fall off, then he has accomplished his life.

(We shall now describe) a more exalted (method) for a well-controlled and instructed monk. (11)

This other law has been proclaimed by Gñatriputra:

He should give up all motions except his own in the thrice-threefold way. (12)

He should not lie on sprouts of grass, but inspecting the bare ground he should lie on it.

Without any comfort and food, he should there bear pain. (13)

When the sage becomes weak in his limbs, he should strive after calmness.

For he is blameless, who is well fixed and immovable (in his intention to die). (14)

He should move to and fro (on his ground), contract and stretch (his limbs) for the benefit of the whole body; or (he should remain quiet as if he were) lifeless. (15)

He should walk about, when tired of (lying), or stand with passive limbs; when tired of standing, he should sit down. (16)

Intent on such an uncommon death, he should regulate the motions of his organs.

Having attained a place swarming with insects, he should search for a clean spot. (17)

He should not remain there whence sin would rise.

He should raise himself above (sinfulness), and bear all pains. (18)

And this is a still more difficult method, when one lives according to it: not to stir from one's place, while checking all motions of the body. (19)

This is the highest law, exalted above the preceding method:

Having examined a spot of bare ground he should remain there; stay O Brahmana! (20)

Having attained a place free from living beings, he should there fix himself.

He should thoroughly mortify his flesh, thinking: There are no obstacles in my body. (21)

Knowing as long as be lives the dangers and troubles, the wise and restrained (ascetic) should bear them as being instrumental to the dissolution of the body. (22)

He should not be attached to the transitory pleasures, nor to the greater ones; he should not nourish desire and greed, looking only for eternal praise. (23)

He should be enlightened with eternal objectss, and not trust in the delusive power of the gods; a Brahmana should know of this and cast off all inferiority. (24)

Not devoted to any of the external objects he reaches the end of his life; thinking that patience is the highest good, he (should choose) one of (the described three) good methods of entering Nirvana. (25) Thus I say.

End of the Seventh Lecture, called Liberation.

**Eighth Lecture,**

**(Called)**

**The Pillow of Righteousness**

**First Lesson**

As I have heard it, I shall tell how the Venerable

Ascetic, exerting himself and meditating, after having entered the order in that winter, wandered about,

'I shall not cover myself with that robe,' only in that winter (he used it). He had crossed (the samsara) for the rest of his life. This (refusing of dress) is in accordance with his doctrine. (1)

More than four months many sorts of living beings gathered on his body, crawled about it, and caused pain there. (2)

For a year and a month he did not leave off his robe. Since that time the Venerable One, giving up his robe, was a naked, world-relinquishing, houseless (sage). (3)

Then he meditated (walking) with his eye fixed on a square space before him of the length of a man. Many people assembled, shocked at the sight; they struck him and cried. (4)

Knowing (and renouncing) the female sex in mixed gathering places, he meditated, finding his way himself: I do not lead a worldly life. (5)

Giving up the company of all householders whomsoever, he meditated. Asked, he gave no answer; he went, and did not transgress the right path. (6)

For some it is not easy (to do what he did), not to answer those who salute; he was beaten with sticks, and struck by sinful people. (7)

Disregarding slights difficult to bear, the Sage wandered about, (not attracted) by story-tellers, pantomimes, songs, fights at quarter-staff, and boxing-matches.(8)

At that time the son of Gñatri saw without sorrow (or pleasure) people in mutual conversation. Gñatriputra obtained oblivion of these exquisite sorrows. (9)

For more than a couple of years he led a religious life without using cold water; he realised singleness, guarded his body, had got intuition, and was calm. (10)

Thoroughly,knowing the earth-bodies and waterbodies and fire-bodies and wind-bodies, the lichens, seeds, and sprouts, (11)

He comprehended that they are, if narrowly inspected, imbued with life, and avoided to injure them; he, the great Hero. (12)

The immovable (beings) are changed to movable ones, and the movable beings to immovable ones; beinas which are born in all states become individually sinners by their actions. (13)

The Venerable One understands thus: he who is under the conditions (of existence), that fool suffers pain. Thoroughly knowing (karman), the Venerable One avoids sin. (14)

The sage, perceiving the double (karman), proclaims the incomparable activity, he, the knowing one; knowing the current of worldliness, the current of sinfulness, and the impulse, (15)

Practising the sinless abstinence from killing, he did no acts, neither himself nor with the assistanceof others; he to whom women were known as the causes of all sinful acts, he saw (the true state of the world). (16)

He did not use what had expressly been prepared for him; he well saw (that bondage comes) through action. Whatever is sinful, the Venerable One left that undone: he consumed clean food. (17)

He did not use another's robe, nor does he eat out of another's vessel. Disregarding contempt, he went with indifference to places where food was prepared. (18)

Knowing measure in eating and drinking, he was not desirous of delicious food, nor had he a longing for it. A sage should not rub his eyes nor scratch his body. (19)

Looking a little sideward, looking a little behind, answering little when spoken to, he should walk attentively looking on his path. (20)

When the cold season has half-way advanced, the houseless, leaving off his robe and stretching out his arms, should wander about, not leaning against a trunk. (21)

This is the rule which has often been followed by the wise Brahmana, the Venerable One, who is free from attachment: thus proceed (the monks).

Thus I say. (22)

**Second Lesson**

Whatever different seats and couches have been told, whatever have been used by the great Hero, these resting-places are thus detailed. (1)

He sometimes lodged in workshops, assembling-places, wells, or shops; sometimes in manufactories or under a shed of straw. (2)

He sometimes lodged in travellers halls, gardenhouses, or towns; sometimes on a burying-ground, in relinquished houses, or at the foot of a tree. (3)

In these places was the wise Sramana for thirteen long years; he meditated day and night, exerting himself, undisturbed, strenuously. (4)

The Venerable One, exerting himself, did not seek sleep for the sake of pleasure; he waked up himself, and slept only a little, free from desires. (5)

Waking tip again, the Venerable One lay down, exerting himself; going outside for once in a night, he walked about for an hour. (6)

In his resting-places he sustained fearful and manifold calamities; crawling or flying animals attack him. (7)

Bad people, the guard of the village, or lance-bearers

attack him; or there were domestic temptations, single women or men; (8)

Fearful and manifold (calamities) of this and the next world; pleasant and unpleasant smells, and manifold sounds: (9)

Always well controlled, he bore the different sorts of feelings; overcoming carelessness and pleasure, the Brahmana wandered about, speaking but little. (10)

In the resting-places there once, in a night, the single, wanderers asked him (who he was, and why he was there); as he did not answer, they treated him badly; but he persevered in his meditations, free from resentment. (11)

(Sometimes to avoid greater troubles when asked), 'Who is there within?' he answered, ' It is I, a mendicant.' But this is the best law: silently to meditate, even if badly treated.(12)

When a cold wind blows, in which some feel pain, then some houseless monks in the cold rain seek a place sheltered from the wind. (13)

(Some heretical monks say), 'We shall put on more clothes; kindling wood or (well) covered, we shall be able (to bear) the very painful influence of the cold.' (14)

But the Venerable One desired nothingof the kind; strong in control, he suffered, despising all shelter. Goina outside once of a night, the Venerable One was able (to endure all hardships) in calmness. (15)

This is the rule which has often been followed by the wise Brilimana, the Venerable One, who is free from attachment: thus proceed (the monks).

Thus I say. (16)

**Third Lesson**

Always well guarded, he bore the pains (caused by)

grass, cold, fire, flies, and gnats; manifold pains. (1)

He travelled in the pathless country of the Udhas, in Vaggabhumi and Subbhabhumi; he used there miserable beds and miserable seats. (2)

In Ladha (happened) to him many dangers. Many natives attacked him. Even in the faithful part of the rough country the dogs bit him, ran at him. (3)

Few people kept off the attacking, biting dogs. Striking the monk, they cried 'Khukkhu,' and made the dogs bite him. (4)

Such were the inhabitants. Many other men.dicants, eating rough food in Vaggabhumi, and carrying about a strong pole or a stalk (to keep off the dogs), lived there. (5)

Even thus armed they were bitten by the dogs, torn by the dogs. It is difficult to travel in Ladha. (6)

Ceasing to use the stick (i. e. cruelty) against living beings, abandoning the care of the body, the houseless (Mahavira), the Venerable One, endures the thorns of the villages (i.e. the abusive language of the peasants), (being) perfectly enlightened. (7)

As an elephant at the head of the battle, so was Mahavira there victorious. Sometimes he did not reach a village there in Ladha. (8)

When he who is free from desires approached the village, the inhabitants met him on the outside, and attacked him, saying, 'Get away from here.' (9)

He was struck with a stick, the fist, a lance, hit with a fruit, a clod, a potsherd, Beating him again and auain, many cried,- (10)

When he once (sat) without moving his body, they cut his flesh,, tore his hair under pains, or covered him with dust. (11)

Throwing him up, they let him fall, or disturbed him in his religious postures; abandoning the care of his body, the Venerable One humbled himself and bore pain, free from desire. (12)

As a hero at the head of the -battle is surrounded on all sides, so was there Mahavira. Bearing all hardships, the Venerable One, undisturbed, proceeded (on the road to Nirvana). (13)

This is the rule which has often been followed, &c.

**Fourth Lesson**

The Venerable One was able to abstain from indulgence of the flesh, though never attacked by diseases. Whether wounded or not wounded, he desired not medical treatment. (1)

Purgatives and emetics, anointing of the body and bathing, shampooing and cleansing of the teeth do not behove him, after he learned (that the body is something unclean). (2)

Being averse from the impressions of the senses, the Brahmana wandered about, speaking but little. Sometimes in the cold season the Venerable One was meditating in the shade. (3)

In summer he exposes himself to the heat, he sits squatting in the sun; he lives on rough (food): rice, pounded jujube, and beans. (4)

Using these three, the Venerable One sustained himself eight months. Sometimes the Venerable One did not drink for half a month or even for a month. (5)

Or he did not drink for more than two months, or even six months, day and night, without desire (for drink). Sometimes he ate stale food. (6)

Sometimes he ate only the sixth meal, or the eighth, the tenth, the twelfth; without desires, persevering in meditation. (7)

Having wisdom, Mahavira committed no sin himself, nor did he induce others to (to so, nor did he consent to the sins of others. (8)

Having entered a village or a town, he begged for food which had been prepared for somebody else. Having got clean food, he used it, restraining the impulses. (9)

When there were hungry crows, or thirsty beings stood in his way, where he begged, or when he saw them flying repeatedly down, (10)

When a Brahmana or Sramana, a beggar or guest, a Kandala, a cat, or a dog stood in his way, (11)

Without ceasing in his reflections, and avoiding to overlook them, the Venerable One slowly wandered about, and, killing no creatures, he begged for his food. (12)

Moist or dry or cold food, old beans, old pap, or bad grain, whether he did or did not get such food, he was rich (in control). (13)

And Mahavira meditated (persevering) in some posture, without the smallest motion; he meditated in mental concentration on (the things) above, below, beside, free from desires. (14)

He meditated free from sin and desire, not attached to sounds or colours; though still an erring mortal (khadmastha), he wandered about, and never acted carelessly. (15)

Himself understanding the truth and restraining the impulses for the purification of the soul, finally liberated, and free from delusion, the Venerable One was well guarded during his whole life. (16)

This is the rule which has been followed, &c.

End of the Ninth Lecture, called the Pillow of Righteousness.

End of the First Book.

## Second Book

## First Part

## First Lecture,

## Called

## Begging of Food.

### First Lesson.

When a male or a fernale mendicant, having entered the abode of a householder with the intention of collecting alms, recognises food, drink, dainties, and spices as affected by, or mixed up with, living beings, mildew, seeds or sprouts, or wet with water, or covered with dust-either in the hand or the pot of another-they should not, even if they can get it, accept of such food, thinking that it is impure and unacceptable. (1)

But if perchance they accept of such food, under preising circumstances, they should go to a secluded spot, a garden, or a monk's hall-where there are no eggs, nor living beings, nor sprouts, nor dew, nor water, nor ants, nor mildew, nor drops (of water), nor mud, nor cobwebs-and rejecting (that which is affected by), and cleaning that which is mixed up (with living beings, &c.), they should circumspectly eat or drink it. But with what they cannot eat or drink, they should resort to a secluded spot, and leave it there on a heap of ashes or bones, or rusty things, or chaff, or cowdung, or on any such-like place which they have repeatedly examined and cleaned. (2)

A monk or a nun on a begging-tour should not accept

as alms whatever herbs they recognise, on examining them, as still whole, containing their source of life, not split longwise or broadwise, and still alive, fresh beans, living and not broken; for such food is impure and unacceptable. (3)

But when they recognise after examination that those herbs are no more whole, do not contain their source of life, are split longwise or broadwise, and no more alive, fresh beans, lifeless and broken, then they may accept them, if they get them; for they are pure and acceptable. (4)

A monk or nun on a begging-tour should not accept as alms whatever flattened grains, grains containing much chaff, or half-roasted spikes of wheat, &c., or flour of wheat, &c., or rice or flour of rice, they recognise as only once worked [pounded or cooked or roasted, because after only one operation sperms of life might be left]; for such food is impure and unacceptable. (5)

But when they recognise these things as more than once worked, as twice, thrice worked, then they may accept them, if they get them; for they are pure and acceptable.(6)

A monk or a nun desiring to enter the abode of a householder for collecting alms, should not enter or leave it together with a heretic or a householder; or a monk who avoids all forbidden food, &c., together with one who does not. (7)

A monk or a nun entering or leaving the out-of-door places for religious practices or for study should not do so together with a heretic or a householder; or a monk who avoids all forbidden food, together with one who does not.(8)

A monk or a nun wandering from village to village should not do so together with a heretic or a householder; or a monk who avoids all forbidden food, together with one who does not. (9)

A monk or a nun on a begging-tour should not give,

immediately or mediately, food, &c., to a heretic or a householder; or a monk who avoids all forbidden food, to one who does not. (10)

A monk or a nun on a begging-tour should not accept food, &c., from a householder whom they know to give out of respect for a Nirgrantha, in behalf of a fellow-ascetic, food, &c., which he has bought or stolen or taken, though it was not to be taken nor given, but was taken by force, by acting sinfully towards all sorts of living beings; for such-like food, &c., prepared by another man or by the giver himself, brought out of the house or not brought out of the house, belonging to the giver or not belonging to him, partaken or tasted of, or not partaken or tasted of, is impure and unacceptable.

In this precept substitute for 'on behalf of one fellow-ascetic,' (2) on behalf of many fellow-ascetics, (3) on behalf of one female fellow-ascetic, (4) on behalf of many female fellow-ascetics; so that there will be four analogous precepts.(11)

A monk or a nun should not accept of food, &c., which they know has been prepared by the householder for the sake of many Sramanas and Brahmanas, guests, paupers, and beggars, after he has counted them, acting sinfully towards all sorts of living beings; for such food, whether it be tasted of or not, is impure and unacceptable. (12)

A monk or a nun should not accept of food, &c., procured in the way described in §11 for the sake of the persons mentioned in §12, if the said food, &c., has been prepared by the giver himself, has been brought out of the house, does not belong to the giver, has not been partaken or tasted of; for such food, &c.,, is impure and unacceptable; but if the food, &c., has been prepared by another person, has been brought out of the house, belongs to the giver, has been partaken or tasted of, one may accept it; for it is pure and acceptable. (13)

A monk or a nun wishing to enter the abode of a householder with the intention of collecting alms, should not, for the sake of food or drink, enter or leave such always liberal, always open houses, where they always give a morsel, always the best morsel, always a part of the meal, always nearly the half of it.

This certainly is the whole duty of a monk or a nun in which one should, instructed in all its meanings and endowed with bliss, always exert oneself.

Thus I say. (14)

**Second Lesson**

A monk or a nun on a begging-tour should not accept food, &c., in the following case: when, on the eighth or paushadha day, on the beginning of a fortnight, of a month, of two, three, four, five, or six months, or on the days of the seasons, of the junction of the seasons, of the intervals of the seasons, many Sramanas and Brahmanas, guests, paupers, and beggars are entertained with food, &c., out of one or two or three or four vessels, pots, baskets, or heaps of food; such-like food which has been prepared by the giver, &c., (all down to) not tasted of, is impure and unacceptable. But if it is prepared by another person, &c. (see first lesson, § 13), one may accept it; for it is pure and acceptable. (1)

A monk or a nun on a begging-tour may accept food, &c., from unblamed, uncensured families, to wit, noble families, distinguished families, royal families, families belonging to the line of Ikshvaku, of Hari, cowherds' families, Vaisya families, barbers' families, carpenters' families, takurs' families, weavers' families; for such food, &c., is pure and acceptable. (2)

A monk or a nun on a begging-tour should not accept food, &c., in the following case: when in assemblies, or during offerings to the manes, or on a festival of Indra or Skanda or Rudra or Mukunda or demons or Yakshas or the snakes, or on a festival in honour of a tomb, or a shrine, or a tree, or a hill, or a cave, or a well, or a tank, or a pond, or a river, or a lake, or the sea, or a mine-when on such-like various festivals many Sramanas and Brahmanas, guests, paupers, and beggars are entertained with food, &c. (all as in .§ 1, down to) acceptable. (3)

But when he perceives that all have received their due share, and are enjoying their meal, he should address the householder's wife or sister or daughter-in-law or nurse or male or female servant or slave and say: 'O long-lived one! (or, O sister!) will you give me something to eat?' After these words of the mendicant, the other may bring forth food, &c., and give it him. Such food, &c., whether he beg for it or the other give it, he may accept; for it is pure and acceptable. (4)

When a monk or a nun knows that at a distance of more than half a yogana, a festive entertainment is going on, they should not resolve to go there for the sake of the festive entertainment. (5)

When a monk hears that the entertainment is given in an eastern or western or southern or northern place, he should go respectively to the west or east or north or south, being quite indifferent (about the feast); wherever there is a festive entertainment, in a village or scot-free town, &c. (see 1, 7, 6, § 4), he should not go there for the sake of the festive entertainment.

The Kevalin assigns as the reason for this precept, that if the monk eats food, &c., which has been given him on such an occasion, he will incur the sin of one who uses what has been prepared for him, or is mixed up with living beings, or has been bought or stolen or taken, though it was not to be taken, nor was it given, but taken by force. (6)

A layman might, for the sake of a mendicant, make small doors large, or large ones small; put beds from a level position into a sloping one, or from a sloping position into a level one; place the beds out of the draught or in the draught; cutting and clipping the grass outside. or within the upAsraya, spread a couch for him, (thinking that) this mendicant is without means for a bed. Therefore should a well-controlled Nirgrantha not resolve to go to any festival which is preceded or followed by a feast.

This certainly is the whole duty, &c. (see end of lesson1).

Thus I say. (7)

**Third Lesson.**

When he has eaten or drunk at a festive entertainment, he might vomit (what he has eaten), or not well digest it; or some other bad disease or sickness might befall him. (1)

The Kevalin says this is the reason:

A mendicant, having drunk various liquors, together with the householder or his wife, monks or nuns, might not find the (promised) -resting-place on leaving the scene of entertainment and looking out for it; or in the resting-place 'he may get into mixed company; in the absence of his mind-or in his drunkenness he may lust after a woman or a eunuch; approaching the mendicant (they will say): 'O long-lived Sramana! (let us meet) in the garden, or in the sleeping-place, in the night or in the twilight! Luring him thus by his sensuality (she says): 'Let us proceed to enjoy the pleasures of love.' He might go to her, though he knows that it should not be done.

These are the causes to sin, they multiply continuously. Therefore should a well-controlled Nirgrantha not resolve to go to any festival which is preceded or followed by a feast.(2)

A monk or a nun, hearing or being told of some festivity, might hasten there, rejoicing inwardly: 'There will be an entertainment, sure enough!' It is impossible to get there from other families alms which are acceptable and given out of respect for the cloth, and to eat the meal. As this would lead to sin, they should not do it. But they should enter there, and getting from other families their alms, should eat their meal. (3)

A monk or a nun, knowing that in a village or a scot-free town, &c. (see 1, 7, 6, § 4), an entertainment will be given, should not resolve to go to that village, &c., for the sake of the entertainment. The Kevalin assigns as the reason herefore: When a man goes to a much-frequented and vulgar entertainment somebody's foot treads on his foot, somebody's hand moves his hand, somebody's bowl clashes against his bowl, somebody's head comes in collision with his head, somebody's body pushes his body, or somebody beats him with a stick or a bone or a fist or a clod, or sprinkles him with cold water, or covers him with dust; or he eats unacceptable food, or he receives what should be given to others. Therefore should a well-controlled Nirgrantha not resolve to go to a much-frequented and vulgar entertainment to partake of it.(4)

A monk or a nun on a begging-tour should not accept such food, &c., about the acceptability or unacceptability of which his (or her) mind has some doebts or misgivings; for such food, &c. (5)

When a monk or a nun wishes to enter the abode of a householder, they should do so with the complete outfit. (6)

A monk or a nun entering or leaving the out-ofdoor places for religious practices or study, should do so with the complete outfit. (7)

A monk or a nun wandering from village to village should do so with the complete outfit. (8)

A monk or a nun should not, with the complete outfit, enter or leave the abode of a householder to collect alms, or the out-of-door places for religious prictices and study, or wander from village to village on perceiving that a strong and widely-spread rain pours down, or a strong and widely-spread. mist is coming on, or a high wind raises much dust, or many flying insects are scattered about and fall down. (9)

A monk or a nun on a begging-tour should not accept food, &c., in the houses of Kshatriyas, kings, messengers, and relations of kings, whether they are inside or outside, or invite them; for such food, &c., is impure and unacceptable. Thus I say. (10)

**Fourth Lesson**

A monk or a nun on a begging~tour should not resolve to go to a festival, preceded or followed by an entertainment, to partake of it, when they know that there will be served up chiefly meat or fish or roasted slices of meat or fish; nor to a wedding breakfast in the husband's house or in that of the bride's father; nor to a funeral dinner or to a family dinner where something is served up,-if on their way there, there are many living beings, many seeds, many sprouts, much dew, much water, much mildew, many drops (of water), much dust, and many cobwebs; or if there have arrived or will arrive many Sramanas and Brahmanas, guests, paupers, and beggars, and if it will be a crowded assembly, so that a wise man may not enter or leave it, or learn there the sacred texts, to question about them, to repeat them, to consider them, to think about the substance of the law. (1)

A monk or a nun may go to such an entertainment (as described in the preceding Sutra), provided that on their way there, there are few living beings, few seeds, &c.; that no Sramanas and Brahmanas, &c., have arrived or will arrive; that it is not a crowded assembly, so that a wise man may enter or leave, &c. (2)

A monk or a nun desirous to enter the abode of a householder, should not do so, when they see that the milch cows are being milked, or the food, &c., is being cooked, and that it is not yet distributed. Perceiving this, they should step apart and stay where no people pass or see them. But when they conceive that the milch cows are milked, the dinner prepared and distributed, then they may circumspectly enter or leave the householder's abode* for the sake of alms. (3)

Some of the mendicants say to those who follow the same rules of conduct, live (in the same place), or wander from village to village: 'This is indeed a small village, it is too populous, nor is it large; reverend gentlemen, go to the outlying villages to beg alms.

Some mendicant may have there kinsmen or relations, e.g. a householder or his wife, or daughters, or daughters-in-law, or nurses, or male and female slaves or servants. Such families with which he is connected by kindred or through marriage, he intends to visit before (the tinic of begging): 'I shall get there (he thinks) food or dainties or milk or thick sour milk or fresh butter or ghee or sugar or oil or honey or meat or liquor, a sesmum dish, or raw sugar, or a meal of parched wheat, or a meal of curds and sugar with spices'; after having eaten and drunk, and having cleaned and rubbed the alms-bowl, I shall, together with other mendicants, enter or leave the abode of a householder to collect alms.' As this would be sinful, he should not do so. (4)

But, at the proper time, entering there with the other mendicants, he may there in these or other families accept alms which are acceptable and given out of respect for his cloth, and eat his meal.

This certainly is the whole duty, &c. (see end of lesson1).

Thus I say. (5)

**Fifth Lesson**

When a monk or a nun on entering the abode of a householder sees that the first portion of the meal is being thrown away' or thrown down, or taken away, or distributed, or eaten, or put off, or has already been eaten or removed; that already other Sramanas and Brahmanas, guests, paupers, and beggars go there in great haste; (they might think), 'Hallo! I too shall go there in haste.' As this would be sinful, they should not do so. (1)

When a monk or a nun on a begging-tour comes upon walls or gates, or bolts or holes to fit them, they should, in case there be a byway, avoid those (obstacles), and not go on straight.

The Kevalin says: This is the reason: Walking there, he might stumble or fall down; when he stumbles or falls down, his body might become contaminated with fxces, urine, phlegmatic humour, mucus, saliva, bile, matter, semen, or blood. And if his body has become soiled, he should not wipe orrub or scratch or clean or warm or dry it on the bare ground or wet earth [or dusty earth] on a rock or a piece of clay containing life, or timber inhabited by worms, or anything containing eggs, living beings, &c. (down to) cobwebs; but he should first beg for some straw or leaves, wood or a potsherd, which must be free from dust, resort with it to a secluded spot, and on a heap of ashes or bones, &c. (see II, 1, 1, §2), which he has repeatedly examined and cleaned, he should circumspectly wipe or rub, warm or dry (his body).(2)

When a monk or a nun on a begging-tour perceives a vicious cow coming towards them, or a vicious buffalo coming towards them, or a vicious man, horse, elephant, lion, tiger, wolf, panther, bear, hyena, sarablia, shakal, cat, dog, boar, fox, leopard coming towards them, they should, in case there be a byway, circumspectly avoid them, and not walk on straight. (3)

When a monk or a nun on a begging-tour comes on their way upon a pit, pillar, thorns, or unsafe, marshy or uneven ground, or mud, they should, in case there be a byway, avoid these (obstacles), and not walk on straight.

When a monk or a nun on a begging-tour perceives that the entrance of a householder's abode is secured by a branch of a thorn bush, they should not, without having previously got the (owner's) permission, and having examined and swept (the entrance), make it passable or enter and leave (the house). But they may circumspectly do so, after having got the (owner's) permission, and having examined and swept it. (4)

When a monk or a nun on a begging-tour knows that a Sramana or a Brahmana, a guest, pauper oe beggar has already entered (the house), they should not stand in their sight or opposite the door.

The Kevalin says: This is the reason: Another, on seeing him, might procure and give him food, &c. Therefore it has been declared to the mendicants: This is the statement, this is the reason, this is the order, that he should not stand in the other mendicant's sight or opposite the door.

Knowing this, he should go apart and stay where no people pass or see him. Another man may bring and give him food, &c., while he stays where no people pass or see him, and say unto him 'O long-lived Sramana! this food, &c., has been given for the sake of all of you; eat it or divide it among you.' Having sileatly accepted the gift, he might think: 'Well, this is just (enough) for me!' As this would be sinful, he should not do so.

Knowing this, he should join the other beggars, and after consideration say unto them: 'O long-lived Sramanas! this food, &c., is given for the sake of all of you; eat it or divide it among you.' After these words another might answer him: 'O long-lived Sramana! distribute it yourself.' Dividing the food, &c., he should not (select) for himself too great a portion, or the vegetables, or the conspicuous things, ,or the savoury things, or the delicious things, or the nice things, or the big things; but he should impartially divide it, not being eager or desirous or greedy or covetous (of anything). When he thus makes the division, another might say: 'O long-lived Sramana! do not divide (the food); but let us, all together, eat and drink.' When he thus eats, he should not select for himself too great a portion, &c.; but should eat and drink alike with all, not being desirous, &c. (5)

When a monk or a nun on a begging-tour perceives that a Sramana or Brahmana, a beggar or guest has already entered the house, they should not overtake them and address (the householder) first. Knowing this, they should go apart and stay where no people pass or see them. But when they perceive that the other has been sent away or received alms, and-has returned, they may circumspectly enter the house and address the householder.

This certainly is the whole duty, &c.

Thus I say. (6)

**Sixth Lesson**

When a monk or a nun on a begging-tour perceives that many hungry animals have met and come together in search of food, e.g. those of the chicken-kind or those of the pig-kind, or that crows have met and come together, where an offering is thrown on the ground, they should, in case there be a byway, avoid them and not go on straight. (1)

A monk or a nun on a begging-tour should not stand leaning against the door-post of the householder's abode, or his sink or spitting-pot, nor in sight of, or opposite to his bathroom or privy; nor should they contemplate a loophole or a mended spot or a fissure (of the house) or the bathing-house, showing in that direction with an arm or pointing with a finger, bowing up and down. (2)

Nor should they beg, pointing with a finger at the householder, or moving him with a finger, or threatening hint with a finger, or scratching him with a finger, or praising him, or using coarse language. (3)

If he sees somebody eating, e.g. the householder or his wife, &c., he should after consideration say: 'O long-lived one! (or, O sister!) will you give me some of that food?' After these words the other might wash or wipe his hand or pot or spoon or plate with cold or hot water'. He should after consideration say: 'O long-lived one! (or, O sister!) do not wash or wipe your hand or pot or spoon or plate! If you want to give me something, give it as it is!' After these words the other might give him a share, having washed or wiped his hand, &c., with cold or hot water. But he should not accept anything out of such a hand, &c., which has been before treated thus; for it is impure and unacceptable. (4)

It is also to be known that food, &c., is impure and unacceptable, which is given with a wet hand, though the hand be not purposely wetted. (5)

The same rule holds good with regard to a moistened hand, &c., and a dusty hand, &c., and a hand which is soiled with clay, dew, orpiment, vermilion, realgar, collyrium, white chalk, alum, rice-flour, kukkusa, ground drugs. (6)

It is also to be known that he may accept such food, &c., which is given with a soiled hand, &c., to one similarly soiled (i.e. with what one is to receive), or to one unsoiled, with hand similarly soiled; for such food, &c., is pure and acceptable. (7)

A monk or a nun on a begging-tour should not accept flattened grains, grains containing much chaff, &c. (see II, 1, 1, §5), which a layman, for the sake of the mendicant, has ground, grinds, or will grind, has winnowed, winnows, or will winnow on a rock or a piece of clay containing life, &c. (see II, 1, 5, §2, all down to) cobwebs; for such large, parched grains, &c., are impure and unacceptable. (8)

A monk or a nun on a begging-tour should not accept fossil salt or sea salt which a householder, for the sake of the mendicant, has ground or pounded, grinds or pounds, will grind or pound on a rock or a piece of clay containing life, &c.; for such-like fossil salt or sea salt is impure and unacceptable. (9)

A monk or a nun. on a begging-tour should not accept food, &c., which is prepared over the fire; for such food is impure and unacceptable. The Kevalin says: This is the reason: A layman will kill the fire-bodies, by wetting or moistening, wiping or rubbing, throwing up or turning down the food, &c., for the sake of the mendicant. Hence. it has been declared to the mendicants: This is the statement, this is the reason, this is the order, that they should not accept food, &c., which has been prepared over the fire, &c.

This certainly is the whole duty, &c. Thus I say. (10)

**Seventh Lesson**

A monk or a nun on a begging-tour should not accept food, &c., which has been placed on a post or pillar or beam or scaffold or loft' or platform or roof or some such-like elevated place; for such food fetched from above is impure and unacceptable. The Kevalin says: This is the reason: The layman might fetch and erect a stool or a bench or a ladder or a handmill, get upon it, and getting upon it fall or tumble down. Thus he might hurt his foot or arm or breast or belly or head or some other part of his body; or he might kill or frighten or bruise or smash or crush or afflict or pain or dislocate all sorts of living beings. Therefore he should not accept such-like food, &c., fetched from above. (1)

A monk or a nun on a begging-tour should not accept food, &c., which a layman, for the sake of the mendicant, has taken from a granary or vault by contorting himself up and down and horizontally; thinking that such-like food is brought from underground. (2)

A monk or a nun on a begging-tour should not accept food, &c., which is kept in earthenware. The Kevalin says: This is the reason: The layman might, for the sake of the mendicant, break the earthen vessel containing the food, &c., and thereby injure the earth-body; in the same way he might injure the fire-body, the wind-body, plants and animals; by putting it again (in earthenware), he commits the pakkhakamma sin. Hence it has been said to the mendicant, &c., that he should not accept food, &c., which is put in earthenware. (3)

A monk or a nun on a begging-tour should not accept food, &c., placed on the earth-body, the wind-body, the fire-body, for such food is impure and unacceptable. The Kevalin says: This is the reason: A layman might, for the sake of the mendicant, stir or brighten the fire, and taking the food, &c., down from it, might give it to the mendicant. Hence it has been said, &c., that he should accept no such food. (4)

When a monk or a nun on a begging-tour sees that a layman might, for the sake of the mendicant, cool too hot food, &c., by blowing or fanning with a winnowing basket or fan or a palm leaf or a branch or a part of a branch or a bird's tail or a peacock's tail or a cloth or a corner of a cloth or the hand or the mouth, they should, after consideration, say (to the householder or his wife): 'O long-lived one! (or, O sister!) do not blow or fan the hot food, &c., with a winnowing basket, &c.; but if you want to give it me, give it as it is.' After these words the other might give it after having blown or fanned it with a winnowing basket, &c.; such-like food they should not accept, because it is impure and unacceptable.(5)

A monk or a nun on a begging-tour should not accept food, &c., which is placed on vegetable or animal matter; for such food is impure and unacceptable. (6)

A monk or a nun on a begging-tour should not accept water which has been used for watering flour or sesamum or rice, or any other such-like water which has been recently used for washing, which has not acquired a new taste, nor altered its taste or nature, nor has been strained; for such-like water is impure and unacceptable. But if it has long ago been used for washing, has acquired a new taste, has altered its taste or nature, and has been strained, it may be accepted, for it is pure and acceptable. (7)

When a monk or a nun on a begging-tour finds water used for washing sesamum, chaff or barley, or rainwater or sour gruel or pure water, they should, after consideration, say (to the householder or his wife): 'O long lived one! (or, O sister!) will you give me some of this water?' Then the other may answer him: 'O long-lived Sramana! take it yourself by drawing it with, or pouring it in, your bowl!' Such-like water, whether taken by himself or given by the other, he may accept. (8)

A monk or a nun on a begging-tour should not accept such water as has been taken from the bare ground, &c. (see II, 1, 5 § 2, all down to) cobwebs, or water which the

to cooked fruits of Atthiya, Tinduka [Aegle Marmelos], Vilva [Diospyros Glutinosa], Sriparni [Pistia Stratiotes]. (14)

A monk or a nun on a begging-tour should not accept such raw, unmodified substances as corn, clumps of corn, cakes of corn, sesamum, ground sesamum, or cakes of sesamum.

This is the whole duty, &c.

Thus I say. (15)

**Ninth Lesson**

In the east or west or south or north, there are some faithful householders, &c., (all down to) servants who will speak thus: 'It is not meet that these illustrious, pious, virtuous, eloquent, restrained, controlled, chaste ascetics, who have ceased from sensual intercourse, should eat or drink food, &c., which is adhakarmika; let us give to the ascetics all food, &c., that is ready for our use, and let us, afterwards, prepare food for our own use.' Having heard such talk, the mendicant should not accept such-like food, &c., for it is impure and unacceptable. (1)

A monk or a nun on a begging-tour or in their residence or on a pilgrimage from village to village, who know that in a village or scot-free town, &c., dwell a mendicant's nearer or remoter relations-viz. a householder or his wife, &c.-should not enter or leave such houses for the sake of food or drink. The Kevalin says: This is the reason: Seeing him, the other might for his sake, procure or prepare food, &c. Hence it has been said to the mendicant, &c., that he should not enter or leave such houses for the sake of food or drink.

Knowing this, he should go apart and stay where no people pass or see him. In due time he may enter other houses, and having begged for alms which are acceptable and given out of respect for his cloth, he may eat his dinner. If the other has, on the mendicant's timely entrance, procured or prepared food, &c., which is adhakarmika, he might silently examine it, and think: 'Why should I abstain from what has been brought.' As this would be sinful, he should not do so. But after consideration he should say: 'O long-lived one! (or, O sister!) as it is not meet that I should eat or drink food, &c., which is .adhakarmika, do not procure or prepare it.' If after these words the other brings and gives him adhakarmika food which he has prepared, he should not accept such-like food, &c., for it is impure and unacceptable. (2)

When a monk or a nun on a begging-tour sees that meat or fish is being roasted, or oil cakes, for the sake of a guest, are being prepared, they should not, quickly approaching, address the householder; likewise if the food is prepared for the sake of a sick person. (3)

A monk or a nun on a begging-tour might, of the received quantity of food, eat only the sweet-smelling parts and reject the bad-smelling ones. As this would be sinful, they should not do so; but they should consume everything, whether it be sweet smelling or bad smelling, and reject nothing. (4)

A monk or a nun on a begging-tour might, of the received quantity of drink, imbibe only the well-flavoured part, and reject the astringent part. As this would be sinful, they should not do so; but they should consurne everything, whether it be well flavoured or astringent, and reject nothing. (5)

A monk or a nun, having received a more than sufficient quantity of food, might reject (the superfluous part) without having considered or consulted fellow-ascetics living in the neighbourhood, who follow the same rules of conduct, are agreeable and not to be shunned; as this would be sinful, they should not do so. Knowing this, they should go there and after consideration say: 'O long-lived Sramanas! this food, &c., is too much for me, eat it or drink it!' After these words the other might say: 'O longlived Sramana! we shall eat or drink as much of this food or drink as we require; or, we require the whole, we shall eat or drink the whole.' (6)

A monk or a nun on a begging-tour should not accept food, &c., which for the sake of another has been put before the door, if the householder has not permitted him to do so, or he gives it him; for such food, &c. But on the contrary he may accept it.

This is the whole duty, &c.

Thus I say. (7)

**Tenth Lesson**

A single mendicant, having collected alms for many, might, without consulting his fellow-ascetics, give them to those whom he list; as this would be sinful, he should not do so. Taking the food, he should go there (where his teacher &c. is) and speak thus: 'O long-lived Sramana! there are near or remote (spiritual) relations of mine: a teacher, a sub-teacher, a religious guide, a Sthavira, a head of a Gana, a Ganadhara, a founder of a Gana; forsooth, I shall give it them.' The other may answer him: 'Well now, indeed, O long-lived'one! give such a portion!' As much as the other commands, thus much he should give; if the other commands the whole, he should give the whole. (1)

A single mendicant, having collected agreeable food, might cover it with distasteful food, thinking: 'The teacher or sub-teacher, &c., seeing what I have received, might take it himself; indeed, I shall not give anything to anybody!' As this would be sinful, he should not do so.

Knowing this, he should go there (where the other mendicants are), should put the vessel in his out-stretched band, show it (with the words): 'Ah, this! ah, this!' and hide nothing. (2)

A single mendicant, having received some food, might eat what is good, and bring what is discoloured and tasteless; as this would be sinful, he should not do so. (3)

A monk or a nun on a begging-tour should not accept any part of the sugar-cane, whether small or large, pea-pods, seed-pods, of which articles a small part only can be eaten, and the greater part must be rejected; for such things are impure and unacceptable. (4)

A monk or a nun on a begging-tour should not accept meat or fish containing many bones, so that only a part of it can be eaten and the greater part must be rejected; for such meat or fish, &c., is impure and unacceptable. (5)

A monk or a nun on a begging-tour may be invited to meat or fish containing many bones, (by the householder who addresses him thus): 'O long-lived Sramana! will you accept meat with many bones?' Hearing such a communication, he should say, after consideration: 'O long-lived one! (or, O sister!) it is not meet for me to accept meat with many bones; if you want to give me a portion of whatever size, give it me; but not the bones!' If after these words the other (i.e.. the householder) should fetch meat containing many bones, put it in a bowl and return with it, (the mendicant) should not accept such a bowl, whether out of the other's hand or a vessel,; for it is impure and unacceptable. But if he has inadvertently accepted it, he should not say: 'No, away, take it!' Knowing this, he should go apart, and in a garden or an upisraya, where there are few eggs, &c., (all down to) cobwebs, eat the meat or fish, and taking the bones, he should resort to a secluded spot and leave them on a heap of ashes,. &c. (See 11, 1, 1, § 2).(6)

If a householder should fetch fossil salt or sea salt, put it in a bowl and return with it, a monk or a nun on a begging-tour should not accept it out of the other's hand or vessel; for, &c.

But if he has inadvertently accepted it, he should return with it to the householder, if he is not yet too far away, and say, after consideration: 'Did you give me this with your full knowledge or without it?' He might answer: 'I did give it without my full knowledge; but indeed, O long-lived one! I now give it you; consume it or divide it (with others)!'

Then being permitted by, and having received it from, the householder, he should circumspectly eat it or drink it, and what he cannot eat or drink he should share with his fellow-ascetics in the neighbourhood, who follow the same rules of conduct, are agreeable, and not to be shunned; but if there are no fellow-ascetics, the same should be done as in case one has received too much food.

This is the whole duty, &c.

Thus I say. (7)

## Eleventh Lesson

Some mendicants say unto (others) who follow the same rules of conduct, or live in the same place, or wander from village to village, if they have received agreeable food and another mendicant falls sick: 'Take it! give it him! if the sick mendicant will not eat it, thou mayst eat it.' But he (who is ordered to bring the food) thinking, 'I shall eat it myself,' covers it and shows it (saying): 'This is the lump of food, it is rough to the taste, it is pungent, it is bitter, it is astringent, it is sour, it is sweet; there is certainly nothing in it fit for a sick person.' As this would be sinful, he should not do so. But he should show him which parts are not fit for a sick person (saying): 'This particle is pungent, this one bitter, this one astringent, this one sour, this one sweet.' (1)

Some mendicants say unto (others) who follow the same rules of conduct, or live in the same place, or wander from village to village, if they have received agreeable food and another mendicant falls sick: 'Take it! give it him! if the mendicant will not eat it, bring it to us!' 'If nothing prevents me, I shall bring it.' (Then he migfit act as stated in § 1, which would be sinful.) (2)

For the avoidance of these occasions to sin there are seven rules for begging food and as many for begging drink, to be known by the mendicants.

Now, this is the first rule for begging food. Neither hand nor vessel are wet: with such a hand or vessel he may accept as pure, food, &c., for which he himself begs or which the other gives him. That is the first rule for begging food. (3)

Now follows the second rule for begging food. The hand and the vessel are wet. The rest as in the preceding rule. That is the second rule for begging food. (4)

Now follows the third rule for begging food. In the east, &c., there are several faithful householders, &c., (all down to) servants: they have put (food) in some of their various vessels, as a pan, a pot, a winnowing basket, a basket, a precious vessel. Now (the mendicant) should again know: is the hand not wet and the vessel wet; or the hand wet and the vessel not wet? If he collect alms with an alms-bowl or with his hand, he should say,- after consideration: 'O long-lived one! (or, O sister!) with your not-wet hand, or with your wet vessel, put (alms) in this my bowl, or hand, and give it me!' Such-like food, for which he himself begs or which the other gives him, he may accept; for it is pure and acceptable. That is the third rule for begging food. (5)

Now follows, the fourth rule for begging food. A monk or a nun may accepr flattened grains, &c. (cf. II, 1, 1, § 5), for which they beg themselves or which the other gives them, if it be such as to require little cleaning or taking out (of chaff); for it is pure, &c. That is the fourth rule for begging food. (6)

Now follows the fifth rule for begging food. A monk or a nun may accept food which is offered on a plate or a copper cup or any vessel, if the moisture on the hands of the giver is almost dried up; for, &c. That is the fifth rule for begging food. (7)

Now follows the sixth rule for begging food. A monk or a nun may accept food which had been taken up from the ground, either taken up for one's own sake or accepted for the sake of somebody else, whether it be placed in a vessel or in the hand; for, &c. That is the sixth rule for begging food.(8)

Now follows the seventh rule for begging food. A monk or a nun may accept food of which only a part may be used, and which is not wanted by bipeds, quadrupeds, Sramanas, Brahmanas, guests, paupers, and beggars, whether they beg for it themselves, or the householder gives it them. That is the seventh rule for begging food. (9)

These are the seven rules for begging food;- now follow the seven rules for begging drink. They are, however, the same as those about food, only the fourth gives this precept: A monk or a nun may accept as drink water which has been used for watering flour or sesamum, &c. (II, 1, 7, § 7), if it be such as to require little cleaning and taking out (of impure) articles; for, &c. (10)

One who has adopted one of these seven rules for

begging food or drink should not say: 'These reverend persons have chosen a wrong rule, I alone have rightly chosen.' (But he should say): 'These reverend persons, who follow these rules, and I who follow that rule, we all exert ourselves according to the commandment of the Gina, and we respect each other accordingly.' This certainly is the whole duty, &c. Thus I say. (11)

End of the First Lecture, called Begging of Food.

**Second Lecture,**

**Called**

**Begging for a Cough**

**First Lesson.**

If a monk or a nun want to ask for a lodging, and having entered a village or scot-free town, &c., conceive that lodging to contain eggs, living beings, &c., they should not use it for religious postures, night's-rest, or study. (1)

But if the lodging contains only few eggs or few living beings, &c., they may, after having inspected and cleaned it, circumspectly use it for religious postures, &c. Now, if they conceive that the householder, for the sake of a Nirgrantha and on behalf of a fellow-ascetic (male or female, one or many), gives a lodging which he has bought or stolen or taken, though it was not to -be taken nor given, but was taken by force, by acting sinfully towards all sorts of living beings , they should not use for religious postures, &c., such a lodging which has been appropriated by the giver himself, &c. (see II, 1, 1, § 11).

The same holds good if there be instead of a fellow-ascetic many Sramanas and Brahmanas, guests, paupers, and beggars. But if the lodging has been appropriated by another man than the giver, &c., they may, after having inspected and cleaned it, circumspectly use it for religious postures, &c. (2)

A monk or a nun, knowing that the layman has, for the sake of the mendicant, matted the lodging. whitewashed it, strewn it (with grass, &c.), smeared it (with cowdung), levelled, smoothed, or perfumed it (or the floor of it), should not use that lodging, which has been prepared by the giver himself, &c., for religious postures. But if it has been prepared by another person, &c., they may circumspectly use it for religious postures. (3)

A monk or a nun, knowing that a layman will, for the sake of a mendicant, make small doors large, &c. (all as in II, 1, 2, § 7, down to) spread his couch or place it outside, should not use such a lodging which has been appropriated by the giver himself, &c., for religious postures, &c. But if it has been appropriated by another person, &c., they may circumspectly use it for religious postures, &c. (4)

Again, a monk or a nun, knowing that the layman, for the sake of the mendicant, removes from one place to another, or places outside, bulbs or roots or leaves or flowers or fruits or seeds or grass-blades of water plants, should not use such a lodging, which is appropriated by the giver himself, for religious postures, &c. But if it has been prepared by another person, &c., they may circumspectly use it for religious postures, &c. (5)

A monk or a nun, knowing that the layman, for the sake of the mendicant, removes from one place to another, or places outside, a chair or a board or a ladder or a mortar, should not use such a lodging-place, &c. (all as at the end of the last paragraph). (6)

A monk or a nun should not use for religious postures, &c., a lodging-place above ground, as a pillar or a raised platform or a scaffold or a second story or a flat roof, likewise no underground place (except under urgent circumstances). If by chance they are thus lodged, they should there not wash or clean their hands or feet or eyes or teeth or mouth with hot or cold water; nor should they put forth there any other secretion, as excrements, urine, saliva, mucus, bilious humour, ichor, blood, or any other part of the bodily humours.

The Kevalin says: This is the reason: Making secretions he might stumble or fall; stumbling or falling he might hurt his hand, &c. (11, 1, 7, § 1), or any other limb of his body, or kill, &c., all sorts of living beings. Hence it has been said to the mendicant, &c., that he should use no above-ground lodging-place for religious postures, &c. (7)

A monk or a nun on a begging-tour should not use, for. religious postures, a lodging-place used by the householder, in which there are women, children, cattle, food, and drink. This is the reason: A mendicant living together with a householder's family may have an attack of gout, dysentery, or vomiting; or some other pain, illness, or disease may befall him; the layman might, out of compassion, smear or anoint the mendicant's body with oil or ghee or butter or grease, rub or shampoo it with perfumes, drugs, lodhra, dye, powder, padmaka, then brush or rub it clean; clean, wash, or sprinkle it with hot or cold water, kindle or light a fire by rubbing wood on wood; and having done so, he might dry or warm (the mendicant's body).

Hence it has been said to the mendicant, &c., that he should not us for religious postures, &c., a lodging-place which is used by the householder. (8)

This is (another) reason: While a mendicant lives in a lodging used by the householder, the householder or his wife, &c., might bully, scold, attack or beat each other. Then the mendicant might direct his mind to approval or dislike: 'Let them bully each other!' or, 'Let them not bully each other!' &c. &c.

Hence it has been said to the mendicant, &c., that he should not use, for religious postures, &c., a lodging-place used by the householder. (9)

This is (another) reason: While the mendicant lives together with householders, the householder might, for his own sake, kindle or light or extinguish a fire-body. Then the mendicant might direct his mind to approval or dislike: 'Let them kindle or light or extinguish a fire-body;' or,'Let them not do so.'

Hence it has been said to the mendicant, &c. (see above). (10)

This is (another) reason: While the mendicant lives together with householders, he might see the householder's earrings or girdle or jewels or pearl. or gold and silver or bracelets (those round the wrist and those round the upper arm) or necklaces (those consisting of three strings, or those reaching halfway down the body, or those consisting of eighty strings or forty strings or one string or strings of pearls, golden beads or jewels) or a decked or ornamented girl or maiden. Thus the mendicant might direct his mind to approval or dislike: 'Let her be thus;' or, 'Let her not be thus.' So he might say, so he might think. Hence it has been said to the mendicant, &c. (see above). (11)

This is (another) reason: While a mendicant lives together with householders, the householder's wives, daughters, daughters-in-law, nurses, slave-girls or servant-girls might say: 'These reverend Sramanas, &c., have ceased from sexual intercourse; it behoves them not to indulge in sexual intercourse: whatever woman indulges with them in sexual intercourse, will have a strong, powerful, illustrious, glorious, victorious son of heavenly beauty.' Hearing and perceiving such talk, one of them might induce the mendicant ascetic to indulge in sexual intercourse.

Hence it has been said to the mendicant, &c., that he should not use for religious postures, &c., a lodging used by the householder.

This is the whole duty, &c.

Thus I say. (12)

**Second Lesson**

Some householders are of clean habits and the mendicants, because they never bathe, are covered with uncleanliness; they smell after it, they smell badly, they are disagreeable, they are loathsome. Hence the householders, with regard to the mendicant, put off some work which otherwise the), would have done before, and do some work which otherwise they would have put off.

Hence it has been said to the mendicant, &c., that he should not use, for religious postures, &c., a lodging used by the householder. (1)

This is the reason: While a mendicant lives together with householders, the householder might, for his own sake, have prepared something to eat. Then, afterwards, he might, for the sake of the mendicant, prepare or dress food, &c., and the mendicant might desire to eat or drink or swallow it.

Hence it has been said to the mendicant, &c. (see above).(2)

This is the reason: While the mendicant lives together with a householder, there may be ready wood cleft for the use of the householder. Then, afterwards, (the householder) might, for the sake of the mendicant, cleave or buy or steal wood, kindle or light, by rubbing wood on wood, the fire-body, and the mendicant might desire to dry or warm himself at, or enjoy, the fire.

Hence it has been said to the mendicant, &c. (see above). (3)

When in the night or twilight a mendicant, to ease nature, leaves the door open, a thief, watching for an occasion, might enter. It is not meet for the mendicant to say: This thief enters or does not enter, he hides himself or does not hide himself, he creeps in or does not creep in, he speaks or does not speak; he has taken it, another has taken it, it is taken from that man; this is the thief, this is the accomplice, this is the murderer, he has done so'. The householder will suspect the ascetic, the mendicant, who is not a thief, to be the thief. Hence it has been said to the mendicant, &c. (4)

A monk or a nun should not use, for religious postures, &c., sheds of grass or straw which contain eggs, living beings, &c. But they may do so if they contain few eggs, few living beings, &c. (5)

A mendicant should not stay in halting-places, garden houses, family houses, monasteries, where many fellow-ascetics are frequently arriving.

1. If the reverend persons continue to live in those places after staying there for a month [or any fixed period, which the mendicant has vowed not to exceed staying in one place] in the hot or cold seasons or for the rain), season (he should say): 'O long-lived one? you sin by overstaying the fixed time.' (6)

2. If the reverend persons repeatedly live in halting-places, &c., after staying there for the proper time, without passing two or three intermediate months somewhere else, (he should say): 'O long lived one! you sin by repeating your retreat in the same place.' (7)

3. Here, in the east, west, north, or south, there are, forsooth, some faithful householders, householders' wives. &c., who are not well acquainted with the rules of monastic life (with regard to the fitness of lodging-places); nevertheless they believe in, perceive, are convinced of, (the merit of) giving lodging, to mendicants. They (accordingly) give lodging-places for the sake of many Sramanas and

Brahmanas, guests, paupers, and beggars, in workshops, chapels, temples, assembly halls, wells, houses or halls for shopkeeping or for keeping or building carriages, distilleries, houses where Darbha-grass, bark, trees, wood or charcoal are being worked, houses on burial-places, rooms for retirement near the place of sacrifice', empty houses, hill-houses, caves, stone-houses, or palaces. He should say to those reverend persons who live in such-like places as workshops, &c., together with other guests: 'O long-lived one! you sin by living in a place frequented by other sectarians.' (8)

4. Here, in the east, &c. They accordingly give, &c. (all as in §8 down to) palaces. If the mendicants come there while the other religious men do not come there, they sin by living in a place not frequented by other mendicants. (9)

5. In the east, west, north, or south there are faithful householders, viz. a householder or his wife, &c., who will speak thus: 'It is not meet that these illustrious, pious, virtuous, eloquent, controlled, chaste ascetics, who have ceased from sexual intercourse, should dwell in a lodging which is adhakarmika: let us give to the mendicants the lodgings which are ready for our use, viz. workshops, &c., and let us, afterwards, prepare lodgings for our own use, viz. workshops, &c.' Hearing and perceiving such talk, if the reverend persons frequent such-like lodgings, viz. workshops, &c., and live in them which are ceded by other people (they should be warned): 'O long-lived one! that (lodging is infected by the sin called) vargakriya.' (10)

6. Here, in the east, &c. (see § 8 all down to) they give lodging-places for the sake of many Sramanas and Brahmanas, guests, paupers, and beggars, after having well counted them, in workshops, &c. If the reverend persons frequent such-like lodgings viz. workshops, &c., and live in them which are ceded by other people (they should be warned): 'O long lived one! that (lodging is

infected by the sin called) mahavargakriya.' (11)

7. Here, in the east, &c. They accordingly give, for the sake of many sorts of Sramanas, after having well counted them, lodging-places, viz. workshops, &c. If the reverend persons frequent such-like lodgings, viz. workshops, &c., and live in them which are ceded by other people (they should be warned): 'O long-lived one! that (lodging is infected by the sin called) savadyakriya.' (12)

8. Here, in the east, &c. They accordingly prepare, for the sake of one sort of Sramanas, lodgings, viz. workshops, &c., for which purpose great injury is done to the earth, water, fire, wind-bodies, plants, and animals, great injury, great cruelty, great and manifold sinful acts; by wasting cold water or strewing (the ground), smearing it with cowdung, shutting the doors and securing the bed, lighting a fire. If the reverend persons' frequent such-like lodgings, viz. workshops, &c., and lead in such ceded lodgings an ambiguous 2 life (they should be warned): ' O long-lived one! that (lodging is infected by the sin called) mahasavadyakriya.' (13)

9. But if the lodgings, viz. workshops, &c., are prepared by the householders for their own sake under the same circumstances as detailed in the preceding paragraph, and the reverend persons frequent such-like lodgings, they lead, in those lodgings, an unambiguous life. 'O long-lived one! that (lodging is infected by the very small sin called) alpasivadyakriya.'

This is the whole duty, &c.

Thus I say. (14)

**Third Lesson**

It' is difficult to obtain pure, acceptable alms; it is indeed not free from such preparations as strewing the ground (with Darbha-grass), smearing it (with cowdung), shutting the doors and securing the beds. And he (the mendicant) delights in pilgrimage, religious exercises, study, begging for a bed, a couch, or other alms.'

Some mendicants explain thus (the requisites of a lodging); they are called upright, searching after liberation, practising no deceit.

Some householders (who, having learned the requisites of a lodging-place, fit one out accordingly, try to deceive the mendicants, saying): 'This lodging, which we offer you, has been assigned to you, it has been originally prepared for our sake, or for the sake of some relations, it has been used, it has been relinquished.'

Explaining thus, he truly explains. (The teacher says): Well, he is (an explainer of the truth). (1)

If a mendicant, at night or at the twilight, leaves or enters a small lodging, one with a small door, a low or crammed lodging, (he should put forward) first his hand, then his foot, and thus circumspectly leave or enter it.

The Kevalin says: This is the reason: There might be a badly.bound, badly placed, badly fastened, loose umbrella, pot, stick, staff, robe, hide, leather boots or piece of leather belonging to Sramanas or Brahmanas; and the mendicant, when leaving or entering (the lodging) at night or twilight, might stumble or fall; stumbling or falling he might hurt his hand or foot, &c. (see IV, 1, 7, § 1), kill, &c., all sorts of living beings.

Hence it has been said to the mendicant, &c., that one (should put forward) first the hand, then the foot, and thus circumspectly leave or enter such a lodging. (2)

He (the mendicant) should, at halting-places, &c., ask for a lodging-place, after having inquired who is the landlord or who is the tenant. He should ask permission to use the lodging-place in this way: 'By your favour, O long-lived one! we shall dwell here for a while (for the time and in the place) which you will concede.' (If the landlord should object and say that he owns the lodging for a limited time only, or if he asks for the number of monks for which the lodging is required, he should answer)': 'As long as this lodging belongs to you, (or) for the sake of as many fellow-ascetics (as shall stand in need of it), we shall occupy the lodging; afterwards we shall take to wandering.' (3)

A monk or a nun may know the name and gotra of him in whose lodging he lives; in that case they should not accept food, &c., in that house whether invited or not invited; for it is impure and unacceptable. (4)

A monk or a nun should not use for religious postures, &c., a lodging-place which is used by the householder, which contains fire or water; for it is not fit for a wise man to enter or leave it, &c. (cf. II, 1, 4, § 1). (5)

A monk or a nun should not use for religious postures, &c., a lodging for which they have to pass through the householder's abode, or to which there is no road; for it is not fit, &c. (see last paragraph). (6)

A monk or a nun should not use for religious postures, &c., a lodging where the householder or his wife, &c., might bully or scold, &c., each other (see 1, 2, 1, § 9); for it is not fit, &c. (7)

A monk or a nun should not use for religious postures, &c., a lodging where the householder or his wife, &c., rub or anoint each other's body with oil or ghee or butter or grease; for it is not fit, &c. (8)

A monk or a nun should not use for religious postures, &c., a lodging where the householder or his wife, &c., rub or shampoo each other's body with perfumes, ground drugs, powder, lodhra, &c. (see 11, 2, 1, § 8); for it is not fit, &c. (9)

A monk or a nun should not use for religious postures,

&c., a lodging where the householder or his wife, &c., clean, wash, or sprinkle each other's body with cold or hot water; for it is not fit, &c. (10)

A monk or a nun should not use for religious postures, &c., a lodging where the householder or his wife, &c., go about naked or hide themselves, or talk about sexual pleasures, or discuss a secret plan; for it is not fit, &c. (11)

A monk or a nun should not use for religious postures, &c., a lodging which is a much-frequented playground; for it is not fit, &c. (12)

1. If a monk or a nun wish to beg for a couch, they should not accept one which they recognise full of eggs, living beings, &c. (i-)

2. If the couch is free from eggs, living beings, but is heavy, they should not accept such a couch. (14)

3. If the couch is free from eggs, living beings, light, but not movable, they should not accept such a couch. (15)

4. If the couch is free from eggs, living beings, &c., light, movable, but not well tied, they should not accept such a couch 2. (16)

5. If the couch is free from eggs, living beings, light, movable, and well tied, they may accept such a couch. (17)

For the avoidance of these occasions to sin there are four rules, according to which the mendicant should beg for a couch.

Now this is the first rule for begging for a couch. If a monk or a nun beg for a couch, specifying (its quality), viz. one of Ikkata-reed, a hard one, one of Gantuka-grass, of Para-grass, of peacock feathers, of hay, of Kusa-grass, of brush-hair, of Pakkaka, of Pippala, of straw, they should, after consideration, say: 'O long-lived one! (or, O sister!) please give me this here!' If the householder prepares one of the above-specified couches, or if the mendicant asks himself, and the householder gives it, then he may accept it as pure and acceptable.

This is the first rule. (18)

Now follows the second rule.

If a monk or a nun beg for a couch (of the abovedetailed description) after having well inspected it, they should, after consideration, say: 'O long-lived one! &c.' (all as in-the first rule).

This is the second rule. (19)

If a monk or a nun beg for a couch of the above-detailed description, viz. one of Ikkata-grass, &c., from him in whose house he lives, they may use it if they get it; if not, they should remain in a,.squatting or sitting posture (for the whole night).

This is the third rule. (20)

Now follows the fourth rule.

If a monk or a nun beg for a couch such as it is spread, either on the ground or on a wooden plank, they may use it if the), get it; if not, they should remain in a squatting or sitting postuire (for the whole night).

This is the fourth rule. (21)

A monk who has adopted one of these four rules, should not say, &c. (all as in II, 1, 11, § 12, down to) we respect each other accordingly. (22)

If a monk or a nun wish to give back a couch, they should not do so, if the couch contains eggs, living beings, &c. But if it contains few living beings, &c., they may restrainedly do so, after having well inspected, swept, and dried it. (23)

A monk or a nun on a begging-tour or in a residence or on a pilgrimage from village to village should first inspect the place for easing nature. The Kevalin says: This is the reason: If a monk or a nun, in the night or the twilight, ease nature in a place which they have not previously inspected, they might stumble or fall, stumbling or falling the), might hurt the hand or foot, &c., kill, &c., all sorts of living beings. (24)

A monk or a nun might wish to inspect the ground for their couch away from that occupied by a teacher or sub-teacher, &c. (see II, 1, 10, § 1), or by a young one or an old one or a novice or a sick man or a guest, either at the end or in the middle, either on even or uneven ground, or at a place where there is a draught or where there is no draught. They should then well inspect and sweep (the floor), and circumspectly spread a perfectly pure bed or couch. (25)

Having spread a perfectly pure bed or couch, a monk or a nun might wish to ascend it. When doing so, they should first wipe their body from head to heels; then they may circumspectly ascend the perfectly pure bed or couch, and circumspectly sleep in it. (26)

A monk or a nun sleeping in a perfectly pure bed or couch (should have placed it at such a distance from the next one's) that they do not touch their neighbour's hand, foot, or body with their own hand, foot, or body; and not touching it, should circumspectly sleep in their perfectly pure bed or couch. (27)

Before inhaling or breathing forth, or coughing or sneezing or yawning or vomiting or eructating, a monk or a nun should cover their face or the place where it lies; then they may circumspectly inhale or breathe forth, &c. (28)

Whether his lodging, be even or uneven; full of, or free from, draughts; full of, or free from, dust; full of, or free from, flies and gnats; full of, or free from, dangers and troubles-in any such-like lodging one should contentedly stay, nor take offence at anything.

This is the whole duty, &c.

Thus I say. (29)

End of the Second Lecture, called Begging for a Couch.

**Third Lecture**

**Called**

**Walking.**

**First Lesson**

When the rainy season has come and it is raining, many living beings are originated and many seeds just spring up, the roads between (different places) contain many living beings, seeds, &c. (see II, 1, 1, § 2), the footpaths are not used, the roads are not recognisable. Knowing this (state of things) one should not wander from village to village, but remain during the rainy season in one place. (I)

When a monk or a nun knows that. in a village or scot-free town, &c. (see I, 7, 6, § 3), there is no large place for religious practices nor for study; that there cannot easily be obtained a stool, bench, bed, or couch, nor pure, acceptable alms; that there have come or will come many Sramanas and Brahmanas, guests, paupers, and beggars; that the means of existence are extremely small; that it is not fit for a wise man to enter or leave it, &c. (see II, 1, 4, § 1); in such a village, scot-free town, &c., they should not remain during the cold season. (2)

When. a monk or a nun knows that in a village or scot-free town, &c., there is a large place for religious practices or for study; that there can easily be obtained a stool, bench, bed, or couch, or pure, acceptable alms; that there have not come nor will come Sramanas and

Brahmanas, guests, paupers, and beggars; that the means of existence are not small, &c., they may remain in such a village, &c., during the rainy season. (3)

Now they should know this - After the four months of the rainy season are over, and five or ten days of the winter have passed, they should not wander from village to village, if the road contains many living beings, &c., and if many Sramanas and Brahmanas, &c., do not yet travel. (4)

But if after the same time the road contains few living beings, and many Sramanas and Brihmanas, &c., travel, they may circumspectly wander from village to village. (5)

A monk or a nun wandering from village to village should look forward for four cubits, and seeing animals they should move on by walking on his toes or heels or the sides of his feet. If there be some bypath, they should choose it, and not go straight on; then they may circumspectly wander from village to village. (6)

A monk or a nun wandering from village to village, on whose way there are living beings, seeds, grass, water, or mud, should not go straight if there be an unobstructed byway; then they may circumspectly wander from village to village. (7)

A monk or a nun on the pilgrimage, whose road (lies through) places belonging to borderers, robbers,

Mlekkhas, non-Aryan people, half-civilised people, unconverted people, people who rise or eat at an improper time, should, if there be some other place for walking about or friendly districts, not choose the former road for their voyage. (8)

The Kevalin says: This is the reason: The ignorant populace might bully, beat, &c., the mendicant, in the opinion that he is a thief or a spy, or that he comes from yonder (hostile village); or they might take away, cut off, steal or rob his robe, alms-bowl, mantle, or broom. Hence it has been said to the mendicant, &c., that one whose road (lies through) places belonging, &c. (all as in the last paragraph); then he may circumspectly wander from village to village.(9)

A monk or a nun on the pilgrimage, whose road (lies through) a country where there is no king or many kings or an unanointed king or two governments or no government or a weak government, should, if there be some other place for walking about or friendly districts, not choose the former road for their voyage. The Kevalin says: This is the reason: The ignorant populace might bully or beat, &c., the mendicant, &c. (all as in § 9). (10)

A monk or a nun on the pilgrimage, whose road lies through a forest which they are not certain of crossing in one or two or three or four or five days, should, if there be some other place for walking about or friendly districts, not choose the former road for their voyage. (11)

The Kevalin says: This is the reason: During the rain (he might injure) living beings, mildew, seeds, grass, water, mud. Hence it has been said to the mendicant that one whose road lies through such a forest, &c. (all as in the last paragraph); then he may circumspectly wander from village to village. (12)

A monk or a nun on the pilgrimage, on whose way there is some watercourse which must be crossed by a boat, should not ascend such a boat which plies up or down or across (the river), neither for one yogana's or half a yogana's distance, neither for a shorter nor a longer voyage, if they know that the householder' will buy or purloin the boat, or doing the work necessary to put the boat in order, pull it ashore out of the water, or push it from the shore into the water, or bale it, if it is filled (with water), or cause a sinking boat to float. (13)

A monk or a nun, knowing that a boat will cross the river, should, after having received the owners permission, step apart, examine their outfit, put aside their provender, wipe their body from head to heels, reject the householder's food, and putting one foot in the water and the other in the air, they should circumspectly enter the boat. (14)

A monk or a nun in entering the boat should not choose for that purpose the stern or the prow or the middle of the boat; nor should they look at it holding up their arms, pointing at it with their finger, bowing up and down.(15)

If, on board, the boatman should say to the monk, O long-lived Sramana! pull the boat forward or backward, or push it, or draw it with the rope towards you, or, let us do it together,' he should not comply with his request, but look on silently. (16)

If, on board, the other should say to him, 'O long-lived Sramana! you cannot pull the boat forward or backward, or push it, or draw it with a rope towards you; give us the rope, we will ourselves pull the boat forward or backward, &c.,' he should not comply with his request, but look on silently. (17)

If, on board, the other should say to him,'O long-lived Sramana! if you can, pull the boat by the oar, the rudder, the pole, and other nautical instruments,' he should not comply with his request, but look on silently. (18)

If, on board, the other should say to him, 'O long-lived Sramana! please, lade out the water with your hand, or pitcher, or vessel, or alms-bowl, or bucket,' he should not comply with his request, but look on silently. (19)

If, on board, the other should say to him,'O long-lived Sramana! please, stop the boat's leak with your hand, foot, arm, thigh, belly, head, body, the bucket, or a cloth, or with mud, Kusa-grass, or lotus leaves,' be should not comply with his request, but look on silently. (20)

If a monk or a nun see that water enters through a leak in the boat, and the boat becomes dirty all over, they should not approach the boatman and say: 'O long-lived householder! water enters through a leak into the boat, and it becomes dirty all over.'

One should not think so or speak so; but undisturbed, the mind not directed outwardly, one should collect one's self for contemplation; then one may circumspectly complete one's journey by the boat on the water.

This is the whole duty, &c.

Thus I say. (21)

**Second Lesson**

If, on board, the boatman should say to the mendicant,'O long-lived Sramana! please, take this umbrella, pot, &c. (see II, 2, 3, § 2), hold these various dangerous instruments, let this boy or girl drink,' he should not comply with his request, but look on silently. (1)

If, on board, the boatman should say to another of the crew,'O long-lived one! this Sramana is only a heavy load for the boat, take hold of him with your arms and throw him into the water!' hearing and perceiving such talk, he should, if he wears clothes, quickly take them off or fasten them or put them in a bundle on his head. (2)

Now he may think: These ruffians, accustomed to violent acts, might take hold of me and throw me from the boat into the water. He should first say to them:'O long-lived householders! don't take hold of me with your arms and throw me into the water! I myself shall leap from the boat into the water!'

If after these words the other, by force and violence,

takes hold of him with his arms and throws him into the water, he should be neither glad nor sorry, neither in high nor low spirits, nor should he offer violent resistance to those ruffians; but undisturbed, his mind not directed to outward things, &c. (see II, 3, 1, § 21), he may circumspectly swim in the water. (3)

A monk or a nun, swimming in the water, should not touch (another person's or their own?) hand, foot, or body with their own hand, foot, or body; but without touching it they should circumspectly swim in the water. (4)

A monk or a nun, swimming in the water, should not dive up or down, lest water should enter into their ears, eyes, nose, or mouth; but they should circurnspectly swim in the water. (5)

If a monk or a nun, swimming in the water, should be overcome by weakness, they should throw off their implements (clothes, &c.), either all or a part of them, and not be attached to them. Now they should know this: If they are able to get out of the water and reach the bank, they should circumspectly remain on the bank with a wet or moist body. (6)

A monk or a nun should not wipe or rub or brush or stroke [The original has six words for different kinds of rubbing, which it would be impossible to render adequately in any other language -tr.] or dry or warm or heat (in the sun) their body. But when they perceive that the water on their body has dried up, and the moisture is gone, they may wipe or rub, &c., their body in that state; then they may circumspectly wander from village to village. (7)

A monk or a nun on the pilgrimage should not wander from village to village, conversing with householders; they may circumspectly wander from village to village. (8)

If a monk or a nun on the pilgrimage come across a shallow water, they should first wipe their body from head to heels, then, putting one foot in the water and the other in the air, they should wade through the shallow water in a straight line. (9)

If a monk or a nun on the pilgrimage come across a shallow water, they should wade through it in a straight line, without being touched by or touching. (another person's or their own?) hand, foot, or body with-their own hand, foot, or body. (10)

A monk or a nun, wading through shallow water in a straight line, should not plunge in deeper water for the sake of pleasure or the heat; but they should circumspectly wade through the shallow water in a straight line. Now they should know this: If one is able to get out of the water and reach the bank, one should circumspectly remain on the bank with a wet or moist body. (11)

A monk or a nun should not wipe or rub, &c. (all as in § 7). (12)

A monk or a nun on the pilgrimage, with their feet soiled with mud, should not, in order that the grass might take off the mud from the feet, walk out of the way and destroy the grass by cutting, trampling, and tearing it. As this would be sinful, they should not do so. But they should first inspect a path containing little grass; then they may circumspectly wander from village to village. (13)

If a monk or a nun on the pilgrimage come upon walls or ditches or ramparts or gates or bolts or holes to fit them, or moats or caves, they should, in case there be a byway, choose it, and not go on straight. (14)

The Kevalin says: This is the reason: Walking there, the mendicant might stumble or fall down; when he stumbles or falls down, he might get hold of trees, shrubs, plants, creepers, grass, copsewood, or sprouts to extricate himself. He should ask travellers who meet him, to lend a hand; then he may circumspectly lean upon it and extricate himself; so he may circumspectly wander from village to village. (15)

If a monk or a nun perceive in their way (transports of) corn, waggons, cars, a friendly or hostile army, some encamped troops, they should, in case there be a byway, circumspectly choose it, and not walk on straight. One trooper might say to another: 'O long-lived one! this Sramana is a spy upon the army; take hold of him with your arms, and drag him hither!' The other might take hold of the mendicant with his arms and drag him on. He should neither be glad nor sorry for it, &c. (see § 3); then he may circumspectly wander from village to village. (16)

If on his road travellers meet him and say, 'O long-lived Sramana! how large is this village or scot-free town, &c.? how many horses, elephants, beggars, men dwell in it? is there much food, water, population, corn? is there little food, water, population, corn?' he should not answer such questions if asked, nor ask them himself.

This is the whole duty, &c.

Thus I say. (17)

**Third Lesson**

A monk or a nun on the pilgrimage, in whose way there are walls or ditches or ramparts or gates, &c. (See II, 3, 2, § 14), hill houses, palaces, underground houses, houses in trees, mountain caves, a sacred tree or pillar, workshops, &c. (see II, 2, 2, § 8), should not look at them holding up their arms, pointing at them with their fingers, bowing up and down. Then they may circumspectly wander from village to village. (1)

A monk or a nun on the pilgrimage, on whose way there are marshes, pasture-grounds, moats, fortified places, thickets, strongholds in thickets, woods, mountains, strongholds on mountains, caves, tanks, lakes, rivers, ponds, lotus ponds, long winding ponds, water-sheets, rows of water-sheets, should not look at them holding up their arms, &c. (see § 1). (2)

The Kevalin says: This is the reason: The deer, cattle, birds, snakes, animals living in water, on land, in the air might be disturbed or frightened, and strive to get to a fold or (other place of) refuge, (thinking): 'The Sramana will - harm me!'

Hence it has been said to the mendicant, &c., that he should not look at the objects (mentioned in § 2) holding up his arms, &c. (3)

A monk or a nun, wandering from village to village together with the master or teacher, should not touch the master's or teacher's hand with their own, &c.; but without touching or being touched they should circumspectly wander from village to village together with the master or teacher.(4)

A monk or a nun, wandering from village to village together with the master or teacher, might be met on the road by travellers and asked: 'O long-lived Sramana! who are you? whence do you come, and where do you go?' The master or teacher may answer and explain; but whilst the master or teacher answers and explains, one should not mix in their conversation. Thus they may wander from village to village with a superior priest. (5)

A monk or a nun, wandering from village to village with a superior priest, should not touch the superior's hand with their own, &c. (see § 4). (6).

A monk or a nun, wandering from villaee to village with superior priests, might be met on the road by travellers, and be asked: 'O long-lived Sramana! who are you?' He who has the highest rank of them all, should answer and explain; but whilst the superior answers and explains, one should not mix in their conversation, &c. (see § 5). (7)

A monk or a nun, wandering from village to village, might be met on the road by travellers, and be asked: 'O long-lived Sramana! did you see somebody on the road? viz. a man, cow, buffalo, cattle, bird, snake, or aquatic animal-tell us, show us!' The mendicant should not tell it, nor show it, he should not comply with their request, but look on silently, or, though knowing it, he should say that he did not know. Then he may circumspectly wander from village to village.(8)

He should act in the same nianner, if asked about bulbs of water-plants, roots, bark, leaves, flowers, fruits, seeds, water in the neighbourhood, or a kindled fire; (9)

Likewise, if asked about (transports of) corn, waggons, cars, &c. (see II, 3, 2, § 16). (10)

Likewise, if asked: ' O long-lived Sramana! how large is this village or scot-free town, &c.?' (11)

Likewise, if asked: 'O long-lived Sramana! How far is it to that village or scot-free town. &c.?' (12)

If a monk or a nun, wandering from village to village, sees a vicious cow coming towards them, &c. (see II, 1, 5, § 3), they should not, from fear of them, leave the road, or go into another road, nor enter a thicket, wood, or stronghold, nor climb a tree, nor take a plunge in a large and extended water-sheet, nor desire a fold or any other place of refuge, or an army or a caravan; but undisturbed, the mind not directed to outward things, they should collect themselves for contemplation; thus they may circumspectly wander from village to village. (13)

If the road of a monk or a nun on the pilgrimage lies through a forest, in which, as they know, there stroll bands of many thieves desirous of their property, they should not, for fear of them, leave the road, &c. (all as in § 13). (14)

If these thieves say, 'O long-lived Sramana! bring us your clothes, &c., give them, put them down!' the mendicant should not give or put them down. Nor should he reclaim (his things) by imploring (the thieves), or by folding his hands, or by moving their compassion, but by religious exhortation or by remaining silent. (15)

If the thieves, resolving to do it themselves, bully him, &c., tear off his clothes, &c., he should not lodge an information in the village or at the king's palace; nor should he go to a layman, and say, 'O long-lived householder! these thieves, resolving to do (the robbing) themselves, have bullied me, &c., they have torn off my, clothes,' &c. He should neither think so, nor speak so; but undisturbed, &c. (see § 13).

This is the whole duty, &c.

Thus I say. (16)

End of the Third Lecture, called Walking.

**Fourth Lecture,**

**Called**

**Modes of Speech**

**First Lesson**

A monk or a nun, hearing and perceiving these uses of speech, should know that the following ones are not to be employed and have not hitherto been employed (by persons of exemplary conduct); those who speak in wrath or in pride, for deception or for gain, who speak, knowingly or unknowingly, hard words. They should avoid all this, which is blamable. Employing their judgment, they should know something for certain and something for uncertain 2: (1) (N. N.) having received food or not having received food, having eaten it or not having eaten it, has come or has not come, comes or does not come, will come or will not come. (2)

Well considering (what one is to say), speaking with precision, one should employ language in moderation and restraint: the singular, dual, plural; feminine, masculine, neuter gender; praise, blame,praise mixed with blame, blame mixed with praise past, present, or future (tenses), the first and second, or third (person). If one thinks it necessary to speak in the singular, he should speak in the singular; if he thinks it necessary to speak in the plural, he should speak in the plural, &c. Considering well: this is a woman, this is a man, this is a eunuch, this is to be called thus, this is to be called otherwise, speaking with precision, he should employ language in moderation and restraint. (3)

For the avoidance of these occasions to sin, a mendicant should know that there are four kinds of speech: the first is truth; the second is untruth; the third is truth mixed with untruth; what is neither truth, nor untruth, nor truth mixed with untruth, that is the fourth kind of speech: neither truth not untruth. Thus I say.

All past, present, and future Arhats have taught and declared, teach and declare, will teach and declare these four kinds of speech; and they have explained all those things which are devoid of intellect, which possess colour, smell, taste, touch, which are subject to decay and increase, which possess various qualities. (4)

A monk (or a nun should know that) before (the utterance) speech is speech in (antecedent) nonexistence; that while uttered, it is (real) speech; that the moment after it has been uttered, the spoken speech is speech in (subsequent) non-existence. (5)

A monk or a nun, well considering, should not use speech whether truth or untruth, or truth mixed with untruth, if it be sinful, blamable, rough, stinging, coarse, hard, leading to sins, to discord and factions, to grief and outrage, to destruction of living beings. (6)

A monk or a nun, considering well, should use true and accurate speech, or speech which is neither truth nor untruth (i.e. injunctions); for such speech is not sinful, blamable, rough, stinging, &c. (7)

A monk or a nun, if addressing a man who, if addressed, does not answer, should not say: 'You loon! you lout! you Sudra! you low-born wretch! you slave! you dog! you thief! you robber! you cheat! you liar! &c.; you are such and such! your parents are such and such!' Considering well, they should not use such sinful, blamable, &c., speech. (8)

But in that case they should say: 'N. N.! O long-lived one! O long-lived ones! O layman! O pupil! O faithful one! O lover of faith!' Considering well, they should use such sinless, blameless, &c., speech. (9)

A monk or a nun, if addressing a woman who, if addressed, does not answer, should not say: 'You hussy! you wench! &c.' (repeat the above list of abusive words adapted to fernales). Considering well, they should not use such sinful, blamable, &c., speech.(10)

A monk or a nun, if addressing a woman who, Waddressed, does not answer, should say: 'O long-lived one! O sister! madam! my lady! O lay-sister! O pupil! O faithful one! O lover of faith!' Considering well, they should use such sinless, blameless, &c., speech. (11)

A monk or a nun should not say: 'The god of the sky! the god of the thunderstorm! the god of lightning! the god who begins to rain! the god who ceases to rain! may rain fall or may it not fall! may the crops grow or may they not grow! may the night wane or may it not wane! may the sun rise or may it not rise! may the king conquer or may he not conquer!' They should not use such speech. (12)

But knowing the nature of things, he should say: 'The air; the follower of Guhya; a cloud has gathered or come down; the cloud has rained.'

This is the whole duty. &c.

Thus I say. (13)

**Second Lesson**

A monk or a nun, seeing any sort (of diseases), should not talk of them in this way: 'He has got boils, or leprosy, &c. (see I, 6, 1, § 3); his hand is cut, or his foot, nose, car, lip is cut.' For as all such people, spoken to in such language, become angry, hence, considering well, they should not speak to them in such language. (1)

A monk or a nun, seeing any sort (of good qualities), should speak thus: 'He is strong, powerful, vigorous, famous, well-formed, well-proportioned, handsome.' For as all such people, spoken to in such language, do not become angry, they should, considering well, speak to them in such language. (2)

A monk or a nun, seeing any sort of such things as walls or ditches, &c. (see II, 3, 2, § 14), should not speak of them in this way; 'This is well-executed, finely executed, beautiful, excellent, (so done) or to be done;' they should not use such sinful, &c., language. (3)

A monk or a nun, seeing walls, &c., should speak about them in this way: 'This has been executed with great effort, with sin, with much labour; it is very magnificent, it is very beautiful, it is very fine, it is very handsome;' considering well, they should use such sinless, &c., language. (4)

A monk or a nun, seeing food, &c., prepared, should

not speak about it in this way: 'This is well executed, finely executed, beautiful, excellent, (so done) or to be done;' considering well, they should not use such sinful, &c., language. (5)

A monk or a nun, seeing food, &c., prepared, should speak about it in this way: 'This has been executed with great effort, with sin, with much labour; it is very good, it is excellent, it is well seasoned, it is most delicious, it is most agreeable;' considering well, they should use such sinless, &c., language. (6)

A monk or a nun, seeing a man, a cow, a buffalo, deer, cattle, a bird, a snake, an aquatic animal of increased bulk, should not speak about them in this way: 'He (or it) is fat, round, fit to be killed or cooked;' considering well, they should not use such sinful, &c., language. (7)

A monk or a nun, seeing a man, a cow, &c., of increased bulk, should speak about them in this way: 'He is of increased bulk, his body is well grown, well compacted, his flesh and blood are abundant, his limbs are fully developed;' considering well, they should use such sinless, &c., language. (8)

A monk or a nun, seeing any sort of cows (or oxen), should not speak about them in this way: 'These cows should be milked or tamed or covered, should draw a waggon or car;' considering well, they should not use such sinful, &c., language. (9)

A monk or a nun, seeing any sort of cows (or oxen), should speak about them in this way: 'It is a young cow, a milch cow, she gives much milk, it is a short or a large one, a beast of burden;' considering well, they should use such sinless, &c., language. (10)

A monk or a nun, seeing big trees in parks, on hills, or in woods, should speak about them in this way: 'These (trees) are fit for palaces, gates, houses, benches, bolts, boats, buckets, stools, trays, ploughs, mattocks(?), machines, poles, the nave of a wheel(?), gandi [a kind of utensil], seats, beds, cars, sheds;' considering well, they should not use such sinful, &c., language. (11)

A monk or a nun, seeing big trees in parks, on hills, or in woods, should speak about them in this way: 'These trees are noble, high and round, big; they have many branches, extended branches, they are very magnificent' &c. (see § 4); considering well they should use such sinless, &c., language. (12)

A monk or a nun, seeing many wild fruits, should not speak about them in this way: 'They are ripe, they should be cooked or eaten, they are just in season, or soft, or they have just split;' considering well, they should not use such sinful, &c., language. (13)

A monk or a nun, seeing many wild fruits, should speak about them in this way: 'They are very plentiful, they contain many seeds, they are fully grown, they have developed their proper shape;' considering well, they should use such sinless, &c., language. (14)

A monk or a nun, seeing many vegetables, should not speak about them in this way: 'They are ripe, they are dark coloured, shining, fit to be fried or roasted or eaten;' considering well, they should not use such sinful, &c., language. (15)

A monk or a nun, seeing many vegetables, should speak about them in this way: 'They are grown up, they are fully grown, they are strong, they are excellent, they are run to seed, they have spread their seed, they are full of sap;' considering well, they should use such sinless, &c., language.(16)

A monk or a nun, hearing any sort of sounds, should not speak about them in this way: 'This is a good sound, this is a bad sound;' considering well, they should not use such sinless, &c., language; but they should call them good, if they are good; bad, if they are bad; considering well, they should use such sinless, &c., language. (17)

In the same manner they should speak about the (five) colours, as black, &c.; as pleasant; the (two) smells, as pleasant or unpleasant; the (five) tastes, as sharp &c.; the (five) kinds of touch, as hard, &c. (18)

A monk or a nun, putting aside wrath, pride, deceit, and greed, considering well, speaking with precision, what one has heard, not too quick, with discrimination, should employ language in moderation and restraint.

This is the whole duty, &c.

Thus I say. (19)

End of the Fourth Lecture, called Modes of Speech.

## Fifth Lecture,

## Called

## Begging of Clothes.

### First Lesson

A monk or a nun wanting to get clothes, may beg for cloth made of wool, silk, hemp, palm-leaves, cotton, or Arkatula,or such-like clothes. If he be a youthful, young, strong, healthy, well-set monk, he may wear one robe, not two; if a nun, she should possess four raiments, one two cubits broad, two three cubits broad, one four cubits broad. If one does not receive such pieces of cloth, one should afterwards sew together onewith the other. (1)

A monk or a nun should not resolve to go further than half a yogana to get clothes. As regards the acceptance of clothes, those precepts which have been given in the (First Lession of the First Lecture, called) Begging of Food.

concerning one fellowascetic, should be repeated here; also concerning many fellow-ascetics, one female fellow-ascetic, many female fellow-ascetics, many Sramanas and Brahmanas; also about (clothes) appropriated by another person. (2)

A monk or a nun should not accept clothes which the layman, for the mendicant's sake, has bought, washed, dyed, brushed, rubbed, cleaned, perfumed, if these clothes be appropriated by the giver himself. But if they be appropriated by another person, they may accept them; for they are pure and acceptable. (3)

A monk or a nun should not accept any very expensive clothes of the following description: clothes made of fur, fine ones, beautiful ones; clothes made of goats' hair, of blue cotton, of common cotton, of Bengal cotton, of Patta, of Malaya fibres, of bark fibres, of muslin, of silk; (clothes provincially called) Desaraga, Amila, Gaggala, Phaliya, Kayaha; blankets or mantles. (4)

A monk or a nun should not accept any of the following plaids of fur and other materials: plaids made of Udra, Pesa fur, embroidered with Pesa fur, made of the fur of black or blue or yellow deer, golden plaids, plaids glittering like gold, interwoven with gold, set with gold, embroidered with gold, plaids made of tigers' fur, highly ornamented plaids, plaids covered with ornaments. (5)

For the avoidance of these occasions to sin there are four rules for begging clothes to be known by the mendicants.

Now, this is the first rule:

A monk or a nun may beg for clothes specifying (their quality), viz. wool, silk, hemp, palm-leaves, cotton, Arkatula. If they beg for them, or the householder gives them, they may accept them; for the), are pure and acceptable.

This is the first rule. (6)

Now follows the second rule:

A monk or a nun may ask for clothes which they have well inspected, from the householder or his wife, &c. After consideration, they should say: 'O long~ lived one! (or, O sister!) please give me one of these clothes!' If they beg for them, or the householder gives them, they may accept them; for they are pure and acceptable.

This is the second rule. (7)

Now follows the third rule:

A monk or a nun may beg for an under or upper garment. If they beg for it, &c. (see § 7)

This is the third rule. (8)

Now follows the fourth rule:

A monk or a nun may beg for a left-off robe, which no other Sramana or Brihmana, guest, pauper or beggar wants. If they beg, &c. (see § 7).

This is the fourth rule.

A monk or a nun who have adopted one of these four rules should not say, &c. (all as in II, 1, 11, § 12, down to) we respect each other accordingly. (9)

A householder may perhaps say to a mendicant begging in the prescribed -way: 'O long-lived Sramana! return after a month, ten nights, five nights, to-morrow, to-morrow night; then we shall give you some clothes.' Hearing and perceiving such talk, he should, after consideration, say: 'O long-lived one! (or, O sister!) it is not meet for me to accept such a promise. If you want to give me (something), give it me now!'

After these words the householder may answer:

O long-lived Sramana! follow me! then we shall give you some clothes.' The mendicant should give the same answer as above.

After his words the householder may say (to one of his people): 'O long-lived one! (or, O sister!) fetch that robe! we shall give it the Sramana, and afterwards prepare one for our own use, killing all sorts of living beings.'

Hearing and perceiving such talk, he should not accept such clothes; for they are impure and unacceptable. (10)

The householder may say (to one of his people): 'O long-lived one! (or, O sister!) fetch that robe, wipe or rub it with perfume, &c. (see II, 2, 1, § 8); we shall give it to the Sramana.'

Hearing and perceiving such talk, the mendicant should, after consideration, say: 'O long-lived one! (or, O sister!) do not wipe or rub it with perfume, &c. If you want to give it me, give it, such as it is!'

After these words the householder might nevertheless offer the clothes after having wiped or rubbed them, &c.; but the mendicant should not accept them, for they are impure and unacceptable. (11)

The householder may say (to another of his people): 'O long-lived one! (or, O sister!) bring that robe, clean or wash it with cold or hot water!'

The mendicant should return the same answer as above (in § 11) and not accept such clothes. (12)

The householder may say (to another of his people): 'O long-lived one! (or, O sister!) bring that cloth, empty it of the bulbs, &c. (see II, 2, 1, § 5); we shall give it to the Sramana.' Hearing and perceiving such talk, the mendicant should say, after consideration: 'O long-lived one! (or, O sister!) do not empty that cloth of the bulbs, &c.; it is not meet for me to accept such clothes.' After these words the householder might nevertheless take away the bulbs, &c., and offer him the cloth; but he should not accept it; for it is impure and unacceptable. (13)

If a householder brings a robe and gives it to the mendicant, he should, after consideration, say: 'O long-lived one! (or, O sister!) I shall, in your presence, closely inspect the inside of the robe.'

The Kevalin says: This is the reason: There might be hidden in the robe an earring or girdle or gold and silver, &c. (see II, 2, 1, § 11), or living beings or seeds or grass. Hence it has been said to the mendicant, &c., that he should closely inspect the inside of the robe. (14)

A monk or a nun should not accept clothes which are full of eggs or living beings, &c.; for they are impure, &c. A monk or a nun should not accept clothes which are free from eggs or living beings, &c., but which are not fit nor strong nor lasting nor to be worn-which though pleasant are not fit (for a mendicant); for they are impure and unacceptable.(15)

A monk or a nun may accept clothes which are fit, strong, lasting, to be worn, pleasant and fit for a mendicant; for they are pure and acceptable. (16),

A monk or a nun should not wash his clothes, rub or wipe them with ground drugs, &c., because they are not new.

A monk or a nun should not clean or wash his clothes in plentiful water, because they are not new. (17)

A monk or a nun should not make his clothes undergo the processes (prohibited in § 17), because they have a bad smell. (18)

A monk or a nun wanting to air or dry (in the sun) their clothes, should not do so on the bare ground or wet earth or rock or piece of clay containing life, &c. (see II, 1, 5, § 2). (19)

A monk or a nun wanting to air or dry (in the sun) their clothes, should not hang them for that purpose on a post of a house, on the upper timber of a door-frame, on a mortar, oil a bathing-tub, or on any such-like above-ground place, which is not well fixed or set, but shaky and movable.(20)

A monk or a nun wanting to air or dry (in the sun) their clothes, should not lay them for that purpose on a dyke, wall, rock, stone, or any such-like above-ground place, &c. (21)

A monk or a nun wajiting to air or dry (in the sun) their clothes, should not do it on a pillar, a raised platform, a scaffold, a second story, a flat roof, or any such-like above-ground place, &c. (22)

Knowing this, he should resort to a secluded spot, and circumspectly air or dry his clothes there on a heap of ashes or bones, &c. (see II, 1, 1, § 1), which he has repeatedly inspected and cleaned.

This is the whole duty, &c.

Thus I say. (23)

**Second Lesson**

A monk or a nun should beg for acceptable clothes, and wear them in that state in which they get them; they should not wash or dye them, nor should they wear washed or dyed clothes, nor (should they) hide (their clothes) when passing through other villages, being careless of dress. This is the whole duty for a mendicant who wears clothes.

A monk or a nun wanting, for the sake of alms, to enter the abode of a householder, should do so outfitted with all their clothes; in the same manner they should go to the out-of-door place for religious practices or study, or should wander from village to village.

Now they should know this: A monk or a nun dressed in all their clothes should not enter or leave, for the sake of alms, the abode of a householder, &c. &c., on perceiving that a strong and widely spread rain pours down, &c. (see II, 1, 3, § 9). (1)

If a single mendicant borrows for a short time a robe

(from another mendicant) and returns after staying abroad for one, two, three, four, or five days, he (the owner) should not take such a robe for himself, nor should he give it to somebody else, nor should he give it on promise (for another robe after a few days), nor should he exchange that robe for another one. He should not go to another mendicant and say: 'O long-lived Sramana! do you want to wear or use this robe?' He (the owner of the robe) should not rend the still strong robe, and cast it away; but give it him (who had borrowed it) in its worn state; he should not use it himself(2)

The same rule holds good when many mendicants borrow for a short time clothes, and return after staying abroad, for one, &c., days. All should be put in the plural.(3)

'Well, I shall borrow a robe and return after staying abroad for one, two, three, four, or five days; perhaps it will thus become my own.' As this would be sinful, he should not do so. (4)

A monk or a nun should not make coloured clothes colourless, or colour colourless clothes; nor should they give them to somebody else thinking that they will get other clothes; nor should they give it on promise (for other clothes); nor should they exchange them for other clothes; nor should they go to somebody else and say: 'O long-lived Sramana! do you want to wear or use these clothes?' They should not rend the still strong clothes, and cast them away, that another mendicant might think them bad ones. (5)

If he sees in his way thieves, he should not from fear of them, and to save his clothes, leave the road or go in to another road, &c. (see II, 3, 3, § 13), but undisturbed, his mind not directed to outward things, he should collect himself for contemplation; then he may circumspectly wander from village to village. (6)

If the road of a monk or a nun on the pilgrimage lies

through a forest in which, as they know, there stroll bands of many thieves desirous of their clothes, they should not from fear of them, and to save their clothes, leave the road or go into another road, &c. (all as in § 6). (7)

If these thieves say: 'O long-lived Sramana! bring us your robe, give it, deliver it!' he should not give or deliver it. He should act in such cases (as prescribed in II, 3, 3, §§ 15 and 16).

This is the whole duty, &c.

Thus I say. (8)

End of the Fifth Lecture, called Begging of Clothes.

**Sixth Lecture,**

**Called**

**Begging for a Bowl.**

**First Lesson**

A monk or a nun wanting to get a bowl, may beg for one made of bottle-gourd or wood or clay, or such-like bowls. If he be a youthful, young, &c. (see II, 5, j, § I) monk, he may carry with hirn one bowl, not two.

A monk or a nun should not resolve to go farther than half a Yogana to get a bowl.

As regards the acceptance of a bowl, those four precepts which have been given in (the First lesson of the First Lecture, called) Begging of Food, concerning One fellow-ascetic, &c., should be repeated here, the fifth is that concerning many Sramanas and Brahmanas.

A monk or a nun should not accept a bowl which the, layman has, for the mendicant's sake, bought, &c. (see the Lecture called Begging of Clothes) (1)

A monk or a nun should not accept any very expensive

consideration, say: 'O long-lived one! (or, O sister!) I shall in your presence closely inspect the interior of the bowl.'

The Kevalin says: This is the reason: In the alms-bowl there might be living beings or seeds or grass. Hence it has been said to the mendicant, &c., that he should closely inspect the interior of the alms-bowl. (11)

All that has been said in the Lecture called Begging of Clothes (II, 5, 1, § 15 down to the end) is mutatis mutandis to be repeated here. (In § 15, add before perfumes) with oil, ghee, butter or marrow.

This is the whole duty, &c.

Thus I say. (12)

**Second Lesson**

A monk or a nun, entering the abode of a householder for the sake of alms, should after examining their alms-bowl, taking out any living beings, and wiping off the dust, circumspectly enter or leave the householder's abode.

The Kevalin says: This is the reason: Living beings, seeds or dust might fall into his bowl. Hence it has been said to the mendicant, &c., that he should after examining his alms-bowl, taking out any living beings, circumspectly enter or leave the householder's abode. (1)

On such an occasion the householder might perbaps, going in the house, fill the alms-bowl with cold water and, returning, offer it him; (the mendicant) should not accept such an alms-bowl' either in the householder's hand or his vessel; for it is impure and unacceptable. (2)

Perhaps he has, inadvertently, accepted it; then he should empty it again in (the householder's) ,water-pot; or (on his objecting to it) he should put down the bowl and the water somewhere, or empty it in some wet place. (3)

A monk or a nun should not wipe or rub a wet or

moist alms-bowl. But when they perceive that on their alms-bowl the water has dried up and the moisture is gone, then they may circumspectly wipe or rub it. (4)

A monk or a nun wanting to enter the abode of a householder, should enter or leave it, for the sake of alms, with their bowl; also on going to the out-of-door place for religious practices or study; or on wandering from village to village.

If a strong and widely spread rain pours down, they should take the same care of their alms-bowl as is prescribed for clothes (in the preceding-, Lecture, Lesson 2, § 1).

This is the whole duty, &c. Thus I say. (5)

End of the Sixth Lecture, called Begging for a Bowl.

**Seventh Lecture,**

**Called**

**Regulation of Possession.**

**First Lesson**

'I shall become a Sramana who owns no house, no property, no sons, no cattle, who eats what others give him; I shall commit no sinful action; Master, I renounce to accept anything that has not been given.' Having taken such vows, (a mendicant) should not, on entering a village or scot-free town, &c., take himself, or induce others to take, or allow others to take, what has not been given. A mendicant should not take or appropriate any property, viz. an umbrella or vessel or stick, &c. (see II, 2, 3, § 2), of those monks together with whom he stays, without getting their permission, and without having inspected and wiped (the object in question); but having got their permission, and having inspected and wiped (the object in question), he may take or appropriate it.(1)

He may beg for a domicile in a traveller's hall, &c.

(see II, 1, 8, § 2), having reflected (on its fitness for a stay); he should ask permission to take Possession of it from him who is the landlord or the steward of that place: 'Indeed, O long-lived one! for the time, and in the space which you concede us, we shall dwell here. We shall take possession of the place for as long a time as the place belongs to you; and of as much of it as belongs to you; for as many fellow ascetics (as shall stand in need of it); afterwards we shall take to wandering.' (2)

Having got possession of some place, a mendicant should invite to that food, &c., which he himself has collected, any fellow-ascetics arriving there who follow the same rules and are zealous brethren; but he should not invite them to anything of which he has taken possession for the sake of somebody else. (3)

Having got possession of some place (in a traveller's hall, &c.), a mendicant should offer a footstool or bench or bed or couch, which he himself has begged, to any fellow-ascetics arriving there who follow other rules than he, yet are zealous brethren; but he should not offer them anything of which he has taken possession for the sake of somebody else. (4)

Having got possession of some lace in a traveller's hall, &c., a mendicant mighpt ask from a householder or his sons the loan of a needle or a Pippalaka [a utensil] or an ear-picker or a nail-parer, he should not give or lend it to somebody else; but having done that for which he wanted one of the above articles, he should go with that article there (where the householder, &c., is), and stretching out his hands or laying the article on the ground, he should, after consideration, say: 'Here it is! here it is.' But he should not with his own hand put it in the hand of the householder.(5)

A monk or a nun should not take possession of anything, on the bare ground, on wet ground, where there are eggs, &c.; nor on pillars or such an above-ground place (II, 2, 1, § 7); nor on a wall, &c.; nor on the trunk of a tree, &c.; nor where the householder or fire or water, or women or children or cattle are, and where it is not fit for a wise man to enter or to leave, &c., nor to meditate on the law; nor where they have to pass through the householder's abode or to which there is no road, and where it is not fit, &c.; nor where the householder or his wife, &c., bully or scold each other, &c. (see II, 2, 1, § 9, and 3, § 7); nor where they rub or anoint each other's body with oil or ghee or butter or grease; nor where they take a bath, &c.; nor where they go about naked, &c. (all as in II, 2, 3, §§ 7-12).

This is the whole duty, &c.

Thus I say. (6-12)

**Second Lesson**

He may beg for a domicile in a traveller's hall, &c. (see II, 1, 8, § 2), having reflected (on its fitness); he should ask permission to take possession of it from the landlord or the Steward of that place: Indeed, O long-lived one! for the time and in the space You concede is, we shall dwell here' &c. (see 1, § 2). Now what further after the place is taken Possession of? He should not remove from without to within, or vice versa, any umbrella or stick, &c. (see II, 2, 3, § 2) belonging to Sramanas or Brallmanas (Previously settled there); nor should he wake up a sleeping person, nor offend or molest the (inmates). (1)

A monk or a nun might wish to go to a mango park; they should then ask the landlord's or steward's permission (in the manner described above). Now what further after the place is taken possession of? Then they might desire to eat a mango. If the monk or the nun perceive that the mango is covered with eggs, living beings, &c. (see II, 1, 1, § 2), they should not take it; for it is impure, &c. (2)

If the monk or the nun perceive that the mango is free from eggs, living beings, &c., but not nibbled at by animals, nor injured, they should not take it; for it is impure, &c. But if they perceive that the mango is free from eggs, living beings, &c., and is nibbled at by animals and injured) then they may take it; for it is pure, &c. (3)

The monk might wish to eat or suck one half of a mango or a mango's peel or rind or sap or smaller particles. If the monk or the nun perceive that the above-enumerated things are covered with eggs, living beings, they should not take them; for they are impure, &c. But they may take them, if they are free from eggs, &c., and nibbled at by animals or injured. (4)

A monk or a nun might wish to go to a sugarcane plantation. They should ask permission in the manner described above. The monk or the nun might wish to chew or suck sugar-cane. In that case the same rules as for eating mango apply also; likewise if they wish to chew or to stick the sugar-cane's pulp, fibres, sap, or smaller particles. (5)

A monk or a nun might wish to go to a garlic field. They should ask permission in the manner described above. The monk or the nun might wish to chew or suck garlic. In that case the same rules as for eating mangoes apply also; likewise if they wish to chew or suck the bulb or peel or stalk or seed of garlics. (6)

A monk or a nun, having got possession of a place in a travellers hall, &c., should avoid all occasions to sin (proceeding from any preparations made by) the householders or their sons, and should occupy that place according to the following rules. (7)

Now this is the first rule:

He may beg for a domicile in a traveller's hall, &c.,

having reflected (on its fitness for a stay), &c. (§ 2 of the preceding Lesson is to be repeated here).

This is the first rule. (8)

Now follows the second rule:

A monk resolves: 'I shall ask for possession of a dwelling-place, &c., for the sake of other mendicants and having taken possession of it for their sake, I shall use it.'

This is the second rule. (9)

Now follows the third rule:

A monk resolves: 'I shall ask for possession of a dwelling-place, &c., for the sake of other mendicants, and having taken possession of it for their sake, I shall not use it.'

This is the third rule. (10)

Now follows thee fourth rule:

A monk resolves: 'I shall not ask for possession of a dwelling-place, &c., for the sake of other mendicants; but if the dwelling-place, &c., has already been ceded to them, I shall use it.'

This is the fourth rule. (11)

Now follows the fifth rule:

A monk resolves: 'I shall ask for possession of a dwelling-place for my own sake, not for two, three, four, or five persons.'

This is the fifth rule. (12)

Now follows the sixth rule:

If a monk or a nun, occupying a dwelling-place in which there is Ikkada reed, &c. (see II, 2, 3, § 18), get this thing, then they may use it; otherwise they should remain in a squatting or sitting posture.

This is the sixth rule. (13)

Now follows the seventh rule:

A monk or a nun may beg for a dwelling-place paved with clay or wood. If they get it, then they may use it; otherwise they should remain in a squatting or sitting posture.

This is the seventh rule.

One who has adopted one of these seven rules, should not say, &c. (all as in II, 1, 1 1, § 12). (14)

I have heard the following explanation by the venerable (Mahavira): The Sthaviras, the venerable ones, have declared that dominion is fivefold: The lord of the gods' dominion; The king's dominion; The houseowner's dominion; The householder's dominion; The religious man's dominion. This is the whole duty, &c. Thus I say. (15)

End of the Seventh Lecture, called Regulation of Possession.

## Second Part

## The Seven Lectures

## Eighth Lecture

When a monk or a nun wishes to perform religious postures:, they should enter a village or a scot-free town, &c.; having entered it, they should not accept a place, even if it is offered, which is infected by eggs or living beings, &c.; for Such a place is impure and unacceptable. In this way all that has been said about couches (in the Second Lecture) should be repeated here as far as water-plants (II, 2, 1, § 5).(1)

Avoiding these occasions to sin, a mendicant may choose one of these four rules for the performance of religious postures.

This is the first rule:

I shall choose something inanimate, and lean against it; changing the position of the body, and moving about a little, I shall stand there.

This is the first rule. (2)

Now follows the second rule:

I shall choose something inanimate, and lean against it; changing the position of the body, but not moving about a little, I shall stand there.

This is the second rule. (3)

Now follows the third rule:

I shall choose something inanimate, and lean against it; not changing the position of the body, nor moving about a little, I shall stand there.

This is the third rule. (4)

Now follows the fourth rule:

I shall choose something inanimate, but I shall not lean against it; not changing the position of the body, nor moving about a little, I shall stand there. Abandoning the care of the body, abandoning the care of the hair of the head, beard, and the other parts of the body, of the nails, perfectly motionless, I shall stand there.

This is the fourth rule. (5)

One who has adopted one of these four rules, &c. (see II, 1,11,§ 12).

This is the whole duty, &c.

Thus I say.

**Ninth Lecture**

When a monk or a nun wishes to go to a pure place for study, they should not accept one which is infected by eggs or living beings, &c.; for it is impure and unacceptable.

But if that place for study to which they wish to go, is free from eggs or living beings, &c., they may accept it; for it is pure and acceptable.

In this way all that has been said in the corresponding passage about couches should be repeated here as far as 'water-plants.' (1)

If parties of two, three, four, or five (mendicants) resolve to go to the place for study, they should not embrace or hug, bite with their teeth or scratch with their nails each other's body.

This is the whole duty, &c.

Thus I say. (2)

**Tenth Lecture**

A monk or a nun being pressed by nature should, in case they have not their own broom, beg for that of a fellow-ascetic. A monk or a nun, seeing that the ground is infected by eggs or living beings, &c., should not ease nature on such an unfit ground. But if the ground is free from eggs or living beings, &c., then they may case nature on such a ground.(1)

A monk or a nun, knowing that the householder with regard to such a place for the sake of one or many, male or female fellow-ascetics, for the sake of many Sramanas or Brahmanas whom he has well counted, kills living beings and commits various sins, should not ease nature on such a place or any other of the same sort, whether that place be appropriated by another person or not, &c. (see II, 1, 1, § 13). (2 and 3).

Now he should know this: If that place has not been appropriated by another person, &c., he may ease nature on such a place (after having well inspected and cleaned it). (4)

A monk or a nun should not ease nature on a ground which for their sake has been prepared or caused to be prepared (by the householder), or has been occupied by main force, or strewn with grass, or levelled, or smeared (with cowdung), or smoothed, or perfumed. (5)

A monk or a nun should not ease nature on a ground where the householders or their sons remove from outside to inside, or vice versa, bulbs, roots, &c. (see II, 2, 1, § 5). (6)

A monk or a nun should not ease nature on a pillar or bench or scaffold or loft or tower or roof. (7)

A monk or a nun should not ease nature on the bare ground or on wet ground or on dusty ground or on a rock or clay containing life, or on timber inhabited by worms or on anything containing life, as eggs, living beings, &c. (8)

A monk or a nun should not ease nature in a place where the householders or their sons have, do, or will put' by bulbs, roots, &c. (9)

A monk or a nun should not ease nature in a place where the householders or their sons have sown, sow, or will sow rice, beans, sesamum, pulse, or barley. (10)

A monk or a nun should not ease nature in a place where there are heaps of refuse, furrows, mud, stakes, sprigs, holes, caves, walls, even or uneven places. (11)

A monk or a nun should not ease nature in fireplaces, layers (or nests) of buffaloes, cattle, cocks, monkeys, quails, ducks, partridges, doves, or francoline partridges. (12)

A monk or a nun should not ease nature in a place where suicide is committed, or where (those who desire to end their life) expose their body to vultures, or precipitate themselves from rocks or trees, or eat poison, or enter fire.(13)

A monk or a nun should not ease nature in gardens, parks, woods, forests, temples, or wells- (14)

A monk or a nun should not ease nature in towers, pathways, doors, or town gates. (15)

A monk or a nun should not ease nature where three or four roads meet, nor in courtyards or squares. (16)

A monk or a nun should not ease nature where charcoal or potash is produced, or the dead are burnt, or on the sarcophagues or shrines of the dead. (17)

A monk or a nun should not ease nature at sacred places near rivers, marshes or ponds, or in a conduit. (18)

A monk or a nun should not ease nature in fresh clay pits, fresh pasture grounds for cattle, in meadows or quarries.(19)

A monk or a nun should not ease nature in a field of shrubs, vegetables, or roots. (20)

A monk or a nun should not ease nature in woods of Asana [Terminalia Tomentosa], Sana [Crotolaria Juncea], Dhataki [Grislea Tomentosa], Ketaki [Pandanus Odoratissimus], Mango, Asoka, Punnaga, or other such-like places which contain leaves, flowers, fruits, seeds, or sprouts.(21)

A monk or a nun should take their own chamberpot or that of somebody else, and going apart with it, they should ease nature in a secluded place where no people pass or see them, and which is free from eggs or living beings, &c.; then taking (the chamber-pot). they should go to a secluded spot, and leave the excrements there on a heap of ashes, &c. (see II, 1, 1, § 2).

This is the whole duty, &c.

Thus I say. (22)

**Eleventh Lecture**

A monk or a nun should not resolve to go where they

will hear sounds of a Mridanga, Nandimi-mridanga, or Ghallarli [different kinds of drums], or any such-like various sounds of drums. (1)

If a monk or a nun hear any sounds, viz. of the Vina, Vipamki, Vadvisaka, Tunaka, Panaka, Tumba-viniki, or Dhamkuna, they should not resolve to go where they will hear any such-like various sounds of stringed instruments.(2)

The same precepts apply to sounds of kettledrums, viz. of the Tala, Lattiya, Gohiya, or Kirikiriya; (3)

Also to sounds of wind instruments, viz. the conch, flute, Kharamukhi, or Piripiriya. (4)

A monk or a nun should not, for the sake of hearing sounds, go to walls or ditches, &c. (see II, 3, 3, §§ 1 and 2); (5)

Nor to marshes, pasture grounds, thickets, woods, strongholds in woods, mountains, strongholds in mountains;(6)

Nor to villages, towns, markets, or a capital, hermitages, cities, halting-places for caravans; (7)

Nor to gardens, parks, woods, forests, temples, assembly halls, wells; (8)

Nor to towers, pathways, doors, or town gates; (9)

Nor where three or four roads meet, nor to courtyards or squares; (10)

Nor to stables (or nests) of buffaloes, cattle, horses, elephants, &c. (see 10, § 12); (11)

Nor to places where buffaloes, bulls, horses, &c., fight;(12)

Nor to places where herds of cattle, horses, or elephants are kept; (13)

Nor to places where story-tellers or acrobats perform, or where continuously story-telling, dramatical plays, singing, music, performance on the Vini, beating of time, playing on the Turya, clever playing on the Pataha is going on; (14)

Nor to places where quarrels, affrays, riots, conflicts between two kingdoms, anarchical or revolutionary disturbances occur; (15)

Nor to places where a young well-attended girl, well-attired and well-ornamented, is paraded, or where somebody is led to death. (16)

A monk or a nun should not, for the sake hearing sounds, go to places where there are many great temptations, viz. where many cars, chariots, Mlekkhas, or foreigners meet. (17)

A monk or a nun should not, for the sake of hearing sounds, go to great festivals where women or men, old, young, or middle-aged ones are welldressed and ornamented, sing, make music, dance, laugh, play, sport, or give, distribute, portion or parcel out plenty of food, drink, dainties, and spices. (18)

A monk or a nun should not like or love, desire for, or be enraptured with, sounds of this or the other world, heard or unheard ones, seen or unseen ones.

This is the whole duty, &c.

Thus I say. (19)

**Twelfth Lecture**

If a monk or a nun see various colours (or forms), viz. in wreaths, dressed images, dolls, clothes, woodwork, plastering, paintings, jewelry, ivory-work, strings, leaf-cutting, they should not for the sake of pleasing the eye resolve to go where they will see various colours (or forms).

All that has been said in the last chapter with regard to sounds should be repeated here with regard to colours (or forms); only the passages on music are to be omitted. (1)

**Thirteenth Lecture**

One should neither be pleased with nor prohibit the action of another which relates to one's self, and produces karman.

One should neither be pleased with nor prohibit it;

If another (i. e. a householder) wipes (or rubs] the mendicant's feet; (1)

If he kneads or strokes them; (2)

If he touches or paints them; (3)

If he smears or anoints them with oil, ghee, or marrow; (4)

If he rubs or shampoos them with Lodhra, ground drugs, powder, or dye; (5)

If he sprinkles or washes them with hot or cold water;(6)

If he rubs or anoints them with any sort of ointment;(7)

If he perfumes or fumigates them with any sort of incense; (8)

If he extracts or removes a splinter or thorn from them; (9)

If he extracts or removes pus or blood from them. (10)

If he wipes or rubs the mendicant's body, &c. (see §§ 2-8 down to) if he perfumes or fumigates it with any sort of incense. (11)

If he wipes or rubs a wound in (the mendicant's) body (&c, down to) if he sprinkles or washes it with hot or cold water; (12)

If he cuts or incises it with any sharp instrument; if after having done so, he extracts or removes pus or blood from it; (13)

If he wipes or rubs a boil, abscess, ulcer, or fistula (&c., down to) if he cuts or incises it with any sharp instrument; if after having done so, he extracts or removes pus or blood from it; (14)

If he removes, or wipes off, the sweat and uncleanliness on his body; (15)

If he removes, or wipes off, the dirt of his eyes, ears, teeth, or nails; (16)

If he cuts or dresses the long hair of his head or his brows or armpits; (17)

If he removes, or wipes off, the hit or lice from his head.(18)

One should neither be pleased with nor prohibit it, if the other, sitting in the Anka or Paryanka posture, wipes or rubs (the mendicant's) feet; in this way the §§ 1-18 should be repeated here. (19)

One should neither be pleased with nor prohibit it, if the other, sitting in the Anka or Paryanka posture, fastens or ties a necklace of many or less strings, a necklace hanging down over the breast, a collar, a diadem, a garland, a golden string; (20)

If the other leading him to, or treating him in, a garden or a park, wipes or rubs (the mendicant's) feet &c. (all as above); similarly with actions done reciprocally. (21)

One should neither be pleased with nor prohibit it, if the other tries to cure him by pure charms;

If the other tries to cure him by impure charms;

If he tries to cure him, digging up and cutting, for

the sake of a sick monk, living bulbs, roots, rind, or sprouts. (22)

For sensation is the result of former actions; all sorts of living beings experience sensation.

This is the whole duty, &c.

Thus I say. (23)

**Fourteenth Lecture.**

One should not be pleased with nor prohibit a reciprocal action, which relates to one's self, and produces karman.

A mendicant should not be pleased with nor prohibit it, if (he and the other) wipe or rub each other's feet, &c.

In this way the whole Thirteenth Lecture should be repeated here.

This is the whole duty, &c.

Thus I say. (1)

End of the Second Part, called the Seven Lectures.

**Third Part.**

**Fifteenth Lecture,**

**Called**

**The Clauses**

In that period, in that age lived the Venerable Ascetic Mahavira, the five (most important moments of whose life happened) when the moon was in conjunction with the asterism Uttaraphalguni; to wit: In Uttaraphalguni he descended (from heaven), and having descended (thence), he entered the womb (of Devananda); in Uttaraphalguni he was removed from the (womb of Devananda) to the womb (of Trisala); in Uttaraphalguni he was born; in

Uttaraphalguni tearing out his hair, he left the house, and entered into the state of houselessness; in Uttaraphalguni he obtained the highest knowledge and intutition, called Kevala, which is infinite, supreme, unobstructed, unimpeded, complete and perfect. But in Svati the Venerable One obtained final liberation. (1)

When in this Avasarpini era, the Sushama-sushama period, the Sushama period, the Sushamaduhshama period and much time of the Duhshamasushami period had elapsed seventy-five years nine and a half months of it being left; in the fourth month Of Summer, in the eighth fortnight, in the light fortnight Of Asudha, on its sixth day, while the moon was in conjunction with Uttaraphalguni, the Venerable Ascetic Mahavira descended from the great Vimana, the all-victorious and all-prosperous Pushpottara, which is like the lotus amongst the best (and highest flowers), and like the Svastika and Vardhamanaka amongst the celestial regions, where he had lived for twenty Sagaropamas till the termination of his allotted length of life, (divine) nature and existence (among gods). Here, forsooth, in the continent of Gambudvipa, in Bharata-varsba, in the southern part of it, in the southern brahmanical part of the place Kundapura, he took the form of an embryo in the womb of Devanandi, of the Galandhariyana gotra, wife of the Brahmana Rishabhadatta, of the gotra of Kodala, taking the form of a lion. (2) The knowledge of the Venerable Ascetic Mahavira (with reference to this transaction) was threefold: he knew that he was to deseend; he knew that he had descended; he knew not when he was descending- For that time has been declared to be infinitesimally small. (3)

Then in the third month of the rain season, the fifth fortnight, the dark (fortnight) of Asvina, on its thirteenth day, while the moon was in conjunction with Uttaraphalguni, after the lapse of eighty-two days, on the eighty-third day current, the compassionate god (Indra), reflecting on what was the established custom (with regard to the birth of Tirthakaras), removed the embryo from the southern brahmanical part of the place Kundapura to the northern Kshatriya part of the same place, rejecting the unclean matter, and retaining the clean matter, lodged the fetus in the womb of Trisali of the Vasishtha gotra, wife of the Kshatriya Siddhartha, of the Kisyapa gotra, of the clan of the Gñatris, and lodged the fetus of the Ksliatriyani Trisala in the womb of Devanandi of the Galandharayana gotra, wife of the Brahmana Risliabhadatta, of the gotra of Kodala, in the southern brahmanical part of the place Kundapuri. (4) The knowledge of the Venerable Ascetic Mahavira (with regard to this transaction) was threefold: he knew that he was to be removed; he knew that he was removed; he also knew when he was being removed. (5)

In that period, in that age, once upon a time, after the lapse of nine complete months and seven and a half days, in the first month of summer, in the second fortnight, the dark (fortnight) of Kaitra, on its thirteenth day, while the moon was in conjunction with Uttaraphalguni, the Kshatriyani Trisali, perfectly healthy herself, gave birth to a perfectly healthy (boy), the Venerable Ascetic Mahavira. (6)

In that night in which the Kshatriyani Trisali, perfectly healthy herself, gave birth to a perfectly healthy (boy), the Venerable Ascetic Mahavira, there was one great divine, godly lustre (originated) by descending and ascending gods and goddesses (of the four orders of) Bhavanapatis, Vyantaras, Gyotishkas, and Viminavssins; and in the conflux of gods the bustle of gods amounted to confusion. (7)

In that night, &c., the gods and goddesses rained down one great shower of nectar, sandal powder, flowers, gold, and pearls. (8)

In that night the gods and goddesses (of the above-mentioned four orders) performed the customary ceremonies of auspiciousness and bonour, and his anointment as a Tirthakara. (9)

Upwards from the time when the Venerable Mahavira, was placed in the womb of the Kshatriyani Trisala, that farnily's (treasure) of gold, silver, riches, corn, jewels, pearls, shells, precious stones, and corals increased!. (10) When the parents of the Venerable Ascetic Mahivira had become aware of this, after the lapse of the tenth day, and the performance of the purification, they prepared much food, drink, sweetmeats, and spices; and having invited a host of friends, near and remote relatives, they distributed, portioned. out, bestowed (the above-mentioned materials) to Sramanas, Brihmanas, paupers, beggars, eunuchs, &c., and distributed gifts to those who wanted to make presents; then they gave a dinner to the host of friends, near and remote relatives, and after dinner they announced the name (of the child) to their guests: (11) 'Since the prince was placed in the womb of the Kshatriyani Trisala, this family's (treasure) of gold, silver, riches, corn, jewels, pearls, shells, precious stones, and corals increased; therefore the prince shall be called Vardhamana (i.e. the Increasing).' (12)

The Venerable Ascetic Mahavira was attended by five nurses: a wet-nurse, a nurse to clean him, one to dress him, one to play with him, one to carry him; being transferred from the lap of one nurse to that of another, he grew up on that beautiful ground, paved with mosaic of precious stones, like a Kampaka, tree growing in the glen of a mountain.(13)

Then the Venerable Ascetic Mahavira, after his intellect had developed and the childhood had passed away, lived in the enjoyment of the allowed, noble, fivefold joys and pleasures: (consisting in) sound, touch, taste, colour, and smell. (14)

The Venerable Ascetic Mahivira belonged to the

Kasyapa gotra. His three names have thus been recorded by tradition: by his parents he was called Vardhamina, because he is devoid of love and hate; (he is called) Sramana (i.e. Ascetic), because he sustains dreadful dangers and fears, the noble nakedness, and the miseries of the world; the name Venerable Ascetic Mahavira has been given to him by the gods.

The Venerable Ascetic Mahivira's father belonged to the Kasyapa gotra; he had three names: Siddhartha, Sreyamsa, and Gasamsa. His mother belonged to the Vasishtha gotra, and had three names: Trisali, Videhadatti, and Priyakirini. His paternal uncle Suparsva belonged to the Kasyapa gotra. His eldest brother, Nandivardhana, and his eldest sister, Sudarsana, belonged both to the Kasyapa gotra. His wife Yasoda belonged to the Kaundinya gotra. His daughter, who belonged to the Kisyapa gotra, had two names: Anogga and Priyadarsana. His granddaughter, who belonged to the Kausika gotra, had two names: Seshavatt and Yasovati. (15)

The Venerable Ascetic Mahavira's parents were worshippers of Parsva and followers of the Sramanas. During many years they were followers of the Sramanas, and for the sake of protecting the six classes of lives they observed, blamed, repented, confessed, and did penance according to their sins. On a bed of Kusa-grass they rejected all food, and their bodies dried up by the last mortification of the flesh, which is to end in death. Thus they died in the proper month, and, leaving their bodies, were born as gods in Adbhuta Kalpa. Thence descending after the termination of their allotted length of life, they will, in Mahavideha, with their departing breath, reach absolute perfection, wisdom, liberation, final Nirvana, and the end of all misery. (16)

In that period, in that age the Venerable Ascetic Mahavira, a Gñatri Kshatriya, Gñatriputra, a Videha, son of Videhadatta, a native of Videha, a prince of Videha, lived thirty years amongst the householders under the name of 'Videha.'

After his parents had gone to the worlds of the gods and he had fulfilled his promise, he gave up his gold and silver, his troops and chariots, and distributed, portioned out, and gave away his valuable treasures (consisting of) riches, corn, gold, pearls, &c., and distributed among those who wanted to make presents to others. Thus he gave away during a whole year. In the first month of winter,in the first fortnight, in the dark (fortnight) of Margasiras, on its tenth day, while the moon was in conjunction with Uttaraphalguni, he made up his mind to retire from the world. (17)

A year before the best of Ginas will retire from the world, they continue to give away their property, from the rising of the sun. i.

One krore and eight lacks of gold is his gift at the rising of the sun, as if it were his morning meal. ii.

Three hundred and eighty-eight krores and eighty lacks were given in one year. iii.

The Kundaladharas of Vaisramana, the Laukantika and Maharddhika gods in the fifteen Karma-bhumis' wake the Tirthakara. iv.

In Brahma Kalpa and in the line of Krishmas, the Laukantika Vimanas are eightfold and infinite in number.v.

These orders of gods wake the best of Ginas, the Venerable Vira: 'Arhat! propagate the religion which is a blessing to all creatures in the world!' vi.

When the gods and goddesses (of the four orders of) Bhavanapatis, Vyantaras, Gyotishkas, and Vimanavasins had become aware of the Venerable Ascetic Mahavira's intention to retire from the world, they assumed their proper form, dress, and ensigns, ascended with their proper pomp and splendour, together with their whole retinue, their own vehicles and chariots, and rejecting all gross matter, retained only the subtile matter. Then they rose and with that excellent, quick, swift, rapid, divine motion of the gods they came down again crossing numberless continents and oceans till they arrived in Gambhudvipa at the northern Kshatriya part of the Place Kundapura; in the north-eastern quarter of it they suddenly halted. (18)

Sakra, the leader and king of the gods, quietly and slowly stopped his vehicle and chariot, quietly and slowly descended from it and went apart. There he underwent a great transformation, and produced by magic a great, beautiful, lovely, fine-shaped divine pavilion, which was ornamented with many designs in precious stones, gold, and pearls. In the middle part of that divine pavilion he produced one great throne of the same description, with a footstool.(19)

Then he went where the Venerable Ascetic Mahavira was, and thrice circumambulating him from left to right, he praised and worshipped him. Leading him to the divine pavilion, he softly placed him with the face towards the east on the throne, anointed him with hundredfold and thousandfold refined oil, with perfumes and decoctions, bathed him with pure water, and rubbed him with beautifying cool sandal, laid on a piece of cloth worth a lack. He clad him in a pair of robes so light that the smallest breath would carry them away; they were manufactured in a famous city, praised by clever artists, soft as the fume of horses, interwoven with gold by skilful masters, and ornamented with designs of flamingos. Then (the god) decked him with necklaces of many and fewer strings, with one hanging down over his breast and one .consisting of one row of pearls, with a garland, a golden string, a turban, a diadem, wreaths of precious stones, and decorated him with garlands, ribbons, scarves, and sashes like the Kalpavriksha. (20)

The god then, for a second time, underwent a great transformation, and produced by magic the great palankin, called Kandraprabha [i.e. shining like the moon], which a thousand men carry. (This palankin) was adorned with pictures of wolves, bulls, horses, men, dolphins, birds, monkeys, elephants, antelopes, sarabhas [a fabulous animal with eight legs], yacks, tigers, lions, creeping plants, and a train of couples of Vidyadharas; it had a halo of thousands of rays; it was decorated with thousands of brilliant glittering rupees; its lustre was mild and bright; the eyes could not bear its light; it shone with heaps and masses of pearls; it was hung with strings and ribbons, and with golden excellent necklaces, extremely beautiful; it was embellished with designs of lotuses and many other plants; its cupola was adorned with many precious stones of five colours, with bells and flags; it was conspicuous., lovely, beautiful, splendid, magnificent. (21)

This palankin was brought for the best of Ginas, who is free from old age and death; it was hung with wreaths and garlands of divine flowers, grown in water or on dry ground. vii.

In the middle of the palankin (was) a costly throne covered with a divine cloth, precious stones and silver, with a footstool, for the best of Ginas. viii.

He wore on his head a chaplet and a diadem, his body was shining, and he was adorned with many ornaments; he had put on a robe of muslin worth a lack. ix.

After a fast of three days, with a glorious resolution he ascended the supreme palankin, purifying all by his light.x.

He sat on his throne, and Sakra and Isana, on both sides, fanned him with chowries, the handles of which were inlaid with jewels and precious stones. xi.

In front it was uplifted by men, covered with joyful horripilation; behind the gods carried it: the Suras and Asuras, the Garudas and the chiefs of Nagas. xii.

The Suras carried it on the eastern side, and the Asuras on the southern one; on the western side the Garudas carried it, and the Nagas on the northern side. xiii.

As a grove in blossom, or a lotus-covered lake in autumn looks beautiful with a mass of flowers, so did (then) the firmament with hosts of gods. xiv.

As a grove of Siddhartha [White mustard], of Karnikara [Cassia Fistula] or of Kampaka [Michelia Champaka] looks beautiful with a mass of flowers, so did (then) the firmament with hosts of. gods. xv.

In the skies and on earth the sound of musical instruments produced by hundreds of thousands of excellent drums, kettle-drums, cymbals, and conches was extremely pleasant. xvi.

Then the gods ordered many hundreds of actors to perform a very rich concert of four kinds of instruments: stringed instruments and drums, cymbals and wind-instruments. xvii.

At that period, in that age, in the first month of winter, in the first fortnight, the dark (fortnight) of Margasiras, on its tenth day, called Suvrata, in the Muhurta called Vigaya, while the moon was in conjunction with the asterism Uttaraphalguni, when the shadow had turned towards the east, and the first Paurushi was over, after fasting three days without taking water, having put on one garment, the Venerable Ascetic Mahivira, in his palankin Kandraprabha, which only a thousand men can carry, with a train of gods, men, and Asuras left the northern Kshatriya part of the place Kundapura by the high way for the park Gñatri Shanda. There, just at the beginning of night, he caused the palankin Kandraprabha to stop quietly on a slightly raised untouched ground, quietly descended from it, sat quietly down on a throne with the face towards the east, and took off all his ornaments and finery. (22)

The god Vaisramana, prostrating himself, cauglit up the finery and ornaments of the Venerable Ascetic Mahavira in a cloth of flamingo-pattern. Mahavira then plucked out with his right and left (hands) on the right and left (sides of his head) his hair in five handfuls. But Sakra, the leader and king of the gods, falling down before the feet of the Venerable Ascetic Mahavira, caught up the hair in a cup of diamond, and requesting his permission, brought them to the Milk Ocean. After the Venerable Ascetic Mahavira had plucked out his hair in five handfuls (as described above), he paid obeisance to all liberated spirits, and vowing to do no sinful act, he adopted the holy conduct. At that moment thewhole assembly of men and gods stood motionless, like the figures on a picture.

At the command of Sakra, the clamour of men and gods, and the sound of musical instruments suddenly ceased, when Mahavira chose the holy conduct. xviii.

Day and night following that conduct which is a blessing to all animated and living beings, the zealous gods listen to him with joyful horripilation. xix.

When the Venerable Ascetic Mahavira had adopted the holy conduct which produced that state of soul in which the reward of former actions is temporarily counteracted, he reached the knowledge called Manahparyaya, by which he knew the thoughts of all sentient beings, with five organs, which are not defective, and possess a developed intellect, (living) in the two and a half continents and the two oceans. Then he formed the following resolution: I shall for twelve years neglect my body and abandon the care of it; I shall with equanimity bear, undergo, and suffer all calamities arising from divine powers, men or animals.(23)

The Venerable Ascetic Mahavira having formed this resolution, and neglecting his body, arrived in the village Kummara when only one Muhurta of the day remained. Neglecting his body, the Venerable Ascetic Mahavira meditated on his Self, in blameless lodgings, in blameless wandering, in restraint, kindness, avoidance of sinful influence (samvara), chaste life, in patience, freedom from passion, contentment; control, circumspectness, practising religious postures and acts; walking the path of Nirvana and liberation, which is the fruit of good conduct. Living thus he with equanimity bore, endured, sustained, and suffered all calamities arising from divine powers, men, and animals with undisturbed and unafflicted mind, careful of body, speech, and mind. (24)

The Venerable Ascetic Mahavira. passed twelve years in this way of life; during the thirteenth year in the second month of summer, in the fourth fortnight, the light (fortnight) of Vaisakha, on its tenth day. called Suvrata, in the Muhurta called Vigaya, while the moon was in conjunction with the asterism Uttaraphalguni, when the shadow had turned towards the east, and the first wake was over, outside of the town Grimbhikagrama, on the northern bank of the river Rigupalika, in the field of the householder Samaga, in a north-eastern direction from an old temple, not far from a Sal tree, in a squatting position with joined heels exposing himself to the heat of the sun, with the knees high and the head low, in deep meditation, in the midst of abstract meditation,he reached Nirvana, the complete and full, the unobstructed, uninipeded, infinite and supreme best knowledge and intuition, called Kevala.(25) When the Venerable One had become an Arhat and Gina, he was a Kevalin, omniscient and comprehending all objects, he knew all conditions of the world, of gods, men, and demons; whence they come,. where they go, whether they are born as men or animals (kyavana), or become gods or hellbeings (upapdda); their food, drink, doings, desires, open and secret deeds, their conversation and gossip, and the thoughts of their minds; he saw and knew all conditions in the whole world of all living beings.(26)

On the day when the Venerable Ascetic Mahavira reached the Kevala, the gods (of the four orders of) Bhavanapatis, Vyantaras, Gyotishkas, and Vimanavasins descended from, and ascended to heaven, &c. (as on the moment of his birth, see above, § 7)- (27)

Then when the Venerable Ascetic Mahavira had reached the highest knowledge and intuition, he reflected on himself and the world: first he taught the law to the gods, afterwards to men. (28)

The Venerable Ascetic Mahavira endowed with the highest knowledge and intuition taught the five great vows, with their clauses, the six classes of lives to the Sramanas and Nirgranthas, to Gautama, &c.

The six classes of lives are earth-body, &c. (down to) animals. (29)

i. The first great vow, Sir, runs thus:

I renounce all killing of living beings, whether subtile or gross, whether movable or immovable. Nor shall I myself kill living beings (nor cause others to do it, nor consent to it). As long as I live, I confess and blame, repent and exempt myself of these sins, in the thrice threefold way, in mind, speech, and body.

There are five clauses.

The first clause runs thus:

A Nirgrantha is careful in his walk, not careless. The Kevalin assigns as the reason,that a Nirgrantha, careless in his walk, might (with his feet) hurt or displace or injure or kill living beings. Hence a Nirgrantha is careful in his walk, not careless in his walk.

This is the first clause. (1)

Now follows the second clause:

A Nirgrantha searches into his mind (i.e. thoughts and intentions). If his mind is sinful, blamable, intent on works, acting on impulses, produces cutting and splitting (or division and dissension), quarrels, faults, and pains, injures living beings, or kills creatures, he should not employ such a mind in action; but if, on the contrary, it is not sinful, &c., then he may put it in action.

This is the second clause. (2)

Now follows the third clause:

A Nirgrantha searches into his speech; if his speech is sinful, blamable, &c. (all down to) kills creatures, he should not utter that speech. But if, on the contrary, it is not sinful, &c., then he may utter it.

This is the third clause. (3)

Now follows the fourth clause:

A Nirgrantha is careful in laying down his utensils of begging, he is not careless in it. The Kevalin says: A Nirgrantha who is careless in laying down his utensils of begging, might hurt or displace or injure or kill all sorts of living beings. Hence a Nirgrantha is careful in laying down his utensils of begging, he is not careless in it.

This is the fourth clause. (4)

Now follows the fifth clause:

A Nirgrantha eats and drinks after inspecting his food and drink; he does not eat and drink without inspecting his food and drink. The Kevalin says: If a Nirgrantha would eat and drink without inspecting his food and drink, he might hurt and displace or injure or kill all sorts of living beings. Hence a Nirgrantha eats and drinks after inspecting his food and drink, not without doing so.

This is the fifth clause. (5)

In this way the great vow is correctly practised, followed, executed, explainedp established, effected according to the precept.

This is, Sir, the first great vow: Abstinence from killing any living beings. i.

ii. The second great vow runs thus:

I renounce all vices of lying speech (arising) from anger or greed or fear or mirth. I shall neither myself speak lies, nor cause others to speak lies, nor consent to the speaking of lies by others. I confess and blame, repent and exempt myself of these sins in the thrice threefold way, in mind, speech, and body.

There are five clauses.

The first clause runs thus:

A Nirgrantha speaks after deliberation, not without deliberation. The Kevalin says: Without deliberation a Nirgrantha might utter a falsehood in his speech. A Nirgrantha -speaks after deliberation, not without deliberation.

This is the first clause. (1)

Now follows the second clause:

A Nirgrantha comprehends (and renounces) anger, he is not angry. The Kevalin says: A Nirgrantha who is moved by anger, and is angry, might utter a falsehood in his speech. A Nirgrantha, &c.

This is the second clause. (2)

Now follows the third clause:

A Nirgrantha comprehends (and renounces) greed, he is not greedy. The Kevalin says: A Nirgrantha who is moved by greed, and is greedy, might utter a falsehood in his speech. A Nirgrantha, &c.

This is the third clause. (3)

Now follows the fourth clause

A Nirgrantha comprehends (and renoundes) fear, he is not afraid. The Kevalin says: A Nirgrantha who is moved by fear, and is afraid might utter a falsehood in his speech. A Nirgrantha, &c.

This is the fourth clause. (4)

Now follows the fifth clause:

A Nirgrantha comprehends (and renounces) mirth, he is not mirthful. The Kevalin says: A Nirgrantha who is moved by mirth, and is mirthful, might utter a falsehood in his speech. A Nirgrantha, &c.

This is the fifth clause. (5)

In this way the great vow is correctly practised, followed, &c.

This is, Sir, the second great vow. ii

iii. The third great vow runs thus:

I renounce all taking of anything not given, either in a village or a town or a wood, either of little or much, of small or great, of living or lifeless things. I shall neither take myself what is not given, nor cause others to take it, nor consent to their taking it. As long as I live, I confess and blame, &c. (all down to) body.

There are five clauses.

The first clause runs thus:

A Nirgrantha begs after deliberation, for a limited ground, not without deliberation. The Kevalin says: If a Nirgrantha begs without deliberation for a limited ground, he inight take what is not given. A Nirgrantha, &c.

This is the first clause. (1)

Now follows the second clause:

A Nirgrantha consumes his food and drink with permission (of his superior), not without his permission. The Kevalin says: If a Nirgrantha consumes his food and drink without the superior's permission, he might eat what is not given. A Nirgrantha, &c.

This is the second clause. (2)

Now follows the third clause:

A Nirgrantha who has taken possession of some ground, should always take possession of a limited part of it and for a fixed time. The Kevalin says: If a Nirgrantha who has taken possession of some ground, should take possession of an unlimited part of it and for an unfixed time, he might take what is not given. A Nirgrantha, &c.

This is the third clause. (3)

Now follows the fourth clause:

A Nirgrantha who has taken possession of some ground, should constantly have his grant renewed. The Kevalin says: If a Nirgrantha has not constantly his grant renewed, he might take possession of what is not given. A Nirgrantha, &c.

This is the fourth clause. (4)

Now follows the fifth clause:

A Nirgrantha begs for a limited ground for his co-religionists after deliberation, not wilhout deliberation.

The Kevalin says: If a Nirgrantha should beg without deliberation, he might take possession of what is not given.. A Nirgrantha, &c.

This is the fifth clause. (5)

In this way the great vow, &c.

This is, Sir, the third great vow. iii.

iv. The fourth great vow runs thus:

I renounce all sexual pleasures, either with gods or men or animals. I shall not give way to sensuality, &c. (all as in the foregoing paragraph down to) exempt myself.

There are five clauses.

The first clause runs thus:

A Nirgrantha does not continually discuss topics relating to women. The Kevalin says: If a Nirgrantha discusses such topics, he might fall from the law declared by the Kevalin, because of the destruction or disturbance of his peace. A Nirgrantha, &c.

This is the first clause. (1)

Now follows the second clause:

A Nirgrantha does not regard and contemplate the lovely forms of women. The Kevalin says: If a Nirgrantha regards and contemplates the lovely forms of women, he might, &c. A Nirgrantha, &c.

This is the second clause. (2)

Now follows the third clause:

A Nirgrantha does not recall to his mind the Pleasures and amusements he formerly had with women. The Kevalin says: If a Nirgrantha recalls to his mind the pleasures and amusements he formerly had with women, he might, &c. A Nirgrantha, &c.

This is the third clause. (3)

Now follows the fourth clause:

A Nirgrantha does not eat and drink too much, nor does he drink liquors or eat highly-seasoned dishes. The Kevalin says: If a Nirgrantha did eat and drink too Much, or did drink liquors and eat highly-seasoned dishes, he might, &c. A Nirgrantha, &c.

This is the fourth clause. (4)

Now follows the fifth clause:

A Nirgrantha does not occupy a bed or couch affected by women, animals, or eunuchs. The Kevalin says: If a Nirgrantha did occupy a bed or couch affected by women, animals, or eunuchs, he might, &c. A Nirgrantha, &c.

This is the fifth clause. (5)

In this way the great vow, &c.

This is, Sir, the fourth great vow. iv.

v. The fifth great vow runs thus:

I renounce all attachments, whether little or much, small or great, living or lifeless; neither shall I myself form such attachments, nor cause others to do so, nor consent to their doing so, &c. (all down to) exempt myself.

There are five clauses.

The first clause runs thus:

If a creature with ears hears agreeable and disagreeable sounds, it should not be attached to, nor delighted with, nor desiring of, nor infatuated by, nor covetous of, nor disturbed by the agreeable or disagreeable sounds. The Kevalin says: If a Nirgrantha is thus affected by the pleasant or unpleasant sounds, he might fall, &c. (see above, IV, 1).

If it is impossible not to hear sounds, which reach the ear, the mendicant should avoid love or hate, originated by them.

A creature with ears hears agreeable and disagreeable sounds.

This is the first clause. (i)

Now follows the second clause:

If a creature with eyes sees agreeable and disagreeable forms (or colours), it should not be attached, &c., to them.

The Kevalin says, &c. (the rest as in the last clause. Substitute only see and forms for hear and sounds).

This is the second clause. (2)

Now follows the third clause:

If a creature with an organ of smell smells agreeable or disagreeable smells, it should not be attached to them. (The rest as above. Substitute smell and nose.)

This is the third clause.

Now follows the fourth clause:

If a creature with a tongue tastes agreeable or disagreeable tastes, it should not be attached, &c., to them. (The rest as above. Substitute taste and tongue.)

This is the fourth clause. (4)

Now follows the fifth clause:

If a creature with an organ of feeling feels agreeable or disagreeable touches, it should not be attached to them. (The rest as above. Substitute feel and touch.) This is the fifth clause. (5) In this way the great vow, &c. (see above). v.

He who is well provided with these great vows and their twenty-five Clauses is really Houseless, if he, according to the sacred lore, the precepts, and the way correctly practises, follows, executes, explains, establishes, and, according to the precept, effects them.

End of the Fifteenth Lecture, called the Clauses.

**Fourth Part.**

**Sixteenth Lecture,**

**Called**

**The Liberation**

The creatures attain only a temporary residence (in one of the four states of being); hearing this supreme truth (i.e. the doctrine of the Tirthakara's) one should meditate upon it. The wise man should free himself from the family bonds; fearless should he give up acts and attachments. (1)

A mendicant, living thus, self-controlled towards the eternal (world of living beings), the matchless sage, who collects his alms, is insulted with words by the people assailing him, like an elephant in battle with arrows. (2)

Despised by such-like people, the wise man, with undisturbed mind, sustains their words and blows, as a rock is not shaken by the wind. (3)

Disregarding (all calamities) he lives together with clever (monks, insensible) to pain and pleasure, not hurting the movable and immovable (beings), not killing, bearing all: so is described the great sage, a good Sramana. (4)

As the lustre of a burning flame increases, so increase the austerity, wisdom, and glory of a steadfast sage who, with vanquished desires, meditates on the supreme place of virtue, though suffering pain. (5)

The great vows which are called the place of peace, the great teachers, and the producers of disinterestedness have, in all quarters of the earth, been proclaimed by the infinite Gina, the knowing one, as light, illumining the three worlds, (repels) darkness. (6)

The unbound one, living amongst the bound (i.e. householders), should lead the life of a mendicant;

unattached to women, he should speak with reverence. Not desiring this or the next world, the learned one is not measured by the qualities of love. (7)

The dirt (of sins) formerly committed by a thus liberated mendicant who walks in wisdom (and restraint), who is constant, and bears pain, vanishes as the dirt covering silver (is removed) by fire. (8)

He lives, forsooth, in accordwice with wisdom (and restraint), and walks free from desire, and with conquered sensuality. As a snake casts off its old skin, so is the Brahmana freed from the bed of pain. (9)

As they call the great ocean a boundless flood of water, difficult to traverse with the arms (alone), so should the learned one know (and renounce) it (the samsara): that sage is called 'Maker of the end.' (10)

Here amongst men bondage and deliverance have been declared; he who, according to that doctrine (of the church), knows bondage and deliverance: that sage is called 'Maker of the end.' (11)

He for whom there is no bondage whatever in this world, and besides in the two (other continents, or heaven and hell), is indeed a (monk needing) no support and no standing place; he has quitted the path of births. (12)

End of the Sixteenth Lecture, called the Liberation.

End of the Second Book.

End of the Akaranga Sutra.

**The Kalpasutra of Bhadrabahu.**

**Lives of The Ginas.**

**Life of Mahavira.**

**First Lecture.**

Obeisance to the Arhats!

Obeisance to the Liberated Ones!

Obeisance to the Religious Guides!

Obeisance to the Religious Instructors!

Obeisance to all Saints in the World!

This fivefold obeisance, destroying all sins, is of all benedictions the principal benediction.

In that period, in that age lived the Venerable Ascetic Mahavira, the five (most important moments of whose life happened) when the moon was in conjunction with the asterism Uttaraphalguni; to wit, in Uttaraphalguni he descended (from heaven), and having descended (thence), he entered the womb (of Devananda); in Uttaraphalguni he was removed from the womb (of Devananda) to the womb (of Trisala); in Uttaraphalguni he was born; in Uttaraphalguni, tearing out his hair, he left the house and entered the state of houselessness; in Uttaraphalguni he obtained the highest knowledge and intuition, called Kevala, which is infinite, supreme, unobstructed, unimpeded, complete, and perfect. But in Svati the Venerable One obtained final liberation. (1)

End of the First Lecture.

## Second Lecture

In that period, in that age the Venerable Ascetic Mahavira, having on the sixth day of the fourth month of summer, in the eighth fortnight, the light (fortnight) of Ashadha, descended from the great Vimana, the all-victorious and all-prosperous Pushpottara, which is like the lotus amongst the best things, where he had lived for twenty Sagaropamas till the termination of his allotted length of life, of his (divine nature, and of his existence (among gods); here in the continent of Gambudvipa, in

Bharatavarsha,-when of this Avasarpini era the Sushamasushama, the Sushama, and Sushamaduhshama periods, and the greater part of the Duhshamasushama period (containing a Kodakodi [a koti of kotis or 100,000,000,000,000] of Sagaropamas, less forty-two thousand years) had elapsed, and only seventy-two years, eight and a half months were left, after twenty-one Tirthankaras of the race of Ikshvaku and of the Kasyapa gotra, and two of the race of Hari and of the Gautama gotra, on the whole twenty-three Tirthakaras had appeared,-the Venerable Ascetic Mahavira, the last of the Tirthakaras, took the form-of an embryo in the womb of Devananda, of the Galandhariyana gotra, the wife of the Brahmana Rishabhadatta, of the gotra of Kodala, in the brahmanical part of the town Kundagrama in the middle of the night, when the moon was in conjunction with the asterism Uttaraphalguni, after his allotted length of life, of his (divine) nature, and of his existence (amongst gods) had come to their termination. (2)

The knowledge of the Venerable Ascetic Mahavira (about this) was threefold; he knew that he was to descend, he knew that he had descended, he knew not when he was descending.

In that night in which the Venerable Ascetic Mahavira took the form of an embryo in the womb of the Brahmani Devananda of the Galandharayana gotra, the Brahmani Devananda was on her couch, taking fits of sleep, in a state between sleeping and waking, and having seen the following fourteen illustrious, beautiful, lucky, blest, auspicious, fortunate great dreams, she woke up.- (3) To wit:

An elephant, a bull, a lion, the anointing (of the goddess Sri), a garland, the moon, the sun, a flag, a vase, a lotus lake, the ocean, a celestial abode, a heap of jewels, and a flame. (4)

When the Brihmani Devananda, having seen these dreams, woke up, she-glad, pleased, and joyful in her mind, delighted, extremely enraptured, with a heart widening under the influence of happiness, with the hair of her body all erect in their pores like the flowers of the Kadamba touched by rain-drops- firmly fixed the dreams (in her mind), and rose from her couch. Neither hasty nor trembling, with a quick and even gait, like that of the royal swan, she went to the Brahmana Rishabhadatta, and gave him the greeting of victory. Then she comfortably sat down in an excellent chair of state; calm and composed, joining the palms of her hands so as to bring the ten nails together, she laid the folded hands on her head, and spoke thus: (5)

O beloved of the gods, I was just now on my couch taking fits of sleep, in a state between sleeping and waking, when I saw the following fourteen .illustrious, &c., great dreams: to wit, an elephant, &c. (6)

'O beloved of the gods, what, to be sure, will be the happy result portended by these fourteen illustrious, &c., great dreams?' (7)

When the Brahmana Rishabhadatta had heard and perceived this news from the Brdhmant Devinanda, he, glad, pleased, and joyful (see § 5, down to) rain-drops, firmly fixed the dreams (in his mind), and entered upon considering them. He grasped the meaning of those dreams with his own innate intellect and intuition, which were preceded by reflection, and thus spoke to the Brahmani Devananda: (8)

'O beloved of the gods, you have seen illustrious dreams; O beloved of the gods, you have seen beautiful, lucky, blest, auspicious, fortunate dreams, which will bring health, joy, long life, bliss, and fortune! We shall have success, O beloved of the gods, we shall have pleasure; we shall have happiness, beloved of the gods, we shall have a son! Indeed, beloved of the gods, after the lapse of nine complete months and seven and a half days you will give birth to a lovely and handsome boy with tender hands and feet, with a body containing the entire and complete five organs of sense, with the lucky signs, marks, and good qualities; a boy on whose body all limbs will be well formed, and of full volume, weight, and length, of a lovely figure like that of the moon! (9) And this boy, after having passed his childhood, and, with just ripened intellect, having reached the state of youth,will repeat, fully understand, and well retain (in his mind) the four Vedas: the Rig-veda, Yag-ur-veda, Sama-veda, Atharva-veda-to which the Itihasa is added as a fifth, and the Nigghantu as a sixth (Veda)-together with their Angas and Upangas, and the Rahasya; he will know the six Angas, he will be versed in the philosophy of the sixty categories, and well grounded in arithmetic, in phonetics, ceremonial, grammar, metre, etymology, and astronomy, and in many other brahmanical [and monastic] sciences besides. (10) Therefore, O beloved of the gods, you have seen illustrious dreams, &c. (see § 9).

In this way he repeatedly expressed his extreme satisfaction. (11)

When the Brahmani Devananda had heard and perceived this news from the Brahmana Rishabhadatta, she-glad, pleased, and joyful, &c. (see § 5) joining the palms of her hands, &c- (see § 5, down to) and spoke thus:(12)

'That is so, O beloved of the gods; that is exactly so, O beloved of the gods; that is true, O beloved of the gods; that is beyond doubt, O beloved of the gods; that is what I desire, O beloved of the gods; that is what I accept, O beloved of the gods; that is what I desire and accept, O beloved of the gods; that matter is really such as you have pronounced it.'

Thus saying, she accepted the true meaning of the

dreams, and enjoyed together with Rishabhadatta the noble permitted pleasures of human nature. (13)

In that period, in that age, Sakra,-the chief and king of the gods, the wielder of the thunderbolt, the destroyer of towns, the performer of a hundred sacrifices, the thousand-eyed one, Maghavan, the punisher of the Daitya Paka, the lord of the southern half of the earth, the lord of the thirty-two thousand celestial abodes, the bestrider of the elephant Airavata, the chief of the Suras, who wears spotless clothes and robes, and puts on garlands and the diadem, whose cheeks were stroked by fine, bright, and trembling earrings of fresh gold [the most prosperous, the most brilliant, the most mighty, the most glorious, the most powerful, and the most happy one], with a splendid body, ornamented with a long down-reaching garland,-this Sakra was in the Saudharma Kalpa, in the celestial abode Saudharma Avatamsaka, in the council-hall Sudharman, on his throne Sakra; he who exercises and maintains the supreme command, government, management, guidance, direction, and sovereign power and generalship ovef-the thirty-two thousand gods of the ceiestial abodes, the eighty-four thousand gods of a rank equal with that of himself, the thirty-two chief gods, the four guardians of the world, the eight principal queens with their trains, the three courts, the seven armies, and the seven commanders of these armies. He was then enjoying the permitted pleasures of divine nature under the great din of uninterrupted story-telling, dramatical plays, singing, and music, as beating of time, performance on the Vina, the Turya, the great drum, and the Patupataha. (14)

And he viewed this whole continent Gambudvipa with his extensive (knowledge called) Avadhi. There he saw in the continent Gambadvipa, in Bharatavarsha, in the southern half of Bharata, in the brahmanical part of the town KundagrAma, the Venerable Ascetic Mahivira taking the form of an embryo in the womb of the Brahmani Devananda of the Galandharayana gotra, wife of the Brahmana Rishabhadatta of the gotra of Kodala; and-glad, pleased, and joyful in his mind, delighted, extremely enraptured, with a heart widening under the influence of happiness, with the hair of his body bristling and erect in their pores like the fragrant flowers of Nipa when touched by rain-drops, with his eyes and mouth open like full blown lotuses, with his excellent, various, trembling bracelets, with diadem and earrings, his breast lighted up by necklaces, wearing long and swinging ornaments with a pearl pendant-the chief of the gods rose with confusion, hasty and trembling from his throne, descended from the footstool, took off his shoes which were by a clever artist set with Vaidurya and excellent Rishta and Añgana [names of precious stones], and ornamented with glittering jewels and precious stones, threw his seamless robe over his left shoulder, and, arranging the fingers of his hands in the shape of a bud, he advanced seven or eight steps towards the Tirthakara.

Bending his left knee and reposing on the right one, he three times placed his head on the ground and lifted it a little; then he raised his bracelet-encumbered arms, and joining the palms of his hands so as to bring the ten nails together, laid the hands on his head and spoke thus: (15)

'Reverence to the Arhats and Bhagavats; to the Adikaras, the Tirthakaras, the perfectly-enlightened ones; to the highest of men, the lions among men, the flowers among mankind 2, the Gandhahastins among men; to the highest in the world, the gUides of the world, the benefactors of the world, the lights of the world, the enlighteners of the world; to the givers of safety, to the givers of sight, to the givers of the road, to the givers of shelter, to the givers of life, to the givers of knowledge; to the givers of the law, the preachers of the law, the lords of the law, the leaders of the law, the universal emperors of the best law; to the light, the help, the shelter, the refuge, the resting-place, the possessors of unchecked knowledge and intuition who have got rid of unrighteousness; to the conquerors and the granters of conquest, the saved and the saviours, the enlightened and the enlighteners, the liberated and the liberators, to the all-knowing ones, the all-seeing ones, to those who have reached the happy, stable, unstained, infinite, unperishable, undecaying place, called the path of perfection, whence there is no return; reverence to the Ginas who have conquered fear.

'Reverence to the Venerable Ascetic Mahavira, the Adikara, the last of the Tirthakaras who was predicted by the former Tirthakaras, &c. I here adore the Revered One yonder, may the Revered One yonder see me here!' With these words he adored, he worshipped the Venerable Ascetic Mahavira, and sat down on his excellent throne facing the east. Then the following internal, reflectional, desirable idea occurred to the mind of Sakra, the chief of kings and gods:(16)

'It never has happened, nor does it happen, nor will it happen, that Arhats, Kakravartins, Baladevas, or Vasudevas, in the past, present, or future, should be born in low families, mean families, degraded families, poor families, indigent families. beggars' families, or brahmanical families. (17) For indeed Arhats, Kakravartins, Baladevas, and Vasudevas, in the past, present, and future, are born in high families, noble families, royal families, noblemen's families, in families belonging to the race of Ikshvaku, or of Hari. or in other such-like families of pure descent on both sides. (18)

Now this is something which moves the wonder of the world: it happens in the lapse of numberless Avasarpinis and Utsarpinis, because the imperishable, indescribable, and undestroyable Karman relating to name and gotra must take effect, that Arhats, &c., in the past, present, and future, descend in (i.e. take the form of an embryo in the womb of a woman belonging to) low families, &c.; but they are never brought forth by birth from such a womb.(19) This Venerable Ascetic Mahavira, now, in the continent Gambudvipa, in Bharatavarsha, in the brahmanical part of the town Kundagrama, has taken the form of an embryo in the womb of the Brahmani Devananda of the Galandharayana gotra, wife of the Brahmana Rishabhadatta of the gotra of Kodala. (20) Hence it is the established custom of all past, present, and future Sakras, chiefs and kings of the gods, to cause the Arhats and Bhagavats to be removed from such-like low, mean, &c., families, to such-like high, noble, &c., families. (21) It is, therefore, better that I should cause the Venerable Ascetic Mahavira, the last of the Tirthakaras who was predicted by the former Tirthakaras, to be removed from the brahmanical part of the town Kundagrama, from the womb of the Brahmani Devananda of the Gilandharayana gotra, wife of the Brahmana Rishabhadatta of the gotra of Kodila, to the Kshatriya part of the town Kundagrama, and to be placed as an embryo in the womb of the Ksbatriyani Trisala of the Vasishtha gotra, wife of the Kshatriya Siddhartha of the Kasyapa gotra, belonging to the clan of the Gñatri Kshatriyas; and to cause the embryo of the Kshatriyani Trisala of the Vasishtha gotra to be placed in the womb of the Brahmani Devanandi of the Galandharayana gotra.'

Thus he reflected and called Harinegamesi, the divine commander of the foot troops; having called him, he spoke thus: (22)

'Well, now, beloved of the gods, it never has happened, &c. (§§ 17-20 are verbally repeated). (23-25)

'Therefore, go now and remove the Venerable Ascetic Mahavira from the brahmanical part, &c., and place the embryo of the Kshatriyani Trisala, &c.

(See § 21). Having done this, return quickly to report on the execution of my orders.' (26)

When Harinegamesi, the divine commander of the foot troops, was thus spoken to by Sakra, the chief and king of the gods, he-glad, pleased, and joyful, &c. (see § 15)-laid his folded hands on his head and modestly accepted the words of command, sayingn 'Just as your Majesty commands.' After this he left the presence of Sakra, the chief and king of the gods, and descended towards the northeastern quarter; then be transformed himself through his magical power of transformation, and stretched himself out for numerous Yoganas like a staff, (during which he seized) jewels, Vagra, Vaidurya, Lohitaksha, Masaragalla, Hamsagarbha, Pulaka, Saugandhika, Gyotisara, Añgana, Añganapulaka, Gatarupa, Subhaga, Sphatika, and Rishta; (of these precious materials) he rejected the gross particles, and retained the subtle particles. (27) Then for a second time he transformed himself through his magical power of transformation, and produced the definitive form (which gods adopt on entering the world of men); having done so, he passed with that excellent, hasty, trembling, active, impetuous, victorious, exalted, and quick divine motion of the gods right through numberless continents and oceans, and arrived in Gambudvipa, in Bharatavarsha, in the brahmanical part of the town Kundagrama, at the house of the Brahmana Rishabhadatta, where the Brahmani Devinanda dwelt. Having arrived there, he made his bow in the sight of the Venerable Ascetic Mahavira, and cast the Brahmani Devananda, together with her retinue, into a deep sleep; then he took off all unclean particles, and brought forth the clean particles, and saying, 'May the Venerable One permit me,' he took the Venerable Ascetic Mahivira in the folded palms of his hands without hurting him. Thus he went to the Kshatriya part of the town Kundagrama, to the house of the Kshatriya Siddhartha, where the Kshatriyani Trisala dwelt; he cast her and her attendants into a deep sleep, took off all unclean particles, and brought forth the clean particles, and placed the embryo of the Venerable Ascetic Mahivira in the womb of the Kshatriyani Trisala, and the embryo of the Kshatriyani Trisala he placed in the womb of the Brihmani Devinanda of the Gandhariyana gotra. Having done so, he returned in that direction in which he had come,. (28) With that excellent, &c. (see § 28), divine motion of the gods, he flew upwards right through numberless continents and oceans, taking thousands of Yoganas in each motion, and arrived in the Saudharma Kalpa, in the divine abode called Saudharma Avatamsaka, where Sakra, the chief and king of the gods, sat on the throne called Sakra, and reported to Sakra, the chief and king of the gods, on the execution of his orders.

In that period, in that age the knowledge of the Venerable Ascetic Mahavira was threefold; he knew that he was to be removed; he knew that he was removed; he knew not when he was being removed. (29)

In that period, in that age, on the thirteenth day of the third month of the rainy season, in the fifth fortnight, the dark (fortnight) of Asvina, after the lapse of eighty-two days, on the eighty-third day current (since his conception), the embryo of the Venerable Ascetic Mahavira was, on the command of Sakra, safely removed by Harinegamesi from the womb of the Brahmani Devinanda to that of the Kshatriyani Trisala, in the middle of the night, when the moon was in conjunction with the asterism Uttaraphalguni. (30)

End of the Second Lecture.

**Third Lecture**

In that night in which the embryo of the Venerable Ascetic Mahavira was removed from the womb of the Brahmani Devananda of the Galandharayana gotra, to that of the Kshatriyani Trisala of the Vaasishtha gotra, the former was on her couch taking fits of sleep in a state between sleeping and waking; and seeing that these fourteen illustrious, beautiful, lucky, blest, auspicious, fortunate, great dreams were taken from her by the Kshatriyini Trisala, she awoke. (31)

In that night in which the embryo of the Venerable Ascetic Mahavira. was removed from the womb of the Brahmani Devananda of the Galandharayana, gotra to that of the Kshatriyani Trisala of the Vasishtha. gotra, the latter was in her dwelling-place, of which the interior was ornamented with pictures, and the outside whitewashed, furbished and cleansed, the brilliant surface of the ceiling was painted, the darkness was dispelled by jewels and precious stones, the floor was perfectly level and adorned with auspicious figures; which, moreover, was furnished with offerings of heaps of delicious, fragrant, strewn flowers of all five colours, was highly delightful through curling, scented fumes of black aloe, the finest Kundurukka and Turuslika [Different kinds of the resin of Boswellia], and burning frankincense; was exquisitely scented with fine perfumes, and turned as it were into a smelling-bottle; on a couch with a mattress of a man's length, with pillows at head and foot, raised on both sides and bollow in the middle, soft as if one walked on the sand of the banks of the Ganges, covered with the cloth of a robe of ornamented linen, containing a well-worked towel, and hung with red mosquito curtains, delightful, soft to the touch like fur, wadding, Pura [name of a tree], butter, or cotton, with all the comforts of a bed, such as fragrant, excellent flowers and sandal-powder-(in such a room and on such a bed Trisala was) taking fits of sleep between sleeping and waking, and having seen the following fourteen, &c. (see § 3), dreams, viz. an elephant, &c. (see § 4), she awoke.(32)

1. Then Trisala saw in her first dream a fine, enormous elephant, possessing all lucky marks, with strong thighs

and four mighty tusks; who was whiter than an empty great cloud, or a heap of pearls, or the ocean of milk, or the moon-beams, or spray of water, or the silver mountain (Vaitadhya); whose temples were perfumed with fragrant musk-fluid, which attracted the bees; equalling in dimension the best elephant of the king of the gods (Airivata); uttering a fine deep sound like the thunder of a big and large rain-cloud. (33)

2. Then she saw a tame, lucky bull, of a whiter hue than that of the mass of petals of thė white lotus, illumining all around by the diffusion of a glory of light; (a bull) whose lovely, resplendent, beautiful hump was delightful through the collection of its charms, whose glossy skin (was covered with) thin, fine, soft hairs; whose body was firm, well made, muscular, compact, lovely, well proportioned, and beautiful; -whose horns were large, round, excellently beautiful, greased at their tops, and pointed; whose teeth were all equal, shining, and pure. He foreboded innumerable good qualities. (34)

3. Then she saw a handsome, handsomely shaped, playful lion, jumping from the sky towards her face; a delightful and beautiful lion whiter than a heap of pearls, &c. (see § 33), who had strong and lovely fore-arms, and a mouth adorned with round, large, and well-set teeth; whose lovely lips, splendent through their proportions, and soft like a noble lotus, looked as if they were artificially ornamented; whose palate was soft and tender like the petals of the red lotus, and the top of whose tongue was protruding; whose eyes were like pure lightning, and revolved like red-hot excellent gold just poured out from the crucible; (a lion) with broad and large thighs, and with full and excellent shoulders, who was adorned with a mane of soft, white, thin, long hair of the finest quality; whose erect, well-shaped, and well-grown tail was flapping; the tops of whose nails were deeply set and sharp; whose beautiful tongue came out of his mouth like a shoot of beauty. (35)

4. Then she, with the face of the full moon, saw the goddess of famous beauty, Sri, on the top of Mount Himavat, reposing on a lotus in the lotus lake, anointed with the water from the strong and large trunks of the guardian elephants. She sat on a lofty throne. Her firmly placed feet resembled golden tortoises, and her dyed, fleshy, convex, thin, red, smooth nails were set in swelling muscles. Her hands and feet were like the leaves of the lotus, and her fingers and toes soft and excellent; her round and well-formed legs were adorned with the Kuruvindavarta [an ornament, according to the commentary], and her knees with dimples. Her fleshy thighs resembled the proboscis of an excellent elephant, and her lovely broad hips were encircled by a golden zone. Her large and beautiful belly was adorned by a circular navel, and contained a lovely row of hairs (black as) collyrium, bees, or clouds, straight, even, continuous, thin, admirable, handsome, soft, and downy. Her waist, which contained the three folds, could be encompassed with one hand. On all parts of her body shone ornaments and trinkets, composed of many jewels and precious stones, yellow and red gold. The pure cup-like pair of her breasts sparkled, encircled by a garland of Kunda flowers, in which glittered a string of pearls. She wore strings of pearls made by diligent and clever artists, shining with wonderful strings, a necklace of jewels with a string of Dinaras, and a trembling pair of earrings, touching her shoulders, diffused a brilliancy; but the united beauties and charms of these ornaments were only subservient to the loveliness of her face. Her lovely eyes were large and pure like the water lily. She sprinkled about the sap from two lotus flowers which she held in her splendid hands, and geacefully fanned herself. Her glossy, black, thick, smooth hair hung down in a braid.(36)

5. Then she saw, coming down from the firmament, a garland charmingly interwoven with fresh Mandara flowers. It spread the delicious smell of Kampaka

[Michelia Champaka], Asoka [Jonesia Asoka], Naga [Mesua Roxburghii], Punnaga [Rottlera Tinctoria], Priyangu [Panicum Italicum], Sirisha [Acacia Sirisa], Mudgara [a species of jasmine], Mallika [Jasminum Zambac], Gati [Jasminum Grandiflorum], Yuthika [Jasminum Auriculatum], Ankolla [Alangium Hexapetalum], Korantakapatra [?], Damanaka [Artemisia Indica], Navamalika [Nykanthes or Jasminum Zambac], Bakula [Mimusops Elengi], Tilaka [Clerodendum Phlomoides or Symplocos Racemosa] Vasantika [Gaertnera Racemosa], Nuphar, Nymphaea, Patala [Bignonia Suaveolens] , Kunda [Fragrant Oleander], Atimukta [Disopyros Glutinos or Dalbergia Ougeinense] and Mango; and perfumed the ten divisions of the universe with its incomparably delightful fragrance. It was white through wreaths of fragrant flowers of all seasons, and brilliant through splendid, beautiful embellishments of many colours. Towards it came humming swarms of different kinds of bees, and filled with their sweet noise the whole neighbourhood.(37)

6. And the moon:white as cow-milk, foam, spray of water, or a silver cup, glorious, delighting heart and eyes, full, dispelling the compact darkness of the thickest wilderness, whose crescent shines at the end of the two halves of the month, opening the blossoms of the groups of Nymphaeas, adorning the night, resembling the surface of a well-polished mirror. She was of a white hue, like a flamingo, the stars' head-ornament, the quiver of Cupid's arrows, raising the waters of the ocean, burning as it were disconsolate people when absent from their sweethearts, the large, glorious, wandering headmark of the celestial sphere-beloved in heart and soul by Rohini. Such was the glorious, beautiful, resplendent full moon which the queen saw. (38)

7. Then she saw the large sun, the dispeller of the mass of darkness, him of radiant form, red like the Asoka, the open Kimsuka, the bill of a parrot, or the Guñgardha,

the adorner of the lotus groups, the marker of the starry host, the lamp of the firmament, throttling as it were the mass of cold, the illustrious leader of the troop of planets, the destroyer of night, who only at his rising and setting may be well viewed, but (at all other times) is difficult to be regarded, who disperses evil-doers that stroll about at night, who stops the influence of cold, who always circles round Mount Meru, whose thousand rays obscure the lustre of other lights. (39)

8. Then she saw an extremely beautiful and very large flag, a sight for all people, of a form attractive to the beholders. It was fastened to a golden staff with a tuft of many soft and waving peacock's feathers of blue, red, yellow, and white colours, and seemed as if it would pierce the brilliant, celestial sphere, with the brilliant lion on its top, who was white like crystal, pearlmother, Anka-stone, Kunda-flowers, spray-6f water, or a silver cup. (40)

9. Then she saw a full vase of costly metal splendent with fine gold, filled with pure water, excellent, of brilliant beauty, and shining with a bouquet of water lilies. It united niany excellencies and all-auspicious marks, and stood on a lotus (shaped foot), shining with excellent jewels. It delighted the eyes, glittered and illumined all about; it was the abode of happy Fortune, free from all faults, fine, splendid, exquisitely beautiful, entwined with a xyreath of fragrant flowers of all seasons. (41)

10. Then she saw a lake, called Lotus Lake, adorned with water lilies. Its yellow water was perfumed by lotuses opening in the rays of the morning sun; it abounded with swarms of aquatic animals, and fed fishes. It was large, and seemed to burn through the wide-spreading, glorious beauty of all kinds of lotuses. Its shape and beauty were pleasing. The lotuses in it were licked by whole swarms of gay bees and mad drones. Pairs of swans, cranes, Kakravakas, ducks, Indian cranes, and

many other lusty birds resorted to its waters, and on the leaves of its lotuses sparkled water-drops like pearls. It was a sight, pleasing to the heart and the eye. (42)

Then she whose face was splendid like the moon in autumn, saw the milk-ocean, equalling in beauty the breast of Lakshmi, which is white like the mass of moon-beams. Its waters increased in all four directions, and raged with ever-changing and, moving, excessively high waves. It presented a splendid and pleasant spectacle as it rushed to and from the shore with its wind-raised, changeable, and moving billows, its tossing waves, and its rolling, splendid, transparent breakers. From it issued camphor-white foam under the lashing (tails) of great porpoises, fishes, whales, and other monsters of the deep. Its agitated waters were in great uproar, occasioned by the vortex Gangavarta, which the vehemence and force of the great rivers produced; they rose, rushed onwards and backwards, and eddied. (43)

12. Then she saw a celestial abode excelling among the best of its kind, like the lotus (among flowers). It shone like the morning sun's disk, and was of a dazzling beauty. Its thousand and eight excellent columns (inlaid with) the best gold and heaps of jewels diffused a brilliant light like a heavenly lamp, and the pearls fastened to its curtains glittered. It was hung with brilliant divine garlands, and decorated with pictures of wolves, bulls, horses, men, dolphins, birds, snakes, Kinnaras, deer, Sarabhas, Yaks, Samsaktas, elephants, shrubs, and plants. There the Gandharvas performed their concerts, and the din of the drums of the gods, imitating the sound of big and large rain-clouds, penetrated the whole inhabited world. It was highly delightful through curling, scented fumes of black aloe, the finest Kundurukka and Turushka, burning frankincense and other perfumes. It (shed) continuous light, was white, of excellent lustre, delighting the best of gods, and affording joy and pleasure.(44)

13. Then she saw an enormous heap of jewels containing Pulaka, Vagra, Indranila, Sasyaka, Karketana, Lohitaksha, Marakata, Prabala, Saugandhika, Sphatika, Hamsagarbha, Añgana, and Kandrakanta. Its base was on the level of the earth, and it illumined with its jewels even the sphere of the sky. It was high and resembled Mount Meru. (45)

14. And a fire. She saw a fire in vehement motion, fed with much-shining and honey-coloured ghee, smokeless, crackling, and extremely beautiful with its burning flames. The mass of its flames, which rose one above the other, seemed to interpenetrate each other, and the blaze of its flames appeared to bake the firmament in some places. (46)

    After having seen these fine, beautiful, lovely, handsome dreams, the lotus-eyed queen awoke on her bed while the hair of her body bristled for joy.

    Every mother of a Tirthakara sees these fourteen dreams in that night in which the famous Arhat enters her womb. (46 b)

    End of the Third Lecture.

## Fourth Lecture

When the Kshatriyani Trisala, having seen these fourteen illustrious, great dreams, awoke, she was glad, pleased, and joyful, &c. (see § 5, down to) rose from her couch, and descended from the footstool. Neither hasty nor trembling, with a quick and even gait like that of the royal swan, she went to the couch of the Kshatriya Siddhartha. There she awakened the Kshatriya Siddhartha, addressing him with kind, Pleasing, amiable, tender, illustrious, beautiful, lucky, blest, auspicious, fortunate, heart-going, heart-easing, well-measured, sweet, and soft words. (47)

Then the Kshatriyani Trisala, with the permission of king Siddhartha, sat down on a chair of state inlaid with various jewels and precious stones in the form of arabesques; calm and composed, sitting on an excellent, comfortable chair, she addressed him with kind, pleasing, &c. (see last paragraph), words, and spoke thus: (48)

'O beloved of the gods, I was just now on my couch (as described in § 32), &c. (see § 5), and awoke after having seen the fourteen dreams; to wit, an elephant, &c. What, to be sure, O my lord, will be the happy result portended by these fourteen illustrious, great dreams?' (49)

When the Kshatriya Siddhartha had heard and perceived this news from the Kshatriyani Trisala, he glad, pleased, -and joyful, &c. (see § 5, down to) firmly fixed the dreams in his mind, and entered upon considering them; he grasped the meaning of those dreams with his own innate intelligence and intuition which were preceded by reflection, and addressing the Kshatriyani Trisala with kind, pleasing, &c., words, spoke thus: (50)

'O beloved of the gods, you have seen illustrious dreams, &c. (see § 9, down to) you will give birth to a lovely, handsome boy, who will be the ensign of our family, the lamp of our family, the crown of our family, the frontal ornament of our family, the maker of our family's glory, the sun of our family, the stay of our family, the maker of our family's joy and fame, the tree of our family, the exalter of our family; (a boy) with tender hands and feet, &c. (see § 9, down to the end). (51) And this boy, after having passed childhood, and, with just ripened intellect, having reached the state of youth, will become a brave, gallant, and valorous king, the lord of the realm, with a large and extensive army and train of waggons. (52) Therefore, O beloved of the gods, you have seen illustrious, &c., dreams, &c. (see § 9).'

In this way he repeatedly expressed his extreme satisfaction.

When the Kshatriyani Trisala had heard and

perceived this news from king Siddhirtha, she glad, pleased, and joyful, &c. (See § 12, down to) and spoke thus: (53)

'That is so, O beloved of the gods, &c. (see § 13, down to) as you have pronounced it.'

Thus saying she accepted the true meaning of the dreams, and with the permission of king Siddhartha she rose from her chair of state, inlaid with various jewels and precious stones in the form of arabesques. She then returned to her own bed, neither hasty nor trembling, with a quick and even gait like that of the royal swan, and spoke thus: (54)

'These my excellent and pre-eminent dreams shall not be counteracted by other bad dreams.'

Accordingly she remained awake to save her dreams by means of (hearing) good, auspicious, pious, agreeable stories about gods and religious men. (55)

At the time of daybreak the Kshatriya Siddhirtha called his family servants and spoke thus: (56)

'Now, beloved of the gods, quickly make ready, or have made ready, the exterior hall of audience; see that it be sprinkled with scented water, cleaned, swept, and newly smeared, furnished with offerings of fragrant, excellent flowers of all five colours, made highly delightful through curling scented fumes, &c. (see § 32, down to) and turned, as it were, into a smelling box; also erect my throne, and having done this quickly return, and report on the execution of my orders.' (57)

When the family servants were thus spoken to by king Siddhartha, they—glad, pleased, and joyful, &c. (See § 12, down to) on their heads, and modestly accepted the words of command, saying, 'Yes, master!' Then they left the presence of the Kshatriya Siddhartha, and went to the exterior hall of audience, made it ready, and erected the throne (as described in the last paragraph). Having done this, they returned to the Kshatriya Siddhirtha; joining the palms of their hands so as to bring, the ten nails together, laid the folded hands on their heads, and reported on the execution of their orders. (58)

Early at the wane of the night, when the bright morning disclosed the soft flowers of the full-blown lotuses and Nymphaeas, rose the sun: he was red like the Asoka, the open Kimsuka, the bill of a parrot or the Guñgardha; of an intense redness like that of the Bandhugivaka [Penatpetes Phoenicea], the feet and eyes of the turtle dove, the scarlet eyes of the Indian cuckoo, a mass of China roses, or vermilion. He, the thousand-rayed maker of the day, shining in his radiance, awakened the groups of lotuses. When in due time the god of the day had risen and by the blows of his hands (or rays) the darkness was driven away, while the inhabited world was, as it were, dipped in saffron by the morning sun, the Kshatriya Siddhartha rose from his bed, (59) descended from the footstool, went to the hall for gymnastic exercises, and entered it. There he applied himself to many wholesome exercises, jumped, wrestled, fenced, and fought till he got thoroughly tired: then he was anointed with hundredfold and thousandfold refined different kinds of oil, which nourished, beautified, invigorated, exhilarated, strengthened, and increased all senses and limbs. On an oiled hide he was shampooed by clever men with soft and tender palms of the hands and soles of the feet, who were well acquainted with the best qualities of the practices of anointing, kneading, and stretching; well trained, skilful, excellent, expert, intelligent, and never tiring. When by this fourfold agreeable treatment of the body the king's bones, flesh, skin, and hair had been benefited, and his fatigues banished, he left the hall for gymnastic exercises, (60) and entered the bathing-house. The pleasant bathing-room was very agreeable, and contained many windows, ornamented with pearls; its floor was decorated with mosaic of various jewels and precious stones. On the bathing-stool, inlaid with various jewels and precious stones in the form of arabesques, he comfortably sat down and bathed himself with water scented with flowers and perfumes, with tepid water and pure water, according to an excellent method of bathing, combined with healthy exercises. When this healthy excellent bathing under many hundred fold pleasures was over, he dried his body with a long-haired, soft, scented, and coloured towel, put on a new and costly excellent robe, rubbed himself with fresh and fragrant Gosirsha [a superior kind of sandal] and sandal, and ornamented himself with fine wreaths and sandal-ointment. He put on (ornaments) of jewels and pearls, hung round his neck fitting necklaces of eighteen, nine, and three strings of pearls, and one with a pearl pendant, and adorned himself with a zone. He put on a collar, rings, and charming ornaments of the hair, and encumbered his arms with excellent bracelets:. he was of excessive beauty. His face was lighted up by earrings, and his head by a diadem; his breast was adorned and decked with necklaces, and his fingers were, as it were, gilded by his rings. His upper garment of fine cloth contained swinging pearl pendants. He put on, as an emblem of his undefeated knighthood, glittering, well-made, strong, excellent, beautiful armlets, made by clever artists of spotless and costly jewels, gold, and precious stones of many kinds. In short, the king was like the tree granting all desires, decorated and ornamented; an umbrella, hung with wreaths and garlands of Korinta flowers, was held above him. He was fanned with white excellent chowries, while his appearance was greeted with auspicious shouts of victory. Surrounded by many chieftains, satraps, kings, princes, knights, sheriffs, heads of families, ministers, chief ministers, astrologers, counsellors, servants, dancing masters, citizens, traders, merchants, foremen of guilds, generals, leaders of caravans, messengers, and frontier-guards, he-the lord and chief of men, a bull and a lion among men, shining with excellent lustre and glory, lovely to behold like the moon emerging from a great white cloud in the midst of the flock of the planets and of brilliant stars and asterisms-left the bathing-house, (61) entered the exterior hail of audience and sat down on his throne with the face towards the east. (62)

On the north-eastern side he ordered eight state chairs, covered with cloth and auspiciously decorated with white mustard, to be set down. Not too far from and not too near to himself, towards the interior of the palace, he had a curtain drawn. It was adorned with different jewels and precious stones, extremely worth seeing, very costly, and manufactured in a famous town; its soft cloth was all over covered with hundreds of patterns and decorated with pictures of wolves, bulls, horses, men, dolphins, birds, snakes, Kinnaras, deer, Sarabhas, Yaks, Samsaktas, elephants, shrubs, and plants. Behind it he ordered to be placed, for the Kshatriyani Trisala, an excellent chair of state, decorated with arabesques of different jewels and precious stones, outfitted with a coverlet and a soft pillow, covered with a white cloth, very soft and agreeable to the touch. Then he called the family servants and spoke thus:(63)

'Quickly, O beloved of the gods, call the interpreters of dreams who well know the science of prognostics with its eight branches, and are well versed in many sciences besides!'

When the family servants were thus spoken to by king Siddhartha, they-glad, pleased, and joyful, &c.-laid the folded hands on their heads and modestly accepted the words of command, saying, 'Yes, master!' (64)

Then they left the presence of the Kshatriya Siddhartha, went right through the town Kundapura to the houses of the interpreters of dreams, and called the interpreters of dreams. (65)

Then the interpreters of dreams, being called by the Kshatriya Siddhartha's family servants, glad, pleased, and joyful, &c., bathed, made the offering (to the house-gods), performed auspicious rites and expiatory acts, put on excellent, lucky, pure court-dress, adorned their persons with small but costly ornaments, and put, for the sake of auspiciousness, white mustard and Durva grass on their heads. Thus they issued from their own houses and went right through the Kshatriya part of the town Kundapura to the front gate of king Siddhirtha's excellent palace, a jewel of its kind. (66)

There they assembled and went to the exterior hall of audience in the presence of the Kshatriya Siddhartha. joining the palms of their hands so as to bring the ten nails together, they laid the folded hands on their heads and gave him the greeting of victory. (67)

The king Siddhartha saluted and honoured the interpreters of dreams, made them presents, and received them with respect. They sat down, one after the other, on the chairs of state which had been placed there before. (68) Then the Kshatriya Siddhartha, placed his wife Trisala behind the curtain, and taking flowers and fruits in his hands, addressed with utmost courtesy the interpreters of dreams: (69)

'O beloved of the gods, the Kshatriyani Trisala was just on her couch, &c. (see § 32, down to the end). (70 and 71) What to be sure, O beloved of the gods, will be the result portended by these fourteen illustrious great dreams?' (72)

When the interpreters of dreams had heard and perceived this news from the Kshatriya Siddhartha, they-glad, pleased, and joyful, &c.-fixed the dreams in their minds, entered upon considering them, and conversed together. (73)

Having found, grasped, discussed, decided upon, and clearly understood the meaning of these dreams, they recited before king Siddhartha, the dream-books and spoke thus:

'O beloved of the gods, in our dream-books are enumerated forty-two (common) dreams and thirty great dreams. Now, O beloved of the gods, the mothers of universal monarchs or of Arhats wake up after seeing these fourteen great dreams out of the thirty great dreams, when the embryo of a universal monarch or an Arhat enters their womb; (74) viz. an elephant, a bull, &c. (75) The mothers of Visudevas wake up after seeing any seven great dreams out of these fourteen great dreams, when the embryo of a Visudeva enters their womb. (76) The mothers of Baladevas wake up after seeing any four great dreams out of these fourteen great dreams, when the embryo of a Baladeva enters their womb. (77) The mother of Mandalikas wake up after seeing a single great dream out of these fourteen great dreams, when the embryo of a Mandalika enters their womb. (78) Now, O beloved of the gods, the Kshatriyani Trisala has seen these fourteen great dreams, &c. (see § 51, down to the end). (79) And this boy, &c. (see § 52, down to) the lord of a realm with a large and extensive army and train of waggons, a universal emperor or a Gina, the lord of the three worlds, the universal emperor of the law. (80). Therefore, O beloved of the gods, the Kshatriyani Trisala has seen illustrious dreams,' &c. (see § 9). (81)

When king Siddhartha had heard and perceived this news from the interpreter of dreams, he-glad, pleased, and joyful, &c.-spoke to them thus: (82)

'That is so, O beloved of the gods, &c. (see § 11, down

to) as you have pronounced it.'

Thus saying he accepted the true meaning of the dreams, and honoured the interpreters of dreams with praise and plenty of food, flowers, perfumes, garlands, and ornaments. He made them a present in keeping with their station in life [or a life annuity] and dismissed them. (83)

After this the Kshatriya Siddhartha rose from his throne, went to the Kshatriyani Trisala behind the curtain, and addressed her thus: (84)

'Now, O beloved of the gods, you have seen these fourteen great dreams, &c. (see § 79, 80, down to) emperor of the law.' (85, 86)

When the Kshatriyani Trisald had heard and perceived this news, she-glad, pleased, and joyful, &c.- accepted the true meaning of the dreams. (87) With the permission of king Siddhirtha she rose from her chair of state which was decorated with arabesques of various jewels and precious stones, and returned to her own apartments, neither hasty nor trembling, with a quick and even gait like that of the royal swan. (88)

From that moment in which the Venerable Ascetic Mahavira was brought into the family of the Gñatris, many demons in Vaisramana's service, belonging to the animal world, brought, on Sakras command, to the palace of king Siddhartha, old and ancient treasures, of which the owners, deponers, and families to whom they originally belonged were dead and extinct, and which were hidden in villages, or mines, or scot-free towns, or towns with earth walls, or towns with low walls, or isolated towns, or towns accessible by land and water, or towns accessible either by land or by water only, or in natural strongholds, or in halting-places for processions or for caravans, in triangular places, or in places where three or four roads meet, or in courtyards, or squares, or high roads, or on the site of villages or towns, or in drains of villages or towns, or in bazaars, or temples, or assembling halls, or wells, or parks, or gardens, or woods, or groves, or burying-places, or empty houses, or mountain caves, or hermits' cells, or secret places between walls, or in houses on an elevation, or houses for audience, or palaces.(89)

In the night in which the Venerable Ascetic Mahavira was brought into the family of the Gñatris their silver increased, their gold increased; their riches, corn, majesty, and kingdom increased; their army, train, treasure, storehouse, town, seraglio, subjects, and glory increased; their real valuable property, as riches, gold, precious stones, jewels, pearls, conches, stones, corals, rubies, &c., the intensity of their popularity and liberality highly increased. At that time the following personal, reflectional, desirable idea occurred to parents of the Venerable Ascetic Mahavira:(90)

'From the inoment that this our boy has been begotten, our silver increased, our gold increased, &c. (see § 90, down to) the intensity of our liberality and popularity highly increased. Therefore when this our boy will be born, we shall give him the fit name, attributive and conformable to his quality Vardhamana [the Increasing One].' (91)

Now the Venerable Ascetic Mahavira, out of compassion for his mother, did not move nor stir nor quiver, but remained quiet, stiff, and motionless. Then the following, &c. (see § go, down to) idea occurred to the mind of theKshatriyani Trisala: 'The fruit of my womb has been taken from me, it has died, it is fallen, it is lost. Formerly it moved, now it does -not move.' Thus with anxious thoughts and ideas, plunged in a sea of sorrow and misery, reposing her head on her hand, overcome by painful reflections, and casting her eyes, on the ground she meditated. And in the palace, of king Siddhartha the music of drums and stringed instruments, the clapping of hands, the dramatical performances, and the amusements of the people ceased, and mournful dejection reigned there. (92)

Then the Venerable Ascetic Mahavira, knowing that such an internal, &c. (see § 90, down to) idea had occurred to the mind of his mother, he quivered a little. (93)

Feeling her child quivering, trembling, moving, and stirring, the Kshatriyani Trisala-glad, pleased, and joyful, &c.-spoke thus: 'No, forsooth, the fruit of my womb has not been taken from me, it has not died, it is not fallen, it is not lost. Formerly it did not move, but now it does move.' Thus she was glad, pleased, and joyful, &c.

Then the Venerable Ascetic Mahavira, while in her womb, formed the following resolution: 'It will not behove me, during the life of my parents, to tear out my hair, and leaving the house to enter the state of houselessness.' (94)

Bathing, making offerings to the house-gods, performing auspicious rites and expiatory acts, and adorning herself with all ornaments, the Kshatriyani Trisala kept off sickness, sorrow, fainting, fear, and fatigue by food and clothing, perfumes and garlands, which were not too cold nor too hot, not too bitter nor too pungent, not too astringent nor too sour nor too sweet, not too smooth nor too rough, not too wet nor too dry, but all just suiting the season. In the proper place and time she ate only such food which was good, sufficient, and healthy for the nourishment of her child. She took her walks in places which were empty and agreeable as well as delightful to the mind; her desires were laudable, fulfilled, honoured, not disregarded, but complied with and executed; she most comfortably dozed, reposed, remained, sat, and laid on unobjectionable and soft beds and seats, and thus most comfortably carried her unborn child. (95)

In that period, in that age the Venerable Ascetic Mahavira-after the lapse of nine months and seven and a half days, in the first month of summer, in the second fortnight, the dark (fortnight) of Kaitra, on its fourteenth day, [while all planets were in their exaltations, the moon in her principal conjunction, and the sky in all its directions clear, bright, and pure; while a favourable and agreeable, low wind swept the earth; at the time when the fields were green and all people glad and amusing themselves] in the middle of the night while the moon was in conjunction with the asterism Uttaraphalguni (Trisala), perfectly healthy herself, gave birth to a perfectly healthy boy- (96)

End of the Fourth Lecture.

**Fifth Lecture**

In that night in which the Venerable Ascetic Mahavira was born, there was a divine lustre originated by many descending and ascending gods and goddesses, and in the universe, resplendent with one light, the conflux of gods occasioned great confusion and noise. (97)

In that night in which the Venerable Ascetic Mahavira was born, many demons in Vaisramana's service belonging to the animal world, rained down on the palace of king Siddhartha one great shower of silver, gold, diamonds, clothes, ornaments, leaves, flowers, fruits, seeds, garlands, perfumes, sandal, powder, and riches. (98)

After the Bhavanapati, Vyantara, Gyotishka, and Vaimanika gods had celebrated the feast of the inauguration of the Tirthakara's birthday, the Kshatriya Siddhartha called, at the break of the morning, together tht: town policemen and addressed them thus: (99)

'O beloved of the gods, quickly set free all prisoners in the town of Kundapura, increase measures and weights, give order that the whole town of Kundapura with its suburbs be sprinkled with water, swept, and smeared (with cowdung, &c.) that in triangular places, in places where three or four roads meet, in courtyards, in squares, and in thoroughfares, the middle of the road and the path along the shops be sprinkled, cleaned, and swept; that platforms be erected one above the other; that the town be decorated with variously coloured flags and banners, and adorned with painted pavilions; that the walls bear impressions in Gosirsha, fresh red sandal, and Dardara [sandal from Dardara] of the hand with outstretched fingers; that luck-foreboding vases be put on the floor, and pots of the same kind be disposed round every door and arch; that big, round, and long garlands, wreaths, and festoons be hung low and high; that the town be furnished with offerings, &c. (see § 32, down to) smelling box; that players, dancers, rope-dancers, wrestlers, boxers, jesters, story-telling ballad-singers, actors, messengers, pole-dancers, fruit-mongers, bag-pipers, lute-players, and many Talakaras [those who by clapping the hands beat the time during the performance of music] be present. Erect and order to erect thousands of pillars and poles, and report on the execution of my orders.' (100)

When the family servants wre thus spoken to by king Siddhartha, they-glad, pleased, and joyful, &c. (see § 58)-accepted the words of command, saying, 'Yes, master!'

Then they set free all prisoners, &c. (see § 100 down to) pillars and poles. Having done this, they returned to king Siddhartha, and laying their hands on their heads, reported on the execution of his orders. (101)

The. king Siddhirtha then went to the hall for gymnastic exercises, &c. (see §§ 60 and 61). (After having bathed) the king accompanied by his whole seraglio, and adorned with flowers, scented robes, garlands, and ornaments, held during ten days the festival in celebration of the birth of a heir to his kingdom; (it was held) under the continuous din and sound of trumpets, with great state and splendour, with a great train of soldiers, vehicles. and guests, under the sound, din, and noise of conches, cymbals, drums, castanets, horns, small drums, kettle drums, Muragas, Mridangas, and Dundubhis [three kinds of drums], which were accompanied at the same time by trumpets. The customs, taxes, and confiscations were released, buying and selling prohibited, no policemen were allowed to enter houses, great and small fines were remitted, and debts cancelled. Numberless excellent actors performed and many Talakaras were present, drums sounded harmoniously, fresh garlands and wreaths were seen everywhere, and the whole population in the town and in the country rejoiced and was in full glee. (102)

When the ten days of this festival were over, the king Siddhartha gave and ordered to be given hundreds and thousands and hundred-thousands of offerings to the gods, gifts, and portions (of goods); he received and ordered to be received hundreds, thousands, and hundred-thousands of presents. (103)

The parents of the Venerable Ascetic Mahavira celebrated the birth of their heir on the first day, on the third day they showed him the sun and the moon, on the sixth day they observed the religious vigil; after the eleventh day, when the impure operations and ceremonies connected with the birth of a child had been performed, and the twelfth day had come, they prepared plenty of food, drink, spices, and sweetmeats, invited their friends, relations, kinsmen, agnates, cognates, and followers, together with the Gñatrika Kshatriyas. Then they bathed, made offerings (to the house-gods), and performed auspicious rites and expiatory acts, put on excellent, lucky, pure court-dress, and adorned their persons with small but costly ornaments. At -dinner-time they sat down on excellent, comfortable chairs in the dining-hall, and together with their friends, relations, kinsmen, agnates, cognates and followers, and with the Gñatrika Kshatriyas they partook, ate, tasted, and interchangred (bits) of a Iarge collation of food, drink, spices, and sweetmeats. (104)

After dinner they went (to the meeting hall) after having cleansed their mouths and washed; when perfectly clean, they regaled and honoured their friends, &c. (see § 104, down to) Gñatrika Kshatriyas with many flowers, clothes, perfumes, garlands,and ornaments. Then they spoke thus to their friends, &c.: (105)

'Formerly,O beloved of the gods, when we had begotten this our boy, the following personal, reflectional, desirable idea occurred to our mind: "From the moment that this our boy has been begotten, our silver increased, our gold increased, &c. (see § 91, down to) Vardhamana. Now our wishes have been fulfilled, therefore shall the name of our boy be Vardhamana."' (106,107)

The Venerable Ascetic Mahavira belonged to the Kasyapa gotra. His three names have thus been recorded - by his parents he was called Vardhamana; because he is devoid of love and hate, he is called Sramana (i. e. Ascetic); because he stands fast in midst of dangers and fears, patiently bears hardships and calamities, adheres to the chosen rules of penance, is wise, indifferent to pleasure and pain, rich in control, and gifted with fortitude, the name Venerable Ascetic Mahavira has been given him by the gods. (108)

The Venerable Ascetic Mahavira's father belonged to the Kasyapa gotra; he had three names: Siddhartha, Sreyamsa, and Gasamsa, &c. (see Akaraga Sutra II, 15, § 15, down to) Seshavati and Yasovati. (109)

The Venerable Ascetic Mahavira -clever, with the aspirations of a clever man, of great beauty, controlling (his senses), lucky, and modest; a Gñatri Kshatriya, the son of a Gñatri Kshatriya; the moon of the clan of the Gñatris; a Videha, the son of Videhadatta, a native of

Videha, a prince of Videha-had lived thirty years in Videha when his parents went to the world of the gods (i. e. died), and he with the permission of his elder brother and the authorities of the kingdom fulfilled his promise. At that moment the Laukantika gods, following the established custom, praised and hymned him with these kind, pleasing, &c. (see § 47, down to) sweet, and soft words: (110)

'Victory, victory to thee, gladdener of the world! Victory, victory to thee, lucky one! Luck to thee, bull of the best Kshatriyas! Awake, reverend lord of the world! Establish the religion of the law which benefits all living beings in the whole universe! It will bring supreme benefit to all living beings in all the world!'

Thus they raised the shout of victory. (111)

Before the Venerable Ascetic Mahavira had adopted the life of a householder (i.e. before his marriage) he possessed supreme, unlimited, unimpeded knowledge and intuition. The Venerable Ascetic Mahivira perceived with this his supreme unlimited knowledge and intuition that the time for his Renunciation had come. He left his silver, he left his gold, he left his riches, corn, majesty, and kingdom; his army, grain, treasure, storehouse, town, seraglio, and subjects; he quitted and rejected his real, valuable property, such as riches, gold, precious stones, jewels, pearls, conches, stones, corals, rubies, &c.; he distributed presents through proper persons, he distributed presents among indigent persons. (112)

In that period, in that age, in the first month of winter, in the first fortnight, in the dark (fortnight) of Margasiras, on its tenth day, when the shadow had turned towards the east and the (first) Paurushi was full and over, on the day called Suvrata, in the Muhurta called Vigaya, in the palankin Kandraprabha, (Mahivira) was followed on his way by a train of gods, men, and Asuras, (and surrounded) by a swarm of shell-blowers, proclaimers, pattivallas, courtiers, men carrying others on the back, heralds, and bell bearers. They praised and hymned him with these kind, pleasing, &c. (see § 47, down to) sweet and soft words: O 13)

'Victory, victory to thee, gladdener of the world! Victory to thee, lucky one! Luck to thee! with undisturbed knowledge, intuition, and good conduct conquer the unconquered Senses; defend the conquered Law of the Sramanas; Majesty, conquering all obstacles, live in Perfection; put down with thy devotion Love and Hate, the (dangerous) wrestlers; vigorously gird thy loins with constancy and overcome the eight Karmans, our foes, with supreme, pure meditation; heedful raise the banner of content, O Hero! in the arena of the three worlds gain the supreme, best knowledge, called Kevala, which is free from obscurity; obtain the pre-eminent highest rank (i. e. final liberation) on that straight road which the best Ginas have taught; beat the army of obstacles! Victory, victory to thee, bull of the best Kshatriyas!

Many days, many fortnights, many months, many seasons, many half-years, many years be not afraid of hardships and calamities, patiently bear dangers and fears; be free from obstacles in the practice of the law!'

Thus they raised the shout of victory. (114)

Then the Venerable Ascetic Mahavira-gazed on by a circle of thousands of eyes, praised by a circle of thousands of mouths, extolled by a circle of thousands of hearts, being the object of many thousands of wishes, desired because of his splendour, beauty, and virtues, pointed out by a circle of thousands of forefingers, answering with (a, salam) of his right hand a circle of thousands of joined hands of thousands of men and women, passing along -a row of thousands of palaces, greeted by sweet and delightful music, as beating of time, performance on the Vina, Turya, and the great drum, in which joined shouts of victory, and the low and pleasing murmur of the people; accompanied by all his pomp, all his splendour, all his army, all his train, by all his retinue- by all his magnificence, by all his grandeur, by all his ornaments, by all the tumult, by all the throng, by all subjects, by all actors, by all timebeaters, by the whole seraglio; adorned with flowers, scented robes, garlands, and ornaments, &c. (see § 102, down to) which were accompanied at the same time by trumpets-went right through Kundapura to a park called the Shandavana of the Gñatris and proceeded to the excellent tree Asoka. (115) There under the excellent tree Asoka he caused his palankin to stop, descended from his palankin, took off his ornaments, garlands, and finery with his own hands, and with his own bands plucked out his hair in five handfuls. When the moon was in conjunction with the asterism Uttaraphalguni, he, after fasting two and a half days' without drinking water, put on a divine robe, and quite alone, nobody else being present, he tore out his hair and leaving the house entered the state of houselessness. (116)

The Venerable Ascetic Mahavira for a year anda month wore clothes; after that time he walked about naked, and accepted the alms in the hollow of his hand. For more than twelve years the Venerable Ascetic Mahivira neglected his body and abandoned the care of it; he with equanimity bore, underwent, and suffered all pleasant or unpleasant occurrences arising from divine powers, men, or animals.(117)

Henceforth the Venerable Ascetic Mahavira was houseless, circumspect in his walking, circumspect in his speaking, circumspect in his begging, circumspect in his accepting (anything), in the carrying of his outfit and drinking vessel; circumspect in evacuating excrements, urine, saliva, mucus, and uncleanliness of the body;

circumspect in his thoughts, circumspect in his words, circumspect in his acts; guarding his thoughts, guarding his words, guarding his acts, guarding his senses, guarding his chastity; without wrath, without pride, without deceit, without greed; calm, tranquil, composed, liberated, free from temptations, without egoism, without property; he had cut off all earthly ties, and was not stained by any worldliness: as water does not adhere to a copper vessel, or collyrium to mother of pearl (so sins found no place in him); his course was unobstructed like that of Life; like the firmament he wanted no support; like the wind he knew no obstacles; his heart was pure like the water (of rivers or tanks) in autumn; nothing could soil him like the leaf of a lotus; his senses were well protected like those of a tortoise; he was single and alone like the horn of a rhinoceros; he was free like a bird; he was always waking like the fabulous bird Bharundal, valorous like an elephant, strong like a bull, difficult to attack like a lion, steady and firm like Mount Mandara, deep like the ocean, mild like the moon, refulgent like the sun, pure like excellent gold'; like the earth he patiently bore everything; like a well-kindled fire he shone in his splendour.

These words have been summarized in two verses:

A vessel, mother of pearl, life, firmament, wind, water in autumn, leaf of lotus, a tortoise, a bird, a rhinoceros, and Bhirunda; I

An elephant, a bull, a lion, the king of the mountains, and the ocean unshaken-tbe moon, the sun, gold, the earth, well-kindled fire. II

There were no obstacles anywhere for the Venerable One. The obstacles have been declared to be of four kinds, viz. with regard to matter, space, time, affects. With regard to matter: in things animate, inanimate, and of a mixed state, with regard to space: in a village or a town or in a wood or in a field or a threshing-floor or a house' or a court-yard; with regard to time: in a Samayas or an Avalika or in the time of a respiration or in a Stoka or in a Kshana or in a Lava or in a Muhurta or in a day or in a fortnight or in a month or in a season or in a half year or in a year or in a long space of time; with regard to affects: in wrath or in pride or in deceit or in greed or in fear or in mirth or in love or in hate or in quarrelling or in calumny or in tale-bearing or in scandal or in pleasure or pain or in deceitful falsehood, &c. (all down to) or in the evil of wrong belief. There was nothing of this kind in the Venerable One. (118)

The Venerable One lived, except in the rainy season, all the eight months of summer and winter, in villages only a single night, in towns only five nights; he was indifferent alike to the smell of ordure and of sandal, to straw and jewels, dirt and gold, pleasure and pain, attached neither to this world nor to that beyond, desiring neither life nor death, arrived at the other shore of the sams.Ara, and he exerted himself for the suppression of the defilement of Karman.(119)

With supreme knowledge, with supreme intuition, with supreme conduct, in blameless lodgings, in blameless wandering, with supreme valour, with supreme uprightness, with supreme mildness, with supreme dexterity, with supreme patience, with supreme freedom from passions, with supreme control, with supreme contentment, with supreme understanding, on the supreme path to final liberation, which is the fruit of veracity, control, penance, and good conduct, the Venerable One meditated on himself for twelve years.

During the thirteenth year, in the second month of summer, in the fourth fortnight, the light (fortnight) of Vaisakha, on its tenth day, when the shadow had turned towards the east and the first wake was over, on the day called Suvrata, in the Muhurta called Vigaya, outside of the town Grimbhikagrama on the bank of the river Rigupalika, not far from an old temple, in the field of the householder Samaga, under a Sal tree, when the moon was in conjunction with the asterism Uttaraphalguni, (theVenerable One) in a squatting position with joined heels, exposing himself to the heat of the sun, after fasting two and a half days without drinking water, being engaged in deep meditation, reached the highest knowledge and intuition, called Kevala, which is infinite, suprême, unobstructed, unimpeded, complete, and full. (120)

When the Venerable Ascetic Mahavira had become a Gina and Arhat, he was a Kevalin, omniscient and comprehending all objects; he knew and saw all conditions of the world, of gods, men, and demons: whence they come, whither they go, whether they are born as men or animals (kyavana) or become gods or hell-beings (upapada), the ideas, the thoughts of their minds, the food, doings, desires, the open and secret deeds of all the living beings in the whole world; he the Arhat, for whom there is no secret, knew and saw all conditions of all living beings in the world, what they thought, rpoke, or did at any moment. (121)

In that period, in that age the Venerable Ascetic Mahavira stayed the first raimy season in Asthikagrama, three rainy seasons in Kampi and Prishtikampi, twelve in Vaisali and Vanigagrima, fourteen in Ragagriha and the suburbs of Nalanda, six in Mithila, two in Bhadrika, one in Alabhika, one in Panitabhumi one in Sravasti, one i.n the town of Papa in king Hastipala's office of the writers: that was his very last rainy season. (122)

In the fourth month of that rainy season, in the seventh fortnight, in the dark (fortnight) of Karttika, on its fifteenth day, in the last night, in the town of Papa, in king Hastipala's office of the writers, the Venerable Ascetic Mahavira died, went off, quitted the world, cut asunder the ties of birth, old age, and death; became a Siddha, a Buddha, a Mukta, a maker of the end (to all misery), finally liberated, freed from all pains. (123)

This occurred in the year called Kandra, the second (of the lustrum); in the month called Pritivardhana; in the fortnight Nandivardhana; on the day Suvratagni, surnamed Upasama; in the night called Devinanda, surnamed Nirriti; in the Lava called Arkya; in the respiration called Mukta; in the Stoka called Siddha; in the Karana called Naga; in the Muhurta called Sarvirthasiddha; while the moon was in conjunction with the asterism Svati he died, &c. (see above, all down to) freed from all pains. (124)

That night in which the Venerable Ascetic Mahavira died, &c. (all down to) freed from all pains, was lighted up by many descending and ascending gods. (125)

In that night in which the Venerable Ascetic Mahavira died, &c. (all down to) freed from all pains, a great confusion and noise was originated by many descending and ascending gods. (126)

In that night in which the Venerable Ascetic Mahavira died, &c. (all down to) freed from all pains, his oldest disciple, the monk Indrabhuti of the Gautama gotra, cut asunder the tie of friendship which he had for his master, and obtained the highest knowledge and intuition, called Kevala, which is infinite, supreme, &c., complete, and full. (127)

In that night in which the Venerable Ascetic Mahavira, died, &c. (all down to) freed from all pains, the eighteen confederate kings of Kasi and Kosala, the nine Mallakis and nine Likkhavis, on the day of new moon, instituted an illuminations on the Poshadha, which was a fasting day; for they said: 'Since the light of intelligence is gone, let us make an illumination of material matter!' (128)

In that night in which the Venerable Ascetic Mahavira died, &c. (all down to) freed from all pains, the great Graha [comet] called Kshudratma, resembling a heap of ashes, which remains for two thousand years in one asterism, entered the natal asterism, of the Venerable Ascetic Mahavira. (129) From the moment in which the great Graha, &c., entered the natal asterism of the Venerable Ascetic Mahavira, there will not he paid much respect and honour to the Sramanas, the Nirgrantha monks and nuns. (130) But when the great Graha, &c., leaves that natal asterism, there will be paid much respect and honour to the Sramanas, the Nirgrantha monks and nuns. (131)

In that night in which the Venerable Ascetic Mahavira died, &c. (all down to) freed from all pains, the animalcule called Anuddhari was originated:. which when at rest and not moving, is not easily seen by Nirgrantha monks and nuns who have not yet reached the state of perfection, but which when moving and not at rest, is easily seen by Nirgrantha monks and nuns who have not yet reached the state of perfection. (132) On seeing this (animalcule) many Nirgrantha monks and nuns must refuse to accept the offered alms.

'Master, why has this been said?' 'After this time the observance of control will be difficult.' (133)

In that period, in that age the Venerable Ascetic Mahavira had an excellent community of fourteen thousand Sramanas with Indrabhuti at their head; (134) thirty-six thousand nuns with Kandana at their head; (135) one hundred and fifty-nine thousand lay votaries with Sankhasataka. at their head; (136) three hundred and eighteen thousand female lay votaries with Sulasa and Revati at their head; (137) three hundred sages who knew the fourteen Purvas, who though no Ginas came very near them, who knew the combination of all letters, and like

Gina preached according to the truth; (138) thirteen hundred sages who were possessed of the Avadhi-knowledge and superior qualities; (139) seven hundred Kevalins who possessed the combined best knowledge and intuition; (140) seven hundred who could transform themselves, and, though no gods, had obtained the powers (riddhi) of gods; (141) five hundred sages of mighty intellect who know the mental conditions of all developed beings possessed of intellect and five senses in the two and a half continents and two oceans; (142) four hundred professors who were never vanquished in the disputes occurring in the assemblies of gods, men, and Asuras; (143) seven hundred male and fourteen hundred female disciples who reached perfection, &c. (all down to) freed from all pains; (144) eight hundred sages in their last birth who were happy as regards their station, happy as regards their existence, lucky as regards their future. (145)

The Venerable Ascetic Mahavira instituted two epochs in his capacity of a Maker of an end: the epoch relating to generations, and the epoch relating to psychical condition; in the third generation ended the former epoch, and in the fourth year of his Kevaliship the latter. (146)

In that period, in that age, the Venerable Ascetic Mahavira lived thirty years as a householder, more than full twelve years in a state inferior to perfection, something less than thirty years as a Kevalin, forty-two years as a monk, and seventy-two years on the whole. When his Karman which produces Vedaniya (or what one has to experience in this world), Ayus (length of life), name, and family, had been exhausted, when in this Avasarpini era the greater part of the Duhshamasushama period had elapsed and only three years and eight and a half months were left, when the moon was in conjunction with the asterism Svati, at the time of early morning, in the town of Papa, and in king Hastipala's office of the writers,

(Mahivira) single and alone, sitting in the Samparyahka, posture, reciting the fifty-five lectures which detail the results of Karman, and the thirty-six unasked questions (the Uttaradhyana Sutra), when he just explained the chief lecture (that of Marudeva) he died, &c. (see § 124, all down to) freed from all pains. (147)

Since the time that the Venerable Ascetic Mahavira died, &c. (all down to) freed from all pains, nine centuries have elapsed, and of the tenth century this is the eightieth year. Another redaction has ninety-third year (instead of eightieth). (148)

End of the Fifth Lecture.

End of the Life of Mahavira.

**Life of Parsva.**

In that period, in that age lived the Arhat Parsva, the people's favourite, the five most important moments of whose life happened when the moon was in conjunction with the asterism Visakha: in Visakha he descended (from heaven), and having descended thence, entered the womb (of his mother); in Visakha he was born; in Visakha, tearing out his hair, he left the house and entered the state of houselessness; in Visakha he obtained the highest knowledge and intuition, called Kevala, which is infinite, supreme, unobstructed, unimpeded, complete, and full; in Visakha he obtained final liberation. (149)

In that period, in that age, in the first month of summer, in the first fortnight, the dark (fortnight) of Kaitra, on its fourth day, the Arhat Parsva, the people's favourite, descended from the Pranata Kalpa [the tenth world of the gods], where he had lived for twenty Sagaropamas, here on the continent Gambudvipa, in Bharatavarsha, in the town of Benares; and in the middle of the night when the. moon was in conjunction with the asterism Visakha, after the termination of his allotted length of life, divine nature, and existence (among the gods), he took the form of an embryo in the womb of the queen Vama, wife of Asvasena, king (of Benares). (150)

The knowledge of the Arhat Parsva, the people's favourite, (about this) was threefold, &c. (repeat §§ 3-95 after making the necessary substitutions, and ornitting what exclusively applies to Mahavira, all down to) comfortably carried her unborn child. (151)

In that period, in that age the Arhat Parsva, the people's favourite-after the lapse of nine months and seven and a half days, in the second month of winter, in the third fortnight, the dark (fortnight) of Paushya, on its tenth day, in the middle of the night when the moon was in conjunction with the asterism Visakha-(Vama), perfectly healthy herself, gave birth to a perfectly healthy boy. (152)

In that night in which the Arhat Parsva, the people's favourite, was born, -&c. (repeat §§ 97-107 with the necessary alterations, all down to) therefore shall the name of our boy be Parsva. (153, 154)

The Arhat Parsva, the people's favourite, clever, with the aspirations of a clever man, of great beauty, controlling his senses, lucky, and modest, lived thirty years as a householder. Then the, Laukantika gods, following the established custom, addressed him with these kind, pleasing, &c., sweet, and soft words: (155)

'Victory, victory to thee, gladdener of the world!' (see § 111, down to) Thus they raised the shout of victory. (156) Before the Arhat Parsva, the people's favotirite, had adopted the life of a householder, &c. (see § 112, down to) indigent persons.

In the second month of winter, in the third fortnight, the dark (fortnight) of Paushya, on its eleventh day, in the middle of the night, riding in his palankin called Visala, followed on his way by a train of gods, men, and Asuras, &c. (Parsva) went right through the town of Benares to the park called Asramapada, and proceeded to the excellent tree Asoka. There, &c. (see § 116, down to) five handfuls.

When the moon was in conjunction with the asterism Visakha, he, after fasting three and a half days without drinking water, put on a divine robe, and together with three hundred men he tore out his hair, and leaving the house entered the state of houselessness. (157)

The Arhat Parsva, the people's favourite, for eighty-three days neglected his body, &c. (see § 117, down to) animals. (158) -

Thereafter the Arhat Parsva, the people's favourite, was houseless, circumspect, &c. (see §§ 118-120, down to) meditated upon himself for eighty-three days.

During the eighty-fourth day-it was in the first month of summer, in the first fortnight, the dark (fortnight) of Kaitra, on its fourth day, in the early part of the day, when the moon was in conjunction with the asterism Visakha-Parsva, under a Dhataki tree, after fasting two and a half days without drinking water, being engaged in deep meditation, reached the infinite, &c. (see § 120, down to) highest knowledge and intuition called Kevala, &c. (see § 121, down to) moment.(159)

The Arhat Parsva, the people's favourite, had eight Ganas and eight Ganadharas (enumerated in a Sloka):

Subha and Aryaghosha, Vasishtha and Brahmakirin, Saumya and Sridhara, Virabhadra and Yasas. (160)

The Arhat Parsva, the people's favourite, had an excellent community of sixteen thousand Sramanas with Aryadatta at their head; (161) thirty-eight thousand nuns with Puslipakula at their head; (162) one hundred and sixty-four thousand lay votaries with Suvrata at their head; (163) three hundred and twenty-seven thousand female lay votaries with Sunandi at their head; (164) three hundred and fifty sages who knew the fourteen Purvas, &c. (see § 138); (165) fourteen hundred sages who were possessed of the Avadhi knowledge; one thousand Kevalins, eleven hundred sages who could transform themselves, six hundred sages of correct knowledge, one thousand male and two thousand female disciples who had reached perfection, seven hundred and fifty sages of vast intellect, six hundred professors, and twelve hundred sages in their last birth, (166)

The Arhat Parsva, the people's favourite, instituted two epochs in his capacity of a Maker of an end: the epoch relating to generations and the epoch relating to psychical condition; the former ended in the fourth generation, the latter in the third year of his Kevaliship. (167)

In that period, in that age the Arhat Parsva, the people's favourite, lived thirty years as a householder, eighty-three days in a state inferior to perfection, something less than seventy years as a Kevalin, full seventy years as a Srarnana, and a hundred years on the whole.

When his fourfold Karman was exhausted and in this Avasarpini era the greater part of the Duhshamasushama period had elapsed, in the first month of the rainy season, in the second fortnight, the light (fortnight) of Sravana, on its eighth day, in the early part of the day when the moon was in conjunction with the asterism Visakha, (Parsva), after fasting a month without drinking water, on the summit of mount Sammeta, in the company of eighty-three persons, stretching out his hands, died, &c. (all down to) freed from all pains. (168)

Since the time that the Arhat Parsva, the people's favourite, died, &c. (all down to) freed from all pains, twelve centuries have elapsed, and of the thirteenth century this is the thirtieth year. (169)

End of the Life of Parsva.

**13**

# Life of Arishtanemi

In that period, in that age lived the Arhat Arishtanemi, the five most important moments of whose life happened when the moon was in conjunction with the asterism Kitra. In Kitra he descended from heaven, &c. (see § 149, down to) obtained final liberation. (170)

In that period, in that age, in the fourth month of the rainy season, in the seventh fortnight, the dark (fortnight) of Karttika, on its twelfth day, the Arhat Arishtanemi descended from the great Vimana, called Aparigita, where he had lived for thirty-six Sagaropamas, here on the continent Gambudvipa, in Bharatavarsha, in the town of Sauripura, and in the middle of the night when the moon was in conjunction with the asterism Kitra, he took the form of an embryo in the womb of the queen Siva, wife of the king Samudravigaya, &c. (the seeing of the dreams, the accumulation of riches, &c., should be repeated here). (17 1)

In that period, in that age the Arhat Arishtanemi- after the lapse of nine months and seven and a half days, in the first month of the rainy season, in the second fortnight, the light (fortnight) of Sravana, on its fifth day, &c.-(Sivi), perfectly healthy herself, gave birth to a perfectly healthy boy. (Repeat the account of the birth, substituting the name Samudravigaya, all down to) therefore shall the name of our boy be Arishtanemi. [His mother saw in a dream a nemi, the outer rim of a wheel, which consisted of rishta stones flying up to the sky. Hence the name Arishtameni.]

The Arhat Arishtanemi, clever, &c. (see §§ 155-157, all down to) indigent persons. (172) In the first month of the rainy season, in the second fortnight, the light (fortnight) of Sravana, on its sixth day riding in his palankin called Uttarakura, and followed on his way by a train of gods, men, and Asuras, &c. (Arishtanemi) went right through the town of Dvaravati to the park called Revatika, and proceeded to the excellent Asoka tree. There, &c. (see § 116, down to) five handfuls. When the moon was in conjunction with the asterism Kitra, after fasting two and a half days without drinking water, he put on a divine robe, and together with a thousand persons he tore'out his hair, and leaving the house entered the state of houselessness. (173)

The Arhat Arishtanemi for fifty-four days neglected his body, &c. (see §§ 117-120). During the fifty-fifth day-it was in the third month of the rainy season, in the fifth fortnight, the dark fortnight of Asvina, on its fifteenth day, in the last part of the day, when the moon was in conjunction with the asterism Kitra-(Arishtanemi) under a Vetasa tree on the summit of mount Girnar, after fasting three and a half days without drinking water, &c., obtained infinite, &c., highest knowledge and intuition called Kevala, &c. (see § 121, down to) moment. (174)

The Arhat Arishtanemi had eighteen Ganas and eighteen Ganadharas. (175)

The Arhat Arishtanemi had an excellent community, of eighteen thousand Sramanas with Varadatta at their head; (176) forty thousand nuns with Arya Yakshini at their head; (177) one hundred and sixty-nine thousand lay votaries with Nanda at their head; (178) three hundred and thirty-six thousand female lay votaries with Mahasuvrata at their head; (179) four hundred sages who knew the fourteen Purvas, &c.; (180) fifteen hundred sages who were possessed of the Avadhi knowledge; fifteen hundred Kevalins; fifteen hundred sages who could transform themselves; one thousand sages of vast intellect; eight hundred professors; sixteen hundred sages in their last birth; fifteen hundred male and three thousand female disciples who had reached perfection.

The Arhat Arishtanemi instituted, &c. (see § 146, down to) the former ended in the eighth generation, the latter in the twelfth year of his Kevaliship. (181)

In that period, in that age the Arhat Arishtanemi lived three centuries as a prince, fifty-four days. in a state inferior to perfection, something less than seven centuries as a Kevalin, full seven centuries as a Sramana, a thousand years on the whole. When his fourfold Karman was exhausted and in this Avasarpini era a great part of the Duhshamasushama. period had elapsed, in the fourth month of summer, in the eighth fortnight, the light (fortnight) of Ashadha, on its eighth day, in the middle of the night when the moon was in conjunction with the asterism Kitra, (Arishtanemi), after fasting a month without drinking water, on the summit of mount Girnar, in the company of five hundred and thirty-six monks, in a squatting position, died, &c. (all down to) freed from all pains. (182)

Since the time that the Arhat Arishtanemi died, &c. (all down to) freed from all pains, eighty-four thousand years have elapsed, of the eighty-fifth millennium nine centuries have elapsed, of the tenth century this is the eightieth year. (183)

End of the Life of Arishtanemi.

**Epochs of the Intermediate Tirthakaras**

Since he time that the Arhat Nami died,&c. (all down to) freed from all pains, 584,979 years have elapsed, this is the eightieth year. (184) Since the death of Munisuvrata this is the year 1,184,980. Since Malli this is the year 6,584,980. Ara died 10,000,000 years before Malli; Kunthu a quarter of a Palyopama before Malli; Santi three-quarters of a Palyopama; Dharma three Sagaropamas before Malli; Ananta seven Sagaropamas before Malli; Vimala sixteen Sagaropamas before Malli; Vasupugya forty Sagaropamas before Malli; Sreyimsa a hundred Sagaropamas before Malli. Sitala died a krore of Sagaropamas, less 42,003 years and eight and a half months, before the death of Vira. Suvidhi, surnamed Pushpadanta, died ten krores of Sagaropamas before Sitala; Kandraprabha a hundred krores of Sagaropamas before Sitala.; Suparsva a thousand krores of Sagaropamas before Sitala; Padmaprabha ten thousand krores of Sagaropamas before Sitala; Sumati one hundred thousand krores of Sagaropamas before Sitala; Abhinandana one million krores of Sagaropamas before Sitala; Sambliava two million krores of Sagaropamas before Sitala; Agita five million krores of Sagaropamas before Sitala. (185-203)

# 14

# Life of Rishabha

In that period, in that age lived the Arhat Rishabha, the Kosalian, four important moments of whose life happened when the moon was in conjunction with the asterism Uttarashadha; the fifth, when in conjunctioin with Ashadha: (204) in Uttarashadha he descended from heaven, &c. (all down to) in Abhigit he obtained final liberation. (205)

In that period, in that age, in the fourth month of summer, in the seventh fortnight, the dark (fortnight) of Ashadha, on its fourth day, the Arhat Rishabha, the Kosalian, descended from the great Vimina called Sarvarthasiddha, where he had lived for thirty-three Sagaropamas, here on the continent Gambudvipa, in Bharatavarsha, in Ikshvakubhumi, and in the middle of the night, &c., he took the form of an embryo in the womb of Marudevi, wife of the patriarch Nabhi. (206)

The knowledge of the Arhat Risliablia about this, &c. (all as in the case of Mahivira., but note the following differences: the first dream is a bull (Coming forward with his face, the other (mothers of Tirthakaras see first) an elephant. She (Marudevi) relates them to Nabhi, the patriarch; there are no interpreters of dreams; Nabhi, the patriarch, himself interprets them). (207)

In that period, in that age the Arhat Rishabha, the Kosalian,-in the first month of summer, in the first fortnight, the dark (fortnight) of Kaitra, on its eighth day, &c.,-(Marudevi), perfectly health), herself, gave birth to a perfectly healthy boy. (208)

(The circumstances connected with the birth of Rishabha are the same as in the case of that of Mahavira, only that the contents of § 100 and 101 do not apply to the present case.) (209)

The Arhat Rishabha, the Kosalian, belonged to the Kisyapa gotra, and he had five names: Rishabha, First Kin, First Mendicant, First Gina, and First Tirthakara. (210)

The Arhat Rishabha, the Kosalian, clever, with the aspirations of a clever man, of great beauty, controlling (his senses), hicky, and modest, lived two millions of former years as a prince, and six millions three hundred thousand former years as a king. During his reign he taught, for the benefit of the people, the seventy-two sciences, of which writing is the first, arithmetic the most important, and the knowledge of omens the last, the sixty-four accomplishments of women, the hundred arts, and the three occupations of men. At last he anointed his hundred sons as kings, and gave each a kingdom. Then the Laukantika god, following the established custom, &c. (see §§ 110-112, down to) indigent persons. In the first month of summer, in the first fortnight, the dark (fortnight) of Kaitra, on its eighth day, in the latter part of the day, riding in his palankin called Sudarsana, followed on his way by a train of gods, men, and Asuras, &c. (Rishabha) went right through the town Vinita to the park called Siddhartha Vana, and proceeded to the excellent tree Asoka. There, &c. (see § 116, down to) four handfuls. When the moon was in conjunction with the asterism Ashadha, he, after fasting two and a half days without drinking water, put on a divine robe, and together with four thousand of high, noble, royal persons, and Kshatriyas, he tore out his hair, and leaving the house entered the state of houselessness. (211)

The Arhat Rishabha, the Kosalian, for one thousand years neglected his body, &c. (see §§ 117-120, down to) meditated upon himself for one thousand years. Thereupon-it was in the fourth month of winter, the seventh fortnight, the dark (fortnight) of Phalguna, on its eleventh day, in the early part of the day, when the moon was in conjunction with the asterism Ashadha, outside of the town Purimatala, in the park called Sakatamukha, under the excellent tree Nyagrodha-(Rishabha) after fasting three and a half days without drinking water, being engaged in deep meditation, reached the infinite, &c. (see § 120, down to) highest knowledge and intuition called Kevala, &c. (see § 121, down to) moment. (212)

The Arhat Rishabha, the Kosalian, had eighty four Ganas and eighty-four Ganadharas. (213)

The Arhat Rishabha, the Kosalian, had an excellent community of eighty-four thousand Sramanas with Rishabhasena at their head; (214) three hundred thousand nuns with Brahmisundari at their head; (215) three hundred and five thousand lay votaries with Sreyamsa at their head; (216) five hundred and fifty-four thousand female lay votaries with Subhadra at their head; (217 four thousand seven hundred and fifty sages who knew the fourteen Purvas, &c.; (218) nine thousand sages who were possessed of the Avadhi knowledge; (219) twenty thousand Kevalins; (220) twenty thousand six hundred sages who could. transform themselves; (221) twelve thousand six hundred and fifty sages of vast intellect, &c.; (222) twelve thousand six hundred and fifty professors; (223) twenty thousand male and forty thousand female disciples who had reached perfection; (224) twenty-two thousand nine hundred sages in their last birth, &c. (225)

The Arhat Rishabha, the Kosalian, instituted, &c. (see § 146, down to) the former ended after numberless generations, the latter from the next Muhurta after his Kevaliship. (226)

In that period, in that age the Arhat Rishabha, the Kosalian, lived two millions of former years as a prince, six millions three hundred thousand former years as a king, together eight millions three hundred thousand former years as a householder; a thousand (former) years in a state inferior to perfection, nine-and-ninety thousand former years as a Kevalin, together a hundred thousand former years as a Sramana, and eight millions four hundred thousand years on the whole. When his fourfoid Karman was exhausted, and in this Avasarpini era the Sushamaduhshami period had nearly elapsed, only three years and eight and a half months being left, in the third month of winter, in the fifth fortnight, the dark (fortnight) of Magha, on its thirteenth day, in the early part of the day when the moon was in conjunction with the asterism, Abhigit, (Rishabha), after fasting six and a half days without drinking water, on the summit of mount Ashapada, in the company of ten thousand monks in the Samparyahka position, died, &c. (all down to) freed from all pains. (227)

Since the time that the Arhat Rishabha, the Kosalian, died, -&c. (all down to) freed from all pains, three years and eight and a half months elapsed; thereupon one koti of kotis of Sagaropamas, less forty-two thousand and three years and eight and a half months, elapsed. At that time the Venerable Ascetic Mahivira died; after his Nirvana nine centuries elapsed, of the tenth century this is the eightieth year.

End of the Life of Rishabha.

End of the Lives of the Ginas.

15

# List of The Sthaviras

At that period, at that age the Venerable Ascetic Mahivira had nine Ganas and eleven Ganadharas.

'Why, now, has it been said, that the Venerable Ascetic Mahavira had nine Ganas, but eleven Ganadharas?'

'The oldest monk of the Venerable Ascetic Mahavira was Indrabhuti of the Gautama gotra, who instructed five hundred Sramanas; the middle-aged monk was Agnibhuti of the Gautama gotra, who instructed five hundred Sramanas; the youngest was Vayabhuti of the Gautarna gotra, who instructed five hundred Sramanas. The Sthavira Arya-Vyakta of the Bharadvaga rotra instructed five hundred Sramanas; the Sthavira Arya-Sudharman of the Agnivesayana gotra instructed five hundred Sramanas; the Sthavira Mandikaputra of the Vasishtha gotra instrticted two hundred and fifty Sramanas; the Sthavira Matiryaputra of the Kasyapa gotra instructed two hundred and fifty Sramanas; the Sthavira Akampita of the Gatitama gotra and Sthavira Akalabhritri of the Harittiyana gotra, both Sthaviras instructed together three hundred Sramanas each; the Sthaviras Metarya and Prabhasa, both of the Kaundinya gotra, instructed together three hundred

Sramanas each. Therefore, Sir, has. it been said that the Venerable Ascetic Mahavira had nine Ganas, but eleven Ganadharas. (1)

All these eleven Ganadharas of the Venerable Ascetic Mahavira, who knew the twelve Angas, the fourteen Purvas, and the whole Siddhanta of the Ganins, died, &c. (all down to) freed from all pains in Ragagriha after fasting a month without drinking water. The Sthaviras Itidrabhuti and Arya Sudharman both died after the Nirvana of Mahavira. The Nirgrantha Sramanas of the present time are all (spiritual) descendants of the monk Arya Sudharman, the rest of the Ganadharas left no descendants. (2)

The Venerable Ascetic Mahavira was of the Kilsyapa gotra. His disciple was:

1. Arya Sudharman of the Agnivesyayana gotra
2. Arya Gambunaman of the Kisyapa gyotra;
3. Arya Prabhava of the Katyayana gotra;
4. Arya Sayyambha, father of Manaka, was of the Vatsa gotra;
5. Arya Yasobhadra of the Tungikayana gotra. (3)

In the short redaction the list of Sthaviras after Arya Yasobhadra is the following:

6. Arya Sambbutavigaya of the Mathara gotra and Arya Bhadrabahu of the Prakina gotra;
7. Arya Sthalabhadra of the Gautama gotra
8. i. Arya Mahagiri of the Ailapatya gotra and

   ii. Arya Suhastin of the Vasishtha gotra;
9. Susthita and Supratibuddha, surnamed Kotika and Kakandaka, of the Vyaghrapatya gotra;
10. Arya Indradatta. (Indadinna) of the Kausika gotra;
11. Arya Datta (Dinna) of the Gautama gotra;

12. Arya Simhagiri Gatismara of the Kausika gotra;

13. Arya Vagra of the Gautama gotra;

14. Arya Vagrasena of the Utkirishta gotra

He had four disciples: Arya Nagila, Arya Padmila, Arya Gayanta, and Arya Tapasa, each of whom founded a Sakha called after his name, viz. the Aryanagila Sakha, the Aryapadmila Sakha, the Aryagayanta Sakha, and the Aryatapasa Sakha. (4)

In the detailed redaction the. list of Sthaviras after Arya Yasobhadra is the following:

6. i. Arya Bhadrabahu of the Prakina gotra, who had four disciples of the Kasyapa gotra:

A. Godasa, founder of the Godasa Gana, which was divided into four Sakhas:

a. The Tamraliptika Sakha,

b. The Kotivarshiyta Sakha,

c. The Pundravardhantya Sakha, and

d. The Disikharhatika Sakha.

B. Agnidatta,

C. Ganadatta,

D. Somadatta.

ii. Arya Sambhutavigaya of the Mithara gotra, who had twelve disciples:

7. A. Nandanabhadra,

B. Upananda,

C. Tishyabhadra

D. Yasobhadra,

E. Sumanobhadra

F. Manibhadra,

G. Punyabhadra

H. Sthulabhadra of the Gautama gotra,

I. Rigumati,

K. Gambu,

L. Dirghabhadra, and

M. PAndubhadra; and seven female disciples:

A. Yaksha

B. Yakshadatta (Yakshadinna),

C. Bhuta,

D. Bhutadatta (Bhutadinna),

E. Sena (also Ena),

F. Vena,

G. Rena.

8. i. Arya Mahagiri of the Aillpatya gotra, who had eight disciples:

A. Uttara,

B. Balissaha, who both together founded the Uttarabalissaha Gana, which was divided into four Sakhas:

a. Kausambika,

b. Sautaptika (Pr. Soittiya),

c. Kautumbini (or Kundadhari),

d. Kandandgari.

C. Dhanarddhi (Pr. Dhanaddha),

D. Sirarddhi (Pr. Siriddha),

E. Kodinya,

F. Naga,

G. Nigaputra,

H. Khaluka Rohagupta of the Kausika gotra, founder of the Trairasika Sakha

ii. Arya Stiliastin of the Vasisshtha gotra, who had twelve disciples

9. A. Arya Rohana. of the Kasyapa gotra, founder of the Uddeha Gana, which was divided into four Sakhas:

a. Udumbarika (Pr. Udumbariggiya),

b. Masapurika,

c. Matipatriki,

d. Purnapatriki (Pr. Punnapattiya, Panna, Sunna, or Suvanna); and into six Kulas:

a. Nagabhuta,

b. Somabhuta,

c. Ullagakkha (or Ardrakakkha?),

d. Hastilipta (Pr. Hatthiligga),

e. Nandika (Pr. Nandigga),

f. Parhasaka.

B. Bhadrayasas of the Bharadvagra gotra, who founded the Uduvatika Gana, which was divided into four Sakhas:

a. Kampiyika (Pr. Kampiggiya),

b. Bhadriyika (Pr. Bhaddiggiya),

c. Kakandika,

d. Mekhaltyika (Pr. Mehaliggiya); and into three Kulas:

a'. Bhadrayaska (Pr. Bhaddagasiya),

b'. Bhadraguptika,

c'. Yasobhadra (Pr. Gasabhadda).

C. Megha.

D. Karnarddhi (Pr. Kamidithi) of the Kundala gotra, who founded the Vesavatika Gana, which was divided into four Sakhas:

a. Sravastika

b. Ragyapalika (Pr. Raggapaliya),

c. Antarañgika (Pr. Antariggiya),

d. Kshemaliptika (Pr. Khemaliggya); and into four Kulas:

a'. Ganika,

b'. Maighika,

c'. Kamarddhika,

d'. Indrapuraka.

E. Srigupta of the Harita gotra. founder of the Karana Gana, which was divided into four Sakhas

a. Haritamalakari,

b. Samkasika,

c. Gavedhuka,

d. Vagranagari; and into seven Kulas:

a'. Vatsaliya (Pr. Vakkhaligga),

b'. Pritidharmika,

c'. Haridraka (Pr. Halligga),

d'. Pushyamitrika (Pr. Pusamittigga).

e'. Malyaka (Pr. Maligga),

f'. Aryaketaka,

g'. Krishnasakha (Pr. Kanhasaha).

F. Rishigupta Kakandaka of the Vasishtha gotra, founder of the Manava Gana, which was divided into four Sakhas:

a. Kasyapiyi (Pr. Kasaviggiya),

b. Gautamiya (Pr. Goyameggiya),

c. Vasishthiya (Pr. Vasitthiya),

d. Saurashtrika; and into three Kulas:

a'. Rishiguptika,

b'. Rishidattika,

c'. Abhiyasasa.

G. and H. Susthita and Supratibuddha, surnamed Kautika and Kakandaka, of the Vyaghrapatya gotra, founders of the Kautika gotra, which was divided into four Sakhas:

a. Ukkanagari,

b. Vidyidhari,

c. Vagri,

d. Madhyamika (Pr. Magghimilla); and into four Kulas:

a'. Brahmaliptaka (Pr. Bambhaligga),

b'. Vatsaliya (Pr. Vakkhaligga, cf. E. a'.),

c'. Vaniya (Pr. Vanigga),

d'. Prasnavahanaka.

Both Sthaviras had together five disciples:

10. A. Arya Indradatta (Pr. Indadinna) of the Kasyapa gotra,

B. Priyagantha, founder of tht Madhyana Sakha,

C. Vidyadharagopala of the Kasyapa gotra, founder of the Vidyadhari Sakha,

D: Rishidatta,

E. Arhaddatta (Pr. Arihadatta).

11. Arya Datta (Pr. Dinna) of the Gautama gotra, who had two disciples:

12. i. Arya Santisenika of the Mathara, gotra, founder of the Ukkanagara Sakha, who had four disciples:

A. Arya Senika, founder of the Aryasenika Sakha,

B. Arya Tapasa, founder of the Aryatapasi Sakha,

C. Arya Kubera, founder of the Aryakubera Sakha, and

D. Arya Rishipalita, founder of the Aryarishipaliti Sakha.

ii. Arya Simhagiri Gatismara of the Gautama gotra, who had four disciples:

13. A. Dhanagiri,

B. Arya Samita of the Gautarna gotra, founder of the Brahmadvipika Sakha,

C. Arya Vagra of the Gautama gotra, founder of the Aryavagra Sakha,

D. Arhaddatta (Pr. Arihadinna).

14. i. Arya Vagrasena, founder of the Aryanagila Sakha,

ii. Arya Padma, founder of the Aryapadmi Sakha,

iii. Arya Ratha of the Vatsa gotra, founder of the Aryag-ayantl Sakha.

15. Arya Pulgyagiri of the Kausika gotra

16. Arya Phalgumitra of the Gautama gotta.

17. Arya Dhanagiri of the Vasishtha gotra.

18. Arya Sivabhuti of the Kautsa gotra.

19. Arya Bhadra of the Kasyapa gotra.

20. Arya Nakshatra of the Kasyapa gotra.

21. Arya Raksha of the Kasyapa gotra.

22. Arya Naga of the Gautama gotra.

23. Arya Gehila of the Vasishtha gotra.

24. Arya Vishnu of the Mathara gotra.

25. Arya Kalaka of the Gautama gotra.

26. Arya Sampalita and Bhadra, both of the Gautama gotra.

27. Arya Vriddha of the Gautama gotra.

28. Arya Sanghapalita of the Gautama gotra.

29. Arya Hastin of the Kasyapa gotra.

30. Arya Dharma of the Suvrata gotra.

31. Arya Simha of the Kasyapa gotra.

32. Arya Dhama of the Kasyapa gotra.

33. Arya Sandilya.

Bowing down my head, I pay my reverence to the Sthavira Gambu of The Gautama gotra, who possessed steady virtue, good conduct, and knowledge. ix.

I prostrate myself before the Sthavara Nandita, of Kasyapa gotra, who is possessed of great clemency and of knowledge, intuition, and good conduct. x.

Then I adore the Kshamasramana Desiganin of the Kasyapa gotra, who, steady in his conduct, possesses.the highest righteousness and virtue. xi.

Then I prostrate myself before the Kshamaramama Sthiragupta of the Vatsya gotra, the preserver of the sacred lore, the wise one, the ocean of wisdom, him of great virtue. xii.

Then I adore the Sthavira prince, Dharma, the virtuous Ganin, who stands well in knowledge, intuition, good conduct, and penance, and is rich in virtues. xiii.

I revere the Kshamasramama Devarddhi of the Kasyapa gotra, who wears, as it were, the jewel of the right understanding of the Sutras, and possesses the virtues of patience, self-restraint, and clemency. xiv.

End of the List of the Sthaviras.

## Rules for Yatis.

1. In that period, in that age the Venerable Ascetic Mahdvira commenced the Paggusan when a month and twenty nights of the rainy season had elapsed.

'Why has it been said that the Venerable Ascetic Mahavira commenced the Paggusan when a month and twenty nights of the rainy season had elapsed?' (1)

'Because at that time the lay people have usually matted their houses, whitewashed them, strewn them (with straw), smeared thein (with cowdung), levelled, smoothed, or perfumed them (or the floor of them), have dug gutters and drains, have furnished their houses, have rendered them comfortable, and have cleaned them. Hence it has been said that the Venerable Ascetic Mahivira commenced the Paggusan when a month and twenty nights of the rainy season had elapsed.' (2)

As the Venerable Ascetic Mahavira, commenced the Paggusan when a month and twenty nights of the rainy season had elapsed, so the Ganadharas commenced the Paggusan when a month and twenty nights of the rainy season had elapsed. (3) As the Ganadharas have done, so the disciples of the Ganadharas have done. (4) As they have done, so the Sthaviras have done. (5) As they have done, so do the Nirgrantha Sramanas of the present time. (6)

As they do, so our masters, teachers, &c. do. (7) As they do, so do we commence the Paggusan after a month and twenty nights of the rainy season have elapsed. It is allowed to commence the Paggusan earlier, but not after that time.(8)

2. Monks or nuns during the Paggusan are allowed to regard their residence as extending a Yogana, and a Krosa all around, and to live there for a moderate time. (9)

3. During the Paggusan monks or nuns are allowed to go and return, for the sake of collecting alms, not farther than a Yogana, and a Krosa (from their lodgings). (10) If there is (in their way) an always flowing river which always contains water, they are not allowed to travel for a Yogana and a Krosa. (11) But if the river is like the Eravati near Kunala, such that it can be crossed by putting one foot in the water and keeping the other in the air, there it is allowed to travel for a Yogana and a Krosa. (12) But where that is impossible, it is not allowed to travel for a Yogana and a Krosa. (13)

4. During the Paggusan the Akarya will say, 'Give, Sir!' Then he. is allowed to give (food to a sick brother), but not to accept himself. (14) If the.Akarya says, 'Accept, Sir!' then he is allowed to accept (food), but not to give. (15) If the Akarya, says, 'Give, Sir! accept, Sir!' then the patient is allowed to give and to accept (food). (16)

5. Monks or nuns who are hale and healthy, and of a strong body, are not allowed during the Paggusan frequently to take the following nine drinks: milk, thick sour milk, fresh butter, clarified butter, oil, stigar, honey, liquor, and meat. (17)

6. During the Paggusan a collector of alms might ask (the Akarya), 'Sir, is (anything of the just-mentioned articles) required for the sick man?' he (the Akarya) says, 'Yes, it is.' Then (the sick man) should be asked, 'How much do you require?' The Akarya says,'So much is required for the sick man: You must take so much as he told you.' And he (the collector of alms) should beg, and begging he should accept (the required food). Having obtained the quantity orderd, he should say, ' No more!' Perchance (the giver of food) might ask, 'Why do you say so, Sir?' (Then he Should answer), 'Thus much is required for the sick man.' Perchance, after that answer the other may say, ' Take it, Sir! You may after (the sick man has got his share) eat it or drink it.' Thus he is allowed to accept it, but he is not allowed to accept it by pretending, that it is for the sick man. (18)

7. In householders' families which are converted, dcvoted, staunch adherers (to the law), and honour, praise, and permit (the visits of monks), Sthaviras, during the Paggusan, are not allowed to ask, 'Sir, have you got such or Such a thing?' if they do not see it.

'Why, Sir, has this been said?' 'Because a devout houscholder might buy it or steal it.' (19)

8. During the Paggusan a monk eats only one meal

a day, and should at one fixed time frequent the abodes of householders for the sake of collecting alms, except when he does services for the Akarya, the teacher, an ascetic, or a sick man, likewise if he or she be a novice who has not yet the marks of ripe age'. (20) To a monk who during the Paggusan eats only one meal on every second day, the following special rule applies. Having gone out in the morning, he should eat and drinks his pure dinner, then he should clean and rub his alms-bowl. If his dinner was sufficient, he should rest content with it for that day; if not, he is allowed for a second time to frequent the abodes of householders for the sake of collecting alms. (21) A monk who during the Paggusan eats on every third day, is allowed twice to frequent the abodes of householders for the sake of collecting alms. (22) A monk who during the Paggusan eats one meal on every fourth day, is allowed three times to frequent the abodes of householders for the sake of collecting alms. (21) A monk who keeps still more protracted fasts, is allowed at all (four) times to frequent the abodes of householders for the sake of collecting alms. (24)

9. A monk who during the Paggusan eats one meal every day, is allowed to accept all (permitted) drinks. A monk who during, the Paggusan eats one meal on every second day, is allowed to accept three kinds of drinks: water used for watering flour, sesamum, or rice. A monk who eats one meal on every third day, is allowed to accept three kinds of drinks: water used for washing sesamum, chaff, or barley. A monk who during the Paggusan eats one meal on every fourth day, is allowed to accept three kinds of water: rain-water, or sour gruel, or pure (i.e. hot) water. A monk who during the Paggusan keeps still more protracted fasts, is allowed to accept only one kind of drink: hot pure water It must contain no boiled rice. A monk who abstains from food altogether, is allowed to accept only one kind of drink: pure hot water. It must contain no boilcd rice; it must be filtered, not unfiltered; it must be a limited quantity,

not an unlimited one; it must be sufficient, not insufficient. (25)

10. A monk Who during the Paggusan restricts himself to a certain number of donations, is allowed to accept (e.g.) five donations of food, and five of drink; or four of food, and five of drink; or five of food, and four of drink. He may accept one donation of salt for seasoning his meat. He should rest content for that day with the dinner he has brought together, and is not allowed a second time to frequent the abodes of householders for the sake of collecting alms. (26) During the Paggusan monks or nuns who restrict their visits to certain houses may go to a place where rice is cooked, if it is the seventh house from that where they are lodged. According to some, the lodging is included in the seven houses which such a mendicant must pass before he may participate in the festive entertainment; but according to others, it is not included in those seven houses. (27)

11. During the Paggusan a monk who collects alms in the hollow of his hand, is not allowed to frequent the abodes of householders, &c., if rain, even in the form of a fine spray, falls down. (28) During the Paggusan a monk who collects alms in the hollow of his hand, is not allowed to stay anywhere except in a house after having accepted alms, for it might begin to rain. But he should eat a part, and put back the rest (if it then begins to rain), covering his hand with the other hand, and laying it on his bosom or hiding it under his armpits; then he should go to well-covered (places), to a cave or the foot of a tree, where no water or drops of water or spray of water falls in his hand. (29)

12. During the Paggusan a monk who collects alms in the hollow of his hand, is not allowed to collect alms if rain, even in the form of a fine spray, falls down. (30)

13. During the Paggusan a monk who uses an alms-bowl is not allowed to frequent the abodes of householders for the sake of collecting alms if it rains fast, but he is

allowed to do so if it rains but little; but they must wear then an under and upper garment. (31) During the Paggusan a monk who has the abode of a householder while there are single showers of rain, is allowed (when the rain ceases for a moment) to stand under a grove, or in his residence, or in the assembling-hall of the village, or at the foot of a tree. (32) If before his arrival a dish of rice was being cooked, and after it a dish of pulse was begun to be cooked, he is allowed to accept of the dish of rice, but not of the dish of pulse. (33) But if before his arrival a dish of pulse was being cooked, and after it a dish of rice was begun to be cooked, he is allowed to accept of the dish pulse, but not of the dish of rice. (34) If both dishes were begun to be cooked before his arrival, he is allowcd to accept of both. If both dishes were begun to be cooked after his arrival, he is not allowed to acccept of either. he is allowed to accept of what was prepared before his arrival; he is not allowed to acccept of what was prepared after his arrival. (35) During the Paggusan, &c. (see § 32, down to) tree; he is not allowed to pass there his time with the food he had collected before. But he should first eat and dring his pure (food and drink), then rub and clean his alms bowl, and, putting his things together, he should, while the sun has not yet set, go to the place where he is lodged; but he is not allowed to pass the night in the former place. (36) During the Paggusan, &c. (see § 32, down to) tree. (37) It is not allowed that there at the same place should stand together one monk and one nun, nor one monk and two nuns, nor two monks and one nun, nor two monks and two nuns. But if there is a fifth person, a male or female novice, or if that place can be seen (by those who pass) of doors open on it, then they are allowed to stand there together. (38) During the Paggusan, &c. (see § 32, down to) tree. It is not allowed that there at the same place should stand together a monk and a lay woman, &c. (through the four cases as in § 28). But if there is a fifth person, a Sthavira or a Sthavirâ or if that place can be seen (by those who pass) or doors open on it, then they are allowed to stand there together. The same rule applies to a nun and a layman. (39)

14. During the Paggusan monks or nuns are not allowed to accept food, drink, dainties, and spices for one who has not asked them, and whom they have not promised to do so. (40)

'Why has this been said, Sir?' 'Because one who collects alms for another without being asked for it, might eat them or not, just as he lists.' (41)

15. During the Paggusan monks or nuns are not allowed to take their meals as long as their body is wet or moist. (42)

'How has this been said, Sir?' 'Seven places which retain the moisture have been declared: the hands, the lines in the hand, the nails, the top of the nails, the brows, the under lip, the upper lip.' But when they perceive that the water on their body has dried up and the moisture is gone, then they are allowed to take their meals. (43)

16. There are these eight classes of small things which a mendicant ought diligently to perceive, observe, and inspect, viz. living beings, mildew, seeds, sprouts, flowers, eggs, layers, and moisture.

What is understood by the small living beings? The small living beings are declared to be of five kinds: black, blue, red, yellow, and white ones. There is an animalcule called Anuddhari, which when at rest and not moving is not easily seen by monks and nuns who have not yet reached perfection, which when not at rest but moving is easily seen by monks and nuns who have not yet reached perfection. Monks and nuns who have not yet reached perfection must diligently perceive, observe, and inspect this. Those are the small living beings. (44)

What is understood by small mildew? Small mildew

has been declared to be of five kinds: black, blue, &c. There is a kind of small mildew which has the same colour as the substance on which it grows. Monks, nuns, &c. (see § 44, down to) inspect this. That is small mildew.

What is understood by small seeds? Small seeds are declared to be of five kinds: black, blue, &c. There is a kind of small seeds of the same colour as grain. Monks and nuns, &c. (see § 44, down to) inspect this. Those are the small seeds.

What is understood by small sprouts? Small sprouts are declared to be of five kinds: black, blue, &c. There is a kind of small sprouts of the same colour as earth. Monks and nuns, &c. (see § 44, down to) inspect them. Those are the small sprouts.

What is understood by small flowers? Small flowers are declared to be of five kinds: black, blue, &c. There is a kind of small flowers of the same colour as the tree (on which they grow). Monks and nuns, &c. (see § 44, down to) inspect them. Those are the small flowers.

What is understood by small eggs? Small eggs are declared to be of five kinds: eggs of biting insects', of spiders, of ants, of lizards (or wasps), and of chameleons. Monks and nuns, &c. (see § 44, down to) inspect them. Those are the small eggs.

What is understood by small caves or lairs? Small caves or lairs are declared to be of five kinds: lairs of animals of the asinine kind, chasms, holes, cavities widening below like the stem of a palm tree, and wasps' nests. Monks and nuns, &c. (see § 44, down to) inspect them. Those are the small caves or lairs.

What is understood by small moisture? Small moisture is declared to be of five kinds: dew, hoarfrost, fog, hailstones, and damps. Monks and nuns, &c. (see § 44, down to) inspect this. That is small moisture.

17. During the Paggusan a monk might wish to frequent the abodes of householders for the sake of collecting alms. He is not allowed to go without asking leave of the teacher, or sub-teacher, or religious guide, or Sthavira, or head of the Gana, or Ganadhara, or founder of the Gana, or whom else he regards as his superior; he is allowed to go after having asked leave of one of these persons (in this way): 'I want with your permission to frequent the abodes of householders for the sake of collecting alins.' If he (the superior) grants permission, one is allowed to go; if not, one is not allowed to go.

'Why has this been said, Sir?' 'The teacher knows how to make good what has been done wrong.' (46) The same rule applies concerning the visits to temples and leaving the house for easing nature, or any other business, also the wandering from village to village. (47)

18. During the Paggusan a monk might wish to take some medicine; he is not allowed to take it without asking leave of the teacher, &c. (see § 47, down to) founder of the Gana; but he is allowed to take it after having asked leave of one of these persons (in this way) 'I want, Sir, with your permission to take some medicine,' viz. so much or so often. If he, &c. (see § 46, down to) wrong. (48) The same rule applies if a monk wants to undergo some medical cure. (49) Also if he wants to do some exalted penance. (50) Also if he intends, after the last mortification of the flesh which is to end in death, to wait for his last hour without desiring it, in total abstinence from food and drink or in remaining motionless; also if he wants to go out or to enter, to eat food, &c., to ease nature, to learn his daily lesson, to keep religious vigils-he is not is allowed to do it without asking leave. (51)

19. If during the Paggusan a monk wants to dry or warm (in the sun) his robe, alms-bowl, blanket, broom, or any other utensil, he is not allowed without asking one or many persons to frequent the abodes of householders for

the sake of collecting alms, to eat food, &c., to visit temples or leave the house for easing nature, to learn his daily lesson, to lie down with outstretched limbs or stand in some posture. If there is somebody near, one or many persons, then he should say: 'Sir, please mind this (robe, &c.) while I frequent the abodes of householders, &c. (see above, down to) posture.' If that person promises to do it, then he (the monk) is allowed to go; if he does not promise it, then he is not allowed to go. (52)

20. During the Paggusan monks or nuns are not allowed to be without their proper bed or bench. This is the reason: A mendicant whose bed and bench are not reserved for his own use, are low and rickety, not sufficiently fastened, without a fixed place, and never exposed to the sun, and who is not circumspect in what he does, nor accustomed to inspect and clean the things of his use, will find it difficult to exercise control; (53) but on the contrary, control will be easy to him. (54).

21. During the Paggusan monks or nuns must always inspect three spots where to ease nature; not so in the summer and winter, as in the rainy season. 'Why has this been said, Sir?' 'For in the rainy season living beings, grass, seeds, mildew, and sprouts frequently come forth.' (55)

22. During the Paggusan monks or nuns must have three pots, one for ordure, one for urine, and a spitting-box. (56) Monks and nuns, who wear after the Paggusan their hair as short as that of a cow, are not allowed to do so during the Paggusan after the night (of the fifth Bhadrapada); but a monk should shave his head or pluck out his hair. Shaving with a razor every month, cutting with scissors every half month, plucking out every six months. (57) This is the conduct cheiflyof the Sthaviras during the rainy season.

23. During the Paggusan monks or nuns should not use harsh words after the commencement of the Paggusan;

if they do, they should be warned: 'Reverend brother (or sister), you speak unmannerly.' One who (nevertheless) uses harsh words after the commencement of the Paggusan, should be excluded from the community. (58)

24. If, during the Paggusan, among monks or nuns occurs a quarrel or dispute or dissension, the young monk should ask forgiveness of the superior, and the superior of the young monk. They should forgive and ask forgiveness, appease and be appeased, and converse without restraint. For him who is appeased, there will be success (in control); for him who is not appeased, there will be no success; therefore one should appease one's self. 'Why has this been said, Sir?' 'Peace is the essence of monachism.' (59)

25. During the Paggusan monks or nuns should have three lodging-places; (two) for occasional use, which must be inspected; one for constant use, which must be swept (60).

26. During the Paggusan monks or nuns should give notice of the direction or intermediate direction in which they intend to go forth for the sake of begging alms. 'Why has this been said, Sir?' 'During the Paggusan the reverend monks frequently undertake austerities; an ascetic becoming weak and exhausted might swoon or fall down. (In case of such an accident the remaining) reverend monds will undertake their search in theat direction or intermediate direction (which the ascetic has named them). (61)

27. During the Paggusan monks or nuns are not allowed to travel further than four or five Yoganas, and then to return. They are allowed to stay in some intermediate place, but not to pass there (at the end of their journey) the night. (62)

Of the Nirgrantha monks who follow, &c. (see Akaranga Sutra II 15, V end, down to) ... there (rules regulating) the conduct of Sthaviras in the rainy season,

# 16

# 24 Tirthankaras

Time rolls along in eternal cycles of rise and decline. Utsarpini is a "rising" era in which human morale and natural conditions improve over time. At the end of Utsarpini, begins Avasarpini, a "declining" era of the same length, in which human morale and virtues deteriorate. During the middle of every rising and declining era twenty-four souls become Tirthankaras. They are the humans like us who rise to that level. While accumulating different karmas, they also accumulate get a special karma called Tirthankar Nam Karma in the last 3rd of their life by performing one or more of the 20 special austerities. Tirthankar Nam Karma matures in the final life and leads the person to become a Tirthankara. After attaining omniscience, Tirthankara reorganize Jain religion to suit the changing times. Tirthankaras are also called Arihantas, Jinas, Kevalis, and Vitragi. Arihant means "destroyer of inner enemies," Jina means "victor of inner enemies," and vitragi means "one who does not have anymore attachment or hatred towards anyone." This means that they are totally detached from worldly aspects. They have destroyed the four ghati karmas, namely Jnanavarniya Karma,

Darshanavarniya Karma, Mohniya Karma, and Antaraya Karma. They are Kevaljnani meaning that they know everything everywhere that happened in the past, that is happening now, and that will happen in the future at the same time. They are also Kevaldarshani, meaning that they can see all that happened in the past, that is happening now, and that will happen in the future all at the same time. They reinstate the fourfold order of sadhus (monks), sadhvis (nuns), shravaks (male householders), and shravikas (female householders).

Jains celebrate five major events in the life of a Tirthankar. They are called Kalyanak (auspicious events). They are:

1. **Chyavana Kalyanak** - This is the event when the Tirthankar's soul departs from its last life, and is conceived in the mother's womb.

2. **Janma Kalyanak** - This is the event when the Tirthankar's soul is born.

3. **Diksha Kalyanak** - This is the event when the Tirthankar's soul gives up all his/her worldly possessions and becames a monk/nun. (Digambar sect does not believe that women can become Tirthankar or be liberated.)

4. **Kevaljnana Kalyanak** - This is event when Tirthankar's soul destroys the four ghati karmas completely and attains the Kevaljnana (absolute knowledge). Celestial angels set Samavsaran for Tirthankars from where he/she delivers the first sermon. This is the most important event for the entire Jain order as the Tirthankar reinstates Jain Sangh and preaches the Jain path of purification and liberation.

5. **Nirvana Kalyanak** - This event is when a Tirthankar's soul is liberated from this worldly physical existence forever and becomes a Siddha. On this day, the Tirthankar's soul destroys the four aghati karmas completely, and attains salvation, the state of eternal bliss.

There are other significant events also in the final life of a Tirthankars. When a Tirthankar's soul is conceived, his/her mother has fourteen dreams (some texts mention sixteen dreams). A Tirthankar's soul, while even in mother's womb, has three types of knowledge, namely Matijnan, Shrutjnan, and Avadhijnan. One year before the time of renunciation, a group of celestial angels come to pay homage to the future Tirthankar. They remind him/her that the time to renounce the world is arriving. When a Tirthankar renounces the worldly life, he attains Manahparyavjnan, the fourth type of the knowledge, which enables him/her to know people's thoughts.

## List of 24 TIRTHANKARS

| Name | Father | Mother | Birth Place |
|---|---|---|---|
| 1.**Rishabha** (Adinath) | Nabhi-raja | Maru-Devi | Ayodhya |
| 2 **Ajitnath** | Jita Satru | Vijaya-Devi | Ayodhya |
| 3 **Sambhava-nath** | Jitari | Sena | Sravasti |
| 4 **Abhinandan-nath** | Samvara | Siddhartha | Ayodhya |
| 5 **Sumatinath** | Megh-Prabha | Sumangala | Ayodhya |
| 6 **Padmabrabha** | Dharana (Sidhara) | Susima | Kausambhi |
| 7 **Suparshva-nath** | Supratishtha | Prithvi | Kasi (Banaras) |
| 8 **Chandra-prabha** | Mahasena | Lakshmana | Chandrapuri |
| 9 **Pushpadanta** (Suvidhinatha) | Sugriva | Rama (Supriya) | Kakandi |

| | | | |
|---|---|---|---|
| **10 Shiatnath** | Dridharatha | Sunanda | Bhadrika-puri |
| **11 Shreyansanath** | Vishnu (Vishna) | Vishnudri | Simhapuri |
| **12 Vasupujya** | Vasupujya | Vijaya | Champapuri |
| **13 Vimalnath** | Kritvarman (Syama) | Suramya | Kampilya |
| **14 Anantnath** | Simhasena | Sarvavasa | Ayodhya |
| **15 Dharmanath** | Bhanu | Suvrata | Ratnapuri |
| **16 Shantinath** | Visvasena | Acira | Hastinapura |
| **17 Kunthunath** | Surya(Sura) | Sri-Devi | Hastinapura |
| **18 Aranath** | Sudarsana | Mitra(Devi) | Hastinapura |
| **19 Malinath** | Kumbha | Rakshita | Mithilapuri |
| **20 Munisuvrata** | Sumitra | Padmavati | Kusagra-nagara (Raj-grih) |
| **21 Nami Natha** | Vijaya (Vipra) | Vapra (Mathura) | Mithilapuri |
| **22 Neminatha** | Samudra-vijaya | Sivadevi | Sauripura (Dvaraka) |
| **23 Parsva Natha** | Asvasena | Vama (Banaras) | Kasi |
| **24 Mahavira** (Vardhamana) | Siddharatha | Priyakarni (Trishala) | Kundapura |

## List of 24 TIRTHANKARS

| Name | Number of Ganadharas | Place of Death | Emblem |
|---|---|---|---|
| **1 Rishabha** | 84 | Mount Kailasa | Bull |
| **2 Ajitnath** | 90 | Mount Parasnath | Elephant |
| **3 Sambhav Nath** | 105 | Samet Sikhar | Horse |
| **4 Abhinandannath** | 103 | Samet Sikhar | Monkey |
| **5 Sumatinath** | 116 | Samet Sikhar | Curlew |
| **6 Padmaprabha** | 111 | Samet Sikhar | Red Lotus |
| **7 Suparshvanath** | 95 | Samet Sikhar | Svastika |
| **8 Chandraprabha** | 93 | Samet Sikhar | Crescent |
| **9 Pushpadanta** (Suvidhinath) | 88 | Samet Sikhar | Dolphin |
| **10 Shitalnath** | 81 | Samet Sikhar | Wishing Tree |
| **11 Shreyamsanath** | 77 | Samet Sikhar | Garuda |
| **12 Vasupujya** | 66 | Champapuri | Buffalo |
| **13 Vimalnath** | 55 | Mount Parasnath | Boar |
| **14 Anantanath** | 50 | Mount Parasnath | Bear |
| **15 Dharmanath** | 43 | Mount Parasnath | Vajardanda |
| **16 Shantinath** | 36 | Mount Parasnath | Deer |
| **17 Kunthunath** | 35 | Mount Parasnath | HeGgoat |
| **18 Aranath** | 30 | Mount Parasnath | Fish |
| **19 Malinath** | 28 | Mount Parasnath | Waterpot |
| **20 Munisuvrata** | 18 | Mount Parasnath | Tortoise |
| **21 Naminath** | 17 | Mount Parasnath | Blue Lotus |
| **22 Neminath** | 11 | Mount Girnar | Conch |
| **23 Parshvanath** | 10 | Mount Parasnath | Serpent |
| **24 Mahavira** (Vardhamana) | 11 | Pava Puri | Lion |

17

# Timeline of Jainism

| | |
|---|---|
| **5th cent. BCE** | Life of Mahavira, the founder of Jainism. |
| **3rd cent. BCE** | A Jain community forms in the trading center of Mathura. |
| **c. 4th-5th cent. CE** | Umasvati codifies Jain texts in the Tattvartha Sutra. |
| **5th cent.** | Schism occurs, forming the Svetambara and Digambara sects. |
| **9th-11th cent.** | Digambara Jainism is frequently supported by south Indian royalty. |
| **12th cent.** | Hemacandra, a Svetambara monk, is tutor to the rulers Siddharaja and his nephew Kumarapala. |
| **17th cent.** | The iconoclastic Sthanakvasis sect emerges. |
| **18th-19th cent.** | Decline of image-worshipping ascetic communities. |
| **21st cent.** | Revival of asceticism and development of mystical sects. Many Jains emigrate to East Africa, the United Kingdom and North America. |

# 18

## Glossary of Jain Words

| | |
|---|---|
| **Abadhita** | With no contradiction of the probandum |
| **Abadhitavisayatva** | Absence of contradiction of the probandum |
| **Abhavya** | One who is incapable of attaining moksa |
| **Abhedavrtti** | Identifying by transference of epithet |
| **Abhedopacara** | Making identical aspect predominant |
| **Abhigraha** | Resolution |
| **Abhikshna-Jnanopayoga** | Ceaseless pursuit of right knowledge. |
| **Abhipsita** | Desirable |
| **Abhiseka** | Anointing ceremony |
| **Abhyasta** | Habituated |
| **Abhyuhana** | Process of understanding |
| **Abrahma** | Unchastity. |

| | |
|---|---|
| **Abrahma-varjana** | Abandonment of all incontinence |
| **Acaksurdarsana** | Perception by means of the senses other than visual |
| **Acara** | Conduct |
| **Acarya** | Head of a mendicant group; spiritual leader; monk-scholar |
| **Achakshu-darshana-varana** | Non-Ocular-Conation-Obscuring |
| **Acharya-Bhakti** | Devotion to Acharyas or Heads of the Orders of Saints. |
| **Achetanatva** | Unconsciousness |
| **Adama-nirjara** | Equanimous submission to the fruition of karma |
| **Adana-niksepana-samiti** | Care in the picking up and putting down of any object |
| **Adattadana-virati** | Not taking anything which has not been given; identical to asteya-vrata |
| **Adeya** | Impressive; appearance such as may affect others. |
| **Adharma** | Principle of Rest |
| **Adharma-dravya** | The principle of rest |
| **Adhigama** | preaching of another. |
| **Adhigamaja** | Grahita |
| **Adhikarana** | Dependance |
| **Adhikaraniki-kriya** | having weapons of hurtfulness. |
| **Adho-loka** | The lower world; the home of infernal beings |
| **Adhyavasaya** | Determinate cognition |
| **Adhyayana** | Lecture |
| **Advaita** | Non-dual; cap., the monistic school of Vedanta |

| | |
|---|---|
| **Agama** | Scripture; canonical literature Verbal testimony |
| **Agamika** | Non-repetitive |
| **Agari** | House-holders(laymen). |
| **Aghatiya** | Karamas that generate embodiment and particular conditions thereof |
| **Aghatiya** | Non-Destructive karmas |
| **Agni** | Fire |
| **Agurulaghu** | Nor heavy-light; neither too heavy to move, nor too light to have stability. |
| **Agurulaghutva** | Capacity by which one attribute or substance does not become another and the substance does not lose the attributes whose grouping forms the substance itself. Individuality; The quality of constancy in space-points |
| **Ahampratyaya** | Self-awareness |
| **Ahara Agrahya-Vargana** | Assimilation-unrecievable-molecule |
| **Ahara-Vargana** | Assimilation-molecule for food |
| **Aharaka** | Assimilative; The spiritual man-like emanation from the head of a saint in doubt, in the sixth spiritual stage. |
| **Aharaka mishra** | Assimitative with physical. |
| **Aharaparyapti** | Taking of morsels of food |
| **Aharyaprasanjana** | Determinate concomitant |
| **Aharyaropa** | Determinate concomitant |
| **Ahavaniya-agni** | One of the sacred fires in the Hindu srauta ritual |
| **Ahimsa** | Nonharming |

| | |
|---|---|
| **Ahimsavrata** | Refraining from harming |
| **Ailaka** | The highest state of a Digambara layman, wherein he retains only one piece of clothing |
| **Ajinana** | Ignorance |
| **Ajiva** | Insentient, Non-Living, Non-Soul, Which is not soul |
| **Ajna-vyapadiki-kriya** | Misinterpreting the scriptural injunctions, which we do not want to follow. |
| **Ajnana** | Ignorance-nivartaka-remover Wrong belief caused by ignorance. Indiscrimination of good and bad. |
| **Ajnanavada** | Agnosticism |
| **Ajnanika** | Agnostic. Everything is not knowable. This is one of the general attributes of all substances. |
| **Ajnavicaya** | Contemplation on the teachings of Jina |
| **Akama-nirjara** | Equanimous submission to the fruition of karma. |
| **Akasa** | Space |
| **Akasha** | Space |
| **Akashaya** | Quasi-passions; slight or minor passions. |
| **Akincitkara** | Immaterial |
| **Akrandana** | weeping |
| **Akriyavada** | Doctrine of non-action |
| **Akriyavadi** | Opposite of Kriyavadi, e.g., the soul does nothing. This undermines all truth. |
| **Aksa** | An organ of sense Self |

| | |
|---|---|
| **Aksara** | Alphabet |
| **Aksata** | Uncooked rice |
| **Aksaya-trtiya** | The "immortal third," a Jaina holiday |
| **Alarikara** | Ornamentation |
| **Alocana** | Critical self-examination |
| | Intuitional cognition |
| **Aloka** | Non-Universe |
| **Aloka-akasa** | Totally empty space |
| **Alokitapana-bhojana** | Thoroughly seeing to one's food and drink. |
| **Amanaska** | Without mind |
| **Amari** | Prohibition of animal sacrifice |
| **Amla** | Acid. |
| **Amsavatara** | Minor incarnation of Visnu |
| **Amudha drishtitva** | Free from superstitious belief. |
| **Amudhadrsti** | Freedom from delusory notions |
| **Amurtatva** | Along with Achetanatva, is common to Space, Motion, Rest and Time. Along with Chetanatva, is a common attributes of the class of substance, or group of attributes, called Soul. Immateriality |
| **Anabhimata** | Undesirable |
| **Anabhoga** | putting down a thing where it ought not to be put. |
| **Anabhoga-kriya** | indifference in dropping things or throwing oneself down upon the earth, i.e. without seeing whether it is swept or not. |
| **Anabhyupagata** | Unproved |
| **Anadeya** | Non-impressive; dull appearance. |

| | |
|---|---|
| **Anadhyavasaya** | Indecision |
| **Anadhyavasita** | Neither known |
| **Anadi** | Having no beginning |
| **Anadinidhana** | Without beginning and without end |
| **Anagara** | House-less(ascetics). |
| **Anagara-dharma** | Mendicant discipline |
| **Anaikantika** | Inconclusive |
| **Anaikantikatva** | Inconclusiveness |
| **Anakanksha-kriya** | Disrespect to scriptural injunctions out of viceor laziness. |
| **Anakaropayoga** | Formless conscious activity |
| **Anaksara** | Non-alphabet |
| **Anangapravista** | Main scriptions |
| **Ananta-sukha** | Infinite bliss |
| **Anantadharma** | Infinite aspects |
| **Anantajnana** | Infinite knowledge; a synonym for kevalajnana |
| **Anantanu-Vargana** | Infinite-atoms-molecule |
| **Anantanubandhi** | Error feeding or wrong-belief-breeding or Right-belief preventing-passions. |
| **Anantanubandhi-kasaya** | Passions that "Pursue from the limitless past," preventing the attainment of samyak-darsana |
| **Anantaviryatva** | Infinite energy |
| **Ananugamika** | Non-following |
| **Ananvaya** | Lacking in positive concomitance |
| **Anarpitabhasa** | False unimplied point of view |
| **Anarpitanaya** | Unimplied view-point |
| **Anartha danda-vrata** | Taking a vow not to commit purposeless sin |

| | |
|---|---|
| **Anarthadandavrata** | Refraining from the five minor types of evil activity |
| **Anasana** | Fasting |
| **Anashana** | Fasting—external austerity. |
| **Anataraya** | Obstructive. |
| **Anavastha** | Regressus ad infinitum |
| **Anekantavada** | The doctrine of manifold aspects |
| **Anekatva** | Multiplicity |
| **Anga** | Limb; cap., a group of twelve Jaina canonical texts |
| **Angabahya** | The subsidiary canon |
| **Angapuja** | Veneration of the limbs of the lord |
| **Angopanga** | Limbs; limbs and minor limbs. |
| **Anigraha** | Free from defect |
| **Anindriyaja** | Non-sensuous, not caused by senses |
| **Anirakrta** | Not refuted |
| **Anisrita** | Independent |
| **Anitya** | Impermanent |
| **Anitya anupreksha** | Everything is subject to change or transitory. transitoriness |
| **Anityavada** | Noneternalism |
| **Anivartin** | That state from which there is no returning |
| **Anivrtti-karana** | The process of suppressing certain mohaniya karmas |
| **Anrita** | Falsehood. |
| **Antar-muhurta** | A period of up to forty-eight minutes |
| **Antara-bhava** | The state of existence between death and rebirth |
| **Antaratman** | The state of perceiving the self within |

| | |
|---|---|
| **Antaraya** | inflow of obstructive karma Obstructive |
| **Antaraya-karma** energy- | Karma that restricts the quality of the soul |
| **Antarjalpa** | Inward repetition |
| **Antarmuhurtta** | For a moment |
| **Antarmuhurttika** | A period of less than forty-eight minutes |
| **Antarvyapti** | Internal concomitance |
| **Antyesti-kriya** | Funeral rites |
| **Anu** | Atom; an indivisible particle of matter |
| **Anu Vargana** | Atom |
| **Anu-Vratas** | Five minor vows. |
| **Anubhaga** | intensity of fruition |
| **Anubhava** | Experience, Retribution of a karma; intensity |
| **Anubhaya-mana** | Neither true nor false. |
| **Anubhaya-vachana** | Neither true or false. |
| **Anubhuta** | Cognised, felt |
| **Anugamika** (Avadhijnana) | Following |
| **Anugamin** | Following |
| **Anukampa** | Compassion |
| **Anumana** | Inference |
| **Anumanika** | Inferential |
| **Anumati-tyaga** | Preparatory to the monk's life. Enjoins a gradual giving up of the world and retiring into some very quiet place to aquire the knowledge of truth and ultimately to become fit to be a teacher of the path to Liberation. |

| | |
|---|---|
| **Anumatityaga-pratima** | The tenth stage in which a layman refrains from all household activities |
| **Anumiti** | Inference |
| **Anupalambha** | Non-observation |
| **Anupatta** | Matter which is not taken in by the soul. |
| **Anupayoga** | Not in actual use |
| **Anupayukta** | Without attention |
| **Anupreksa** | Reflection, twelve kinds |
| **Anupreksha** | Meditation. |
| **Anupurvi** | Migratory form; the power of retaining the form of the last incarnation during transmigration, i.e., in the passage from one to another condition of existence. |
| **Anutseka** | not being proud of one's own achievement or attainments. |
| **Anuvichi-bhashana** | Speaking in accordance with scriptural injunctions. |
| **Anuvratas** | Minor vows pertaining only to laypeople |
| **Anuyoga** | Exposition; a group of postcononical texts |
| **Anvaya** | Concomitance in agreement |
| **Anvayadharma** | Quality |
| **Anyatarasiddha** | Unproved for either of the two |
| **Anyathanupapatti** | Logical impossibility in the absence of the other |
| **Anyatva anupreksha** | Sepatateness. Otherness. The world, my relations and friends, my body, and mind, they are all distinct and separate from my real self. |

| | |
|---|---|
| **Apadhyana** | Thinking ill of others. |
| **Apara** (Samgrahanaya) | Non-ultimate (generic) |
| **Aparamarthika** | Empirical |
| **Aparigraha** | Nonpossession |
| **Aparinamin** | Unchanging |
| **Aparyapti** | Undevelopable; Incapable of developing the body fully. |
| **Aparyavasita**(Srutajnana) | Having no end |
| **Apavartana** | Energy that hastens the time and decreases the intensity of karmic fruition |
| **Apaya** | Perceptual judgment |
| **Apayavicaya** | Contemplation on the means by which beings can be saved |
| **Apo-kayika** | Water-bodies |
| **Apradhanacarya** | Nominal acarya |
| **Apramanatva** | Invalidity |
| **Apramatta-virata** | Restraint not vitiated by carelessness, the seventh gunasthana |
| **Apramatva** | Non-organ of knowledge |
| **Aprapyakaritva** | The quality of acting from distance |
| **Apratipatina** | Non-extinguishing |
| **Apratita** | Neither known |
| **Apratya Vekshita** | Putting down a thing without seeing. |
| **Apratyakhyana-kriya** | not renouncing what ought to be renounced. |
| **Apratyakhyanavarana** | Obstructors of partial renunciation |
| **Apratyakhya-navaraniya** | Partial vow-preventing passions including anger, pride, deceit and greed. |

| | |
|---|---|
| **Aprayojaka** | Immaterial |
| **Apta** | Authentic |
| **Apta-vacana** | Statement of an authentic personality |
| **Apurva-karana** | The process by which the soul attains to an unprecedented degree of purity |
| **Arahamta** | Prakrit for arhat |
| **Arambha** | Commencement of a thing - compare attempt in Criminal Law. |
| **Arambha-tyaga** | Abandonment of merely worldly engagements and occupations. |
| **Arambhatyaga- pratima** | The eighth stage in which a layman withdraws from all professional commitments |
| **Arambhaya-himsa** | Violence occurring either accidentally or through the performance of an acceptable occupation |
| **Arapa** | Hot light; radiant heat;possessed of a brilliant body, which is hot to others but not to the possessor, as the gross radiant earth bodied beings in the sun. |
| **Arati** | Displeasure in regard to sense activities dissatisfaction. The lamp-waving ceremony |
| **Arcana** | Worship |
| **Ardha naracha samhanana** | Semi-unbreakable joints and bones. |
| **Ardha-phalaka** | Loincloth worn by Svetambara monks |
| **Ardha-pudgala-paravartana-kala** | The amount of time required for a soul to take in and use up half |

| | |
|---|---|
| | of the available karmic matter in the universe |
| **Arghya** | Respectful offering |
| **Arham** | Identical to arhat |
| **Arhat** | "Worthy to worship"; an epithet of one who has attained kevalajnana; a synonym for kevalin |
| **Arhat Kevali** | Omniscient Lord |
| **Arhat-Bhakti** | Devotion to Arhats or Omniscient Lords. |
| **Arihamta** | A variant for arahamta |
| **Arpitanaya** | Implied point of view |
| **Arpitanayabhasa** | False implied point of view |
| **Artha** | Meaning of a word |
| **Artha (Kaladigata)** | Object |
| **Artha-kriya** | Exercise of casual efficiency |
| **Artha-kriyasamartha** | Capable of performing any action |
| **Artha-naya** | Point of view of meaning |
| **Artha-nayabhasa** | False point of view of meaning |
| **Artha-paryaya** | Mode of the object |
| **Artha-prapakatva** | Conveyance of the sense |
| **Artha-pratipadaka** | Support of truth |
| **Artha-samvedana** | Manifested in the statement |
| **Arthavagraha**(Matijnana) | Object-awareness |
| **Arupi-ajiva** | The four insentient, formless dravyas |
| **Aryika** | Nuns of the Digambara sect |
| **Asad guna udbhavana** | proclaiming in oneself the good qualities which one does not possess. |
| **Asamgrahika** (Naigamanaya) | Non-generic |

| | |
|---|---|
| **Asamjni** | Unable to reason about spiritual matters |
| **Asamkhyata** | Innumerable |
| **Asamprapta sripatika samhanana** | Loosely jointed bones. |
| **Asamyama** | Nonrestraint |
| **Asankyatanu-Vargana** | Innumerable-atoms-molecule |
| **Asarira** | Free from embodiment; a siddha |
| **Asat-khyati** | Knowledge of a non-existent thing |
| **Asata-vedaniya** | Pain-feeling; that which brings pain. The inflow of pain-bringing-feeling |
| **Asata, Asatavedaniya** | Experience of pain |
| **Asatana** | Disrespect |
| **Asatavedaniya** | Unpleasant-feeling |
| **Asatpratipaksatva** | Non-conclusive |
| **Asatva** | Non-existence |
| **Asatya** | Lying |
| **Asatya mana** | False mind |
| **Asatya-Vachana** | False |
| **Ascarya** | Extraordinary event |
| **Asharana anupreksha** | Unprotectiveness; helplessness. The soul is unprotected from the fruition of karmas. Death, pain, pleasure, success, failure are the necessary results of our acts in this or past lives. |
| **Ashrava** | Inflow, The attraction of good or bad matter by the soul in virtue of its mental, vocal, or bodily activity. |
| **Ashrava anupreksa** | Inflow. The inflow of karma is the cause of my mudane |

| | |
|---|---|
| | existence and it is the product of passions, etc. |
| **Ashubha** | Ugly (body). |
| **Ashubha-nama** | A Bad-body-making karma |
| **Ashuchi anupreksha** | Impurity. The body is impure and dirty. |
| **Asi** | "Sword"; government |
| **Asiddha** (Hetvabhasa) | Non-existence |
| **Asiddhata** | Unproved state |
| **Asiddhatva** | Non-existent |
| **Asiddhi** | Whose existence cannot be proved |
| **Aspasta** | Indistinct |
| **Asrava** | Karmic influx The thought-activity invites the karmic |
| matter | into the soul. |
| **Asraya** | Substratum |
| **Astanga** | Eight limbs (of samyak-darsana) |
| **Asteya** | Not stealing |
| **Asthira** | (unsteady circulation of blood, etc.). |
| **Asti-kaya** | Having extension |
| **Astikya** | Affirmation |
| **Astitva** | Existence |
| **Asubha-karma** | Unwholesome karma |
| **Asva** | Horse |
| **Aticara** | Infractions committed by accident |
| **Atidesavakya** | Analogical sentence |
| **Atisaya-ksetra** | Places where miraculous events associated with great monks have occurred |

| | |
|---|---|
| **Atithi-samvibhaga** | Sharing with (ascetic) guests Taking a vow to take one's food only after feeding the ascetivs with a part of it. |
| **Ativyapti** | Undesirable extension |
| **Atma ninda** | denouncing one's self |
| **Atma prashansa** | Praising oneself |
| **Atman** | Soul; self |
| **Atmanubhava** | Abiding in one's own nature |
| **Atmarthatva** | Meant for the self |
| **Atmarupa** (Kaladigata) | Form |
| **Atmasad-guna uchchhadana** | not proclaiming one's own good qualities. |
| **Attara guna** | A kind of production of the dependance relating to the non-soul, i.e., production of books, pictures, statues, etc. |
| **Audarika** | Physical, The physical body of all men and animals. |
| **Audarika mishra** | Physical with karmic. |
| **Audarikasarira** | Gross-body of Lord |
| **Aupapadika** | Born spontaneously |
| **Aupasamika** | Subsidence |
| **Aushbha** | Awkward. |
| **Avadhi** (Jnana) | Clairvoyance |
| **Avadhi-darshanavarana** | Visual-conation-obscuring. |
| **Avadhi-jnanavarana** | Visual-knowledge-obscuring |
| **Avadhidarsana** | The indistinct type of awareness preceding |
| **Avadhijnana** | Supermundane knowledge such as clairvoyance |
| **Avagaha** | Penetrability |
| **Avagraha** (Matijnana) | Determinate perception |

| | |
|---|---|
| **Avaharana** | Distinguishing |
| **Avaktavya** | Indescribable, Inexpressible |
| **Avamaudarya** | Eating only a very small portion of food |
| **Avamodarya** | Eating less than one's fill, or less than one has appetite for-external austerity. |
| **Avantara samanya** | General substance |
| **Avapodvapa** | Elimination and addition |
| **Avarana** | The veil |
| **Avarana ksaya** | Destruction of veil |
| **Avaraniya** | Obscuring |
| **Avarnavada** | Causes the right-belief-deluding karmic matter (Darshana). |
| **Avasarpini** | Descending round Regressive half-cycle |
| **Avashyaka-parihari** | Not neglecting one's six important daily duties |
| **Avastu-nirbhasa** | Dealing with no object |
| **Avasyaka** | Essential duty |
| **Avaya (Matijnana)** | Perceptual judgment |
| **Avayava** | Part |
| **Avicyuti** | Absence of lapse |
| **Avidya** | Ignorance |
| **Avinayeshu** | Those who are uncivil or ill-behaved. |
| **Avipaka-nirjara** | Inducing a karma to leave the soul by means of a contrary karma, or by means of ascetic practices. |
| **Avirata** | Vowlessness, non-renunciation. |
| **Avirati** | Nonrestraint |

| | |
|---|---|
| **Aviruddhanupalabdhi** (Hetu) | Non-availability of non-contradictory |
| **Aviruddhopalabdhi** (Hetu) | Availability of non-contradictory |
| **Avisamvadakatva** | Non-discrepancy |
| **Avisvagbhava** | All-pervasiveness |
| **Aviveka** | Lack of discrimination |
| **Avrta** | Obscured |
| **Avyakta** | Indeterminate |
| **Avyaktaksara** | Indistinct sound |
| **Ayaga-pata** | Votive slabs |
| **Ayariya** | Prakrit for acarya |
| **Ayashah kirti** | Notoriety; bringing bad name, even if one does good actions. |
| **Ayoga-kevalin** | The fourteenth gunasthana, attained by the kevalin when, in the instant before death, all his activities cease |
| **Ayu** | Age-karma age. |
| **Ayu-karma** | Karma that determines the span of a given lifetime |
| **Badara** | Gross (body). |
| **Badha** | Depriving of vitality |
| **Badhita-visaya** | Subject being hindered |
| **Bahiratman** | (Perceiving) The self in externals |
| **Bahirvyapti** | External concomitance |
| **Bahu (Matijnana)** | Many |
| **Bahu-shruta-bhakti** | Devotion to Upakhyayas or teaching Saints. |
| **Bahuvidha** (Matijnana) | Multiplied |
| **Bala tapa** | austerities not based upon right knowledge |

| | |
|---|---|
| **Balabhadra** | A Jaina literary type; the hero and companion of narayana |
| **Balatapa** | Austerities not based upon right knowledge. |
| **Bandah** | Bound |
| **Bandha** | Attracted matter had actually become a part of our body, i.e., when it has become bound to the soul as the body is already bound to it. |
| **Bandhana** | Bondage; molecular bondage. Energy that brings about karmic influx |
| **Bhagavan** | Venerable |
| **Bhaikshya-shuddhi** | Purity of alms, according to the scriptures. |
| **Bhajana** | Option |
| **Bhakti** | Devotionalism |
| **Bhanga** | Infractions committed intentionally One of the seven-fold ways of statement |
| **Bhasa** | Language |
| **Bhasa-samiti** | Care in speaking |
| **Bhasha Agrahya-Vargana** | Speech-unrecievable-molecule |
| **Bhasha-Vargana** | Speech-molecule |
| **Bhasya** | Commentary |
| **Bhattaraka** | Venerable ones; a class of Jaina clerics |
| **Bhava** | Function, Internal; states of a dravya; a synonym for paryaya |
| **Bhava-jiva** | Real symbol of soul |
| **Bhava-puja** | The internal aspect of a devotional practice |

| | |
|---|---|
| **Bhava-samyaktva** | The internal aspect of true insight |
| **Bhavana** | Meditation. Practice; a section of the Acaranga-sutra |
| **Bhavanavasi** | Those (gods) who reside in mansions |
| **Bhavasruta** | Real functioning knowledge |
| **Bhavatmaka** | Real |
| **Bhavatva** | Real |
| **Bhavollasa** | Aroused emotions |
| **Bhavya** | One who is capable of attaining moksa |
| **Bhavyatva** | Capability of attaining moksa |
| **Bhaya** | Fear. |
| **Bheda** | Disjunction |
| **Bheda-vivaksa** | Desired difference |
| **Bheda-vrtti** | Attitude of difference |
| **Bhedopacara** | Secondary use of difference |
| **Bhekta-pana** | mixing up food and drink. |
| **Bhiksu-pratima** | Difficult asuterities recommended for a mendicant |
| **Bhirutva-pratyakhyana** | Giving up cowardice or fear. |
| **Bhoga** | Enjoyment;experience |
| **Bhoga Antaraya** | obstructive of Enjoyment, of non-comsumable things.Karma that restricts enjoyment |
| **Bhoga-bhumi** | Realm of enjoyment |
| **Bhogopabhaga-parimanavrata** | Restraint against practicing certain professions and partaking of certain foods |
| **Bhojana-Katha** | Food |
| **Bhumi** | Realm |
| **Bhuta-anukampa** | compassion for all living beings. |

| | |
|---|---|
| **Bhutacatustaya** | Division of four matters |
| **Bija** | Seed |
| **Bijapuraka-kataha** | A seed-filled fruit, probably; Aegle Marmelos, used for medicinal purposes |
| **Bodhi** | Enlightnenment |
| **Bodhi durlabha anupreksha** | Rarity of Right path. It is difficult to attain right-belief, knowledge and conduct. |
| **Bodhi-durlabha** | The rarity of enlightenment |
| **Bodhisattva** | One who follows the career of a Buddha |
| **Bodiya** | Naked |
| **Brahma-charya** | Celibacy. |
| **Brahmacari** | Celibate; one who has reached the seventh pratima |
| **Brahmacarya-pratima** | The seventh pratima, in which absolute continence is observed |
| **Brahman** | The unitary Absolute postualted by the Vedanta school |
| **Brahmana** (Brahman) | A member of the priestly caste |
| **Brahmavrata** | Refraining from all illicit sexual activities |
| **Caitanya** | Consciousness |
| **Caitya** | Temple |
| **Caityavasi** | Temple-dweller |
| **Cakravartin** | Universal monarch |
| **Caksuradijanita** | Effected by eyes etc. |
| **Caksurdarsana** | Visual perception |
| **Candala** | Untouchable; a synonym for svapaka |
| **Candana** | Sandalwood paste |
| **Carana** | Practice |

| | |
|---|---|
| **Caritra** | Conduct |
| **Caritra-mohaniya** | Conduct-deluding karmas |
| **Caru** | Sweet |
| **Catuhsarana** | The four refuges |
| **Caturvimsati-stava** | Sanskrit caturyama-samvara; a synonym for caujjama-dhamma |
| **Caujjama-dhamma** | Sanskrit caturyama-dharma, the fourfold restraint ascribed to Parsva |
| **Chadmastha** | A person in the state of bondage in this universe. |
| **Chakshu-darshanavarana** | Ocular-Conation-obscuring. |
| **Charitras** | Right-conduct. |
| **Chaundriya** | Four-sensed. |
| **Cheda** | Reduction in seniority |
| **Cheda-sutra** | A law book dealing with monastic offences |
| **Chetanatva** | along with Amurtatva, is a common attribute of the class of substance, or group of attributes,called Soul. Consciousness |
| **Citrajnana** | Knowledge of the picture |
| **Culika** | Appendix; a class of Jaina cononical texts |
| **Cyavamana** | Negligent |
| **Daksina-agni** | One of the sacred fires in the Hindu srauta ritual |
| **Dana** | Charity; alms-giving |
| **Dana Antaraya** | Charity-Obstructive. |
| **Dana-antaraya** | A type of karma that hinders the practice of charity |
| **Dandin** | One who carries a staff |

| | |
|---|---|
| **Darsana** | Indeterminate intuition, faith Intuition; a system of philosophy; insight; perception |
| **Darsana-mohaniya** | Insight-deluding karmas |
| **Darsana-pratima** | The first step on the ladder of pratima |
| **Darsanavaraniya** | Perception-obscuring karmas |
| **Darsantika** | Thesis |
| **Darshana** | Faith. |
| **Darshana mohaniya** | right-belief-deluding karmic matter |
| **Darshana-kriya** | infatuated desire to see a pleasing form. |
| **Darshana-mohaniya** | Right-belief-deluding. |
| **Darshana-vishuddhi** | purity of right-belief |
| **Darshanavarana** | Conation-obscuring |
| **Dasa-dharma** | Ten forms of righteousness |
| **Dashaya** | Astringent, (Saline). |
| **Desa-virata** | The fifth gunasthana where desa-virati is attained |
| **Desa-virati** | The set of restraints prescribed for a Jaina layman |
| **Desana-labdhi** | Obtaining instruction in the Jaina teachings |
| **Desavakasika** | Limiting the area of one's movement |
| **Desha-Katha** | Scandal |
| **Deshavrata** | Taking a vow to limit worldly activity to fixed points for a short period of time, for example,for one's weely or daily worldly activity. |
| **Deva** | Celestial.Heavenly beings; |

| | |
|---|---|
| | untimate divinity. The Celestial beings |
| **Deva Anupurvi** | Celestial—migratory form. |
| **Deva-Ayu** | Celestial-age-karma |
| **Deva-brahmana** | Divine brahman, i.e., a Jaina brahman |
| **Deva-dusya** | "Divine" cloth; a finely woven piece of cloth |
| **Deva-mudhata** | Delusion pertaining to gods |
| **Deva-nikayas** | The four orders of gods |
| **Devagama** | The arrival of gods at a holy gathering |
| **Devajiva** | Soul of the god |
| **Devanupurvi** | The power of retaining the last form whatever it was, in going to the celestial condition of existence. |
| **Devapuja** | Worship of the Tirthankaras |
| **Devayu** | Celestial age. |
| **Dharana** | Retention |
| **Dharma** | Attribute, Holy law; elements in Buddhist doctrine; righteousness, ten forms Observances, Principle of Motion, The true Religion |
| **Dharma svakhya tattvanupreksha** | Nature of Right-Path as said by the conquerors. The true nature of Truth, i.e., the three fold path to real Liberation. |
| **Dharma-dravya** | The principle of motion |
| **Dharma-katha** | Religious tale |
| **Dharma-labha** | Increase in righteousness |
| **Dharma-svakhyatatva** | The absolutely true teachings of the Jinas |
| **Dharma-tirtha** | Holy path |

| | |
|---|---|
| **Dharmadhyana** | Virtuous concentration |
| **Dharmin** | Subject |
| **Dhrauvya** | Continuance |
| **Dhruva** (Matijnana) | Constant |
| **Dhruva Shunya-Vargana** | Fixed-indifferent-molecule |
| **Dhruva Vargana** | Fixed-molecule |
| **Dhupa** | Incense |
| **Dhvani** | The word |
| **Dhyana** | Concentration—internal austerity. Meditation |
| **Digambara** | Sky-clad; name of the Jaina sect whose mendicants practice ascetic nudity |
| **Digha-tapassi** | One who engages in extended penances |
| **Digvrata** | Restriction on the distances a person may travel Taking a life-long vow to limit his wordly activity to fixed points in all the 10 directions; East, West, North, South, South-east, East-north, North-west, West-south, and Up and Down. |
| **Diksa** | Initiation |
| **Dipa** | Lamp |
| **Divyadhvani** | Miraculous sound |
| **Dosa** | Imperfection |
| **Dravya** | Substance; external |
| **Dravya** (Niksepa) | Substance |
| **Dravya-carya** | Nominal acarya |
| **Dravya-mana** | Mind-qua-substance; The physical basis of the mind |

| | |
|---|---|
| **Dravya-puja** | Form of worship employing external objects |
| **Dravya-samyaktva** | The external aspect of true insight |
| **Dravyadeva** | Substantial symbol of god |
| **Dravyajiva** | Substantial soul |
| **Dravyajivatva** | Substantial soul |
| **Dravyakalpana** | Distinction of substance |
| **Dravyakriya** | Pseudo-action |
| **Dravyanikaramba** | Substance transformed into sense-data |
| **Dravyartha** | Through the substance |
| **Dravyarthika** | Of the substance |
| **Dravyarthikabhasa** | False point of view of substance |
| **Dravyarthikanaya** | Point of the substance |
| **Dravyastikanaya** | Material point of view |
| **Dravyatmaka** | Substantial |
| **Dravyatva** | capacity by which it is always changing in modifications. Change-ability; Substantial soul |
| **Dravyendra** | Sense qua substance |
| **Drsta** | Perception |
| **Drstanta** | Example |
| **Drstanta-dosa** | Fallacy of example |
| **Duh-pramrishta** | Putting down a thing petulantly or peevishly. |
| **Duhshruti** | Reading or hearing bad books. |
| **Duhsvara** | Harsh-voiced, noisy. |
| **Dukha** | Pain |
| **Durbhaga** | unprepossessing; even though beautiful. |
| **Durbhiksa** | Famine |

| | |
|---|---|
| **Durgamdha** | Evil-smelling; mal-odorous. |
| **Dusama** | Unhappy |
| **Dusama-dusama** | Extremely unhappy |
| **Dvesa** | Hatred; aversion |
| **Dvesha** | Hatred in the pleasing and displeasing wordly objects of the five senses. |
| **Dvija** | Twice-born |
| **Dvindriya** | Two-sensed. |
| **Dvipa** | Island |
| **Dvipa-samudra** | Island-continent |
| **Eka** | One; unitary |
| **Eka-ksetravagaha** | Occupying the same locus |
| **Eka-phalaka** | Probably identical to eka-sataka |
| **Eka-sataka** | A mendicant who wears a single piece of cloth |
| **Ekanta** | One-sided Taking only one aspect of a many-sided thing e.g., man is mortal and immortal, regarded from the point of view of body and soul respectively. Taking only one view. |
| **Ekanta-nitya** | Absolutely eternal |
| **Ekantavada** | Extremism; absolutist doctrine |
| **Ekantavadin** | One who holds an absolutist doctrine |
| **Ekartha-samavayin** | Co-inherent in the same substratum |
| **Ekatva** | Unity |
| **Ekatva anupreksha** | Loneliness, I am alone the doer of my actinos and the enjoyer of the fruits of them. |
| **Ekatvajnana** | Knowledge of oneness |

| | |
|---|---|
| **Ekendriya** | A being with only one (namely, the tactile) sense faculty; a synonym for sthavara beings One-sensed creature |
| **Ennui** | dissatisfaction. |
| **Esana-samiti** | Care in accepting alms |
| **Eva** | In fact; an important term in the formula of the sapta-bhangi-naya |
| **Evambhuta** (Naya) | The such-like |
| **Evambhutabhasa** | False such-like view point |
| **Gaccha** | A chapter of monks |
| **Gajanimilika** | Closing of eyes like an elephant |
| **Gamdha** | Smell. |
| **Gamika** (Sruta) | Scriptures containing repetitions |
| **Gana** | A residence unit for monks |
| **Ganadhara** | Direct disciple of the Tirthankaras Supporters of the order, i.e., the first mendicant disciples of a Tirthankara |
| **Gandha** | Smell |
| **Gandharva** | Celestial musician |
| **Gani-pidaga** | Basket of the ganadharas, i.e., the canon ofthe Jainas |
| **Ganin** | Leader of the order |
| **Garbha** | Conception |
| **Garhapatya-agni** | One of the sacred fires of the Hindu srauta ritual |
| **Gati** | Birth; destiny condition of existence Condition; Condition of existence. |
| **Gau** | Cow (animal) or the action of going |
| **Ghana-ambu** | Humid air |

| | |
|---|---|
| **Ghana-vata** | Dense air |
| **Ghatanama** | Name of pitcher |
| **Ghatikarman** | Destructive karmans |
| **Ghatiya** | Destructive<br>Karmas that have a vitiating effect upon the qualities of the soul |
| **Ghoratavassi** | One who practices severe austerities |
| **Gorji** | A term used for yati |
| **Gotra** | Exogamous groups |
| | Family-determining. |
| **Gotra-karma** | Karmas that determine environmental circumstances |
| **Grahana** | Cognition |
| **Grahya** | Cognitum |
| **Granthi** | Knot |
| **Gumma** | A chapter of monks |
| **Guna** | Attribute |
| | Quality |
| **Guna** (Kalpana) | Quality |
| **Guna sthana** | Fourth spiritual stage. |
| **Guna vratas** | Special vows relating to the limitation and determination of his daily work, food and enjoyment. |
| **Guna-adhikshu** | The path of liberation. |
| **Guna-sabda** | Word indicating quality |
| **Gunasthana** | The fourteen stages of purification |
| **Gunavratas** | Restraints that reinforce the practice of the anuvratas |
| **Guni-desa** (Kaladigata) | Territory of object |

| | |
|---|---|
| **Gupti** | Preservation; Restraint |
| **Guru** | Heavy; Spiritual teacher |
| **Guru-mudhata** | False beliefs pertaining to teachers |
| **Guru-upasti** | Listening to and venerating teachers |
| **Hamsa** | Swan |
| **Hasya** | Laughter; Risible or Laughter-producing. |
| **Hasya-pratyakhyana** | Giving up of frivolity. |
| **Hetu** | Reason |
| **Hetu-dosa** | Fallacy in the cause |
| **Hetu-samarthana** | Support by cause |
| **Hetvabhasa** | Fallacies of reasons |
| **Himsa** | Injury, harming violence |
| **Himsa** | Injury. |
| **Himsadana** | Giving objects of offence to others. |
| **Hiyamana** (avadhijnana) | Decreasing |
| **Hundaka** | Unsymmetrical; disproportionate, deformed. |
| **Hundavasarpini** | A period of avasarpini in which extraordinary events may take place |
| **Idantollekha** | Indication |
| **Iha** | Speculation |
| **Indrasthapana** | Which has the shape of India |
| **Indriya** | An organ of sense, Sense organ |
| **Indriyaja** | Sensuous |
| **Irya** | Care in walking. |
| **Irya-samiti** | Care in walking |
| **Iryapatha-kriya** | walding carefully, i.e., looking on the ground for protecting |

| | |
|---|---|
| | living beings which may be trod upon and thus injured. |
| **Isat-pragbhara-bhumi** | "Slightly bent region," the name of the final abode of the liberated souls [the siddhas] |
| **Ista-devata** | Chosen deity |
| **Isvara** | God |
| **Jaina** | Follower of Jina, a synonym for Nigantha; one who has samyak-darsana |
| **Jaina-brachman** | Laypeople in charge of priestly functions within certain Jaina communities |
| **Jaina-sasana** | Teaching of the Jainas |
| **Jainabhasa** | False Jainas |
| **Jala** | Water |
| **Janma** | Birth |
| **Janma-kalyana** | Birth; one of the five auspicious events in the career of a Tirthankara |
| **Jara** | Old age |
| **Jarisabda** | Root word |
| **Jati** | Birth, caste; species within a gati Genus of beings. Genus. |
| **Jati** (Kalpana) | Sophism |
| **Jati-karma** | The variety of nama-karma that determines one's specific destiny |
| **Jati-mantra** | A litany used in celebrating the birth of a child |
| **Jayamala** | Garland of victory; a hymn in praise ofthe Jinas |
| **Jigisu katha** | A debate which is held for victory |
| **Jijnasa** | Curiosity |
| **Jina** | Spiritual victor; a synonym for Tirthankara |

| | |
|---|---|
| **Jina-agama** | Jaina scripture |
| **Jina-bhavana** | Jaina temple |
| **Jina-bimba** | Image of Jina |
| **Jina-nama** | Name of Jina |
| **Jinakalpin** | A monk whose conduct is modeled upon that of Mahavira |
| **Jinasthapana** | Image of Jina |
| **Jiva** | living, Soul; sentient |
| **Jiva Kanda** | Fifth of the Sacred Books of the Jainas |
| **Jivatva** | Soul |
| **Jnana** | Knowledge |
| **Jnana-cetana** | Consciousness characterized as knowing itself |
| **Jnananaya** | Point of view of knowledge |
| **Jnananayabhasa** | False point of view of knowledge |
| **Jnanavarana** | Knowledge-obscuring |
| **Jnanavaraniya** | Knowledge-obscuring |
| **Jugupsa** | Disgust; aversion. Hiding one's own, and publishing other people's shortcomings. |
| **Jyotiska** | The steller gods |
| **Kaivalya** | Pure knowledge |
| **Kala** | Time stages within the progressive and regressive half-cycles; time as a dravya |
| **Kala** (Drvyadigata) | Periodically |
| **Kala** (Kaladigata) | Time |
| **Kala** (Kalakarakadigata) | Time |
| **Kalanu** | Time-points |
| **Kalatyayapadista** | Mistimed (contradicted) |
| **Kalikasruta** | A Jain scripture |

| | |
|---|---|
| **Kalpatita** | Born in the highest heavenly abodes |
| **Kalpopapanna** | Born in the kalpa heavens |
| **Kalyanaka** | Auspicious moments |
| **Kanyadana** | Ceremony of giving away the bride |
| **Kapota-lesya** | Gray karmic strain |
| **Karaka** | Case |
| **Karana** | Cause |
| **Karana** (Hetu) | Cause |
| **Karanantarasakalya** | Co-operation of all other causes |
| **Karananupalabdhi** | Non-availability of the cause |
| **Karanatva** | As the cause |
| **Karanollekha** | Mention of instrument |
| **Karma** | Action |
| **Karma-bhumi** | Realm of action |
| **Karma-cetana** | Consciousness of oneself as the doer of actions |
| **Karma-phala-cetana** | Consciousness of oneself as the enjoyer of the karmic fruits |
| **Karma-prakrti** | The particular form into which karmic matter is differentiated |
| **Karman** | Action |
| **Karmana** | karmic. |
| **Karmana-sarira** | The transmigrating body of karmic matter |
| **Karmana-Vargana** | Karmic-molecule |
| **Karsapana** | Coin |
| **Karta** | Agent |
| **Karunya** | Pity, Compassion for the afflicted. |
| **Karya** (Hetu) | Effect |
| **Karyanupalabdhi** | Non-availability of the effect |

| | |
|---|---|
| **Kasaya** | Passions |
| **Katha** | Debate, Narrative literature Talk |
| **Kathora** | Hard |
| **Katuka** | Bitter. |
| **Kavala-ahara** | Food in morsels; ordinary human food |
| **Kaya** | Movement by body. |
| **Kaya klesha** | Mortification of the body, so long as the mind is not disturbed—external austerity. |
| **Kaya-klesa** | Mortifications of the body |
| **Kayiki-kriya** | a wicked man's readiness to hurt others. |
| **Kayotsarga** | Abandonment of the body, a standing or sitting posture of meditation |
| **Kesa-loca** | The practice of pulling out one's hair in five handfuls |
| **Kevala** (Jnana) | Perfect knowledge |
| **Kevala-darshanavarana** | Perfect-conation-obscuring. |
| **Kevala-jnanavarana** | Perfect-knowledge-obscuring. |
| **Kevaladarsana** | Perception associated with kevalajnana |
| **Kevalajnana** | Knowledge isolated from karmic obstruction; infinite knowledge; omniscience; knowledge involving awareness of every existent in all its qualities and modes Kevalin One who has attained kevalajnana; a synonym for arhat |
| **Kilita samhanana** | Riveted bones. |
| **Klishyamaneshu** | The afflicted. |
| **Komala** | Soft |

| | |
|---|---|
| **Krama** | Order Sequential order |
| **Kramabhavi** | Occurring successively |
| **Kramayaugapadya** | Simultaneity or order |
| **Krishna** | Black. |
| **Kriya** (Kalpana) | Activity |
| **Kriya naya** | Point of view of action |
| **Kriyanayabhasa** | False point of view of action |
| **Kriyas** | Actions; a Jaina term for sacred rites |
| **Kriyasabda** | Root word |
| **Kriyavadi** | belief in time, soul, etc., as causing everything in the world. All the substances perform their functions and become |
| **Krodha** | Anger |
| **Krodha-pratyakhyana** | Giving up anger. |
| **Krsi** | Farming |
| **Krsna-lesya** | Black karmic stain |
| **Ksama** | Forgiveness |
| **Ksamasramana** | An ascetic who suffers with equanimity; title used in addressing a monk during the ritual fo confession |
| **Ksanika** | Momentary |
| **Ksanti** | Forbearance |
| **Ksapana** | Destruction |
| **Ksatriya** | Member of a warrior caste |
| **Ksaya** | Destruction |
| **Ksayika-samyak-darsana** | True insight achieved by the destruction of darsana-mohaniya karmas |
| **Ksayopasama** | Cessation and subsidence of karmic veil |

| | |
|---|---|
| **Ksayopasama-labdhi** | Attainment of purity by the destruction-cumsuppression of certain karmas |
| **Ksayopasamika-samyaktva** | True insight achievedby the destruction cum-suppression of darsana-mohaniya karmas; identical to vedakasamyaktva |
| **Ksetra** | Territory |
| **Kshanti** | Forgiveness |
| **Kshaya** | Destruction |
| **Ksina-moha** | Permanent dissociation from all caritra-mohaniya karmas and from the passions which they produce, the twelfth gunasthana |
| **Ksipra** (Matijnana) | Quick |
| **Ksullaka** | Minor; junior monk; a Jaina layman on the eleventhpratima; one who wears three pieces of clothing |
| **Kubjaka** | Hunchback. |
| **Kula** | Family |
| **Kumara-sramana** | A life-long celibate |
| **Kundalini-cakra** | Mystical centers of psychic energy |
| **Kutastha-nitya** | Eternal and unchangeable |
| **Labdhi** | Attainment |
| **Labdhi** (Aksara-sruta) | Potential auditory attainment |
| **Labdhi** (Indriya) | Sense qua attainment |
| **Labdhyaksara** | Potential auditory attainment |
| **Labha** | Attainment |
| **Labha Antaraya** | Gain-Obstructive. |
| **Labha-anfaraya** | Hindrance to the attainment of something |
| **Laghu** | Light; loss |

| | |
|---|---|
| **Laukika** | Mundane |
| **Lesya** | Karmic stain, the color of which indicates a soul's degress of purity |
| **Linga** | Gender |
| **Lobha** | Greed |
| **Lobha-pratyakhyana** | Giving up greed. |
| **Loka** | Universe |
| **Loka anupreksha** | Universe. The nature of the Universe and its constituent elements in all thei vast varity proving the insignificance and miserable nothingness of man in time and space. |
| **Loka-akasa** | The inhabited universe |
| **Loka-mudhata** | False beliefs pertaining to everyday religious practices |
| **Madhu** | Honey |
| **Madhura** | Sweet. |
| **Madhya-loka** | Middle of terrestrial world |
| **Madhyasthya** | Tolerance or indifference to those who are uncivil or ill-behaved. |
| **Madya** | Alcohol |
| **Maha-Skandha-Vargana** | Great-molecule-molecule |
| **Mahana** | Prakrit for Sanskrit brahmana |
| **Mahavira-jayanti** | Birth anniversary of Mahavira |
| **Mahavrata** | The five great vows of a mendicant |
| **Maitri** | Benevolence for all living beings. |
| **Mamsa** | Flesh; meat |
| **Mana** | Movement by mind. Pride |
| **Manah-paryaya** | Psychic mode |

| | |
|---|---|
| **Manah-paryaya** (Jnana) | Intuition of the modes of other minds Telepathy |
| **Manah-paryaya-darsana** | Intuition of the psychic mode |
| **Manahparyaya-jnanavarana** | Mental-knowledge-obscuring. |
| **Manahparyayajnana** | Direct awareness of thought forms of others without the aid of mind or senses |
| **Manas** | Mind |
| **Manasatva** | Mental cognition |
| **Manastambha** | A characteristic Jaina pillar |
| **Mano Agrahya-Vargana** | Mind-unreceivable-molecule |
| **Mano-Vargana** | Mind-molecule |
| **Manodravya** | Mind substance |
| **Manogupti** | Preservation of mind. |
| **Manojanma** | Born of mind |
| **Manojanya** | Born of mind |
| **Mantra** | Holy litany |
| **Manushya** | Human. |
| **Manushya Anupurvi** | Human—Migratory form. |
| **Manushya-Ayu** | Human-age-karma |
| **Manushyayu** | Human age. |
| **Manusya** | Human being |
| **Manusya-gati** | Human destiny |
| **Marga prabhavana** | Propagation of the path of Liberation. |
| **Masi** | Ink; writing |
| **Mastakabhiseka** | Head-anointing [ceremony] |
| **Mati** (Jnana) | Perceptual |
| **Mati-jnanavarana** | Sensitive-knowledge-obscuring. |

| | |
|---|---|
| **Matijana** | Mind-based knowledge |
| **Maulahetu** | Original cause |
| **Maya** | Causes inflow of sub-human age karma Cheating others, preaching the false doctrines, etc. Deceit. |
| **Maya-shalya** | The thorn of deceit. |
| **Mayakriya** | Deceitful disturbance of some one's right knowledge and faith. |
| **Mayavada** | Illusionism |
| **Mithya** (Sruta) | False |
| **Mithya darshana** | Wrong belief. |
| **Mithya-darshana-kriya** | Praising actions due to wrong belief. |
| **Mithya-drsti** | Perverted vision |
| **Mithya-shalya** | The thorn of wrong-belief. |
| **Mithyadarsana** | Synonymous with mathyadrsti and mithyatva |
| **Mithyadarshana** | wrong-belief |
| **Mithyadrsti** | Incorrect viw of reality, the first gunasthana |
| **Mithyatva** | Lack of insight; synonymous with mithyadarsana and mithyadrsti wrong belief. |
| **Mithyatva-kriya** | That which strengthenswrong belief, e.g., superstition, etc. |
| **Mohaniya** | Deluding |
| **Mohaniya-karma** | Karma that prevents the true perception of reality and the purity of the soul; karma that defiles the bliss-quality of the soul |
| **Moksa** | Liberation, Salvation; emancipation from the cycle of birth and death |
| **Moksa-marga** | The path of salvation |

| | |
|---|---|
| **Moksha** | Liberation The total separation of Soul from the bondage of all matter Muh-patti A small piece of cloth worn over the mouth by Sthanakavasi mendicants to protect airbodies from harm |
| **Mukta** | The Liberated Soul. |
| **Mula Guna** | a kind of production of the dependance relating to the non-soul, i.e., of the body, speech, mind and respiration. |
| **Mulagunas** | The eight basic restraints of a Jaina layman |
| **Mulasutra** | A group of texts belonging to the subsidiary canon |
| **Muni** | Mendicant; sage |
| **Murccha** | Delusion |
| **Murtatva** | Along with Achetanatva, is common to Matter. Materiality |
| **Nabho-Vargana** | Sphere-molecule |
| **Naicayika** | Transcendental |
| **Naigama** (Naya) | Non-distinguished |
| **Naigamabhasa** | False point of view of the non-distinguished |
| **Nama** | Body-making Karma |
| **Nama** (Niksepa) | Symbol of name |
| **Nama-Jaina** | Nominal Jaina |
| **Nama-karma** | Karma that determines destinies and body types |
| **Namadinayasa-mudayavada** | Combination of the points of view of name etc. |
| **Namadiniksepa** | Symbols of names etc. |
| **Namajiva** | Name symbol of soul |
| **Namaskara-mantra** | Reverent salutation to the [five] holy beings |

| | |
|---|---|
| **Namaskaraniksepa** | Symbol of salutation |
| **Namatmaka** | Form of the name |
| **Namendra** | The name 'Indra' |
| **Nandyavarta** | A kind of diagram |
| **Napumsaka Veda** | Common sex. |
| **Napumsakaveda** | Sexual cravings for a hermaphrodite |
| **Naracha-Samhanana** | Unbreakable joints and bones. |
| **Naraka** | Hell; the world of infernal beings Hellish. |
| **Naraka Anupurvi** | Hellish—migratory form. |
| **Narakayu** | hellish age. |
| **Narakayu karma** | Hellish age karma |
| **Naraki** | Hell beings |
| **Narayana** | A Jaina literary type; the hero's companion and slayer of the villian |
| **Nasti** | Does not exist; the second member of the sapta-bhangi-naya |
| **Nastitva** | Non-existence |
| **Naya** | Partial truth View; partial expression of truth |
| **Nayabhasa** | False point of view |
| **Nayana** | Sight |
| **Nayavada** | Doctrine of nayas |
| **Nayavakya** | Statement from a point of view |
| **Nicha** | Gotra Low family. |
| **Nichaih Vritti** | an attitude of humility towards one's betters. |
| **Nidana** | Seeking worldly gain from the performance of good deeds and austerities |

| | |
|---|---|
| | The thorn of desire for future sense-pleasures. |
| **Nidhatti** | Energy that renders karmas incapable of all activity save changes in fruition time and intensity |
| **Nidra** | Sleep |
| **Nidra-Nidra** | Deep sleep. |
| **Nigamana** | Conclusion |
| **Nigantha** | Nirgrantha, Unattached, without possessions; ancient name for the Jaina community |
| **Nigoda** | The lowest form of life |
| **Nigraha** | Defeat proper control over mind, speech and body. |
| **Nigrahadhikarana** | Place for defeat |
| **Nigrhita** | Defeated |
| **Nihkamksita** | Freedom from anticipation |
| **Nihksepa** (Niksepa) | The different ways of putting a thing |
| **Nihnava** | Falsehood, heresy |
| **Nihpratikara** | Unavoidable |
| **Nihsankita** | Freedom from doubt |
| **Nikacana** | Energy that renders karmas incapable of all activity |
| **Nila** | Blue |
| **Nila-lesya** | Blue karmic stain |
| **Nimitta-karana** | External efficient cause |
| **Nir vichikitsita** | Free from repulsion from anything. |
| **Nirakrta** | Refuted |
| **Niranvaya** | Discrete |
| **Nirjara** | Dissociation of karmas; The falling away of karmic matter |

| | |
|---|---|
| | from the soul. The gradual shedding of the matter already boundis shedding |
| **Nirjara anupreksha** | Shedding. Karmic matter must be shed from or shaken out of the soul. |
| **Nirmana** | Formation; proper formation of limbs and minor limbs in relation to their situation and dimensions. |
| **Nirnitavipaksavrttika** | Whose existence in the hetrologous is decisive |
| **Nirukti** | Etymology |
| **Nirvana** | Release from bondage; the final death of an enlightened human being [arhat] followed immediately by moksa |
| **Nirvana-bhumi** | The place at which a Tirthankara attained nirvana |
| **Nirvicikitsa** | Freedom from disgust |
| **Nirvrttindriya** | Physical sense-organ shaped like Kadamba flower |
| **Niryukti** | Prakrit verse commentary |
| **Nisarga** | inborn error |
| **Nisarga Kriya** | Admiration of hurtful or unrighteous things. |
| **Nisargaja** | Agrahita |
| **Niscaya** (Naya) | Consideration |
| **Niscaya-naya** | Nonconventional view |
| **Niscayabhasa** | False real point of view |
| **Niscita** (Matijnana) | Determined |
| **Nisedha** | Negation |
| **Nisedhakalpana** | Negative aspect |
| **Nisedhasakhaka** (Hetu) | Which proves negation |

| | |
|---|---|
| **Nishkankshita** | Free from wordly desire. |
| **Nisshankita** | Free from all doubt. |
| **Nitya** | Eternal |
| **Nityavada** | Eternalism |
| **Niyati** | Fate |
| **Niyativada** | Fatalism |
| **No-kasaya** | Subsidiary passions |
| **No-kashaya** | Quasi-passions; slight or minor passions. |
| **Nyag rodha parimandala** | Banyan like; short in lower but large in upper extremities like a banyan-tree. |
| **Om** | Sacred sound formed by combining the first syllable of each word in the namaskara-mantra |
| **Pada** | Word |
| **Padartha-pratibandha** | Indirectly connected with an object |
| **Padastha-dhyana** | Concentration upon holy chants |
| **Padma-lesya** | Lotus-pink karmic stain |
| **Paduka** | Footprint |
| **Paindastha-dhyana** | Concentration upon certain objects made up of the elements of matter |
| **Paksa** | Thesis |
| **Paksa-sadhya-samsarga** | Association of the subject with the probandum |
| **Paksa-suddhi** | Purification of the thesis |
| **Paksabhana** | Knowledge of the subject |
| **Paksadharmata** | Subsistence in the subject |
| **Paksadharmatva** | Subsistence in the subject |
| **Paksadosa** | Fallacy in the thesis |

**Paksavacana** Statement of the subject

**Paksiya sadhya-sadhana sambandha** Relationship of the probandum and the probane of the subject

**Pamana-siddha** Proved by definite organ of knowledge

**Panca-kalyana** The five auspicious events in the life of a **Tirthankara; -mahotsava** (the celebration of these events)

**Panca-mahavrata** see also mahavrata

**Panca-namaskara-mantra** see also namaskara-mantra

**Panca-rupya** Five characteristics

**Panchendriya** Five-sensed.

**Pani-patra** Hand-bowl

**Papa** Unwholesome karmas

**Papopadesha** Preaching of sin to others.

**Para** (Samgraha naya) Ultimate

**Para prashansa** praising others

**Para-dravya** The being, location, time, or state, respectively, of other objects

**Para-pratipatti** Understanding of others

**Paraghata** Destructive; Possessing a limb or organ fatal to others, as a lion's claws, etc.

**Paramanu** Atom

**Paramatman** The highest [the liberated] soul

**Paramesthin** The supreme divinity

**Paramita** Perfection

**Paraninda** Speaking ill of others.

**Parartha** For others (eye etc.)

**Parartha** (Anumana) For others (i.e. syllogistic)

| | |
|---|---|
| **Pararthya** | Meant for others |
| **Parasamaya** | The tenants of others |
| **Paridevana** | Piteous or pathetic moaning to attract compassion. |
| **Parigraha** | Possession |
| | Worldly attachment. |
| **Parigraha-tyaga** | Preparatory to the monk's life. enjoins a gradual giving up of the world and retiring into some very quiet place to acquire the knowledge of truth and ultimately to become fit to be a teacher of the path to Liberation. |
| **Parigrahatyaga-pratima** | The ninth stage in which a layman abandons the cares of worldly possessions |
| **Parihara-vishuddhi** | Ideal and passionless conduct. |
| **Pariksa** | Examination |
| **Parinama** | Modification |
| **Parinami-nitya** | Eternal but constantly changing |
| **Parinamika** | Existence of knowledge |
| **Parinamin** | Changing |
| **Paripurna** (Naigama) | Non-distinguished in general |
| **Parisaha-jaya** | Victory over the afflictions |
| **Parishaha** | Sufferings. |
| **Parishaha-jaya** | Sub-dual of sufferings |
| **Paritapiki-kriya** | Anything which may cause mental pain to oneself or others. |
| **Parivrajaka** | A non-Jaina mendicant |
| **Parmarthika** (Pratyaksa) | Transcendental |
| **Paroksa** | Indirect perception, accomplished through the senses, inference, etc. non-perceptual |

| | |
|---|---|
| **Paroparodhakarana** | Residence in a place where one is not likely to be prohibited by others nor where one should be likely to prohibit others. |
| **Parsad gunaudbhavana** | proclaiming the good qualities of others. |
| **Parthivi-dharana** | Visualization of certain scenes by means of the earth element |
| **Parvan** | Jaina holy days |
| **Paryapta** | rational five-sensed, fully developable soul. |
| **Paryapti** | Developable; capable of developing the body. |
| **Paryaya** | Mode; a synonym for bhava<br>Modification, Modifications |
| **Paryaya** | Synonym |
| **Paryayarthikabhasa** | False point of view of mode |
| **Paryayastikanaya** | Point of view of the mode |
| **Paryusana-parva** | A ten-day holy period for fasting during the rainy season |
| **Pasavaccijja** | Those who follow the discipline of Parsva |
| **Patra** | Bowl |
| **Paudgalika** | Material |
| **Phaddaga** | A chapter of monks |
| **Phala** | Fruit, Resultant |
| **Pinchi** | A peacock-feather whiskbroom |
| **Pita** | Yellow. |
| **Pita-lesya** | Yellow karmic stain |
| **Pitr-loka** | World of the Manes |
| **Posadhopavasa** | The third siksavrata and fourth pratima; fasting on the eighth and fourteenth days of each lunar fortnight |

| | |
|---|---|
| **Posaha-sala** | Fasting hall |
| **Prabhavana** | Illumination, Propagation of the path of Liberation. |
| **Prachala** | Drowsiness. |
| **Prachala-prachala** | Heavy drowsiness. |
| **Pradesa** | Space-point; amount of karma |
| **Pradesha** | Quantity |
| **Pradesha-bandha** | The particular number of the molecules actually absorbed. |
| **Pradeshatva** | Capacity of having some kind of location in space. Spatiality |
| **Pradoshiki-kriya** | Tendency to accuse others in anger |
| **Prajna** | Wisdom |
| **Prakaranasama** (Hetvabhasa) | Inconclusive |
| **Prakirnaka** | Miscellaneous; a group of Jaina canonical texts; scatterd stars |
| **Prakriti** | kind |
| **Prakrti** | Original nature of mind and matter in the Samkhya doctrine; types of karma |
| **Pralaya** | Demanifestation |
| **Pramada** | Carelessness Negligence; carelessness; apathy |
| **Pramada-charitra** | Thoughtless or inconsiderate conduct, such as plucking flowers or breaking branches of trees, without any purpose. |
| **Pramana** | Dimensions, Organ of knowledge |
| **Pramana-prasiddhatva** | Definitelly proved |
| **Pramana-vikalpa-prasiddatva** | Optionally proved |

| | |
|---|---|
| **Pratyaksagamya** | Perceived directly |
| **Pratyayiki-kriya** | Inventing new sense-enjoyments. |
| **Pratyeka** | Individual; solitary |
| **Pratyeka sharira** | Individual body; A body enjoyable by one soul only. |
| **Pratyeka Sharira-Vargana** | Individual body-molecule |
| **Pravacana-matrka** | The eight exercises that prepare a monk for advanced meditational states |
| **Pravachana-bhakti** | Devotion to Scriptures. |
| **Pravachanavatsalatva** | Tender affection for one's brothers on the path of liberation. |
| **Pravrajya** | Renunciation |
| **Pravrttinimitta** | Usage |
| **Prayascitta** | Repentence of transgressions |
| **Prayashchitta** | Expiation—internal austerity. |
| **Prayoga-kriya** | bodily movement. |
| **Prayogya-labdhi** | Reduction of karmic matter in soul attainment of purity due to such a reduction |
| **Prayojaka-vrddha** | A man, who comprehends the word |
| **Prayojya-vrddha** | Elder person, who is asked to do a thing |
| **Proshadhopavasa** | Fortnightly must fast. Taking a vow to fast on 4 days of the month,viz. the two 8th and the two 14th days of every lunar fortnight. |
| **Prthvi-kayika** | Earthbodies |
| **Psadha-pratima** | The fourth sravaka-pratima |
| **Pudgala** | Matter |
| **Pudgala Dravya** | Matter-Substance |

| | |
|---|---|
| **Pudgala-skandha** | Aggregate of matter |
| **Pudgalavadin** | Follower of Buddhist school which upholds a theory of soul |
| **Puja** | Worship |
| **Pumveda** | Masculine. Sexual cravings for a female |
| **Punya-karma** | Wholesome karma |
| **Punya-ksetra** | Field of merit |
| **Puranas** | Name of a class of sacred texts dealing with the lives of Tirthankaras |
| **Purusa** | Person, Soul |
| **Purusa-visesa** | Special soul, i.e., the God (Isvara) of the Yoga school |
| **Purusaveda** | Male-sex-consciousness |
| **Purva** | A group of fourteen Jaina canonical texts, now extinct |
| **Purva ratanu smarana-tyaga** | Renouncing of thinking over, remembrance of past enjoyment of women. |
| **Purvacara** (Hetu) | Predecessor |
| **Purvacaranupalabdhi** | Non-availability of the predecessor |
| **Puspa** | Flower |
| **Raga** | Desire; passion; attachment Giving up infatuation. |
| **Rajas** | Principle of motion in the Samkhya doctrine |
| **Rajoharana** | A whiskbroom |
| **Rajya-Katha** | politics |
| **Rakta** | Rad. |
| **Rasa** | Taste |
| **Rasa parityaga** | Daily renunciation of one or more |

| | |
|---|---|
| | of six kinds of delicacies Ghee, milk, curd, sugar, salt, and oil—external austerity. Abandonment of stimulating or delicious food |
| **Rati** | Indulgence, Pleasure in sense activity |
| **Ratnatraya** | The three jewels right faith or insight, right knowledge, right conduct |
| **Ratre-bhukta-tyaga** | Abstinence from eating at night. |
| **Ratri-bhojana** | Eating at night |
| **Ratribhakta-pratima** | The sixth stage, in which one limits all sexual activity to nighttime hours |
| **Raudradhyana** | Meditation on the perverse pleasure of causing injury to others |
| **Rju** | Analytic |
| **Rju-sutrabhasa** | False analytical view point |
| **Rjumati** | Straight intelligence |
| **Rjusutra** (Naya) | Analytic stand, point |
| **Rjusutra**-naya | "Straight-thread" view |
| **Rta** | Vedic concept of cosmic law |
| **Ruja** | Illness |
| **Ruksha** | Rough. |
| **Rupastha-dhyana** | Concentration on the form of the Jina |
| **Rupatita-dhyana** | Concentration on that which transcends form the nature of the siddha |
| **Sabala** | "Disfigured"; offence |
| **Sabda** | Verbal testimony |
| **Sabda** (Kaladigata) | Word |
| **Sabda** (Naya) | The verbal |

| | |
|---|---|
| **Sabdabhasa** | The false verbal view-point |
| **Sabdadyullekha** | Mention of word etc. |
| **Sabdallekha** | Mention of word |
| **Sabdanayabhasa** | False point of view of word |
| **Sachitta-tyaga** | Abstinence from the flesh of conscious creatures. |
| **Sacittatyaga-pratima** | The fifth stage, in which a layman ceases to take certain vegetable life as food |
| **Sad gunochchhadana** | concealing the good qualities of others |
| **Sada-mukta** | Forever free of bondage |
| **Saddharma-vrddhi** | Increase in righteousness |
| **Sadhana** | Probans |
| **Sadharana** | Common body; Possessed and enjoyable by many souls as a potato. |
| **Sadharana-vanaspati** | Souls which exist together with many others in a common plant body |
| **Sadharma avishamvada** | Not disputing with one's co-religonists, as to "mine" and "thine". |
| **Sadhu** | Mendicant |
| **Sadhu-Samadhi** | Protecting and reassuring to saints or removing their troubles. |
| **Sadhya** | Probandum |
| **Sadhya-dharma-visista** | The object which is qualified by the quality to be proved |
| **Sadhya-dharmadhara** | The substratum of the quality to be proved |
| **Sadhya-sadhana-bhava** | Probaundum and probane relationship |

| | |
|---|---|
| **Sadhyiji** | A nun of the Svetambara or Sthanakavasi sect |
| **Sadi** | Having a beginning |
| **Sadrsa** | Similar |
| **Sadrsya** | Similarity |
| **Sadrsya-jnana** | Knowledge fo similarity |
| **Sahabhavin** | Simultaneous |
| **Sahacara** | Futile invention, Simultaneous |
| **Sahacaranupalabdhi** | Non-availability of one which is simultaneous |
| **Sahasa** | putting down a thing hurriedly |
| **Sakala-pratyaksa** | Perfect perception |
| **Sakaladatti** | Transference of property prior to renunciation |
| **Sakaladesa** | Full statement |
| **Sakara** | Having a form |
| **Sallekhana** | Ritual death by fasting |
| **Sallekhanavrata** | The decision to perform **sallekhana** |
| **Samabhirudha** (Naya) | Subtle |
| **Samabhirudhabhasa** | False subtle view |
| **Samachaturasra** | Symmetrical; perfect symmetry all round. |
| **Samadana-kriya** | tendency to neglect vows, after having taken them. |
| **Samadhi-marana** | Death while in meditation |
| **Samanadhikaranya** | Co-existence |
| **Samanaska** | Endowed with the mental capacity Possessed of mind |
| **Samantanupatana-kriya** | Answering call of nature in a place frequented by men, women or animals. |
| **Samanya** | Generality |

| | |
|---|---|
| **Samanya-guna** | Common Attributes |
| **Samanyalaksana pratyasatti** | Relatonship of generalisation |
| **Samarambha** | Preparation for a thing i.e. collecting materialsfor it. Compare in Criminal Law the conduct of the criminal before committing the offence. |
| **Samarthana** | Corroboration |
| **Samarthana-nyaya** | Acceptance of the propriety of the cause |
| **Samarthyapratibandha** | Non-hindrance in capability |
| **Samavasarana** | Holy assembly of the Jina |
| **Samavayi-dravya-sabda** | Word indicating a collection |
| **Samaya** | Moment |
| **Samayika** | Attaining equanimity; fusion with the true self Taking a vow to devote so much time eveyday, once, twice or three times, at sunrise, sunset, and noon for contemplation of the self for spiritual advancement. Worship—self-contemplation and purifying one's ideas and emotions. |
| **Samayika-caritra** | Avoiding all evil actions, identical to the assumption of the five mahavratas |
| **Samayika-pratima** | The third stage of practicing samayika |
| **Samayika-samyama** | A synonym for samayika-caritra |
| **Samayikavrata** | Cultivation of equanimity; the second of the siksavratas |
| **Sambandha** | Relationship |
| **Sambandha** (Kaladigata) | Relationship |

| | |
|---|---|
| **Sambandhin** | Which are related |
| **Samgha** | Order of monks, nuns, laymen, and laywomen |
| **Samgha-pati** | Leader of lay community |
| **Samghata** | Aggregation |
| **Samgraha** (Naya) | Generic |
| **Samgrahabhasa** | False generic point of view |
| **Samgrahika** (Naigama) | Generic |
| **Samhanana** | Bones, muscle, etc. |
| **Samhata-pararthatva** | Collection, meant for others |
| **Samiti** | (Self-) regulation, Carefulness |
| **Samjni** | Able to think abstractly about spiritual matters |
| **Samjvalana** | Perfect conduct preventing. This is the slightest degree of passion and co-exists with self-restraint of a high order. Smoldering; -kasaya, subtle passions which are removed as one progresses from the sixth to the twelfth gunasthana |
| **Samkalpaja-himsa** | Intentional, premeditated violence |
| **Samkramana** | Energy that contributes to the differentiation or transformation of karmas |
| **Sampada** | Qualifications (of an acarya) |
| **Sampurna-naigama** | Full non-distinguished |
| **Samrambha** | Determination to do a thing - compare intention for an offence in Criminal Law. |
| **Samsara** | Cycle of transmigration Mudane Life |
| **Samsara anupreksha** | Mudaneness. Soul moves in the |

| | |
|---|---|
| | cycle of existences and cannot attain true happiness till he is out of it. |
| **Samsarga** (Kaladigata) | Contact |
| **Samsargin** | Which comes in contact |
| **Samsari-jiva** | Mundane soul |
| **Samsaya** | Doubt |
| **Samshaya** | Doubt, scepticism, hesitaion, e.g., as to path of Liberation |
| **Samskara** | Latent mental trace |
| **Samskara-prabodha** | Awakening of the latent impression |
| **Samskaras** | Sacred rites |
| **Samsthana** | Figure; figure of the body. |
| **Samsthanavicaya** | Contemplation of the structure of the universe |
| **Samudayavada** | Collective |
| **Samudghata** | Bursting forth; expansion of the soul to the limits of the loka-akasa |
| **Samudita** | Jointly |
| **Samvara** | Spiritual path; the stoppage of karmic influx Stoppage of Inflow Stopped. The stoppage of inflow of karmic matter into the soul. |
| **Samvara anupreksha** | Stoppage. The inflow must be stopped. |
| **Samvatsari** | Annual ceremony of public confession |
| **Samvega** | Agitation leading to disenchantment Perpetual apprehension of mundane niseries. The apprhension of the miseries of the world. |

**Samvyavahara** Transaction

**Samvyavaharika** Empirical (intuition)

**Samvyavaharika-pratyaksa** Direct perception, in the conventional sense

**Samyag mithyatva** (mishra) Right-wrong belief;mixed wrong and right belief.

**Samyag-darsana** Right faith

**Samyag-drsti** Right vision

**Samyag-jnana** Right cognition

**Samyak** (Srutajnana) Authentic

**Samyak-caritra** Proper conduct

**Samyak-darsana** Correct view of reality; true spiritual insight; faith in the teachings of the Jina

**Samyak-drsti** The fourth gunasthana, in which one attains samyak-darsana

**Samyak-jnana** Correct knowledge; knowledge associated with samyak-darsana

**Samyak-mithyatva** A state of transition in which both correct and incorrect views are present; the third gunasthana

**Samyaka adana nikshepa samiti** Proper care in lifting and laying.

**Samyaka bhasha samiti** Proper care in speaking.

**Samyaka eshana samiti** Proper care in eating.

**Samyaka irya samiti** Proper care in walking.

**Samyaka utsarga Samiti** Proper care in excreting.

**Samyaktva** Authenticity

**Samyaktva Prakriti** Clouded-right-belief; right belief clouded by slight wrong belief. Full right belief of the

| | |
|---|---|
| | subsidential or destructive knid, being a characteristic |
| **Samyaktva Prakriti** | primary attribute of the soul, manifests itself at thesubsidence or destruction of this sub-class. |
| **Samyaktva-kriya** | that which strengthens right belief e.g., worship, etc. |
| **Samyam-asamyama** | restraint by vows of some, but not of others. |
| **Samyama** | Restraint |
| **Samyamasamyama** | Restraint of some vows, but not of others, found in laymen only. |
| **Samyogi-dravya-sabda** | Word indicating a union |
| **Sandeha** | Doubt |
| **Sandigdha-vipaksa-vrttika** (Hetvabhasa) | Whose existence in the heterologous is doubtful |
| **Sangha** | The Saints' brotherhoods. |
| **Sangraha-naya** | Synthetic view |
| **Sanjna (Aksarasruta)** | Script |
| **Sanjna-sanjni-sambandha** | Relationship of word and its meaning |
| **Sanjnin** (Srutajnana) | Discursive |
| **Sanka-matra-vighataka** | Being a remover of the doubt in general |
| **Sankalana** | Synthetic judgment |
| **Sankalanatmaka** | Synthetic |
| **Sankhya** | Number |
| **Sankhyatanu-Vargana** | Numerable-atoms-molecule |
| **Sankita** | Doubtful |
| **Sannikarsa** | Approximity |
| **Santara-Shunya-Vargana** | Inter-non-inter-indifferent molecule |
| **Santara-Vargana** | Inter-non-inter molecule |

**Sapaksa** Homologous instance

**Saparyavasita** (Srutajnana) Having end

**Sapindikarana** A ritual connected with offering of food to the Manes

**Sapta-bhangi-naya** The sevenfold predication

**Saptabhanga** Seven aspects

**Saptabhangi** Seven-fold statement

**Saptapadi** That portion of the Hindu wedding ceremony in which the couple takes seven steps around the fire

**Saraga-samyama** self-control with slight attachment; etc.

**Sarage-samyama** Self-control with slight attachment found in monks only.

**Sarana** Refuge

**Sarira** Body

**Sarva-virata** Attainment of sarva-virati; the sixth gunasthana

**Sarva-virati** Total restraint of a mendicant

**Sarvajna** An omniscient being; a synonym for kevalin

**Sasana-devata** Guardian spirits

**Sastra** Scripture

**Sasvadana** State of "mixed taste"; the second gunasthana

**Sat** Being

**Sat-jiva-nikaya** The six kinds of living beings, namely, the five ekendriyas and the trasa

**Sata-vedaniya** Pleasure-feeling; that which brings pleasure.

**Sata-vendaniya** Pleasure-bearing feeling karmic matter

| | |
|---|---|
| **Sata, Satavedaniya** | Experience of pleasure |
| **Satpratipaksa** | Inconclusive reason |
| **Satrsanac** | Continuous participles |
| **Sattadvaita** | Non-duality of the existence |
| **Sattveshu** | Living beings. |
| **Satya** | Truth Vrata - the vow to abstain from lying |
| **Satya mana** | True mind |
| **Satya-vachana** | True |
| **Savicara** | Accompanied by applied thinking |
| **Savipaka** | The ripening of fruit by itself. |
| **Savipaka-nirjara** | The natural maturing of a karma and its separation from the soul. |
| **Sayoga-kevalin** | A kevalin still possessed of the activities of body, speech, and mind; the thirteenth gunasthana |
| **Shaktitas-tapa** | The practice of austerities, according to one's capacity. |
| **Shaktitas-tyaga** | Giving to others, gift of knowledge, food, medicine, etc., according to one's capacity. |
| **Shalya** | A thorn; a blemish. |
| **Sharira** | Bodies. The body. |
| **Sharitra** | Conduct. |
| **Sharitra-mohaniya** | Right-conduct-deluding. |
| **Shaucha** | contentmant |
| **Shiksha-vratas** | Four vows relating to meditation in the morning, noon, and evening, to keeping fast on certain days, and to his duty of daily giving charity in the form of knowledge, medicine, comfort, and food. |
| **Shila** | Restrictions |

| | |
|---|---|
| **Shila vrateshvanatichara** | Faultless observance of the Five Vows, and faultless subdual of the passions. 'Shita' Cold. |
| **Shoka** | Sorrow |
| **Shruta** | Scriptures |
| **Shruta-jnanavarana** | Scriptural-knowledge-obscuring. |
| **Shubha** | Beautiful (body). Graceful. |
| **Shukla** | White. |
| **Siddha** | A liberated soul; a kevalin freed from all activities whatsoever Liberated soul, Proved, The Realised Soul. |
| **Siddha sadhana** | The means to prove |
| **Siddha-gati** | The destiny of the siddha |
| **Siddha-loka** | The permanent abode of the siddha; a synonym for isat-pragbhara-bhumi |
| **Siddhanta** | Doctrine |
| **Siddhi** | Yogic power |
| **Siksavratas** | Vows of spiritual descipline |
| **Sila** | Conduct |
| **Silpa** | Handcrafts |
| **Skandha** | Aggregate |
| **Smarana** | Recollection |
| **Smrta** | Remembered |
| **Smrti** | Memory |
| **Smrti-jnanavarana** | Knowledge-obscuring karman of memory |
| **Snapana** | The ceremony of sprinkling or bathing the Jina-image |
| **Snigdha** | Smooth. |
| **Snigdha-ruksatva** | Moisture and dryness (of atoms) |

| | |
|---|---|
| **Soka** | Sorrow |
| **Sparsa** | Touch |
| **Sparsha** | Touch |
| **Sparshana-kriya** | Frivolous indulgence in touching. |
| **Spasta** | Obvious |
| **Spastata** | Clarity |
| **Sraddha** | Faith, Offering of food to the Manes |
| **Sramana** | A non-Vedic mendicant, usually a Jaina or a Buddhist |
| **Sramanabhuta** | A novice about to become a mendicant |
| **Sramanopasaka** | A disciple of the ascetics; a synonym for sravaka |
| **Sravaka** | A layman; a synonym for upasaka and sramanopasaka |
| **Sravaka-pratima** | The eleven stages of the path of the layman; a synonym for upasaka-pratima |
| **Sravakacara** | Book of the layman's discipline |
| **Sreni** | Ladder A term applied to the eighth, ninth, and tenth gunasthanas |
| **Srotra** | Ear |
| **Sruta** | Scriptural (cognition) The oral tradition of Jaina scripture |
| **Sruta-pancami** | The "scripture-fifth," a Jaina holiday |
| **Srutajnana** | Knowledge derived from instruction and reasoning |
| **Srutanusarana** | Basing on word |
| **Srutanusarin** | Based on word |
| **Srutanusaritva** | Based on word |

| | |
|---|---|
| **Srutopayoga** | Conscious activity towards verbal thinking |
| **Stava** | Hymn of praise |
| **Steya** | Theft. |
| **Sthana** | Situation. |
| **Sthanakavasi** | Dwellers in halls; name of a Jaina sect whose members do not worship in temples |
| **Sthapana** | Replacement |
| **Sthapana** | Ritual act of asking a monk to stop for alms |
| **Sthapanacarya** | Sacred objects used as a substitute for a teacher |
| **Sthapanajina** | Symbol of Jina |
| **Sthapanajiva** | Image symbol of soul |
| **Sthapanendra** | Symbol of Indra |
| **Sthavara** | Immobile beings, such as plants Immobile, with bodies having one sense only, i.e., the sense of touch. |
| **Sthavira** | Elder (of the monastaries) |
| **Sthavirakalpin** | A monk who lives in an ecclesiastical community |
| **Sthira** | Steady (circulation of blood, bile, etc.). |
| **Sthitapaksatva** | Real doctrine |
| **Sthiti** | Duration |
| **Sthiti karana** | To help oneself or others to remain steady in thepath of truth. |
| **Sthtikarana** | Acting to promote the stability of another's faith in the Jaina path |
| **Stotra** | A philosophical hymn |

| | |
|---|---|
| **Stri-Katha** | Women |
| **Strimukti** | Attainment of moksa in a female incarnation |
| **Striraga-katha-shravana tyaga** | Renouncing of(reading or) hearing stories exciting attachment for women |
| **Striveda** | Feminine inclination. Sexual cravings for a male |
| **Stupa** | Reliquary mound |
| **Styanagriddhi** | Somnambulism. |
| **Styanarddhi-nidra** | Somnambulism |
| **Subhaga** | Amiable; amaiable personality, even though not beautiful. |
| **Suddha dravya** | Pure existence of the substance |
| **Suddhi** | Purity |
| **Sudra** | A member of the fourth caste |
| **Sugamdha** | Sweet-smelling; fragrant. |
| **Sukha** | Bliss |
| **Sukha-vedana** | Feeling of happiness |
| **Sukla** | White |
| **Sukla-lesya** | Luminous white karmic stain |
| **Sukshma** | Fine (body) uncuttable and all-pervasive. |
| **Sukshma Nigoda-Vargana** | Fine-common-body-molecule |
| **Suksma-samparaya** | The state of having only the subtle passions; the tenth gunasthana |
| **Suksmakriya-anivartin** | The state of subtle movement |
| **Sunyagara** | Residence in a solitary place, like a mountain or cave, etc. |
| **Susama** | Happy |
| **Susama-dusama** | More happy than unhappy |

| | |
|---|---|
| **Susama-susama** | Extremely happy |
| **Susvara** | Sweet-voiced, musical. |
| **Sutra** | Style Aphoristic mode of presentation; the canonical scriptures |
| **Suya-nana** | Scriptural knowledge |
| **Sva sharira sanskara-tyaga** | Renouncing of beautifying one's own body; self-adornment. |
| **Sva-dravya** | Specific being, location, time, and state, respectivelyof oneself |
| **Sva-para-vyavasayin** | Definiitive cognition of the self and others |
| **Sva-samviditva** | Self-illuminating |
| **Svabhava** | Own nature |
| **Svabhava-parinama** | Undefiled change |
| **Svabhava-sthita** | Established in one's own nature |
| **Svabhava-viruddha** | Contradiction in nature |
| **Svabhavanupalabdhi** | Non-availability of the nature |
| **Svadeha-parimana** | The physical dimensions of the soul identical to those of its current body |
| **Svadhyaya** | Study—internal austerity. The study of the scriptures |
| **Svahasta-kriya** | Undertaking to do by one's own hand, what should be done by others. |
| **Svamitva** | The knower |
| **Svanuraktatvakarana** | Sustaining object in its own form |
| **Svapaka** | The lowest class in Indian society |
| **Svartha** (anumana) | For oneself (inference) |
| **Svartha-vyavasiti** | Definite cognition of the self |
| **Svarupa** | Form |
| **Svarupa-pratiti** | Indetermination of knowledge |

| | |
|---|---|
| **Svarupa-prayukta-vyabhicara** | Characterised by the innate nature of the object |
| **Svarupa-visesana** | Indication of nature |
| **Svasamaya** | One's own doctrine |
| **Svastika** | Well-being; the stylized wheel of life |
| **Svati** | Tapering; like a snake-hole, broad in lower but short in the upper extremities, reverse of Nyag- rodha parimandala. |
| **Svetambara** | White [cotton]-clad; name of Jaina sect whose mendicants wear white garments |
| **Svetapata** | A synonym for Svetambara |
| **Syadvada** | The doctrine of qualified assertion |
| **Syat** | From a particular point of view In some respect |
| **Syatkara** | Marked by syat |
| **Sykladhyana** | Pure concentration |
| **Taijasa** | Electric body, Electric body of mundane souls which always accompanies them.Electric. |
| **Taijasa Agrahya-Vargana** | Electric-unrecievable-molecule |
| **Taijasa Vargana** | what the electric body is made of. |
| **Taijasa-sarira** | Heat body |
| **Taijasa-Vargana** | Electric Molecule |
| **Tamas** | The principle of inertia in the Samkhya doctrine |
| **Tan-manohara anga-nirikshana-tyaga** | Renouncing of seeing their beautiful bodies. |
| **Tanu-vata** | Rarefied air |
| **Tapa** | Austerities. Repentance,remorse |

| | |
|---|---|
| **Tapas** | Austerity |
| **Taranapantha** | A Jaina reform movement started by Taranasvami |
| **Tarka** | Reduction and absurdum |
| **Tattva** | The [nine] "reals," regarded as objects of faith for a Jaina |
| **Tattva-rupavati** | The meditative practice of envisioning the body as totally pure |
| **Tejo-kayika** | Fire bodies |
| **Tendriya** | Three-sensed. |
| **Terapantha** | Path of the thirteen; name of a subsect of the Sthanakavasi |
| **Tika** | Commentary |
| **Tikta** | Pungent. |
| **Tirtha** | Ford; the path of Jaina practice; the monastic order |
| **Tirtha-ksetra** | A place where arhats have attained moksa |
| **Tirthamkara** | A Tirthamkara's career with all its grandeur when He preaches and completes His Ministry. |
| **Tirthankara** | Builders of the ford; the omniscient spiritual teachers of the Jainas; a synonym for Jina |
| **Tirthankara-prakrti** | Karmas that determine the body of a Tirthankara |
| **Tiryanca** | Animals and plants, sub-human. |
| **Tiryancha Anupurvi** | Sub-human—migratory form. |
| **Tiryancha-ayu** | Sub-human age karma |
| **Tiryanchayu** | Sub-human age. |
| **Titthiya** | Pali for Tirthankara |
| **Trairupya** | Triple characteristic |
| **Trasa** | Mobile being A being having two |

| | |
|---|---|
| | or more senses Mobile, with bodies having 2, 3, 4, and 5 senses. |
| **Trasa-nadi** | Channel of the mobile beings; that portion of the lokakasa in which the trasas abide |
| **Trilaksana** | Three characteristics |
| **Ubhaya mana** | Mixed true and false mind. |
| **Ubhaya-Vachana** | Both true and false. |
| **Ubhayasambandha** (Vyanjana) | Relation of the two, i.e. contact-awareness and object-awareness |
| **Ubhayasiddha** | Proved both ways |
| **Ubhayasiddha** (Hetvabhasa) | Unproved for both |
| **Ucchedavada** | Doctrine of annihilation after death |
| **Ucchedavadin** | Annihilationist |
| **Ucchvasa** | Sigh |
| **Uchcha** | Gotra high family. |
| **Uchchhvasa** | Respiration. |
| **Udaya** | Arising |
| **Uddistatyaga-pratima** | The eleventh stage, in which a layman renounces any food or lodging that has been specifically prepared for him |
| **Uddistha-tyaga** | Preparatory to the monk's life. enjoins a gradual giving up of the world and retiring into osme very quiet place to acquire the knowledge of truth and ultimately to become fit to be a teacher of the path to Liberation. |
| **Udirana** | Energy that makes possible the premature fruition of karmas |

| | |
|---|---|
| **Udumbara** | Fig |
| **Udvartana** | Energy that delays the time and increases the intensity of karmic fruition |
| **Udyota** | cold light, phosphorescence; cold light like moonshine. |
| **Uha** (Pramana) | Inductive reasoning |
| **Ullekha** | Mention |
| **Upa-brimhana** | Also Upa guhana, advancement in one's own attributes. Free from a tendency to proclaim the foults of others. |
| **Upabhoga** | Repeated enjoyment |
| **Upabhoga-antaraya** | Hindrance to repeated enjoyment |
| **Upabhoga, pari bhoga parimana** | Taking a vow every day limiting one's enjoyment of consumable and non-consumable things. |
| **Upabhogha Antaraya** | obstuctive of Re-enjoyment of non-consumable things. |
| **Upacara** | Transference of epithet |
| **Upadana-karana** | Material cause |
| **Upadhyaya** | Preceptor |
| **Upaghata** | Self-destructive; Having a self-destructive limb or organ, as a stag's horns. |
| **Upaguhana** | Protecting a fellow Jaina |
| **Upakara** | Effect |
| **Upakarana** | Mixing up of things necessary for doing any act. |
| **Upakaranendriya** | Physical sense-organ |
| **Upakarin** | Effect |
| **Upalambha** | Observation |
| **Upamana** (Pramana) | Analogy |

| | |
|---|---|
| **Upanaya** | Application |
| **Upanayana** | Ceremony of initiation |
| **Upanga** | Minor limb, Subsidiary to the Anga; a group of twelve canonical texts |
| **Upaniti** | The ceremony of initiation for a layman |
| **Upapata** | Rebirth in hell or heaven |
| **Upapatti** | Concomitant |
| **Upasaka** | A Jaina layman; a synonym for sravaka |
| **Upasaka-pratima** | The eleven stages of laymanship, a synonym for sravaka-pratima |
| **Upasama** | Suppression |
| **Upasamana** | Energy that temporarily prevents karmas from coming to fruition |
| **Upasamharavacana** | Concluding words |
| **Upasanta-moha** | The eleventh gunasthana, in which all caritra-mohaniya karmas are briefly rendered inoperative |
| **Upasarga** | Calamity, Preposition |
| **Upatta** | Of the matter assimilated as karma and non-karma by the soul, that which is accepted by the soul. |
| **Upayoga** | Applied consciousness, Conscious activity |
| **Upayogendriya** | Functioning sense |
| **Urdhva-loka** | The celestial world |
| **Ushna** | Hot. |
| **Utkrama** | Perverted order |
| **Utpada** | Birth, Comes into existence Origin; acquisition |

| | |
|---|---|
| **Utpala-patra-satavyati-bheda** | Like the piercing of the hundred petals of a lotus |
| **Utsarga-samiti** | Care in performing the excretory functions |
| **Utsarpini** | Ascending round, Progressive half-cycle |
| **Uttama arjava** (Honesty). | Supreme Straight-forwardness, |
| **Uttama mardava** | Supreme Jumility |
| **Uttama samyama** | Supreme Restraint. |
| **Uttama satya** | Supreme truth. |
| **Uttama-akinchanya** | Supreme non-attachment. Not taking the non-self for one's own self. |
| **Uttama-brahmacharya** | Supreme Chastity. |
| **Uttama-kshama** | Supreme Forgiveness |
| **Uttama-shaucha** | Supreme contentment. |
| **Uttama-tapa** | Supreme Austerities. |
| **Uttama-tyaga** | Supreme Renunciation. |
| **Uttaracara** | Successor |
| **Uttaracaranupalabdhi** | (Hetu) Non-availability of the follower |
| **Uvajjhaya** | Prakrit for upadhyaya |
| **Vacana** | Statement |
| **Vacya-vacaka-bhava** | Relationship of the word and its meaning |
| **Vada** | Legitimate discourse |
| **Vadara Nigoda Shunya-Vargana** | Gross common-body-indifferent -molecule |
| **Vadara Nigoda-Vargana** | Gross common-body-molecule |
| **Vadin** | Proponent |
| **Vaggupti** | Preservation of speech. |
| **Vaidriyika** | fluid. |

| | |
|---|---|
| **Vaikalika** | [Texts studied] beyond the prescribed hours |
| **Vaikriyika** | Fluid, the body of hellish and celestial beings, which they can change at will. |
| **Vaikriyika-mishra** | Fluid with karmic. |
| **Vainayika-mithyatva** | Mithyatva due to indiscriminate openmindedness |
| **Vaineyika** | Religion is identical with veneration of parents, king, etc., e.g., Confucianism. |
| **Vairagya** | Aversion leading to renunciation, The non-attachment to sense pleasures. |
| **Vaisya** | A member of the merchant caste |
| **Vaivahiki-kriya** | The wedding ceremony |
| **Vaiyavrittya-karana** | Serving the meritorious.. |
| **Vaiyavritya** | Service of the saints or worthy people—internal austerity. |
| **Vaiyavrttya** | Respectful service |
| **Vajra** | Diamond adamantine |
| **Vajra-naracha-Samhanana** | Adamantine, joints and bones. |
| **Vajra-rishabha-aracha-Samhanana** | Adamantine, nerves, joints and bones. |
| **Vakprayoga** | Statement |
| **Vakya** | Sentence |
| **Valaya** | Layer of the atmosphere |
| **Vamana** | Dwarf. |
| **Vanaspati-kaya** | Plant beings |
| **Vanavasi** | Forest dweller |
| **Vandana** | Reverent salutation |
| **Vang** | Movement by speech |
| **Vardhamana** (Avadhi) | Augmenting |

| | |
|---|---|
| **Varna** | Caste hierarchy/ class; color; a quality of matter Color. Letters |
| **Varna-vyavastha** | Class/ caste system |
| **Varnalabha** | Ritual celebrating the establishment of a new household by a married son |
| **Varsa** | Continent |
| **Varuni-dharana** | A process of meditational "cleansing,"accompanied with the water element. |
| **Vasana** | Memory impression, Trace |
| **Vastu** | Real |
| **Vastutva** | capacity by which a substance has a fuction.Functionality |
| **Vatsalya** | Disinterested affection, Tender affection for one's brother on the path of Liberation. |
| **Vayu-kayika** | Air-bodies |
| **Veda** | Sex-consciousness, Sexual feelings |
| **Vedaka-samyaktva** | A synonym for ksayopasamika-samyaktva |
| **Vedaniya** | Feeling Karma |
| **Vedaniya-karma** | Karma responsible for mundane experience of pain and pleasure |
| **Vibhava** | Defiled; impure |
| **Vibhu** | All-pervasive |
| **Vicara** | Shifting attention from one mode to another |
| **Vidarana-kriya** | Proclaiming other's sins. |
| **Vidhana** | Ritual |
| **Vidhi** | Positively |

| | |
|---|---|
| **Vidhi-sadhaka** (Hetu) | Positive, which proves something positive |
| **Vidhikalpana** | Positive aspect |
| **Vidhirupa** (Hetu) | Positive |
| **Vidya** | The arts |
| **Vigraha-gati** | Movement of a soul to its new destiny |
| **Vihayogati** | Movement; capacity of moving in space. |
| **Vijigisu** | Who wants victory |
| **Vikala-pratyaksa** | Partial perception |
| **Vikaladesa** | Partial reference |
| **Vikalpa** | Idea |
| **Vikalpa-prasiddhatva** | Optional |
| **Vikalpa-siddha** | Optionally proved |
| **Vikalpagamya** | Optional knowledge |
| **Vikalpatmika** | Optional only |
| **Vikrti** | Defiled modification |
| **Vimochitavasa** | Residence in a deserted place. |
| **Vinaya** | Reverence to the elders Reverence-internal austerity. Veneration. Taking all religions and gods, even the so-called religions which enjoin cruel or immoral practices, to be equally worthy of pursuit. |
| **Vinaya-sampannata** | Reverence for means of Liberation and for those who follow them. |
| **Vipaka** | Karmic retribution |
| **Vipakavicaya** | Meditation on karmic fruition |
| **Vipaksa** | Heterologous |
| **Vipaksabadhaka-pramana** | Proof which obstructs the opponent's view |

| | |
|---|---|
| **Vipaksasattva** | Presence in heterologous cases |
| **Viparita** | Contradictory, Perverse belief, e.g., animal sacrifices lead to heaven.Injury to anyone cannot be a cause of merit. |
| **Viparita-mithatva** | Perverted or incorrect view |
| **Viparitaropa** | Contrary imposition |
| **Viparyaya** | Error |
| **Vipulamati** | Ample intelligence |
| **Vira-nirvana** | Beginning of the Jaina era; death [anniversary] of Mahavira |
| **Virodha** | Contradiction |
| **Virodhi-himsa** | Injury generated by standing in |
| **Virodhi-himsa** | opposition to an enemy |
| **Virodhi-sanka** | Doubt of the opponent |
| **Viruddha** | Contradictory |
| **Viruddha sahacaranu palambha** | Non-availability of the concomitant contradictory to the probandum |
| **Viruddha-dharmadhyasa** | Which imposes the opposite quality |
| **Viruddha-karyanupalambha** | Non-availability of the effect contradictory to the probandum |
| **Viruddha-svabhavanu palambha** | Non-availability of the nature contradictory to the probandum |
| **Viruddha-vyapakanu palambha** | Non-availability of the determinant concomitant contradictory to the probandum |
| **Viruddhakarananu palambha** | Non-availability of the cause contradictory to the probandum |
| **Viruddhanupalabdhi** | Non-availability of the contradictory |
| **Viruddhopalabdhi** | Availability of the contradictory |

| | |
|---|---|
| **Virya** | Energy |
| **Virya Antaraya** | obstructive of power of exercise of one's capacities. |
| **Viryantaraya** | Energy-obstruction |
| **Visadrsa** | Dissimilar |
| **Visamvada** | Wrangling, etc., wrong-belief, envy, back-biting, self-praise, censuring others, etc., and causes a bad-body-making karma. |
| **Visani** | An animal possessed of horns |
| **Visesa-darsana** | Particular observation |
| **Visesavamarsa** | Inference of the particular |
| **Vishesha-guna** | Special Attributes |
| **Visistapratyaksa** | Qualified direct perception |
| **Visuddhi** | Purity |
| **Vitaraga** | Free from passion; an epithet for an arhat |
| **Vivaksa** | Aspect emphasized by a speaker |
| **Vivarta** | Mode |
| **Vivartavada** | The theory of illusory causation in monistic Vedanta |
| **Vivikta-sayyasana** | Solitary place of rest |
| **Vivikta-shayyasana** | Sitting and sleeping in a lonely place, devoid of animate beings—external austerity. |
| **Vrata** | Restraint, Vow. |
| **Vrata-pratima** | The second stage where a layman assumes the anuvratas |
| **Vratyanukampa** | Compassion for the vowers. |
| **Vrishyeshta rasa-tyaga** | Renouncing of exciting and aphrodisiac food or drinks. |
| **Vritti-parisankhyana** | Taking a mental vow to accept food from a house-holder, only if a certain dition is fulfilled, |

| | |
|---|---|
| | without letting anyone know about the vow—external terity. |
| **Vrtti** | Subcommentary |
| **Vrtti-parisamkhyana** | Limiting the extent of one's begging rounds |
| **Vyabhicara** | Contradiction |
| **Vyabhicarin** | One who contradicts |
| **Vyanjana** | That which manifests |
| **Vyanjana** (Aksarasruta) | Consonant |
| **Vyanjanaksara** (Sruta) | Alphabet |
| **Vyanjanaparyaya** | Manifest modes |
| **Vyanjanavagraha (Mati)** | Contact-awareness |
| **Vyantaravasi** | The peripatetic gods |
| **Vyapaka** | Determinant concomitant |
| **Vyapakanupalabdhi** | Non-availability of the determinant concomitant |
| **Vyapti** | Necessary concomitance |
| **Vyaptigraha** | Cognition of the concomitance |
| **Vyaptigrahana** | Cognition of the concomitance |
| **Vyaptijnana** | Knowledge of necessary concomitance |
| **Vyapya** | Determinate concomitant |
| **Vyapya** (Hetu) | Determinate concomitant |
| **Vyapyopalabdhi** | Availability of concomitant |
| **Vyatikrama** | Disturbed order |
| **Vyatireka** | Disagreement |
| **Vyatireka-dharma** | Disagreement |
| **Vyavahara** | Convention; appropriate proceedings Practical |
| **Vyavahara** (Naya) | Empirical |
| **Vyavaharabhasa** | False empirical point of view |
| **Vyavaharika** | Empirical |
| **Vyavasayin** | Definitive |